NOKIA® MOBILE DEVELOPER SERIES

Developing Scalable Series 40 Applications

NOKIA® MOBILE DEVELOPER SERIES

Developed by Nokia and Addison-Wesley Professional Publishing, the Nokia® Mobile Developer Series focuses on application development using Nokia's feature-rich software platforms for mobile phones. The series presents "best practices" guidelines for mobile application development through the presentation of real-world examples that have been reviewed and tested by Nokia's subject matter experts. The Nokia® Mobile Developer Series, published and made available around the world by Addison-Wesley, is authorized and approved by Nokia.

Also in this Series:

Developing Series 60 Applications: A Guide for Symbian OS C++ Developers
Edwards, Barker and the Staff of EMCC Software Ltd.

NOKIA® MOBILE DEVELOPER SERIES

Developing Scalable Series 40 Applications:

A Guide for Java Developers

Michael Juntao Yuan
Kevin Sharp

✦✦ Addison-Wesley

Upper Saddle River, NJ • Boston • Indianapolis • San Francisco
New York • Toronto • Montreal • London • Munich • Paris
Madrid • Capetown • Sydney • Tokyo • Singapore • Mexico City

The publisher offers excellent discounts on this book when ordered in quantity for bulk purchases or special sales, which may include electronic versions and/or custom covers and content particular to your business, training goals, marketing focus, and branding interests. For more information, please contact:

    U. S. Corporate and Government Sales
    (800) 382-3419
    corpsales@pearsontechgroup.com

For sales outside the U. S., please contact:

    International Sales
    international@pearsoned.com

Visit us on the Web: www.awprofessional.com

For more information on titles in the Nokia Mobile Developer Series, please go to:
www.forum.nokia.com/books

Library of Congress Catalog Number:
2004112280

ISBN 0-32-126863-6

Text printed in the United States on recycled paper at Phoenix Book Tech in Hagerstown, MD.

First printing December 2004

Contents

Foreword

It started as a wild idea, emerged as a standard, and grew into a phenomenon. Applications that go with you, whenever and wherever you are, and the infrastructure that lets you find them, buy them, and use them. With hundreds of millions of mobile Java-capable devices out there, the potential for developers is really amazing, and because the market is still young, there is still lots of room for innovative applications. There is still plenty of opportunity to get in on the "ground floor" of this industry and then ride the wave...to the top.

Ever since we first developed the DoCoMo Java architecture that started it all, people have been asking me "What is the killer application for mobile Java?" My answer has stayed pretty much the same... it is the application *right now* that solves a need that a user has *right now*! So what do users want? What will they pay for? How do you learn how to build it? And who do you partner with? The answers are here in this book, in readable, practical form.

So what will you build? To date we have seen a tremendous growth in the availability of high-quality, entertainment-focused applications for the mobile marketplace. These applications have been very successful in delivering a good experience to the user even though they have not tried to create an online- or community-based entertainment experience. Using MIDP 2.0, the next generation of applications can take advantage of the capability of the newer mobile devices to connect to other local devices and the wider service network. This will enhance existing types of entertainment applications and facilitate the creation of new communication and community applications that are interesting for both the consumer and the business user.

Who do you partner with? Nokia developer platforms offer the highest volume opportunity for mobile developers, with an installed base measured in the hundreds of millions. Series 40 Developer Platform offers the highest volume opportunity in the family, and offers a robust technical platform, including secure communications, mobile media, messaging, graphics, and Bluetooth (MIDP 2.0, JSR 120, JSR 135, JSR 82).

How do you build it? *Developing Scalable Series 40 Applications* is an end-to-end solutions guide for Java programmers focusing on Nokia's Series 40

Developer Platform. It brings together two of the largest segments of the mobile marketplace—Nokia Series 40 handsets and the worldwide mobile Java developer community—and provides thorough and specific information on how to create scalable mobile applications. These applications will work on the newest Series 40 handsets (based on MIDP 2.0), serve the large installed base of MIDP 1.0 handsets, and scale up to serve owners of smartphones based on Series 60 Developer Platform, enterprise communicators based on Series 80 Developer Platform, and rich media devices based on Series 90 Developer Platform.

Developing Scalable Series 40 Applications details the technical underpinnings of the Series 40 Developer Platform. It includes not only the available APIs but also coding best practices, architectural considerations, and fully tested sample applications ready for download. This book includes plenty of specific tips; for example, pointing out the choices Nokia made when implementing optional APIs.

This book goes beyond presentation of methods and classes. Mobile devices serve a variety of highly specialized customer segments, and some differentiation among devices is necessary to create the high-volume opportunity developers can now tap. Additional differentiation occurs as new devices add features on top of existing feature sets. To serve the mobile mass market at a profit, the right technical approach is critical to avoid fragmenting an application's code base. This book addresses development approaches that allow applications to scale across devices and time. The authors devote a full chapter to code management, sharing tips on how to optimize the mobile experience for a variety of users without fragmenting the code base.

The authors and Nokia are uniquely positioned to guide developers through the process of profitable end-to-end Java application development. Nokia has offerings at all levels: clients (Series 40 through Series 60, 80 and 90); servers (SMSC, MMSC, Nokia Mobile Services SDK); and technology leadership, including the specification leadership of a number of JSRs involving communication, UI, mobile management, and architecture. Author Michael Juntao Yuan is a developer and software architect for open-source mobile software. Kevin Sharp is a consultant and professional engineer specializing in mobile logistics and supply chain infrastructure. Both authors are frequent contributors to Forum Nokia and have had extensive access to and support from Nokia software designers, technical architects, tools developers, and technical support teams throughout the company.

Developing Scalable Series 40 Applications steps the Java developer through the process of end-to-end application development for today's highest volume mobile platform. It includes lots of code and examples, plus 11 end-to-end projects including client-side source code, server code, and tips on how to scale the client side to encompass other device families including Series 60 Developer Platform. Every code sample has been tested and is available for download. Developers can just load a sample and get started on projects of their own.

I have had the good fortune to be involved with mobile Java from the very beginning and I know what it takes to be successful in this marketplace. I believe that this book can really help you be successful with mobile Java application design and development. If you take the information in this book and sprinkle it with some imaginative application ideas, I think you will have a winning combination. I have seen from the inside how committed Nokia is to make a successful developer community, and I think that passion shows in this book and the other resources available from Forum Nokia.

Go fast... Go mobile.

Jon Bostrom, Sr. Director,
CTO Java Technology Platforms,
Nokia

NOKIA® MOBILE DEVELOPER SERIES

Developing Scalable Series 40 Applications

chapter

1

Mobility Explained

What is mobile computing? Why does it matter? Why should you care? What are the mobile killer applications?

Mobile technologies are changing how we live and work. They are truly revolutionary forces that shape the future economy and society. As smart programmable devices and high-speed wireless networks get more pervasive, they create tremendous opportunities for software developers. In this chapter, we introduce basic concepts and applications of mobile commerce from a developer's perspective. Key topics in this chapter include

- **The Freedom Economy:** discusses the revolutionary nature of mobile commerce. We cover the business landscape (value chain) and developer opportunities.

- **Mobile Killer Applications:** covers key mobile tasks and applications. We identify mobile entertainment applications and mobile enterprise applications as the key drivers for mobile commerce.

- **Developer Skill Migration:** discusses how developers from different domains can migrate their skills and become successful mobile application developers. To avoid blind skill transfer, we compare mobile applications' usage and design patterns to their counterparts in the PC world.

This chapter is a high-level overview. Details of key enabling technologies, design patterns, and programming techniques are covered in the rest of this book.

The Freedom Economy

Throughout history, the growth of human knowledge is strongly associated with innovations in information delivery technologies:

- Printed books preserve and spread accurate information. They broaden the reach of information to most of the educated population in the world and make the information available over a long period of time.

- Newspapers, radio, and televisions spread the latest news quickly around the world. They speed up information delivery drastically.

- The emergence of the Internet allows every connected computer user to access information on demand from all over the world. Internet enables fast and personalized information access from large data sources.

Mobile computing is the natural evolution of Internet computing. In the next section, we cover the key advantages of mobile applications over wired Internet applications.

Mobile Advantages

Wired information access applications, such as a Web browser on a desktop PC, require the user to be at certain places at certain times. The usage pattern of wired applications is often exploratory: the user spends long hours of dedicated time to research a specific task. Furthermore, the computer is often shared by several users and requires setup for each use. That model does not fit the needs of today's busy consumers and business professionals who are constantly on the go. Mobile users need the ability to quickly drill down to specific pieces of information at the spot. They also need to multitask across several different business and personal domains at the same time to make the maximum use of idle time when traveling.

Mobile applications support access to extremely personalized information at anytime, anywhere. By cutting the wires, information can now flow freely into every aspect of life. The economic opportunities associated with this freedom of information access are tremendous.

Extreme Personalization

Studies have shown that among the most carried personal items, the mobile phone ranks only behind the key and the wallet. The personal nature of mobile devices requires us to develop applications that can be highly customized to satisfy the user's personal preferences. The customized preferences enable the device application to locate relevant information quickly with minimum user intervention. The better user experience encourages users to further incorporate pervasive digital technologies into their everyday life. For developers, the billions of smart mobile devices tightly integrated into everyday life is a market far larger than today's personal computer market.

Information Access Anytime, Anywhere

Connected pervasive devices allow us to work, shop, or play regardless of our location and time. For the first time in history, a person's information access can be disassociated from her environment. Important information can be accessed on demand or even pushed to us while we are multitasking. Seemingly conflicting tasks such as "pick the kids up from school," "shop for dinner," and "watch the stock market" can now be done at the same time. While you are waiting in the car for your kids, you can shop online at a local grocery store and have any important market updates pushed to your mobile phone. This technology brings about fundamental lifestyle changes, as we can organize our time around high-priority tasks rather than being limited by physical constraints.

Application Areas

Mobile technologies can improve customer satisfaction and worker productivity in many application areas. In this section, we focus on the value proposition of mobile commerce applications.

Business-to-Consumer Applications

Mobile commerce allows consumers to personalize existing Internet-based electronic commerce applications and shop online at anytime, anywhere. Consumers get the benefit of convenient and speedy services. For example, we can compare prices online while shopping at a local store; we can trade stocks while riding on a commuter train. Many online stores and financial information service sites have already provided mobile interfaces to their services.

Mobile commerce also makes it possible to deliver digital goods to nomad users. The success of portable MP3 and DVD players proves the value of mobile entertainment. Connected mobile devices enable users to buy and enjoy music, pictures, books, movies, and games on the move. The convenience of mobile digital content download fits well with the impulsive nature of entertainment consumption.

In addition to improving existing services, the freedom of information enables new breeds of consumer information services. For example, with smart in-home monitoring devices, patients may now stay with their families instead of in hospital observation rooms. Another example is customized marketing messages. Marketing firms can take advantage of the human desire for instant gratification and design more effective product promotions based on consumers' real-time experiences. Those new applications improve our lives directly and create huge opportunities for mobile commerce firms.

Business-to-Business Applications

Mobile commerce could create value by improving efficiency in business operations. A good example is mobile supply chain management. Today's business supply chains consist of many suppliers and sellers across many different countries. They often form a complex web rather than a linear chain. Managing those entities and tracking their products in real time is a very challenging job. A poorly managed supply chain can create redundant inventories or insufficient supplies. In highly competitive business sectors, such as the PC hardware business, efficient supply chain management can determine the survival of a firm.

In a mobile supply chain management system, warehouse workers and truck loaders use mobile devices to track inventory and shipment data. The data is uploaded into enterprise backend systems in real time. Managers make timely decisions based on the most up-to-date supply chain information. Real-time information also allows the management team to quickly identify and correct bottlenecks in supply chains. Purchase authorization, billing, and payment are also completed by field agents in real time, streamlining the whole process and reducing turnaround time for goods, information, and payment. Supply chain management innovation is often custom done inhouse.

Better managed and more transparent supply chains can ultimately benefit a business's bottom line by increasing customer satisfaction at the end of the supply chain. Mobile technology enables vendors to ship goods faster and to better predict the availability or arrival dates. UPS's and FedEx's package-tracking services have become hugely popular. In a world of mobile commerce, real-time order tracking would be the norm of retail business. Highly visible supply chains allow customers to adjust their schedules to meet the product delivery time.

Business-to-Employee and Workplace Automation Applications

Mobile commerce allows firms to reduce operational costs for their mobile employees, including sales force, field agents, and factory floor workers.

Pharmaceutical companies rely on physicians to sell new medicines. Pharmaceutical sales representatives and doctors often meet at lunchtime outside of the doctor's office—it is easier to make personal connections during an informal lunch. However, it is difficult to hook up a networked computer on a dining table. If the doctor wants to make a purchase, the sales representative has to come back later with price and inventory quotes—a lengthy and costly process. With the help of mobile commerce, the salesperson can quote prices and close the deal right on the dining table, and the doctor can then track the shipment. Of course, mobile sales automation can go far beyond the pharmaceutical industry. Combined with leading CRM (customer relationship management) software, companies of all sizes, such as Nokia, IBM, and SAP, offer a range of mobile sales solutions.

Like sales representatives, field agents also need to access their company's enterprise information system on the run. Durable equipment vendors such as Xerox and Otis equip their field service technicians with mobile devices with which they can check technical information as well as conduct asset management on customer sites.

Even for factory workers who do not work outside the company premises, mobile information access can still be very useful. Boeing has huge plants to build commercial jet airliners. It is impossible to wire the plant with Ethernet cables, since there are so many moving parts. Technicians working inside a plane often need to make little trips to a nearby computer terminal to check digital blueprints. Such interruptions are not only inefficient but prone to error as well—humans can recall wrong details even after a short walk. Mobile information devices make it possible for technicians to check blueprints inside the plane right at the problem spot, improving efficiency, reducing error, and hence saving operational costs.

Government and Public Services Applications

Government sectors are among the first to adopt sophisticated mobile applications. For government employees, mobile technologies improve their ability to serve the public the same way as business-to-employee mobile technologies enable mobile workers to improve efficiency. Police officers need to check driver's license, license plate, and vehicle identification numbers whenever they stop a driver. Emergency medical workers at an accident scene need to check drug conflicts and other life-critical information, and emergency response systems have to be coordinated wirelessly. The military requires real-time updates from soldiers and commanders in the battlefield.

For average citizens, mobile access to government information would allow us to make better use of public services. One obvious example is the 911 emergency call centers. Future government mobile data services would allow citizens to check the status of their tax returns and financial aids.

The events of September 11, 2001, in the United States showed the tremendous value in government mobile information systems. When all the fixed-voice and data lines were knocked off by the terrorist attacks, the cell network was still functional. Cell phone calls and wireless email messages became the last words we heard from many people in the World Trade Center and in the hijacked planes.

The Technology Diffusion Curve

Every 18 months, hardware innovations double computer capability while dropping half of the price (Moore's law). Today's high-end consumer devices from Nokia have more computing power than most 10-year-old desktop PCs. However, powerful hardware alone is not sufficient. In order for mobile commerce to realize its promises, innovative software and services are necessary to drive the customer adoption of the new technologies. Early adopters stand to make a great impact (and profit) before the technology finally matures. In general, the diffusion of innovations goes through five stages: visionary, missionary, ordinary, commodity, and maturity (Figure 1–1). The characteristics of each stage are listed below.

1. **Visionary:** The technology has just come out. Few people see its business value. The technology proponents in the visionary stage base their arguments on advocacy rather than on solid value propositions. A famous advocacy slogan in this stage is, "You need this. You just do not know it yet." In this stage, few companies except infrastructure builders can make money.

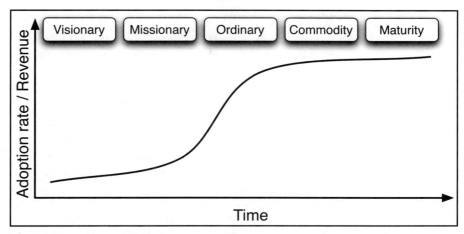

Figure 1–1 The technology diffusion curve.

2. **Missionary:** Business practitioners start to see the value of the innovation. Pioneer companies or employees become early adopters of the new technology and start to profit from it.

3. **Ordinary:** The value of the technology is well accepted by mainstream business executives, and most companies have developed plans to implement solutions based on the new technology. In this stage, the developers and enablers of the new technology make the bulk of profits.

4. **Commodity:** In this stage, the adoption of the technology becomes common practice. The technology has started to generate profits industry-wide. However, since implementations have been standardized, the barrier of entry becomes substantially lower, which results in intense competition in the enablers' sector.

5. **Maturity:** In a mature market, most commodity technology suppliers are consolidated to a few dominant players. The technology takes on a business utility model. Innovation no longer gives the competitive edge and outsourcing becomes the norm.

On a typical innovation diffusion curve, the transition period between missionary and ordinary stages are associated with explosive growth of adoptions and a limited number of technology firms who have the expertise to implement viable solutions. The unbalanced demand and supply creates golden opportunities for developers. We have seen this pattern repeated throughout history. At the time of writing, leading companies have already started to implement their mobile commerce strategies. All these signs indicate that mobile commerce is currently moving toward the ordinary stage. As developers, we not only want to be part of revolution but also want to make a profit during the explosive growth period, which requires us to understand how the money flows in mobile commerce—the mobile value chains.

Mobile Value Chains

For desktop and server-side developers, the mobile commerce value chain (Figure 1–2) is considerably different from that of traditional software sectors.

- **Developers:** Software developers drive the value chain by creating great applications. However, most developers do not have the capacity to handle mass marketing. They also lack the distribution channels to reach consumers.

- **Publishers:** Application publishers aggregate titles from developers. They build a brand name, certify the application for technical correctness, promote the application, and build business relationships with wireless carriers. Publishers also handle billing on the developer's behalf and typically share revenue with the developer. For mobile enterprise applications developed for internal use, the publisher is the deployment company itself.

- **Wireless carriers:** Wireless carriers are at the center of mobile application distribution channels. They include national cellular network operators as well as wireless fidelity (WiFi) providers. Carriers not only control the network but also own the customer information. It is up to them to decide which devices and services to support. Carriers take a big chunk of money out of the overall profit. They can also bill the customers through existing service agreements.

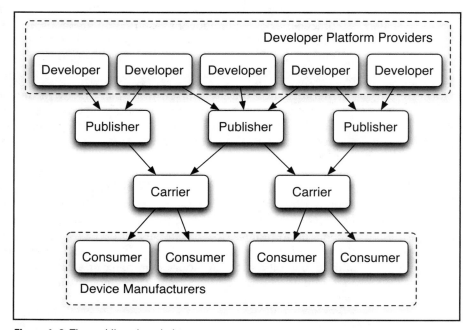

Figure 1–2 The mobile value chain.

- **Wireless device manufacturers:** Device manufacturers drive the technical innovation. They make new hardware and support development platforms. Device manufacturers represent an independent force between carriers and consumers.

- **Mobile developer platform providers:** The platform providers develop a common set of programming languages, APIs, and developer tools across many devices and networks. They focus on the software side of the development cycle. Large device manufacturers, such as Nokia, are often also platform providers.

- **Consumers:** Consumers eventually pay for the costs and margins incurred for the providers along the chain.

For individual developers, it is hard to manage all those complex business relationships. Fortunately, as Nokia developers, you can leverage Nokia's relationship with publishers and carriers. Forum Nokia provides several free programs to facilitate the entire application development and deployment process. We refer to many free documents and tools from Forum Nokia throughout this book. For leading development organizations, Forum Nokia PRO offers elite services. For a small annual fee, it provides early access to devices, confidential documents, and technical support for your entire company. For more details about Forum Nokia PRO, please refer to its Web site at address, *http://www.forum.nokia.com/pro*.

Mobile Killer Applications

The growth of the Internet and electronic commerce has largely been driven by a few "killer applications" such as email, World Wide Web, instant messaging, online auction, and peer-to-peer file sharing. To duplicate the success in the mobile space, it is widely expected that a set of mobile killer applications can also jump-start the adoption of mobile commerce. To identify those killer applications early is critically important for developers. However, after years of searching, the mobile killer application remains elusive to us. Given the revolutionary nature of mobile commerce, many thinkers and researchers have concluded that mobile killer applications will not be in the form of single applications. Rather, they will emerge as groups of related applications forming their own ecosystems. More specifically, we will now discuss emerging "killer application groups" in the mobile entertainment and mobile enterprise arenas. A common characteristic of those killer applications is that they all leverage the extensive connectivity of modern wireless devices. In the rest of this book, we show you exactly how to leverage the well-connected Nokia phones to develop such end-to-end solutions.

Mobile Entertainment

Mobile applications can deliver games or personal entertainment content to end users. In 2003, more than $3.5 billion worth of mobile phone ringtones were downloaded by mobile subscribers. That is 10 percent of today's world music market. This trend will only grow as highly interactive games and rich multimedia content delivery become available on mass consumer phones. Leading wireless carriers (e.g., Vodafone in Europe, DoCoMo in Japan, and Verizon in the United States) have all made significant in-roads in selling mobile games and Multimedia Messaging Services (MMS) for camera phones. In his 2003 wireless industry outlook, Nokia CEO Jorma Ollila identified mobile entertainment as the most important growth area for future smart phones. Several of the high-profile new Nokia devices such as the N-Gage game deck and Series 90 multimedia phone squarely target this application area. Three types of mobile entertainment applications are emerging as market leaders.

- **Multiplayer games:** These games could provide mobile access to established online game communities. Or, they could create completely different social structures taking advantage of mobile-specific features such as the multimedia messaging and location-based services. Good game design and management are crucial to this type of game's success.

- **Content-based applications:** These applications deliver copyrighted multimedia entertainment content, such as celebrity photos, video clips, voice ringtones, and personalized sports games to music/movie/sports fans. Peer-to-peer content generated by camera phone users and bloggers (Web log owners) could also be shared. The key to success is sufficient copyright protection and a flow of high-quality content that justifies the subscription cost.

- **High-impact visual games:** PC and console games have evolved from 2D to 3D. Mobile games will follow this trend too. There are already several mobile 3D toolkits and handsets available. However, 3D games are very resource-intensive. They require expertise from both developers and graphic designers. Professional shops will most likely develop these games.

Most example applications covered in this book are given in the context of mobile entertainment.

Mobile Enterprise

According to a study released by the research firm International Data Corporation (IDC), the number of mobile workers in the United States will reach 105 million by the year 2006. That is almost two-thirds of the total U.S. workforce. In 2003, 50 million workers in Europe already spent at least one day per week out of the office. Improving the productivity of mobile workers is a key strategic goal for enterprise IT departments. The mobile workflows must be fully integrated into the IT infrastructure through enterprise mobility solutions.

Mobile workers perform complex and essential enterprise tasks. The following list shows some examples of those tasks. It is not intended to be a complete list.

- **Connection to company events:** requires access to email, instant messaging systems, and databases from the mobile handhelds.
- **Access to files:** requires the mobile client to download, view, and synchronize document files through secure network connections.
- **Respond to calls and requests sent through messaging services:** requires push-based data delivery (e.g., Short Message Service, or SMS) and signaling protocols.
- **Access to company Web portal:** requires mobile device to fetch and render HTML content and support popular MIME plugins.
- **Optimize scheduling and movement in the field:** requires location-aware software to dynamically optimize the best route, given the current location and overall plan.
- **Connect to legacy applications:** requires virtual private network (VPN) connections to legacy gateway servers that bridge mobile middleware to text-based mainframe applications.

As we can see, the primary focus of mobile enterprise applications is network connectivity, which includes multiple channels for information delivery, integration with enterprise middleware servers, and access to mobile services (e.g., messaging, location and gateway servers). The future trend for mobile phones is clearly to converge voice, entertainment, data access, and PDA features into a single device. It is major challenge for enterprise IT developers to integrate those super mobile phones into the existing infrastructure.

With devices like the Nokia Communicators and Nokia 6800 messaging phones, Nokia has a strong focus on enterprise applications. Nokia Networks also builds mobile services tools that can integrate with enterprise backend applications via XML Web services. Several key examples in this book are end-to-end applications with the networked servers performing key tasks. Popular mobile-to-backend integration schemes are explored in detail through those examples.

Developer Skill Migration

As mobile commerce moves up along the technology diffusion curve, there will soon be a huge demand for end-to-end mobile developers. Today, millions of IT developers are already working on Internet-based applications. The mobile developer platform that can leverage this large talent pool will be greeted with great success.

Unfortunately, in the past decade, mobile development has not been friendly to desktop developers. Device software developers have to learn device-specific languages, core APIs, and development tools separately. Server-side content developers must learn a variety of Web frameworks, mobile-specific markup languages, and messaging protocols. That situation not only diminishes developer productivity but also confuses new developers and raises the barrier of entry for mobile development.

The new generation of mobile developer platforms addresses those issues by reusing common programming languages, APIs, architectural designs, and tools from the desktop PC world. They typically strip down the PC platform to an essential set of core features and then add mobile-specific APIs and tools in the way that conforms to the overall design of the rest of the platform. Nokia Developer Platforms provide a stable foundation of core technologies common across a large installed base, then differentiate individual devices within each platform in order to serve a variety of consumer and operator tastes. The approach puts great emphasis on lowering the barrier of entry for the 3 million existing Java developers. We cover the details of the Nokia Developer Platforms and how they benefit Java developers in the next chapter. In this section, we look at some general issues of developer skill migration and common pitfalls we need to avoid during the transition from wired to wireless.

Migration Paths

Different developers take different paths to enter the mobile application development space. The exact optimal path depends on your past expertise and your target mobile application. In this section, we give a very brief, high-level overview.

Java Server-side Developers

Java server-side developers can start by learning flexible Web application frameworks that separate the presentation layer from business logic layers. Most of those frameworks (e.g., JavaServer Faces and the Java Portlets) have built-in support for mobile browsers that allows us to quickly add support for mobile devices in our Web-based applications. A tutorial of mobile browser applications is available in Chapter 15, "Browser Applications."

Browser applications require always-on wireless connections. For many mobile workers, it is more realistic to synchronize with enterprise servers whenever there is a connection and work offline the rest of the time. Special gateway servers can be developed to support mobile synchronization of enterprise groupware and email servers via SyncML or custom protocols.

Java server-side developers could also look into Java mobile services APIs for server-side messaging, presence, and location-based services. Those APIs support server-driven applications that tightly integrate into the mobile infrastructure and make the best use of mobile devices. Please see Chapter 14, "Multimedia Messaging Service" for more information on this subject.

However, although browser and messaging applications will continue to be popular in mobile commerce, the majority of future mobile applications are smart client applications that run directly on devices. Java server-side developers are well trained in design patterns and enterprise integration. They can quickly move into the smart client market together with existing Java desktop developers.

Java Desktop Developers

Java desktop developers can leverage the power of occasionally connected smart clients using the Java 2 Micro Edition (J2ME) technology. J2ME supports most standard Java language and runtime features. A core set of J2SE (Java 2 Standard Edition) APIs plus a mobile-specific lightweight API extension is also supported. J2ME is the only platform to develop on-device smart clients for Nokia Series 40 devices. A large portion of this book (Chapters 3 to 13) is devoted to J2ME topics with many sample applications.

As a managed environment, J2ME applications are separated from the underlying hardware by the Java runtime. There are many benefits to this approach, as we discuss in Chapter 2, "Introducing Nokia Developer Platforms." However, for applications that require access to low-level device features and aggressive optimizations, the Java runtime may prove limiting. For those applications, we need to rely on native C/C++ platforms built into the device OS itself. Nokia uses the Symbian OS C++ technology on all its Series 60 (including the N-Gage game deck), Series 80, and Series 90 devices. Nokia Mobile Developer Series book *Developing Series 60 Applications: A Guide for Symbian OS C++ Developers* by Leigh Edwards and Richard Barker (published by Addison-Wesley in 2004) is an excellent tutorial and reference book for Symbian C++.

Visual Basic Corporate Developers

Visual Basic corporate developers are accustomed to visual Rapid Application Development (RAD) tools. Their skills in UI building and fast prototyping are desirable in many mobile projects. Commercial Java Integrated Development Environments (IDEs) support visual RAD tools to build J2ME-based smart client as well as J2EE-based mobile Web UIs. Java is clearly the best migration path for Visual Basic developers who are interested in developing applications for Nokia devices.

If for some reason you have to use Visual Basic to develop device applications, third-party vendors such as AppForge sell cross-compilers that can generate Symbian OS binary executables from Visual Basic .NET source code.

Mobile Application Design Concerns

Although the common design goal of modern mobile development platforms is to ease the transition from PC developers to device developers, blind skill transfer does not produce good results. We cannot simply recompile a desktop application, deploy it on devices, and hope for great user experiences. In fact, miniscule desktop UIs are often entirely unusable on limited devices operated by one hand. Technical limits of mobile hardware and social usage patterns of mobile users dictate the design of mobile applications. In this section, we go over the key issues to consider as a PC developer enters the world of mobile application development. Technical solutions raised in the following two sections are covered in the rest of this book through detailed examples.

Mobile Device Characteristics

Although mobile hardware is getting more powerful every day, it will always lag behind the state-of-the-art desktop hardware by several years. In addition, mobile devices often have physical constraints that do not exist in the PC world. We cannot just apply programming techniques in the PC world to mobile devices. The characteristics of mobile devices, their implications, and their proposed solutions are listed in Table 1–1.

Mobile Network Characteristics

Another key difference between mobile and wired applications is that most mobile applications do not have the luxury of broadband Internet access. Popular wireless networking technologies are as follows.

- **The digital voice and analog data networks (second-generation, or 2G networks):** These networks have digital voice infrastructure but require users to dial an analog modem call over the digital voice in order to connect to the data service. They are slow and expensive. Examples of 2G networks are the GSM Data and CDMA networks.

- **The packet-switch networks (2.5G networks):** Devices on 2.5G networks are always connected. There is no need to dial the modem before sending or receiving data. The data communication is packet-based. However, these networks are not very fast. Examples of 2.5G networks are the General Packet Radio Service (GPRS) and Enhanced Data Rates for Global Evolution (EDGE) networks.

- **The 3G networks:** These are designed from ground up to handle fast data traffic. An example of a 3G network is the Universal Mobile Telecommunications system (UMTS) network. However, due to high construction costs, 3G networks are not widely available yet.

- **WiFi networks:** Unlike the national cellular networks mentioned above, WiFi networks provide wireless data services to a local area, such as a building or a shop. WiFi networks are fast and reliable, but their coverage is very limited and the billing is complex. Most mobile phones cannot access WiFi networks directly. However, many PDA phone combos are WiFi ready.

- **Short range radio networks:** Personal range wireless networks, such as those based on the Bluetooth technology, are gaining momentum these

Table 1–1 Limits of Mobile Devices

Device Characteristics	Description	Solution
Slow processor	Mobile device CPUs typically have clock speed from 20 MHz to 400 MHz.	Do not perform computational intensive tasks on device. It is a good design to delegate complex tasks to the server side.
Small heap memory	Mobile devices only have from tens of kilobytes to several megabytes of application heap memory space. The application's runtime objects and data variables are allocated from the heap space.	We should minimize object creation and release big in-memory objects as soon as possible. In native environments, we need to carefully manage pointers and avoid memory leaks.
Small application storage space	The typical storage space on a mobile phone for applications and other downloaded materials ranges from tens of kilobytes to several megabytes.	We need to reduce the overall size of the final application package by removing unnecessary library code and optimizing images and music files. For large applications, we can distribute them on flash memory cards.
Small screen size	Mobile devices must be small. Their screen sizes are typically smaller than 250 by 250 pixels.	Use small images in the application. To make the details stand out in small images, a good idea is to add a dark outline to small figures.
Limited color depth	Early mobile phones have black and white screens. The color phone LCD on many Nokia Series 40 devices supports 4096 colors. Support for 16-bit true colors is available only on high-end devices.	Graphics must be optimized for low-color-depth display. PNG images with indexed color palates are good choices.
Limited audio capability	Most mobile phones can play back only MIDI ringtones. Some can play voice tones or .wav files. Only special multimedia devices (e.g., the Nokia 3300 phone) can play mp3 music files.	Use simple music as much as possible. Simple music files also take much smaller memory space.
Awkward text input methods	It is awkward to input text on a small numeric keypad. Even for devices that come with ASCII keyboards, it is still awkward to type with your thumbs.	Design the UI so that the user primarily selects from lists rather than entering text. Use cache to remember what the user entered before and make autocomplete suggestions in the future. Also, we can use desktop clients to enter

Table 1–1 Limits of Mobile Devices (continued)

Device Characteristics	Description	Solution
		and store URLs and other text information on a gateway server, which makes them available to mobile clients for user selection.
Short battery life	Bright LCDs and fast CPUs are battery hogs. Given the size of cell phones, it is impossible to pack in large batteries. Today's smart phones often need daily recharge.	Reduce the use of LCDs, audio, and device vibration features. The application should provide ways to pause and quit quickly.

days. They connect personal devices, such as a phone in the pocket, a laptop in the backpack, and an earplug in the ear, to a seamless network. Most Nokia phones now have built-in Bluetooth support as an alternative to data cables and infrared ports.

The characteristics of mobile networks, their implications, and their proposed solutions are listed in Table 1–2. The proposed solution for each problem is by no means complete or exclusive. For example, reducing round trips helps fix all the listed problems. Most of those solutions come from good end-to-end architectural designs.

Table 1–2 Limits of Mobile Networks

Network Characteristics	Description	Solution
Slow data rate	The current breed of 2–2.5G wide area cellular networks only has data transfer rates comparable to dial-up modems.	Reduce the need to send large amounts of data over the wireless network. Do caching and incremental updates. Mobile-specific gateways could play an important role here.
Long latency	Wireless data packets need to be relayed multiple times by routers and gateways before they can reach the wired Internet. It takes time to set up an end-to-end connection with so many intermediaries. It is not uncommon for a wireless connection to have a latency of several seconds.	Avoid network round trips with multiple connections. Use the Web application paradigm cautiously. Web frameworks that require round trips for each Web UI event are not suitable for mobile applications.

Table 1–2 Limits of Mobile Networks (continued)

Network Characteristics	Description	Solution
Limited coverage area	In the United States, data services are only available in major metropolitan areas or along major highways. Even if you are inside the coverage area, you might not have radio signal as the reception of wireless radio signal is dependent on the user's surroundings and the distance to radio communication towers.	Design the application flexibly so that the user can choose when and where to send the data— that allows the user to send data when she has a stable connection. We can also develop mechanisms to automatically detect the status of the network. If the network is not available, the application can automatically queue the data for a future request.
Unreliable connections	Environmental changes can easily interfere with or even interrupt wireless radio signals. Dropped data connection is common on mobile phones.	Advanced mobile messaging services can guarantee data deliveries. For synchronous applications, we could group data communications into transactions and provide a rollback mechanism when the transaction fails.
Expensive	Mobile data traffic is typically charged at a much higher rate than wired bandwidth. Some networks (e.g., the GSM data network) charge a rate based on the amount of time you are connected to the data network.	Reduce network data traffic as well as excessive round-trip connections.
Insecure	Radio signals are easy to intercept. Major security issues for WiFi routers and WAP gateways have been uncovered in the past.	End-to-end secure communication protocols such as the HTTPS should be used when transmitting sensitive data.
Limited protocol support	Not all Internet data protocols are supported on wireless networks. Support for real-time protocols such as the UDP is especially weak. Some networks do not even support TCP/IP sockets.	Use commonly supported protocols such as HTTP and WAP as data carriers and use mobile gateways to integrate mobile data with the rest of the Internet.

Social Design Considerations

Limited mobile device hardware and networks are only part of the reason why mobile applications are different from their desktop counterparts. Mobile applications often have different usage patterns and social context than desktop applications, further requiring different application designs. The following are some of the social factors to consider when designing pervasive mobile applications.

- **Easy to learn:** Since users perceive their mobile phones as consumer electronic devices, not computers, mobile applications cannot have steep learning curves. Consumers will not spend hours studying an operation manual of a three-dollar game. Mobile applications must work correctly out of the box.

- **Focused scope:** While desktop applications are often used for exploratory tasks such as Web browsing, writing, and research, mobile applications must be much more focused in scope. Mobile users typically use the device for quick access to a particular piece of information. The application must help the user to find information with minimum navigation and must focus on providing the best user experience for that specific task.

- **Interruptible:** Multitasking is a basic characteristic of the mobile lifestyle. Although each mobile application has a focused scope, the device itself is used for many tasks. A mobile user often has small chunks of free time available between tasks (e.g., while waiting for an email or a taxi to arrive). The same device is used for games, calendar management, messaging, and work data access. A good mobile application should provide value for short time periods and allow users to switch smoothly between modes.

- **Responsive UI:** Due to their personal nature, mobile devices must be responsive to user commands at all times. A mobile application that hangs the device is simply unacceptable. The application should acknowledge all user input. When it is performing long operations, the application should alert the user and preferably display the progress at all times.

- **Subscription based:** Financial success of consumer mobile applications depends on their large volumes. In the case of mobile games, it is expensive to design and develop each game from scratch. For a mobile game developer to make money, it is important to offer multiple titles from the same game engine along similar basic storylines. Subscription-based applications are the best way to generate sustained revenue.

- **Take advantage of mobile innovations:** A huge amount of mobile technology research dollars have been spent on improving the usability and reliability of devices and networks. As a result, the mobile device hardware and network protocols are very different from the desktop/console world— for example, Global Positioning System (GPS) extensions, barcode scanner, and SMS/MMS messaging. Good mobile applications should take advantage of those innovative device features and network infrastructures.

Summary

In this chapter, we discussed basic concepts behind mobile commerce. As mobile entertainment and mobile enterprise applications become the driving force for a new wave of IT revolution, the economic incentives for developers are tremendous. Hopefully, we have convinced you to read on and explore how you can become a successful mobile developer for hundreds of millions of Nokia mobile users.

The number one concern developers have when entering a new market is how they can leverage their existing skills. The Nokia Developer Platforms make extensive use of the Java technology to ease the migration for PC developers. Near the end of this chapter, we discussed various migration paths and high-level mobile application design issues. The proposed solutions are covered in detail throughout the rest of this book. Welcome to the brave world of mobile computing!

chapter

2

Introducing Nokia Developer Platforms

The Nokia Developer Platforms allow developers to write scalable applications across a range of Nokia devices.

The mobile handset industry has seen fast-paced innovation in the last several years. Nokia alone has been announcing more than a dozen new devices every year. That is great news for consumers, since Nokia offers choices. But for mobile application developers, it is tough to make sure that applications work correctly on all handsets. The Nokia Developer Platforms aim to solve this problem by standardizing developer APIs among Nokia phones. Each Developer Platform supports a standard set of technologies on a series of Nokia devices. In 2004, more than 100 million Developer Platform devices will be sold worldwide.

Key technologies supported on Nokia Developer Platforms are open industry standards. In particular, Java technology plays a crucial role. Client-side and server-side Java technologies can be used to develop applications for all Developer Platform devices. That helps 3 million existing Java developers to enter this exciting new market. In this chapter, we discuss the big pictures and architectures behind the Nokia Developer Platforms as well as the technical specifications of the most popular Series 40 and 60 Developer Platforms. From a Java developer's perspective, we cover the four technology pillars on the Series 40 and 60 Developer Platforms: Wireless Markup Language (WML), and Extensible Hypertext Markup Language (XHTML) browsers, Multimedia Message Services (MMS), Java 2 Micro Edition (J2ME), and Symbian C++. Strengths and weakness of each technology are addressed. Key topics in this chapter include

- **Open Standard Mobile Technologies:** explains the synergy between open standards and mobile technologies.

- **Nokia Developer Platform Architecture:** covers the basic architecture, device characteristics, and supported technologies on each Nokia Developer Platform.

- **Pervasive Client Technologies:** discusses the thin-client application paradigm using browser and MMS technologies. They are available on all Nokia Developer Platforms.

- **Managed Smart-Client Technology:** introduces Java technology for smart-client development on Series 40, 60, 80, and 90 devices.

- **Tightly Integrated Smart-Client Technology:** introduces the Symbian C++ technology for native smart-client applications on Series 60, 80 and 90 devices.
- **Get Connected:** gives a brief overview of services from Forum Nokia that help developers, operators, and business leaders to take advantage of the Nokia Developer Platforms.

In this chapter, we cover the technologies from a bird's-eye view. Development tools, API tutorials, design patterns, and best practices are covered in later chapters. In a sense, the rest of this book is to elaborate the concepts discussed in this chapter and put them into practical terms through real-world code examples.

Open Standard Mobile Technologies

Mobile commerce and mobile entertainment present users and developers with tremendous opportunities. But in order to realize those promises, the enabling technologies must keep up with the customer demands. We need continued innovations in both device hardware and software. The successes of the PC and the Internet industries have taught us that standardization and open platforms are the keys to sustainable innovations. In the mobile space, open standards are crucial to both device manufacturers and software developers.

- For developers, standards-based technologies lower the barrier of entry for development and reduce the time and effort required to learn new proprietary APIs and tools. Developers can easily optimize standard-technology-based applications for several different devices.
- For device manufacturers, standards-based technologies allow them to reach out to developer communities. A large portfolio of innovative third-party applications is crucial to the market success of any new device.

However, traditionally, mobile device manufacturers have been slow to embrace open standards. Closed platforms are often considered more secure and more efficient for small consumer devices. Proprietary solutions are developed to take advantage of special hardware optimizations. But that practice has hindered the independent developer's ability to write applications for these smart devices. As the computing power of mobile devices increases exponentially according to Moore's law, a smart phone today can easily have more processing power and memory than a 10-year-old desktop PC. The need for innovative software outweighs the benefits of proprietary optimizations. Today, all major mobile device manufacturers have their own open standards strategies. Nokia is leading the way with the Nokia Developer Platforms.

The Nokia Developer Platforms allow developers to write applications for almost all Nokia devices using open standard technologies. Such platform-enabling technologies include the following.

- Java 2 Micro Edition (J2ME) is a smart-client platform developed by the Java Community Process (JCP), which includes Nokia and all other major wireless handset vendors. J2ME specifications define the programming language, the virtual machine, and programming APIs. It is available on all Nokia Developer Platform devices.

- WML and XHTML are markup languages for authoring Web pages. They are standardized by the World Wide Web Consortium (W3C). Dynamic Web pages can be served by Java-enabled application servers via the HTTP network. All Nokia Developer Platform phones have WML or XHTML browsers.

- MMS is the standard way to deliver multimedia content asynchronously to mobile devices. The Third-Generation Partnership Project (3GPP) defines an open XML/SOAP API (MM7) to access MMS service-center servers in wireless carrier networks. We can use Java Web services toolkits to send and receive MMS messages to handsets from the desktop or server computers. All Nokia Developer Platforms support sending and receiving MMS messages.

- Digital Rights Management (DRM) enables content publishers to provision copyrighted material with special metadata that prevents the receiving device from copying and forwarding it to third parties. The content is typically downloaded from the HTTP network or via MMS. Nokia's DRM solutions are based on the Open Mobile Alliance (OMA) standard.

- The OMA Client Provisioning solution enables developers and wireless operators to send device configuration settings to supported Nokia Developer Platform phones over the air.

- Symbian OS is an open standard mobile operating system developed by a group of leading mobile handset manufacturers, each owning a stake in Symbian. It is the operating system for all Nokia high-end smart phones and enterprise and mobile media devices. The Symbian C++ native programming API can be used to develop applications for Symbian devices.

The audience of this book is primarily Java developers who are interested in developing end-to-end applications for Nokia devices. Throughout the book, we cover, in detail, the use of both client-side and server-side Java technologies to develop smart-client or server-driven mobile applications. In this chapter, we introduce Nokia Developer Platforms from a Java developer's perspective (Figure 2–1).

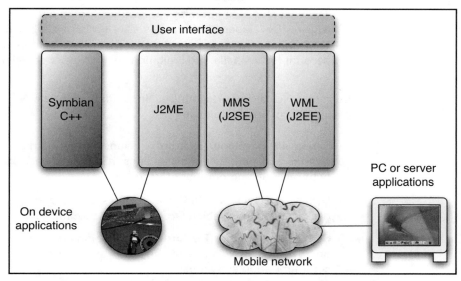

Figure 2–1 Nokia Developer Platform technologies from a Java developer's point of view.

Nokia Developer Platform Architecture

Standardized and open technologies enable developers to develop and optimize portable applications across different devices using the same APIs and tools. However, mobile devices are often used in specific application areas with very different requirements. Not all technologies are available on all devices. As a result, a monolithic Developer Platform does not work. Nokia divides its developer platform into several series, each targeting a specific device market segment. Hence, the Developer Platforms are not just about enabler technologies. They are about devices and user experiences as well.

NOTE

Nokia recommends a "develop-and-optimize" approach to building applications. You first write applications for the key technology enabler (such as Symbian/C++ or Java MIDP), which you select for the application's requirements, your expertise/preference, and the desired market.

From here, you can target specific Developer Platform versions and develop an application against the Developer Platform specifications. The key to leveraging the Nokia Developer Platforms and minimizing device-specific development is to remain as abstract as possible for as long as possible when developing mobile applications.

The next step is to optimize applications for the different user interfaces on a given Developer Platform (file size, screen size, key mapping, etc.) and then finally to take any device-specific hardware limitations or issues into account (such as file size limitations or processor speeds).

Currently, Nokia supports four Developer Platforms. The devices covered under each platform are the following.

- **Series 40 Developer Platform** includes mass-market phones with LCD screens and multimedia capabilities. It is the biggest platform in terms of both revenue and number of users.

- **Series 60 Developer Platform** includes smart phones and mobile game decks based on Symbian OS v6, v7, and beyond.

- **Series 80 Developer Platform** includes high-end enterprise devices based on Symbian OS v7 and beyond, with a full stack of enterprise communication software.

- **Series 90 Developer Platform** includes high-end mobile media devices with advanced multimedia (audio and video) features. Those devices are based on Symbian OS v7 and beyond.

Developer Platforms are not static. They have to evolve to keep up with innovations in device technologies. The Series 40 and 60 Developer Platforms 1.0 mainly apply to devices released before 2004; the Developer Platforms 2.0 apply to most devices that came out in and after 2004.

In this book, we focus on the Series 40 Developer Platform 2.0 and cover important aspects of the Series 60, 80, and 90 Developer Platforms. This approach encourages Series 40 developers to design applications compatible with higher series devices and provides a path for Series 40 developers to extend their skills. Now, let's look at the technical specifications of those platforms.

 NOTE   Nokia Developer Platforms are independent from the user interface. In fact, one of the major strengths of Developer Platforms is that they allow Nokia to implement multiple UI flavors on a common set of device technologies. However, currently, most devices in a series have very similar UI designs. Throughout this book, when we discuss UI designs for a particular series, we refer to the typical and most popular UI design for devices in this series.

Series 40 Developer Platform

The Series 40 Developer Platform targets mass-market consumer devices with hundreds of millions of users. Series 40 devices are very important to developers due to their large market penetration. On the other hand, they also present the biggest challenge to developers due to their limited size and resource constraints. In this section, we first look at the enabler technologies that make up this platform. Then we check out the device characteristics and user interfaces of the current Series 40 devices.

Software Stack

The basic technology stack on a Series 40 device is illustrated in Figure 2–2. At the bottom, there are device hardware and Nokia's proprietary operating system (Nokia OS). The Nokia OS is closed to developers outside of Nokia. On top of the Nokia OS, all Series 40 devices support a common set of native client applications:

- Telephony applications such as speed dialing, call logs, and mobile messaging clients.

- Personal information management (PIM) applications, including calendar, to-do lists, and phonebook.

- Synchronization applications that synchronize the PIM database with desktop PCs via the Nokia PC suite.

- Application installation and management utilities, including over-the-air (OTA) download, wallpaper, and ringtone managers.

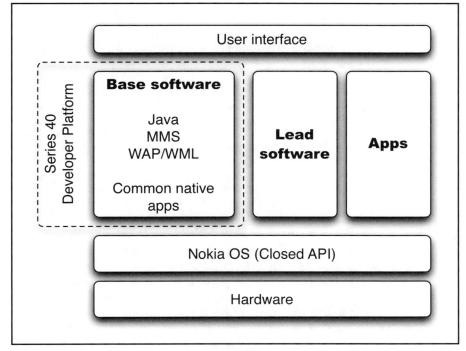

Figure 2–2 Software stack on Series 40 devices.

The common native applications are not customizable by third-party developers and hence not as interesting to the readers of this book. For developers, the key value proposition of the Nokia Developer Platforms is the support for technologies that enable third-party applications on the device. The Series 40 Developer Platform supports the following enabler technologies and APIs: the J2ME MIDP and its optional packages, WML, XHTML Mobile Profile, MMS, OMA DRM (forward lock), and OMA client provisioning technologies. The common native applications and the open API implementations constitute the base software in the Series 40 Developer Platform.

Nokia and wireless operators can also differentiate device offerings by installing "lead software," which are device-specific technologies or native applications. For example, the Nokia 6800 messaging phone for GSM networks extends Series 40 Developer Platform 1.0 with a very capable native email client; the Nokia 6255 imaging phone for Code Division Multiple Access (CDMA) networks extends Series 40 Developer Platform 2.0 with JSR-184 (Mobile 3D API).

Device Characteristics

A typical Nokia Series 40 device features a 128 by 128 LCD display with 4,096 colors. Some devices have 96 by 65 or 128 by 160 LCD screens and other color depths. It typically displays five lines of text plus headers. The keypad has the traditional alphanumeric keys, a four-way scroll key, the Send/End keys, and two or three generic soft keys. The device displays images in common file formats, receives AM/FM radio station signals, records voice messages, and plays Musical Instrument Digital Interface (MIDI) polysynthetic ringtones. Series 40 devices have multiple connectivity protocol support built into their hardware and OS.

- Series 40 devices support 2G and 2.5G wireless networks compatible with mobile operators throughout the world. Some work over GSM and GRPS, while others support CDMA networks.

- Some Series 40 devices support EDGE networks and 3G UMTS networks for fast wireless data transfer.

- All Series 40 devices support one or several of the following local network connectivity protocols: Bluetooth, USB, or Infrared Data Association (IrDA).

Device extensions such as cameras, full alphabetic keyboards, and MP3 players are available on selected Series 40 device models that target specific market segments. Figure 2–3 also shows the Nokia 7210 and 6230 devices, which are the first devices for the Series 40 Developer Platforms 1.0 and 2.0 respectively. The Nokia 6230 device supports a VGA camera, MP3 playback, and add-on MultiMedia Card (MMC) memory cards. The figure also shows a Nokia 6800 messaging phone (full keyboard) and a Nokia 3300 music phone (deck key layout and MP3 support).

Nokia 7210   Nokia 6230   Nokia 6800 folded

Nokia 6800 opened

Nokia 3300

Figure 2–3 Important Series 40 Developer Platform devices.

TIP

We do not print the detailed physical characteristics and application limitations for each individual device in this book. For the most updated information about individual devices, please refer to the device specification document from Forum Nokia, available at *http://forum.nokia.com/devices.*

User Interface

The user interface on Series 40 devices is based on view-switch screens. It is designed specifically for one-hand operations.

1. An idle Series 40 device displays its home screen. After the user presses the Menu soft key, the device shows its top-level menu, which consists of a series of screens, each representing a different native application (e.g., the Web browser or messaging client) or content folder. The content folder could contain media files (i.e., pictures in the Gallery folder) or installed applications (i.e., Java MIDlets in the Applications folder). The user can navigate through the top-level menu items using the arrow navigation keys. The menu content and presentation of each menu item screen are determined by Nokia and the wireless operator. Developers cannot change them from J2ME applications.

2. When we select a top-level menu item by pressing the Select key, the next screen is a list menu. Each menu item takes up one line. For a native application, the list menu consists of available actions. For a content folder, the list menu shows content files, installed applications, or subfolders.

3. A Series 40 application typically consists of multiple screens. Application and navigation actions are assigned to each screen for the users to select. These actions are typically mapped to the soft keys. If there are more than two options, the left soft key becomes an Options key, which opens a full-screen selection list when pressed.

The above menu hierarchy is illustrated in Figure 2–4. Figure 2–5 shows the use of the Options soft key. The user interface on Series 40 devices is very screen-centric. Attempt to interact with individual UI elements (e.g., menu, selection list, options, or editable text box) often brings up a separate screen (see Figure 2–6 for examples). In Chapter 4, "MIDP User Interface," we cover how to program the UI elements shown in Figure 2–6. This UI design is a proven success on small phone screens. Hundreds of millions of existing Nokia users are already familiar with it.

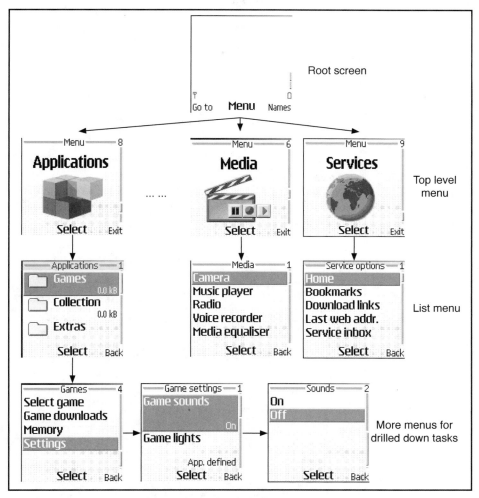

Figure 2–4 The UI menu for devices in the Series 40 Developer Platform.

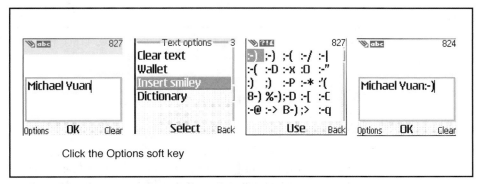

Figure 2–5 The use of the Options soft key in Series 40 devices.

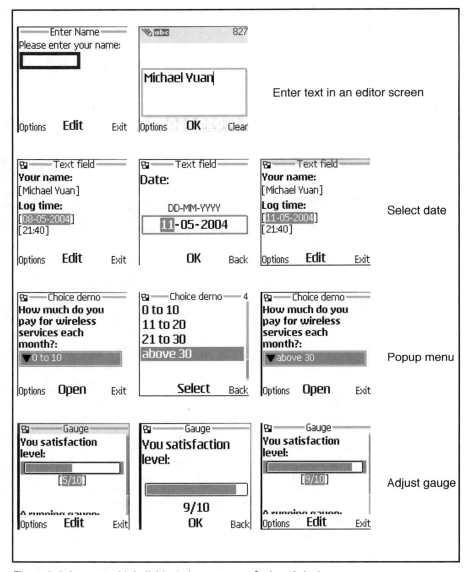

Figure 2–6 Interact with individual elements on a Series 40 device.

Series 60 Developer Platform

The Series 60 Developer Platform targets the world's best-selling smart phones produced by seven (as of April 2004) different vendors, including Nokia. More than 10 million Series 60 smart phones will be sold in 2004. There are a lot of overlaps between the Series 40 and 60 Developer Platforms. In this section, we focus on the enhancements brought by the Series 60 devices.

The Series 60 Developer Platform is different from the Series 60 Platform. The latter is a licensable product from Nokia. It is licensed to seven other device makers. Fourteen (as of April 2004) Series 60 smart phones have been launched. Series 60 Developer Platform is the platform for the developers. This book deals with Developer Platforms.

All Series 40 core native applications and most lead software are available on Series 60 devices. A significant difference between the Series 40 and 60 Developer Platforms is that Series 60 devices are based on Symbian OS instead of the proprietary Nokia OS. Developers can access the OS functionalities directly using Symbian C++ language and APIs. Users can install Symbian C++ applications into the device via OTA downloading or via a flash memory card. For example, most commercial games for the N-Gage game deck are written in Symbian C++. We give a brief introduction to Symbian OS later in this chapter. Figure 2–7 shows the software stack on Series 60 devices.

A Nokia Series 60 device typically has a 176 by 208 LCD screen capable of displaying 65,536 (16-bit) colors. More devices with other UI configurations will come in the future. Compared with a standard Series 40 keypad, a Series 60

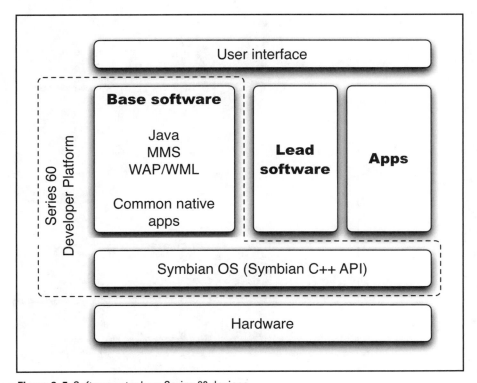

Figure 2–7 Software stack on Series 60 devices.

keypad has several additional keys, including an Application key, a Clear key, and an Edit key. A Series 60 device plays the Audio/Modem Riser (AMR) voice tones as well as other Series 40 audio formats. We can expand the data storage space of Series 60 devices using add-on flash cards. As a result, Series 60 devices can support large downloadable applications up to 4MB. The Nokia 3650 and 6600 smart phones are the first devices for the Series 60 Developer Platforms 1.0 and 2.0, respectively. A particularly interesting Series 60 device is the Nokia N-Gage mobile game deck. It is optimized for connected mobile games. Figure 2–8 shows the important Series 60 devices.

Compared with the typical user interface on a Series 40 device, a Series 60 device looks more like a minicomputer or PDA. The top-level menu and submenus can be displayed in a grid of icons or in a selection list. It supports popups (e.g., menus, option lists, and alerts) and directly editable widgets.

Nokia 3650

Nokia 6600

Nokia N-Gage

Figure 2–8 Important Series 60 Developer Platform devices.

Series 80 Developer Platform

The Series 80 Developer Platform is based on Symbian OS v7 and above. It is designed to support business productivity applications. A significant Series 80 addition to the Developer Platform base software is the support for J2ME Personal Profile. The J2ME Personal Profile is a more powerful Java environment than the MIDP, which is also supported on Series 80. The Personal Profile allows us to run enterprise mobile middleware, including many from IBM, on Series 80 devices. J2ME Personal Profile is not covered in this book. Series 40 and 60 MIDP, WAP, and MMS applications should work well on Series 80 devices. The Series 80 Developer Platform includes an array of enterprise-oriented lead software, including email client, messaging client, and VPN software.

The Series 80 Developer Platform was introduced in February 2004 with the Nokia 9500 Communicator device. It is a platform for enterprise devices. The Nokia 9500 Communicator features two user interfaces. An external 128 by 128 LCD screen and alphanumeric keypad are very similar to the UI design on Series 40 devices. But when opened, the device reveals a 640 by 200 large LCD screen and a full alphabetic keyboard. There are four soft keys along with the large LCD (see Figure 2–9). The Nokia Communicator 9500 user interface is clearly designed for two-hand operations. More UI designs will be available for Series 80 devices in the future.

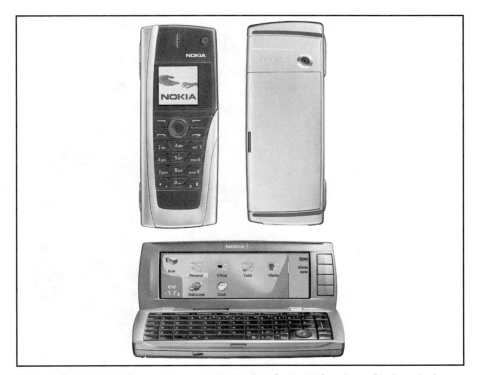

Figure 2–9 The Nokia Communicator 9500 is the first Series 80 Developer Platform device.

Series 90 Developer Platform

The Series 90 and 80 Developer Platforms are similar. The Series 90 is based on Symbian OS v7.0 and is primarily designed to support multimedia applications. For MIDP, WAP, and MMS applications, the multimedia enhancements and pen-based input methods are transparently available to developers. But for Symbian C++ developers, the Series 90 exposes more APIs to manipulate multimedia contents and UI events. Most Series 40 and 60 applications should run correctly on Series 90 devices with little or no change.

The Series 90 Developer Platform was introduced in late 2003. A typical Series 90 device features a 320 by 240 color display with 16-bit colors. It supports many audio and video playback formats and could allow users to watch TV programs or movies on the device. Series 90 devices feature a major UI upgrade from the Series 60: they support pen-based input methods (see Figure 2–10).

Other Nokia Device Series

In addition to Developer Platform devices, Nokia makes other devices. These devices are either legacy devices being phased out or devices that do not offer a significant opportunity for third-party developers. These are not the focus of this book.

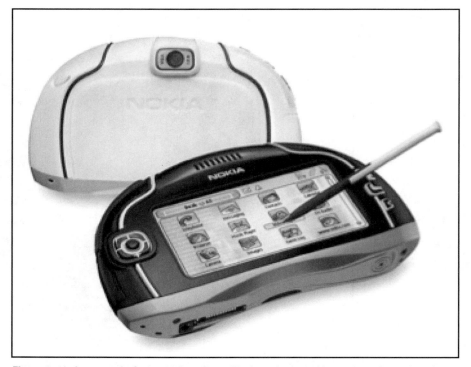

Figure 2–10 An example Series 90 Developer Platform device with pen-based user interface.

Pervasive Client Technologies: WAP and MMS

WAP browser and MMS messaging client are two technology pillars supported by all Nokia Developer Platforms. We cover the basics of those two technologies in this section.

Introducing WAP

A WAP browser works pretty much the same way as the HTML Web browser on a desktop PC. The user interacts with the remote application server by following dynamic links and submitting forms. The handset renders the content provided by the server. All the application logic is processed on the server side.

Although mobile and desktop browser applications share the same application model, the actual network architecture and markup languages are different. We check out those differences in the next several sections.

Network Architecture

While an HTML Web browser can make direct HTTP connections to the server, the WAP browser must go through a gateway server to connect to the general TCP/IP Internet. The WAP infrastructure is illustrated in Figure 2–11. The gateway converts data packets from the wireless network to TCP/IP format and then forwards them onto the wired Internet, and vice versa.

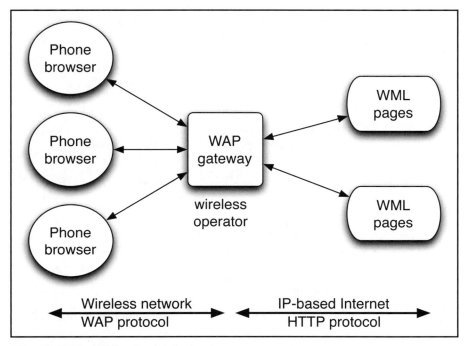

Figure 2–11 The WAP network infrastructure.

From the Web application developer's point of view, however, the gateway is almost completely transparent. All the developer needs to do is set up a normal HTTP server to serve the markup pages and other media objects. HTTP headers, including cookies and authentication credentials, pass through the gateway transparently. The gateway also handles encrypted HTTPS connections automatically.

WML

For developers, the biggest difference between an HTML Web application and a WAP wireless application is the different markup languages. Most mobile browsers support the Wireless Markup Language (WML), and all Nokia Series 40 and 60 devices support the WML specification. A core element in WML is <card>. Unlike HTML, where one page corresponds to one screen, one WML download page can contain a deck of cards denoted by the <card> tag. Each card corresponds to one screen and mobile device, and the user can navigate between cards using internal reference links. The cards help to break long content into several screens without requiring multiple round trips to fetch them one by one from the server. For example, the WML snippet below shows a deck of WML cards in one page, and Figure 2–12 shows how it looks on a device. The <do> tag maps a text label to a soft key. When the user presses on the soft key, the browser navigates to the page or card URL specified in the enclosed <go> tag.

```
<?xml version='1.0'?>
<!DOCTYPE wml PUBLIC "-//WAPFORUM//DTD WML 1.2//EN"
          "http://www.wapforum.org/DTD/wml_1.2.xml">
<wml>
  <card id="Name" title="Enter Name">
    <do type="accept" label="SayHello">
      <go href="#Hello"/>
    </do>
    <p>Please enter your name:
      <input type="text" name="name"/>
    </p>
  </card>

  <card id="Hello" title="Say Hello">
    <p>Hello, $(name)</p>
  </card>
</wml>
```

XHTML MP

The XHTML markup language is developed by the W3C to replace HTML. It is HTML-defined as an XML document with cleaner and stricter syntax. Series 60

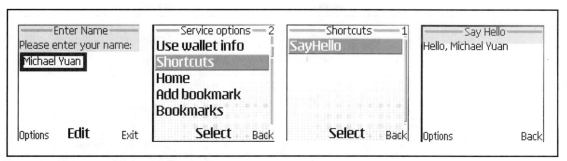

Figure 2–12 A deck of WML cards displayed on a cell phone screen.

devices and some Series 40 devices feature dual-mode WAP browsers that support both WML and XHTML. The browser conforms to the XHTML Mobile Profile (MP) specification, which contains a subset of most widely used XHTML tags. A key benefit of the dual-mode browser is that it allows users to access the vast amount of Web content out there on the wired Internet. The XHTML browser also supports WAP cascading style sheets (CSS) for styling.

Details about the WAP infrastructure, applications, markup languages, and Nokia device browsers can be found in Chapter 15, "Browser Applications."

Introducing MMS

An MMS message is analogous to an email message on the wired Internet. It contains a text body and any number of multimedia file attachments. The MMS client in Nokia Series 40 and 60 devices supports all popular attachment types, including JPEG, GIF, PNG, and MIDI. Some devices support advanced formats such as AMR TrueTone audio and 3GPP mobile video clips. You can send an MMS message to any MMS-enabled phone or ordinary email address. The message is delivered as follows:

1. The sender composes a message and sends it to the carrier's Multimedia Messaging Service Center (MMSC).

2. The MMSC forwards the message to the recipient carrier's MMSC or email server via the wired Internet.

3. The message is delivered to the recipient's phone or email inbox.

As we can see, the MMSC is central to the MMS architecture. We can write applications that connect to the MMSC directly over the wired Internet and send automated messages to a large number of users (see Figure 2–13).

An interactive MMS application functions like an automated email information service. It works as follows:

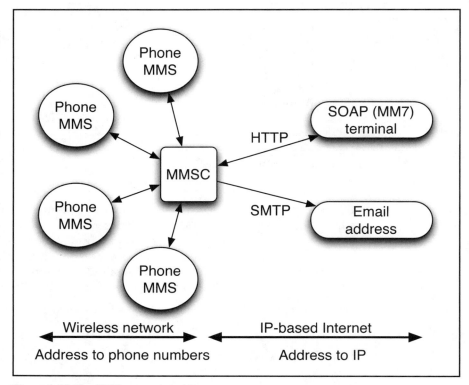

Figure 2–13 The MMS network architecture.

1. The user requests an application action by sending messages to the server.

2. The server returns the results via messages delivered to the phone.

3. The user then makes a further request by replying to that message.

This process goes on until the user stops replying to the message, thereby ending the session (see Figure 2–14).

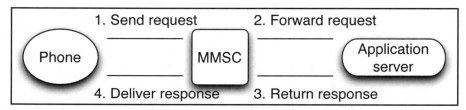

Figure 2–14 The MMS application interaction diagram.

NOTE A major difference between WAP and MMS applications is that MMS applications are not "instantaneous." The message can be queued at the MMSC and scheduled for delivery later. The asynchronous messaging model trades the real-time performance for reliability. Temporary network problems do not cause the application to fail, since the message can be automatically scheduled for a later delivery time when the network recovers. If the delivery fails after a certain amount of time, the user can get a notification message.

SMIL

In addition to the text and multimedia components, the MMS message can also include a presentation component written in a special XML format called Synchronized Multimedia Integration Language (SMIL), which is also a W3C standard. A SMIL document contains time sequence instructions on how to display the attached multimedia components. The following SMIL example code instructs the MMS client to display image demo.gif and text demo.txt simultaneously on different parts of the screen for four seconds. At the same time, the client should play the demo.midi audio file.

```xml
<?xml version="1.0" encoding="utf-8"?>
<!DOCTYPE smil PUBLIC "-//W3C//DTD SMIL 2.0//EN"
      "http://www.w3.org/2001/SMIL20/SMIL20.dtd">
<smil xmlns="http://www.w3.org/2001/SMIL20/Language">
  <head>
    <layout>
      <root-layout width="320" height="240"
                      title="Demo"/>
        <region id="Image" width="150" height="60"
                                    left="0" top="0"/>
        <region id="Text" width="150" height="35"
                                    left="0" top="70"/>
    </layout>
  </head>
  <body>
    <par dur="4s">
      <img src="demo.gif" region="Image"/>
      <text src="demo.txt" region="Text"/>
      <audio src="demo.midi"/>
    </par>
  </body>
</smil>
```

Not all devices support the SMIL component in MMS messages. Some earlier Series 40 devices ignore the SMIL attachment altogether but still allow the user to access other attachments in the MMS message. More details of the MMS infrastructure, applications, and SMIL are available in Chapter 14, "Multimedia Messaging Service."

The Thin-Client Application Paradigm

The WAP and MMS applications both run on servers. The handsets merely render the content and capture user interaction. This is commonly known as the *thin-client* application paradigm. It is a proven success in the Internet-based applications. Key advantages of this thin-client application model include the following:

- **The clients are pervasively available**. WAP browsers are almost universally supported by all device manufacturers and network carriers. The SMS and MMS messaging services are also widely available throughout the world. Several factors contribute to the pervasiveness of those technologies:

  - Since the device only handles presentation, it does not require much processing power. WAP browsers and messaging clients can be implemented on small, low-end devices with high sales volumes and long battery lives.

  - Since WAP has been around for a long time, most wireless data networks are well equipped to handle WAP traffic reliably. That makes thin-client applications available all over the world.

  - WML, XHTML, SMIL, and MIME attachments are standard technologies with a huge installed base worldwide. Most compatibility problems have been worked out over the years.

- **Thin-client applications and developers are readily available.**

  - The Web application and email application models are well known to today's Internet developers. They can easily migrate their skills to the new wireless arena.

  - A large number of Web applications are available today. It is relatively easy to make changes to their presentation layer so that they generate WML pages instead of HTML pages.

- **Thin-client applications are installed and deployed on the server end**. There are no complex and costly provisioning process, license management, security update, and so forth.

However, a crucial disadvantage of the thin-client paradigm is that it requires the mobile device to be always connected. Today's wireless data networks are slow, unreliable, and expensive. They cover only limited areas. Those limitations have severely hindered the adoption of thin-client applications. To get around the network problem, we have to rely on the other two pillars in the Nokia Developer Platforms: J2ME and Symbian C++.

Managed Smart-Client Technology: J2ME

J2ME brings rich and high-availability applications to occasionally connected mobile devices. It is universally supported by all versions of Nokia Developer Platforms as well as all other major mobile handset manufacturers. In this introductory chapter, we have a high-level overview of J2ME.

A Brief History of Java

The Java technology is emerging as one of the most important enablers for mobile applications. In 2007, Java handset shipments will reach more than 450 million, constituting 74 percent of all handset shipments. Java mobile devices will soon surpass Wintel PCs and become the dominant information access clients. Nokia is a major player in the Java landscape. The technical benefits of Java include:

- **Crossplatform:** This is very important in the diverse mobile device market. For example, the same J2ME MIDP application runs on all Nokia Developer Platform devices with relatively small amount of modification, representing huge cost savings for developers.

- **Robust:** Since Java applications run in a managed environment, the bytecode is verified before execution, and unused objects are reclaimed by garbage collectors (see the tip). Even if a Java application does crash, it is contained within the virtual machine. It will not affect other applications on the device.

- **Secure:** The Java runtime provides advanced security features through a domain-based security manager and standard security APIs.

- **Object oriented:** The Java language is a well-designed, object-oriented language with vast library support. There is a vast pool of existing Java developers.

- **Wide adoption at the backend:** It is relatively easy to make Java clients work with Java application servers and messaging servers. Due to the wide adoption of Java 2 Enterprise Edition (J2EE) on the server side, J2ME is the leading candidate for end-to-end mobile applications.

TIP

The garbage collector periodically travels the directed graph of allocated objects and frees up all objects that cannot be reached via a valid reference. That could create certain conditions for memory leaks. For example, if a long-lived object holds references to short-lived objects, even after the short-lived objects are no longer used, their memory cannot be freed because they are still reachable in the linked graph from the long-lived object. As a result, we should be extremely careful when adding object references to collections held in long-lived objects such as the root UI window, the MIDlet object itself, or Singleton objects. Since the heap space on mobile devices is limited and the garbage collector takes time to run, it is generally considered a best practice to minimize object creation and reuse objects as much as possible.

For memory-intensive applications, it is sometimes hard for the garbage collector to keep up. Failures to free stale objects in time could cause out-of-memory errors. To correct this problem, you can manually invoke the garbage collector by calling the `System.gc()` method in your code. It asks the JVM runtime to make best effort to reclaim memory space before it returns.

From WORA to Java Everywhere

For early Java, the term *crossplatform* has a strict meaning: the same bytecode application should run without modification on any computer that has a Java runtime. The original vision is that Java-based software agents could roam over the network automatically. That not only requires bytecode compatibility but also runtime library compatibility. But as Java evolves, it is used in many different application scenarios. The single class library approach no longer fits the needs.

Recognizing that one size does not fit all, the Java 2 Platform is divided into three editions. The Java 2 Standard Edition contains the basic JVM and core class libraries; the Java 2 Enterprise Edition provides additional class libraries and tools for enterprise server applications; the Java 2 Micro Edition consists of stripped-down virtual machines (called KVMs—Kilobyte Virtual Machines) that can run on devices with kilobytes of memory. For mobile devices, a subset of the standard edition class library and new libraries for mobile-specific tasks. It is clear that a Java bytecode application written for an enterprise server will not run crossplatform on a PDA device without modification.

In June 2003, during the eighth JavaOne conference in San Francisco, Sun Microsystems brought up a new slogan for Java: "Java Everywhere." The emphasis is no longer on direct portability of bytecode applications. The focus now is to provide the same language, consistent architectures, and similar APIs across all computing platforms. Java Everywhere allows developers to port their skills to new application arenas.

The J2ME Architecture

The separation of J2EE, J2SE, and J2ME is a step in the right direction. However, a single monolithic J2ME is still too inflexible for mobile devices. There is a huge variety of mobile devices, designed for different purposes and with different features. For example, applications on an automobile-mounted system are much more complex than those on a cell phone. Even among similar devices, such as high-end and low-end cell phones, portability can cause underutilization of resources on one device and strain on another. Device manufacturers and developers need fine-grained API differentiation among devices, not the "lowest common denominator."

To balance portability with performance and feasibility in the real world, J2ME contains several components known as configurations, profiles, and optional packages (Figure 2–15). Each valid combination of a configuration and a profile targets a specific kind of device. The configurations provide the most basic and generic language functionalities. The profiles sit on top of configurations and support more advanced APIs, such as a graphical user interface (GUI), persistent storage, security, and network connectivity. The optional packages can be bundled with standard profiles to support specific application needs.

NOTE Even with J2ME, device-specific optimization is still a major challenge in mobile application development. A single Java code base cannot account for the different screens, CPUs, memory sizes, Java API libraries and even JVM implementation bugs, found on different devices. As we discussed, Nokia reduces the required optimization work by developing relatively consistent handsets within each Developer Platform. The focus of this book is to help the readers understand the J2ME characteristics of Nokia Series 40 devices and then develop applications optimized for those devices. In Chapter 12, "Developing Scalable Applications," we cover how to scale J2ME applications across different devices within and beyond the Nokia Series 40 Developer Platform.

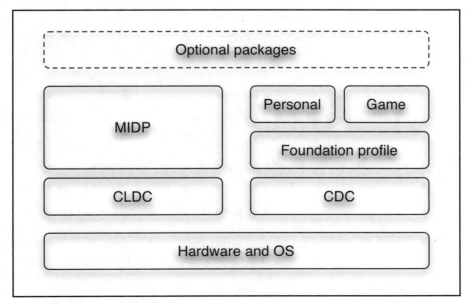

Figure 2–15 The J2ME architecture.

The two most important J2ME configurations are as follows.

- **The Connected Limited Device Configuration (CLDC)** is for the smallest wireless devices with 160KB or more memory and slow 16/32-bit processors. The CLDC has limited math, string, and I/O functionalities, and lacks features such as the Java Native Interface (JNI) and custom class loaders. Only a small subset of J2SE core libraries is supported by the CLDC virtual machines (KVMs). The most recent version of the CLDC is version 1.1. It was developed by the JSR 139 and released in March 2003.

- **The Connected Device Configuration (CDC)** is for more capable wireless devices with at least 2MB of memory and 32-bit processors. Unlike the CLDC, the CDC supports a fully featured Java 2 virtual machine and therefore can take advantage of most J2SE libraries. The CDC 1.0 was developed by the JSR 36, and it became available in March 2001. The new CDC 1.1 is currently being developed by the JSR 218 and is expected before the end of year 2004.

Important J2ME profiles include the following. The **Mobile Information Device Profile (MIDP)** is built on top of the CLDC to provide support for smart phones; the **Foundation Profile** is built on top of CDC to provide support for networked embedded devices; the **Personal Basis Profile (PBP)** and **Personal Profile (PP)** are built on top of the CDC and the Foundation Profile to provide support for GUI-based powerful mobile devices such as high-end PDA devices. The standard UI library in the current PBP and PP editions is the Java AWT (Abstract Widget Toolkit).

On the CDC and Personal Profile stack, important optional packages include the following: the RMI (Remote Method Invocation) Optional Package (JSR 66) supports remote object sharing between Java applications; the JDBC (Java DataBase Connectivity) Optional Package (JSR 169) provides a uniform interface to access structured query language (SQL) databases from Java applications; the Advanced Graphics Optional Package (JSR 209) aims to add Swing and Java 2D API libraries into the CDC/PP stack.

Although CDC and PP have their places in the mobile market, they are not nearly as popular as the MIDP. All major mobile device manufacturers, including Nokia, are committed to support MIDP. In the next section, we take a deeper look at MIDP and its optional packages.

NOTE

The concept of open interfaces is core to the Java technology. It works as follows: For a given computing task, a set of standard APIs is defined by a standards committee. Individual vendors then provide competing libraries that implement those APIs. The application code using the API is completely decoupled from the specific implementation provider. That approach minimizes the developer's learning cost and improves code portability. Yet, it also protects the freedom of choosing vendors. The Java Community Process (JCP) is an effort to develop standard Java API specifications.

JCP Executive Committees (ECs) consist of industry-leading companies. Anyone in the general public can submit a new Java Specification Request (JSR) for a new API. The appropriate EC decides whether to accept this new JSR. Once approved, the JSR lead can recruit more companies or individuals to develop the API specification together. Every specification goes through multiple stages of community and public reviews before it becomes an official Java standard.

MIDP and Its Optional Packages

The most important and successful J2ME profile is the CLDC-based MIDP. The MIDP targets the smallest devices, such as smart phones. It is already deployed on millions of handsets, including all Nokia Series 40 and 60 devices. Hence, the MIDP is a key technology that all Nokia developers need to learn.

An MIDP application consists of a suite of MIDlets. Each MIDlet can be independently installed, started, paused, and stopped by the application management software (AMS) on the device. The AMS can be controlled by the user, using the phone keypad. The MIDlet API specification provides a set of abstract life-cycle methods that hook into the AMS. Developers must implement these methods to specify the runtime behavior of each MIDlet. The code for a minimal MIDlet that displays a `Hello World` string on the screen is as follows. The details of the code are explained in Chapter 3, "Getting Started."

```
package com.buzzphone.hello;

import javax.microedition.midlet.*;
import javax.microedition.lcdui.*;

public class HelloMidlet extends MIDlet {

  Form form;

  // Called by the AMS when the MIDlet is instantiated
  public HelloMidlet () {
    form = new Form ("Hello");
  }

  // Called by the AMS when it starts the MIDlet
  protected void startApp() {
    form.append ("Hello World");
  }
```

```
// Called by the AMS when it stops the MIDlet
protected void destroyApp(boolean unconditional) {
  destroyApp(false);
  notifyDestroyed();
}

// Called by the AMS when it pauses the MIDlet
protected void pauseApp() {
  }
}
```

As of late 2003, most mobile phones in the market support the MIDP 1.0 specification. However, the MIDP 1.0 lacks some important features, such as security and advanced UI controls. As a result, device vendors often supply their own MIDP extensions to provide advanced custom features. Vendor-specific extensions undermine the portability of J2ME applications. Many problems with the MIDP 1.0 have been fixed in the MIDP 2.0, which came out of JCP in August 2002. The Nokia Developer Platforms 2.0 for Series 40 and 60 mandate MIDP 2.0 and optional packages on new Nokia phones.

Table 2–1 lists MIDP-compatible optional packages. Most of the MIDP optional packages run on CDC profiles as well. Nokia supports the optional packages at different levels:

- **Device available:** The optional package is already factory-installed on some Nokia devices.

- **Coming soon:** Device implementation of the optional package is currently being developed by Nokia engineers. It will be available on new devices soon.

- **Specification:** The optional package specification is still being developed by the JCP. Nokia supports that specification by contributing to the expert group.

- **No plan:** Nokia currently has no plan to support this optional package on its devices.

NOTE   The Java Technology for the Wireless Industry (JTWI) specification is a guidance and roadmap document for Java handset manufacturers and developers. It specifies the minimal software and hardware requirements for Java smart phones that can be marketed with the JTWI logo. A JTWI-compatible handset must support MIDP, the Wireless Messaging API, and the Mobile Media API.

Table 2–1 MIDP Optional Packages

Name	JSR	Nokia Support	Description
File I/O and PIM	75	Device available	This optional package has two modules: the file I/O module supports access to file systems on a PDA device; the PIM module allows the MIDP application to integrate with the device's native PIM clients.
Mobile Media	135	Device available	Provides audio and video capture and playback APIs. The exact supported media formats vary by devices. It is covered in detail in Chapter 9.
Wireless Messaging	120/205	Device available	Provides an API for the MIDP application to send and receive SMS and MMS messages. It is covered in detail in Chapter 8.
Location	179	Coming soon (1H2005)	Supports location tracking for devices. The location information can come either from a GPS device module or from the network carrier.
Web Services	172	Coming soon	Provides XML APIs for generic XML parsing as well as SOAP Web Services clients.
Bluetooth	82	Device available	Supports access to Bluetooth data channels and protocol libraries from an MIDP application. It is covered in detail in Chapter 10.
Security and Trust	177	Coming soon (1H2005)	Allows MIDP applications to interact with the phone's embedded security module such as the SIM card for GSM phones.
3D Graphics	184	Device available	Provides an API to display 3D scenes on a mobile device. A lightweight mobile 3D data format for the art works is also defined.
Content Handler	211	Coming soon (1H2005)	Allows devices to associate MIME types with MIDlet applications. Media files with certain MIME types will be automatically opened by the associated MIDlet.
Scalable 2D Vector Graphics	226	Coming soon (1H2005)	Provides capability to render 2D vector images in the SVG (Scalable Vector Graphics) format.

Table 2–1 MIDP Optional Packages (continued)

Name	JSR	Nokia Support	Description
SIP (Session Initiation Protocol)	180	Coming soon (1H2005)	Provides support for SIP-based communication. It will allow data to be pushed to mobile devices.
Presence and IM	165/187	No plan	Supports presence and instant messaging applications based on the SIP.
Data Sync	230	Specification	Supports synchronizing PIM databases over the network. This optional package also provides APIs to process most common PIM data formats.

The Smart-Client Paradigm

Microbrowser-based thin-client technologies were instrumental in bringing mobile Internet to masses in the early days of mobile commerce. But WAP-based mobile commerce has never taken off due to the poor usability on the client side. The new generation of smart-client and mobile middleware technology (e.g., J2ME and Microsoft's .NET Compact Framework) promises to bring feature-rich clients to mobile applications. The benefits of smart clients over thin clients include the following:

- **Smart clients have richer and more pervasive user interfaces.** In particular, the judicial use of threads can drastically improve user perception of the application performance.

- **Smart clients can be more easily personalized.** Extreme personalization is one of the most touted benefits of the freedom (mobile) economy.

- **On-device data storage reduces network traffic, especially unnecessary round trips.** It enables transactions; supports the "offline" mode when the network is temporarily unavailable; and hence improves overall performance, reliability, and availability of mobile applications.

- **Smart clients can leverage device extensions.** For example, a smart-client program can talk with the device's built-in (or attached) GPS module and barcode scanners. A smart client can also integrate with device-specific software (e.g., email and messaging clients) to improve the user's workflow.

- **Smart clients support more powerful and flexible security schemes.** They enable content-based security and distributed single sign-on.

- **Smart clients support advanced integration technologies**. They are easy to plug into existing corporate infrastructure. Supports for asynchronous messaging and XML Web Services are crucial for reliable and maintainable mobile solutions.

Tightly Integrated Smart-Client Technology: Symbian C++

The Symbian OS is a sophisticated 32-bit operating system designed specifically for mobile devices. It consumes few resources and yet has a modular, object-oriented C++ architecture. It is based on preemptive multitasking and supports threading and asynchronous processing. It was anticipated that Symbian devices could run for years without being switched off, so reliability and stability were key design goals for the OS.

The Symbian C++ API provides complete access to services, such as messaging and multimedia, as well as device and OS functionality that is not available through the use of J2ME. Symbian OS is an open developer platform available on Nokia Series 60 and higher devices as well as on devices manufactured by other Symbian OS licensees.

The Evolution of Symbian OS

Symbian devices are proliferating because of Symbian's position as an open operating system for data-enabled mobile phones. Currently, Symbian has the most partners and licensees of any mobile OS, including Nokia, Sony Ericsson, Motorola, Siemens, Fujitsu, Samsung, Sanyo, and others.

The operating system began as software for PDAs from a company called Psion. Symbian was formed in 1998 to evolve this OS primarily for phones. These high-end phone handsets are now known as smart phones. The Symbian OS is layered to support different device designs while retaining core functionality across all products. Three families of product lines emerged:

- **Keypad-based:** These are designed for one-handed operation and do not have a touch screen. They are currently the most common type of Symbian devices, and Series 60 exemplifies this design. Nokia created the Series 60 platform on top of Symbian OS and licenses it to other manufacturers such as Siemens, Samsung, Panasonic, and Sendo. This gives consumers more choice while allowing them to exchange data, use compatible software, and switch smart phones without having to learn a new interface.

- **Pen-based:** These phones include a stylus for touch-screen operation. There are now two lines of pen-based Symbian handsets: UIQ phones and the Series 90 Developer Platform. The Sony Ericsson P800 was the first device with a UIQ user interface. Nokia does not make UIQ devices but has introduced the Series 90 Developer Platform, which represents the latest in mobile technologies.

- **Keyboard-based:** These phones, such as the Nokia 9500 Communicator, are the most similar to handheld personal organizers. They have a full keyboard as well as a touch screen for pen-based input.

In the future, user input will not be the primary distinction between these designs. There will be some convergence of product features, and the addition of new features will add different distinctions between product lines.

Symbian OS Architecture

Symbian OS API (Figure 2–16) contains hundreds of C++ object classes grouped in subsystems. We can also group these subsystems in layers.

In general, we can think of the Symbian architecture in four layers or groupings: the application utility layer, the GUI framework and services, communications, and base system APIs.

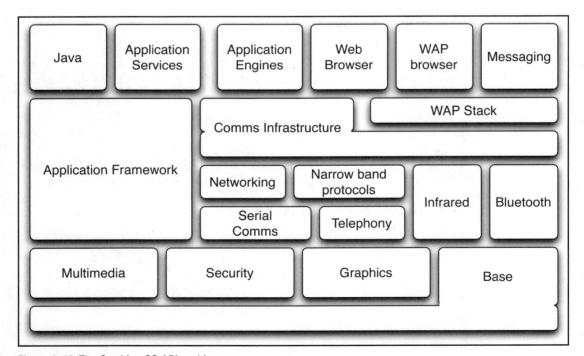

Figure 2–16 The Symbian OS API architecture.

- **The application utility layer:** This includes a variety of application-oriented utilities. Application engines give access to the data from built-in PIM applications, such as contacts and calendar schedules. This allows third-party applications to integrate with core applications easily. Other application services include specialized data management and data exchange.

- **The GUI framework and services:** The framework APIs give structure to third-party applications and provide for UI handling. These include UI controls and lower level APIs for multimedia handling of sounds and graphics. Symbian platforms such as Series 60 and UIQ extend the UI frameworks to provide for different UI designs. When developing Symbian applications, it's best to separate the UI and application logic. This limits the amount of code that needs to be ported between platforms.

- **Communications:** There's a broad stack of communication-related APIs. At a high level, there are messaging and browsing utilities. Beneath that is support for networking interfaces such as Bluetooth, infrared (IrDA), and USB; protocols such as TCP/IP, HTTP, and WAP; and of course mobile telephony services.

- **Base system APIs:** The base APIs encompass class libraries for data structures, file and memory access, date and time, and other basic system APIs.

Although it is more effort to develop Symbian C++ applications, there are compelling reasons to do so. As natively compiled C++ applications, Symbian applications can run much more quickly than J2ME applications. Depending upon the requirements of the solution, a Symbian application may be the only choice available. Symbian provides extensive APIs that give access to almost all the functionality in a handset now, whereas not all the MIDP 2.0 optional packages are available yet.

Get Connected

The success of Nokia Developer Platforms will be ultimately tested by developer adoption. Nokia provides valuable services to wireless operators, developers, content owners, and business managers who want to leverage the Developer Platforms to reach hundreds of millions of device users.

Leading Platforms

The core value behind the Nokia Developer Platforms is the large volume of shipped devices. By March 2004, more than 40 Developer Platform devices had been launched. More than 100 million Developer Platform device units will be shipped in 2004. As the mobile handset market leader, Nokia's commitment to Developer Platforms allows developers and content owners to connect to the volumes via the minimum learning curves. It also eases the decision-making process for business managers who need to identify which handsets to support.

Developer Resources

Forum Nokia, the developer arm of Nokia, provides superb support for the Developer Platforms. Forum Nokia publishes software development tools, documentations, and white papers. The white papers cover a wide range of topics from technical tutorials to best practices to business case studies. Developers can access the latest devices and mobile service servers via the Forum Nokia loaner device and developer hub services. Forum Nokia also provides technical support via telephone and Internet discussion forums. It has more than 1.35 million registered users, more than 460,000 tool and document downloads every month, and more than 17,000 unique visitors everyday. Forum Nokia allows developers to connect to Developer Platform–related answers.

In early 2004, Nokia launched the Forum Nokia PRO service. For a small annual fee, companies can gain early access to tools, the latest prototype devices, confidential documents, and proprietary technical support from Nokia.

Business Generation

Nokia helps developers to get applications to the market. For large developers, Nokia provides opportunities to include custom applications directly on shipped devices. For example, Developer Platform devices can be shipped with add-on MMC flash cards that have third-party applications preinstalled. For smaller developers, the Nokia Tradepoint program is a worldwide online application and service catalog. In March 2004, there were more than 2,500 applications and 200 buyers in the Tradepoint channels. In addition, Nokia sponsors co-marketing events with local developers and buyers around the globe.

Together with Sun Microsystems and other mobile handset vendors, Nokia provides certification services for Java applications. A certificate guarantees that the application works correctly with Nokia Developer Platform devices and hence makes it eligible for software publisher catalogs.

Nokia's catalog, co-marketing, and certification services help developers connect with customers.

Summary

The Nokia Developer Platforms enable us to develop portable and scalable mobile applications for hundreds of millions of Nokia devices. In this chapter, we covered the Series 40 and 60 Developer Platforms and introduced the four enabler technology pillars. They are WAP, MMS, J2ME, and Symbian C++. We reviewed the application paradigms each technology enables and discussed their strengths and shortcomings. It is crucial for us to understand those technologies and know how to apply them correctly to suit specific application needs. Near the end of this chapter, we also covered Nokia's developer support programs that connect developers to volumes, answers, and customers.

chapter

3

Getting Started

Write and deploy your first smart-client application for Series 40 and Series 60 phones.

Java is a key technology pillar supporting the Nokia Developer Platforms. On Nokia Series 40 devices, Java MIDP is the only way to develop smart-client applications. This chapter is an introduction to MIDP application development using Nokia tools. We assume that you already have basic knowledge of the Java programming language. We start from the basics of the MIDlet programming model and APIs. Then, we move on to discuss how to use Nokia tools to build, test, and provision an example MIDlet. The topics covered in this chapter are as follows:

- **Introducing MIDlets:** discusses the basic concepts of MIDlet, including the application life cycle and the UI model.

- **The Photo Viewer example:** uses a simple yet useful example application to illustrate how to construct a MIDlet. We discuss the details of the MIDlet life cycle and how it is implemented on Nokia devices. We also cover basics of multi-thread programming using the `Timer` API.

- **Preparing the tools:** covers the installation and configuration of Nokia development tools as well as third-party integrated development environments (IDEs). We use those tools to build the Photo Viewer example MIDlet as well as other example applications throughout the book.

- **Building the application:** provides step-by-step instructions on how to build deployable MIDP applications from the Java source files. We also discuss how to use Ant script to automate the build process.

- **Over-the-air provisioning:** discusses how to make the MIDP application available for download to the general public. We provide in-depth discussion on the Java Application Descriptor (JAD) file. As a bonus, we also explore other provisioning options using cables and Bluetooth connections.

For beginners, this chapter is a "getting started" guide that teaches you how to write your first MIDlet and deploy it to Nokia devices. For experienced MIDP developers, this chapter explains important concepts in depth and provides Nokia-specific development tips. It helps you understand the MIDP specification and the choices Nokia made when implementing the specification.

Introducing the MIDlet

The structure of a managed mobile-phone Java application is quite different from standalone Java applications on desktops or enterprise servers. To write a standalone application on the desktop, the developer needs to implement the `main()` method, which serves as the entry point of the execution. The standalone application takes control of the resources provided by the Virtual Machine (VM) and does not stop until the `main()` method exits. An MIDP application works differently. It consists of one or many MIDlets that are managed by the Java Application Manager Software (AMS). Instead of a single `main()` method, the MIDP developer needs to implement several life-cycle methods that are called by the AMS. The AMS is implemented on every MIDP-compatible device. Similar to Applets that live in a browser sandbox and servlets that live in J2EE containers, MIDlets live in the AMS. The AMS provides the following key functionalities:

- Downloads and installs the MIDlet.

- Handles MIDlet registration, authentication, and authorization.

- Starts, pauses, and stops the MIDlet upon user requests.

- Allows the MIDlet to access application metadata (e.g., JAD and manifest attributes) and resource files.

- Acts as a communication endpoint for incoming messages and connections.

The `MIDlet` abstract class provides methods that interface between the MIDlet and the AMS. Now, let's look at the `MIDlet` class.

MIDlet Life Cycle

The MIDP specification defines three states for MIDlets:

- **Active:** The MIDlet is currently running and has control over system resources such as the screen and the keypad.

- **Destroyed:** The MIDlet is shut down by the AMS. All its resources have been released. If we want to run the MIDlet again, we must call its constructor to instantiate a new object.

- **Paused:** The MIDlet is in the background. It cannot respond to any UI events but could be wakened to the active state. On Nokia devices, it is not possible to put an active MIDlet into the paused state. However, it is possible for the device to put the UI of a MIDlet into background (see the next section for details).

The user requests the AMS to change the MIDlet state via the phone's keypad. For example, when the user launches a MIDlet, the MIDlet is instantiated and put into the active state. When the user exits the MIDlet by pressing the End key on a Series 40 device, the AMS destroys the MIDlet. The application developer decides what the MIDlet should do when the state changes. For instance, when the MIDlet is put into the active state, we probably want it to display a UI screen to the LCD. The `MIDlet` class defines several abstract methods that are called by the AMS upon state change. They must be implemented by the MIDlet developer.

```
protected abstract void startApp()
protected abstract void destroyApp(boolean b)
protected abstract void pauseApp(); //Never called
```

The `startApp()` method is called before the AMS puts the MIDlet to active state. The `destroyApp()` is called after the user requests to terminate the MIDlet. The `boolean` argument of the `destroyApp()` method specifies whether this is an unconditional shutdown. The `pauseApp()` method is never called by the Nokia AMS, since Nokia devices do not provide an external mechanism for users to put the MIDlet into paused state.

The MIDlet could also request the AMS to change its own state programmatically via the following methods. Notice that they are all final methods and cannot be overridden by application developers.

```
public final void notifyDestroyed()
public final void notifyPaused() // No effect
public final void resumeRequest() // No effect
```

The `notifyDestroyed()` method requests the AMS to destroy the current MIDlet. In this case, the AMS does not automatically call `destroyApp()` before the actual state change. So, if the `destroyApp()` method contains logic to release system resources and clean up, the MIDlet should explicitly call it first. The `notifyPaused()` method and the `resumeRequest()` method have no effect on Nokia devices. Figure 3–1 shows the life-cycle states of a MIDlet on Nokia devices.

The Background and Foreground UI States

Although Nokia devices do not support the paused state for MIDlets, they do support the concept of background and foreground MIDlet UI. The background and foreground UI states are not part of the MIDlet life cycle, and hence no life-cycle method is invoked during the state changes.

On Series 40 devices, only one MIDlet can be actively running at any given time. If the user needs to access another MIDlet or native application, he would have to exit the MIDlet first. However, it is possible for the device to put a temporary system screen in front of the MIDlet screens to deliver messages that require immediate user attention without actually interrupting the MIDlet execution

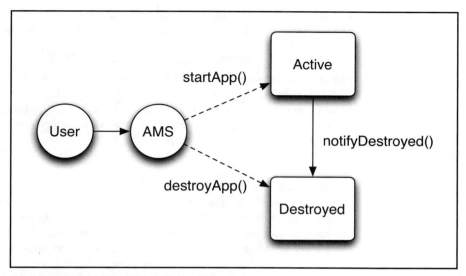

Figure 3–1 MIDlet life cycle on Nokia devices.

flow. For example, if we receive a voice call on a Series 40 device while running a MIDlet, the system screen asking us to accept or reject the call is displayed in the foreground. Once we make a selection, the MIDlet UI is returned to the foreground again.

On Nokia Series 60 devices, multiple MIDlets and native applications can run concurrently. We can use the End key to put an active MIDlet into background and use the system menu to bring a background MIDlet back to foreground. The `pauseApp()` method is never called during the process. In the "Background MIDlet on Series 60 Devices" section in Chapter 4, "MIDP User Interface," we discuss how to programmatically switch Series 60 MIDlets between background and foreground. It provides a simple workaround for the `notifyPaused()` and `resumeRequest()` methods. We also provide a workaround for the `pauseApp()` method in special scenarios.

Accessing the AMS

The `MIDlet` also provides several methods to access configuration data and external applications via the AMS. The implementations of those methods are provided by the MIDP runtime environment. Since they are final, developers cannot change the behavior of those methods.

```
public final String getAppProperty(String s)
public final boolean platformRequest(String url)
public final int checkPermission(String permission)
```

The `getAppProperty()` method retrieves the named property values from the application descriptor file (JAD file) or the JAR manifest file. The `checkPermission()` method checks whether a specific permission is granted to this MIDlet. We check out the usage of those two methods later in this chapter. When `platformRequest()` is called with an `http://host` or `https://host` URL, the device requests the user's permission to start the native Web browser and direct it to the page provided in the URL. When the method is called with a `tel:<phone number>` URL, the user is asked if he wants to initiate a voice call to the given phone number. The `platformRequest()` method call returns immediately and does not block the rest of the MIDlet execution flow.

TIP

When we use the `platformRequest()` method to launch a browser, the exact behavior is dependent on the device. Current Series 40 devices do not support concurrent browser and MIDlet applications. The MIDlet would have to exit before the browser could be launched. Furthermore, on some Series 40 devices, the browser is only launched after the MIDlet is terminated by the `notifyDestroyed()` method. Simply pressing the End key to terminate the MIDlet does not launch the browser. On Series 60 devices, the device puts the MIDlet screen into background and brings the browser screen to the foreground. Once we quit the browser, the MIDlet is brought back to the foreground again. On the other hand, the request to make a voice call is executed immediately while the MIDlet is still running on both Series 40 and Series 60 devices.

MIDlet UI Basics

Once the MIDlet is in the active state, it is responsible for handling displays and user inputs. A large part of the MIDP API is UI related. In this section, we give a quick and brief introduction of the MIDP UI so that we can proceed to discuss the example application. Details on the design and usage of the API are covered in Chapter 4. "MIDP User Interface" and Chapter 5, "Developing Action Games."

The `Display` class provides access to the physical LCD screen. We can display content to the screen by calling the `setCurrent()` method.

```
Display.setCurrent(Displayable d)
```

The `Displayable` object passed to the above method could be a `Form` object that contains several UI widgets (i.e., the high-level UI paradigm) or a `Canvas` object that renders itself (i.e., the low-level UI paradigm). In order for the `Displayable` object to receive user interactions, we could add `Command` objects into it.

```
Displayable.addCommand (Command c)
```

The `Command` object shows a text label mapped to one of the phone's soft keys. Once the user presses the key, a UI event is generated and passed to its parent

Displayable object. The Displayable object then further passes the event to a registered CommandListener.commandAction() callback method. The application developer provides an implementation of the CommandListener interface and registers it with the Displayable object. A majority of MIDlets extensively use an event-driven programming model with listener callbacks.

```
Displayable.setCommandListener (CommandListener cl)
```

In the CommandListener.commandAction() callback, the developer decides how to respond to the UI events raised from the Command buttons.

The Photo Viewer Example: Life Cycle

The Photo Viewer example is a simple application to illustrate MIDlet basic concepts and the procedures of MIDP development. We add more functionality to it in later chapters to show the usage of MIDP APIs. All the code examples and build scripts in this book are available for free download from the book's Web sites (*http://www.forum.nokia.com/books* and *http://www.MichaelYuan.com/Series40/*). Now, let's look inside the Photo Viewer MIDlet. We focus on how the life-cycle methods are implemented.

Starting and Running the MIDlet

The primary functionality of the application is to browse a set of digital photos (i.e., an album) on a mobile phone. All the photos are bundled into the application at build time. When the user starts up the application, she sees the first picture on the screen; then she can use the Next soft key on the phone to move to the next picture until she reaches the last picture in the album. The process is demonstrated in Figure 3–2.

NOTE   In this example application, for the sake of simplicity and clarity, the content of the album is built into the application. Hence, you have to download and install a new version of the application to change to another album. However, in real-world applications, we would probably require the application to update its album by downloading new contents via the Internet. MIDP network APIs and related issues are covered in Chapter 7, "Data Connectivity."

NOTE   Today, it is very convenient to host your photo albums on a Web site. Many sites generate mobile phone–friendly pages with WML markups and images with reduced sizes. However, the MIDP application has a key advantage: the user does not need a wireless connection to view the pictures. So, you can view the pictures on an airplane. A bonus benefit is that there is no need to wait for each page to download.

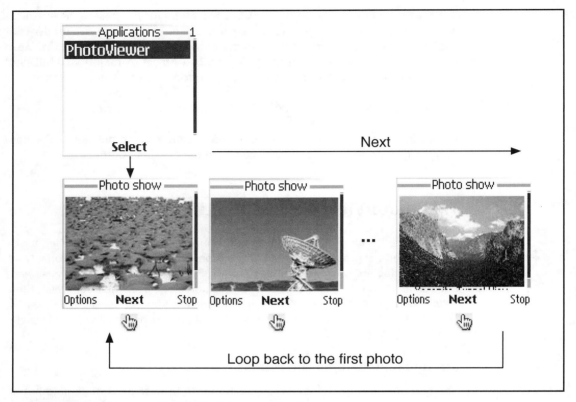

Figure 3–2 Browse pictures with the photo viewer application.

Code Walkthrough

When the user runs a MIDlet, the AMS first calls the MIDlet's constructor to instantiate a new object and then calls the startApp() method. In our Photo Viewer MIDlet, the constructor and startApp() methods are as follows:

```
import javax.microedition.lcdui.*;
import javax.microedition.midlet.*;
import java.util.*;

public class PhotoViewer extends MIDlet
               implements CommandListener {

   private Display display;
   private Command next;
   private Command exit;
   // Other commands
```

```java
private Form imageForm;

private String [] imageNames;
private String [] imageFileNames;
private int imageIdx;
// ... ...

boolean exitConfirmed;

public PhotoViewer () {

  int numOfImages =
Integer.parseInt(getAppProperty("NumberOfImages"));
  imageNames = new String [numOfImages];
  imageFileNames = new String [numOfImages];
  for (int i = 0; i < numOfImages; i++) {
    int tmpi = i + 1;
    String tmp = getAppProperty("Image-" + tmpi);
    int cIdx = tmp.indexOf(",");
    imageFileNames[i] = tmp.substring(0, cIdx).trim();
    imageNames[i] = tmp.substring(cIdx+1).trim();
  }
  imageIdx = 0;

  display = Display.getDisplay (this);
  imageForm = new Form ("Photo show");

  next = new Command ("Next", Command.OK, 1);
  imageForm.addCommand (next);
  exit = new Command ("Exit", Command.EXIT, 1);
  imageForm.addCommand (exit);
  // Other commands ...
  imageForm.setCommandListener (this);
}

protected void startApp () {
  showImage(imageIdx);

  // The following statement is not necessary on
  // Series 40 devices since there is no re-entry.
  exitConfirmed = false;
}

protected void pauseApp () {
  // Not called in Nokia devices
}
```

```java
   private void showImage (int index) {

     imageForm.deleteAll ();

     /* Use the following alternative on MIDP 1 devices
     try {
       imageForm.delete(0);
     } catch (Exception e) {
       e.printStackTrace ();
     }
     */

     Image img;
     try {
       img = Image.createImage("/" +
                       imageFileNames[index]);
     } catch (Exception e) {
       e.printStackTrace ();
       img = null;
     }
     ImageItem imgItem =
        new ImageItem(imageNames[index], img,
                       ImageItem.LAYOUT_CENTER, "image");
     imageForm.append(imgItem);

     display.setCurrent(imageForm);
   }

   public void showNext () {
     imageIdx++;
     if (imageIdx > imageNames.length - 1) {
       imageIdx = 0;
     }
     showImage (imageIdx);
   }

   // ... ...

   public void commandAction (Command c, Displayable d) {
     if (c == exit) {
       safeShutdown ();
     } else if (c == next) {
       showNext ();
     }
     // Handle other commands
   }
}
```

The `PhotoViewer` MIDlet constructor does two things: it first reads in the album information, including the number of images, their file names, and image descriptions, from the application descriptor or manifest file using the `getAppProperty()` method. Then, the constructor instantiates and composes the `Form` object. It also adds `Command` buttons and a `CommandListener` to the `Form`.

The `startApp()` method calls the `showImage()` method to instantiate and display the first photo image on the `Form`. It then displays the `Form` to the LCD screen. After the MIDlet enters the active state, it waits for user input.

TIP

Notice that the `PhotoViewer` class is both a `MIDlet` and a `CommandListener`. From a developer point of view, it is often a good idea to piggyback the `CommandListener` on top of an existing `MIDlet` or `Displayable` object so that the `commandAction()` method will have access to internal data members of UI components. For more information, see the "Overall Architecture" section of Chapter 11, "End-to-End Design Patterns."

When the user presses the Next soft key on the screen (or in the Options menu on a device with two soft-keys), the `commandAction()` method increases the image index by one and calls the `showImage()` method again to refresh the image on the displayed `Form` object. It is a relatively straightforward process.

Exiting the MIDlet

After we are done viewing the album, there are two ways to exit the MIDlet. On a Series 40 device, we could just press the End key to exit immediately (Figure 3–3). Or, we could use the MIDlet's Exit soft key to exit more elegantly (Figure 3–4).

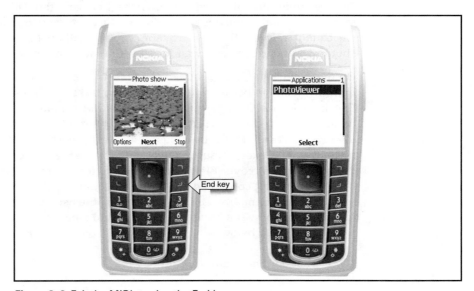

Figure 3–3 Exit the MIDlet using the End key.

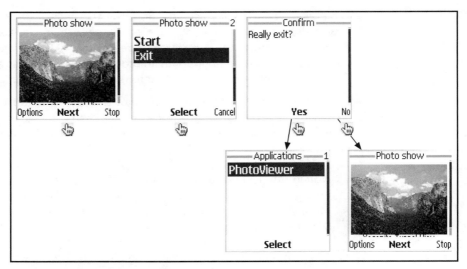

Figure 3–4 Exit the MIDlet using the Exit command.

On a Series 60 device, the End key puts the MIDlet UI into background rather than terminating it.

Code Walkthrough

When the user presses the End key, the AMS calls destroyApp(true) and then terminates the MIDlet unconditionally. On a Series 40 device, if the destroyApp() method call blocks, the AMS will wait for it for five seconds. Five seconds after the user presses the End key, the MIDlet is terminated regardless whether the destroyApp() call has returned. So, using the End key, we cannot rely on the destroyApp(true) method to complete a lengthy shutdown process (e.g., to wait for a user input or to notify a remote server).

On the other hand, using a Command object to exit the MIDlet gives us much more flexibility in performing the shutdown tasks. When the user chooses the Exit item in the Options menu on the MIDlet screen, the command action handler calls the safeShutdown() method, which in turn calls destroy(false). If the user has confirmed the shutdown, the destroy() method would execute successfully, and the safeShutdown() method then calls notifyDestroyed() to ask the AMS to terminate the current MIDlet. But if the user has not confirmed shutdown, the destroy() method would throw a MIDletStateChangeException and prompt the user with a new screen asking for confirmation. The source code for safeShutdown() and destroy() methods is listed below.

```
// Inside the PhotoViewer class

public void safeShutdown () {
```

```
    try {
      destroyApp (false);
      notifyDestroyed ();
    } catch (MIDletStateChangeException me) {
      display.setCurrent(new ConfirmExitScreen(this));
    }
}

protected void destroyApp (boolean unconditional)
                    throws MIDletStateChangeException {
  // Clean up ...

  // Only check confirmation if this is a conditional
  // shutdown (i.e., not shutdown by pressing the
  // End key.
  if (!unconditional) {
    if (!exitConfirmed) {
      throw new MIDletStateChangeException ();
    }
  }
}
```

The confirmation screen provides two Command buttons. If the user selects yes, the exitConfirmed variable is set to true, and the shutdown procedure continues with another call to safeShutdown(). If the user selects no, we will resume the view session of the MIDlet. The confirmation screen class is listed here. Please notice that, again, the ConfirmExitScreen class is a Form that acts as its own CommandListener.

```
public class ConfirmExitScreen extends Form
                    implements CommandListener {

  private PhotoViewer viewer;
  private Command yes;
  private Command no;

  public ConfirmExitScreen (PhotoViewer v) {
    super ("Confirm");
    viewer = v;

    yes = new Command ("Yes", Command.OK, 1);
    no = new Command ("No", Command.BACK, 1);

    append ("Really exit?");
    addCommand (yes);
    addCommand (no);
    setCommandListener (this);
```

```
    }


    public void commandAction (Command c, Displayable d) {
      if ( c == yes ) {
        viewer.exitConfirmed = true;
        viewer.safeShutdown ();
      } else {
        viewer.exitConfirmed = false;
        viewer.resume();
      }
    }
}
```

The resume() method in the PhotoViewer class is shown below.

```
  // Inside the PhotoViewer class

 public void resume () {
    display.setCurrent(imageForm);
  }
```

Automatically Start MIDlets via the Push Registry

So far, we discussed how to change MIDlet life cycle states instantaneously via the AMS or programmatically from inside the MIDlet. We cannot start a MIDlet programmatically from within another one. However, the MIDP Push Registry provides a mechanism to have the AMS start any MIDlet in the suite in a future time or upon a trigger caused by a network external event. The PushRegistry class contains static methods to interact with the AMS. The Push Registry is only supported on MIDP 2.0 devices. The execution can be scheduled after the specified delay time (in milliseconds) via the registerAlarm() method. The midlet argument is the full class name of the MIDlet. For security reasons, a MIDlet can only register MIDlets in the same MIDlet suite (inside the same JAR file). Series 40 devices cannot run two MIDlets at the same time, so the registered MIDlet might not run at the expiration time if there is already another MIDlet running in the foreground.

```
static long registerAlarm(String midlet, long time)
```

The MIDlet execution can also be automatically triggered by an incoming network connection. The registerConnection() method registers incoming connections and security filters with the AMS. The incoming connection URL conforms to the MIDP Generic Connection Framework specification, discussed in Chapter 7, "Data Connectivity" and Chapter 8, "Wireless Messaging." The security filter specifies the allowed originators of the incoming push connections. It could be a combination of numerical IP addresses with * and ?

wildcards. The `PushRegistry` class also provides classes to unregister connections and query the existing Push Registry.

```
static void registerConnection(String url,
                 String midlet, String filter)
static boolean unregisterConnection (String url)
static String [] listConnections (boolean available)
static String getFilter (String url)
static String getMIDlet (string url)
```

As we will see later, we can even declaratively register execution triggers in the JAD file.

The Photo Viewer Example: Thread and Timer

In the previous example, we showed how the Photo Viewer MIDlet responds to AMS and user events. MIDlets can also update their own application state without user intervention by running a separate controller thread. As we see again and again throughout this book, the concept of multi-thread programming is absolutely key to effective MIDP applications. Hence, we cover multi-thread programming in this first sample application of this book.

The example scenario we demonstrate here is an automatic slide show. We can start the show by choosing the Start command option. The slide show displays each photo for five seconds before moving on to the next one. It is as if the user is pressing the Next key every five seconds. During the slide show, we can choose the Stop option to stop it. Figure 3–5 shows the slide show in action.

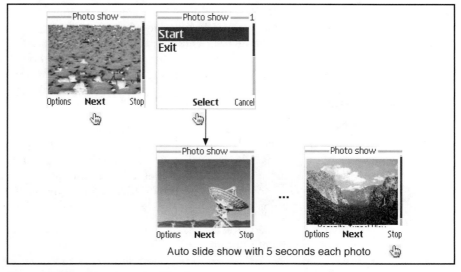

Figure 3–5 Run the automatic slide show.

Why Multi-threading?

At a glance, it seems trivial to start the automatic slide show. Maybe we could just run a loop to change the photo every five seconds inside the Start command handler method. It could be something like the following.

```
// The following code does not work
public void commandAction (Command c, Displayable d) {
  if (c == start) {
    // For simplicity, assume that the automatic slide
    // show runs for ever and ignore the Stop command
    // at this time.
    while (true) {
      // Change the photo
      showNext ();
      // Sleep for five seconds
      Thread.sleep (5000);
    }
    // ... ...
  }
}
```

However, if you really try out the above code, you would notice that the photo is never changed and the MIDlet appears to be frozen. Why is that? The reason lies in the underlying mechanism of how the MIDlet works.

According to the MIDP specification, the device runs the MIDlet in a single thread known as the UI thread. When the MIDlet is running, the UI thread updates and renders the display, listens for user input, and runs the UI event handler methods (e.g., the commandAction() method) as needed. By definition, a thread is a CPU process that handles computing tasks linearly. It cannot do two things at the same time. So, in the above code, when the commandAction() method is running, the UI thread is not able to update the display or listen for further user input. All the UI changes requested by the commandAction() method are rendered after it returns and the UI thread becomes idle again. In fact, the MIDP specification requires the commandAction() method to return immediately to avoid freezing the user interface.

The correct way to implement the automatic slide show feature is to spawn a new thread from the commandAction() method. The commandAction() method returns as soon as the new thread is started. Multiple threads allow the MIDlet to run multiple tasks parallel to each other. In this case, the new thread runs the code for the slide show and leaves the UI thread idle for rendering the display changes and listening for UI events.

In the MIDP API, the TimerTask and Timer classes help us start threads automatically at future times. They are widely used in a variety of applications. Now, let's check out how to use them in the Photo Viewer example.

The TimerTask

In the Photo Viewer example, the AutoShowTask class, which inherits from the TimerTask abstract class, updates the photo for the scheduled slide transition. The TimerTask class represents a task that can be executed in the future. It is a Runnable type, which indicates that it runs as a thread. Hence, the TimerTask can run lengthy tasks in the background without freezing the user interface. The developer must extend the TimerTask class and implement the task itself in the abstract run() method. The code for the AutoShowTask class is shown below.

```
class AutoShowTask extends TimerTask {

  private PhotoViewer viewer;

  public AutoShowTask (PhotoViewer s) {
    viewer = s;
  }

  public void run () {
    viewer.showNext ();
  }
}
```

Upon execution, the AutoShowTask.run() method calls the PhotoViewer.showNext() method to update the screen to the next photo. The idle UI thread does the actual work to render the updated screen. Since the task can be executed multiple times and set up for recurring execution, the TimerTask has two public methods to manage scheduling:

- The cancel() method cancels all future scheduled execution of this task.

- The scheduledExecutionTime() method returns the scheduled execution for the most recent actual execution of this task. This method is often used in the run() method to determine whether the current task is executed on time. If the actual execution time is much later than the scheduled time, we might skip the task completely by immediately returning from the run() method.

The Timer Class

The Timer class is used to schedule the execution of TimerTask objects. We can schedule the execution to happen at a given time or after a given delay from now.

```
public void schedule(TimerTask task, Date date)
public void schedule(TimerTask task, long delay)
```

The delay argument is the delay time in milliseconds. The Timer class can also schedule recurring executions at a given time interval after an initial delay or from a specific time point in the future. The schedule() method schedules them at fixed-delay. That means the next execution happens after the specified time delay from the current execution. If the current execution is delayed for some reason, the next execution will be delayed as well. The scheduleAtFixedRate() method schedules tasks at fixed-rate from the first execution. That means future executions will always happen at specified times. Any unexpected delay of any particular execution in the series would not affect the timing of the next execution in the line.

```
public void schedule(TimerTask task,
                          long delay, long period)
public void schedule(TimerTask task,
                          Date firstTime, long period)
public void scheduleAtFixedRate(TimerTask task,
                          long delay, long period)
public void scheduleAtFixedRate(TimerTask task,
                          Date firstTime, long period)
```

The cancel() method cancels all future scheduled executions of this Timer object. In the PhotoViewer MIDlet, we start and stop the scheduled Timer execution using the following code.

```
public class PhotoViewer extends MIDlet
                implements CommandListener {

  // ... ...
  private Command start;
  private Command stop;

  // ... ...
  private Timer autoShowTimer;

  public PhotoViewer () {
    // ... ...

    start =
        new Command ("Start", Command.SCREEN, 1);
    imageForm.addCommand (start);

    stop = new Command ("Stop", Command.STOP, 1);
    imageForm.addCommand (stop);
```

```java
      // ... ...
  }

  // ... ...

  private void stopShow () {
    if (autoShowTimer != null) {
      autoShowTimer.cancel ();
    }
  }

  private void startShow () {
    stopShow ();
    autoShowTimer = new Timer ();
    AutoShowTask r = new AutoShowTask (this);
    autoShowTimer.schedule(r, 0, 5000);
  }

  // ... ...

  protected void destroyApp (boolean unconditional)
                      throws MIDletStateChangeException {
    // Stop any auto show
    stopShow ();

    // ... ...
  }

  // ... ...

  public void commandAction (Command c, Displayable d) {
    if (c == exit) {
      safeShutdown ();
    } else if (c == start) {
      startShow ();
    } else if (c == stop) {
      stopShow ();
    } else if (c == next) {
      showNext ();
    }
  }
}
```

Preparing the Tools

Now, we have written the code for all the three classes, `PhotoViewer`, `ConfirmExitScreen`, and `AutoShowTask`, in our simple Photo Viewer application. To build, test, and deploy the application, we need to use J2ME development tools. In this section, we cover how to install key tools from Nokia and how those tools fit into a full development environment. In later sections, we discuss how to use them to build and deploy the application step by step.

Nokia Developer's Suite for J2ME

The Nokia Developer's Suite (NDS) for J2ME contains a set of essential tools for developing J2ME applications for Nokia devices. It can be used as a standalone application or integrated with existing Java IDEs. In this book, we cover NDS 2.1 for J2ME, which enables Java smart-client development for Nokia devices supporting MIDP 1.0 and MIDP 2.0. The NDS runs on the Windows 2000/XP and RedHat Linux v7.2 platforms. It might also run on other flavors of Linux OSes, but they are neither tested nor supported. The Windows and Linux editions of the NDS are very similar. Although all our examples and discussions in this book are based on the Windows edition, Linux developers can easily apply them. The NDS installer and its software components are all Java-based. Please make sure that you have a recent version of Sun Java runtime environment (JDK 1.4.1 or later) installed on your computer. If not, you can download the JDK software from *http://www.java.sun.com*.

Install the NDS for J2ME

You can download the most recent version of NDS for J2ME from Forum Nokia's tools section at *http://www.forum.nokia.com/tools*. You need to register a free account with Forum Nokia before you can download it. After downloading the zip installer, you can extract the files into a temporary folder and run the `setup.exe` program. Just follow the on-screen instructions to finish the installation. We recommend that you install the NDS into the default `C:\Nokia` directory. Since we will install many Nokia software components throughout this book, using the default installation directories minimizes the chance for undesired crosstalk between the components. You will have a choice to install NDS as a standalone application or part of an existing IDE. We use the standalone installation for all our examples. The IDE integrated edition is discussed briefly in the next section.

TIP

The NDS installer requires you to enter your Forum Nokia username and a product serial number before it can finish installing. You can request a serial number to be emailed to your registered email address from the NDS download page. Or, you can request the serial number from within the installation program using your Forum Nokia username and password. Again, the serial number will be delivered to your email address registered with Forum Nokia. You have to receive that email before you can proceed.

A Quick Tour of the NDS

After installation, you can start the NDS from the Windows Start | Programs | Nokia Developer Tools | Nokia Developer's Suite 2.1 for J2ME menu. The tool bar on the left side of the main window shows the major features of the NDS (see Figure 3–6).

- The Create Class screen allows developers to create the skeleton source code for Java classes via an easy-to-use wizard. Figure 3–6 shows how to use this wizard and the generated code. We can fill in those empty methods in the generated code as necessary.

- The Create Package screen helps to build the application descriptors and JAR archives for deployment.

- The Sign Application screen provides tools to digitally sign your MIDP applications for secure distribution.

- The Deployment screen allows developers to deploy their MIDP applications to Nokia devices connected through serial ports, Bluetooth connection, or ftp to over-the-air (OTA) provisioning servers.

- The Start Emulators screen lists installed emulators of Nokia devices. We must test our applications against emulators before deploying them to actual devices.

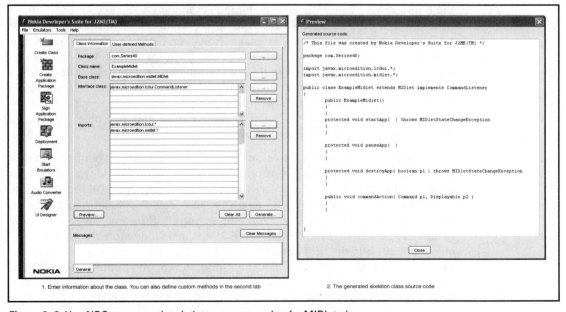

Figure 3–6 Use NDS to create the skeleton source code of a MIDlet class.

- The Audio Converter screen provides tools to convert audio files to ringtone and ToneXML formats, which Nokia devices can play. It can even convert a midi file into a Java array that can be directly copied and pasted into MIDP application source code.

- The UI designer screen is a visual UI code generator for MIDP applications. We introduce it in Chapter 4.

For developers, the unique value of the NDS is its support for Nokia devices. However, the NDS itself does not "know" any particular device. Device-related features, such as the emulator and class libraries, are included in the device SDKs that work with the NDS. Out of the box, the NDS comes with the Nokia 7210 MIDP SDK and Series 60 MIDP Concept SDK pre-installed. More SDKs are available from the Forum Nokia Web site free of charge. To run the example applications in this book, you need to download and install the Nokia Series 40 Developer Platform 2.0 SDK, which is a device SDK for the Nokia 6230 device.

Install Device SDKs

The device SDK contains the entire software stack on that particular device, including the JVM, the Java AMS, and the Java API libraries. The SDK also knows the physical constraints (e.g., the heap memory size) of the device. Since the development PC uses different operating systems and CPUs than the actual device, all the components in the device SDK are ported to the PC platform. Nokia engineers made the greatest effort to ensure that the port is done accurately to reflect the device characteristics (even including bugs) on the development PC. The SDK also contains a device emulator that emulates the entire device user interface, including screen sizes and key layouts, on the development PC. The SDK allows us to develop and run device applications on a PC and get realistic user experiences. However, please note that application performance on emulators is often different from that on real devices and in real wireless networks. We should always stress test our application on live devices after we pass the emulator test. You can download all necessary device SDKs from the *http://www.forum.nokia.com/tools* Web site. As is the case in NDS download, you need a valid Forum Nokia account and must request a serial number for each SDK.

It is strongly suggested that you stop the NDS before installing additional device SDKs. Running the `setup.exe` program in the installer zip file, you can install each SDK into the default `C:\Nokia\Devices` directory. The SDK registers itself with the NDS during installation. Hence, the new device emulator automatically becomes available in the Start Emulator screen. If, for some reason, the SDK failed to register itself with NDS or if the SDK is installed before the NDS, we can also manually add the SDK emulator into the NDS: click the Configure button on the Start Emulator screen and click the Add button on the popup window. Then, you can direct the NDS to find the SDK installation directory in the file dialog box. After adding the SDK, we can run any MIDP application simultaneously in any number of selected device emulators (Figure 3–7).

Figure 3–7 Run the MIDP application in emulators.

TIP

Some Nokia device SDKs are labeled as "concept SDK." The Java runtime in a concept SDK is not ported from the software on actual devices. Instead, it is adapted from the SUN MIDP reference implementation with a "skin" that emulates the device UI. So, the behavior of the concept emulator might differ from that of the real device. Developers must test all MIDlets developed on a concept SDK on the real device.

NOTE

The Sun J2ME Wireless Toolkit (J2ME WTK) is a very popular J2ME development tool. Like the NDS, it provides some basic project management tools and a device emulator. The device emulator in the WTK does not reflect any real-world device. It is a reference implementation reflecting the device capabilities and behaviors specified in the MIDP specification. The WTK imposes no limit on heap memory, storage space, and so on, so it is great for prototyping MIDP applications. We use the J2ME WTK occasionally in this book to crosscheck the results from the Nokia emulators. Figure 3–8 shows the Photo Viewer MIDlet in action on a WTK emulator.

Inside the SDK

The device SDKs can be used independently from the NDS user interface. In order to access the SDK from other development tools (e.g., from command line or Ant) or to diagnose errors, we need to understand the structure inside the SDK. The two most important Series 40 SDKs for Nokia 7210 and 6230 devices have similar file structures.

- At the top level, several XML files or property files specify the SDK configuration for NDS and other integration tools.
- The `lib` directory contains the Java API classes supported on that device. The API library is typically stored in a file named `classes.zip`.

Figure 3–8 The Sun J2ME Wireless Toolkit.

- The doc directory contains the API documentation, installation guide, and tools guide.

- The examples directory contains sample MIDlet applications.

- All the important SDK tools, such as the emulator and preverifier, are in the bin directory.

The bin directory in the SDK contains the following files and directories.

- The preverify.exe program is used to preverify MIDlet classes.

- The 7210.exe program in the Nokia 7210 SDK and S40_DP20_em.exe program in the Nokia Series 40 Developer Platform 2.0 (i.e., Nokia 6230) SDK are used to start device emulators.

- There are a number of JAR, DLL, and media files to support the emulator.

- The device.profile file contains the emulator configuration data. It can be manually edited or changed from the emulator's Preference menu.

- The jam-apps directory contains all the MIDlet suites installed on this device. Each MIDlet suite has its own subdirectory, which stores the persistent data specific to this MIDlet suite (i.e., the MIDP Record Management System, see Chapter 6, "Handling Application Data").

Apache Ant

Now with the NDS and Nokia device SDK installed, we have all the necessary tools to build, run and deploy our MIDP applications. In fact, we show you how to do that "by hand" in the next section to illustrate the key concepts. For most practical projects though, an automated build system is essential for developer productivity. The Apache Ant project is the most popular build system in the Java world. It supports an extensible XML-based script language to control the entire build process. The Ant distribution package supports a number of core tasks. For example, the core tasks allow us to copy and move files, compile, package a JAR file, and execute any program. You can also write your own custom Ant task using its Java APIs. We show you how to write a simple Ant build script for our MIDP project later in the next section and you will see how much easier it is compared with the manual building approach. Throughout the book, we encounter several Ant scripts. They are discussed with the example projects in relevant chapters. In this section, we discuss how to install Ant on your development computer.

The first step is to download the Ant distribution package from the *http://ant.apache.org/* Web site. Since Ant is Java-based, it is the same zip file for all OSes. You can unzip the downloaded file into any directory on your hard drive. That's it for the installation part! Now, we have to configure some environment variables to make the Ant executables accessible to us. On Windows 2000 and XP, the environment variables are accessible from Control

Panel I System I Advanced I Environment Variables (see Figure 3–9). On Linux, the environment variables can be set using your favorite shell scripts. You have to configure the following variables:

- `JAVA_HOME`: It points to your JDK installation directory (e.g., `C:\Java\j2sdk1.4.2\`).

- `ANT_HOME`: It points to your Ant installation directory (e.g., `C:\Java\ant-1.6.0\`).

- `PATH`: You should append the `bin` directory in your Ant installation (e.g., `C:\Java\ant-1.6.0\bin\`) to the end of the existing `PATH` variable. It is also advisable to attach your JDK `bin` directory (e.g., `C:\Java\j2sdk1.4.2\bin\`) to the system `PATH` variable.

Now, if you have an Ant build script `build.xml` in your current directory, you can execute `ant` directly from your command line and start the build process. We use Ant to build most of the example applications in this book.

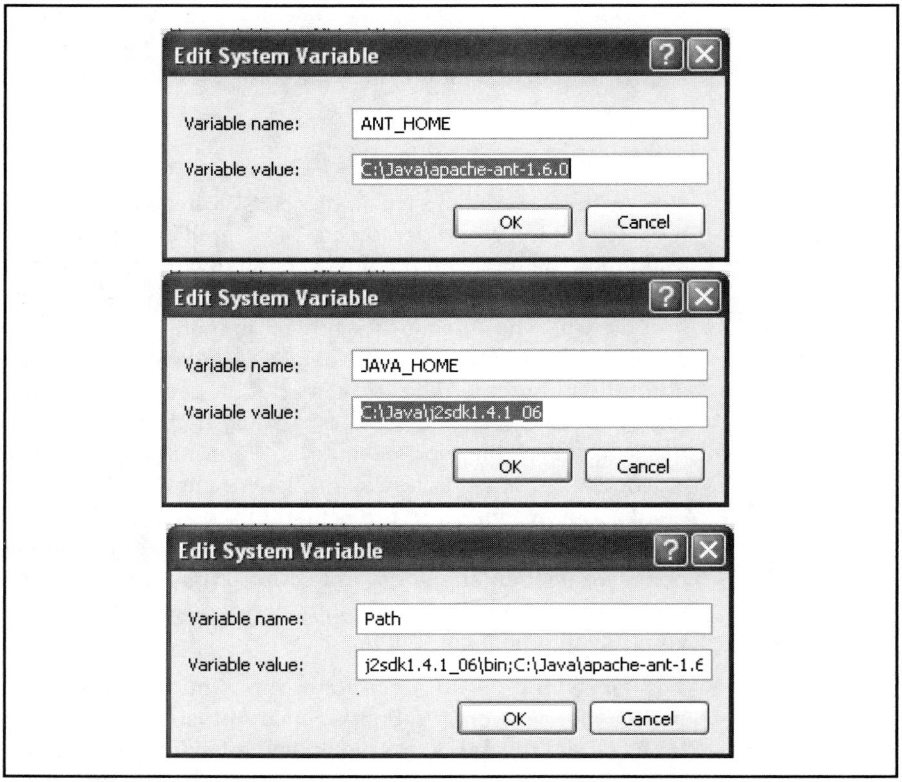

Figure 3–9 Set environment variables on Windows 2000/XP.

Integrated Development Environments

Integrated development environments are very useful developer productivity tools. IDEs can help us visualize the code, collaborate with peers, streamline the development process, and inspect the execution flow in debugging. Many IDE products support the Java programming language, and some of them support J2ME development for Nokia devices. In this section, we introduce several of these IDEs. Experienced Java developers can continue to use familiar IDEs when moving into the J2ME space.

NOTE
All the IDEs discussed in this section support Apache Ant, meaning that we can run Ant tasks directly from the IDE and use Ant script to substitute the IDE's own build environment.

Borland JBuilder

Borland JBuilder is a popular IDE among corporate Java developers. The Borland Mobile Studio (*http://www.borland.com/mobile/*) contains JBuilder Mobile Edition, which comes bundled with popular Nokia SDKs, and has a visual UI builder for the MIDP. We can drag and drop MIDP widgets directly on to the designer form and let JBuilder generate the UI code for us. After we write the application, JBuilder automatically builds and packages it. All the necessary descriptor files and manifest files are automatically generated. We can test and debug it on Nokia emulators from within the IDE.

The Borland Enterprise Studio for Mobile contains additional enterprise design tools (e.g., TogetherSoft), process management tools (e.g., CaliberRM and StarTeam), performance analysis tools (e.g., OptimizeIt), as well as enterprise server and database development tools. It supports the entire development life cycle for end-to-end projects that have both mobile and server components.

The Sun Java Studio

The Sun Java Studio (formerly know as SunONE Studio) is Sun's commercial Java IDE based on the NetBeans open source project. The Sun Java Studio Mobile edition (*http://developers.sun.com/prodtech/javatools/jsmobility/index.html*) supports compilation, preverification, execution, and obfuscation of MIDP applications. It comes default with the Sun J2ME WTK. Nokia device SDKs can be integrated easily via the device emulator registry.

Eclipse

Eclipse is a very popular open source Java IDE originally developed by IBM. You can download it for free from *http://www.eclipse.org*. Out of the box, Eclipse provides excellent support for key IDE features such as context-aware editing, team collaboration, project management and advanced debugger.

However, the real strength of Eclipse is its open plugin architecture that allows third party open source or commercial developers to extend its functionalities.

The Nokia Developer's Suite 2.2 for J2ME can be installed as an Eclipse plugin to support MIDP application development for Nokia devices. With the NDS plugin, we can develop, test, debug, package and deploy the entire MIDP application from within Eclipse. You can find a detailed tutorial on how to develop MIDlets using Eclipse with NDS on the author's Web site at *http://www.MichaelYuan.com/Series40/*.

In this book, we decide not to tie our solutions to any specific IDE tool. Using Apache Ant, you have the freedom to build the source code from the command line or from any of your favorite IDE's Ant console. This way, we can reach the maximum number of readers and explain the technology in more generic terms. Without the constraints of the IDE, we are also able to come up with more powerful and flexible solutions (see Chapter 12, "Developing Scalable Applications"). For readers who are interested in building and running the sample applications in IDEs, short instructions and pointers to further readings are available from the author's Web site at *http://www.MichaelYuan.com/Series40/*.

Building the Photo Viewer MIDlet

With JDK, ANT, and Nokia MIDP class libraries, we can now build the executables to be run in the SDK emulators and real devices.

A Step-by-Step Tutorial

In this section, we illustrate how to build and test the application primarily using command-line tools. The advantage of command-line tools is that they let us clearly understand the interactions between tools such as the compiler, preverifier, and packager. Once you master the command-line tools, it is very easy to switch to IDE tools or automated build scripts.

Before we start, let's review the structure of our project. We can put the entire project in any directory on the hard drive. The name and location of the project directory does not matter. What matters is the file structure under it. The project directory contains four subdirectories:

- The `src` directory contains the entire source code tree. As the Java language specification requires, each Java package is mapped to a subdirectory with the same name.

- The `res` directory contains all the resource files, including the photos to display.

- The `bin` directory contains deployable files and manifest files.

- The `tmp` directory contains the immediate files such as the compiler output. It also serves as the staging area for the final JAR archive contents. We assemble the Java class files, manifest files, and resource files in this directory before generating the deployment JAR file.

The directory structure before we start the build process is illustrated in Figure 3–10.

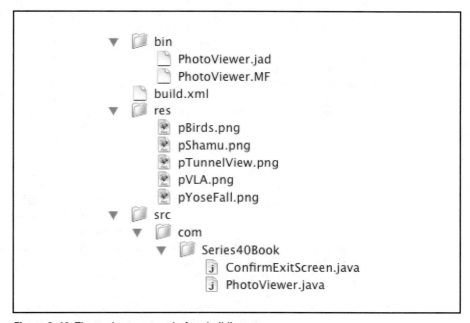

Figure 3–10 The project content before building.

Compiling

First off, we need to compile the Java source code files into Java bytecode class files. This can be done by any standard JDK compiler `javac`. The `javac` utility only compiles the source code. We have to manually set up the output directory tree `tmp\tmpclasses\com\Series40Book` before invoking `javac`. Since the MIDP application uses a different set of base class libraries than standard J2SE applications, we have to manually specify the `classpath` and `bootclasspath` options from the command line. The `bootclasspath` tells the compiler how to look for the most basic Java bootstrap classes, such as `java.lang.Object` and `java.lang.Exception`. The MIDP class library comes from the Nokia device SDK we plan to use. The compiling command, invoked inside the project root directory, is as follows (all in one line).

```
javac -classpath
C:\Nokia\Devices\Nokia_S40_DP20_SDK_1_0\lib\classes.zip
-bootclasspath
C:\Nokia\Devices\Nokia_S40_DP20_SDK_1_0\lib\classes.zip
-sourcepath src -d tmp\tmpclasses
src\com\Series40Book\*.java
```

TIP

To bring up a command-line window under the Windows OS, you could click on the Run item under the Start menu. In the command box, enter `cmd` and hit the Execute button. That gives you a basic DOS window.

More sophisticated command-line shells, such as `bash` and `csh`, are also available on Windows from the open source Cygwin project. You can download their software for free at *http://www.cygwin.com/*.

Preverifying

A major difference between the MIDP's KVM and the standard JVM is that the KVM requires the developer to preverify the bytecode application before deployment in order to reduce the runtime cost. The preverification process adds a `stackmap` attribute to each method in the class files. A `stackmap` attribute itself consists of zero or more stackmap frames. Each stackmap frame specifies an offset, an array of verification types for the local variables, and an array of verification types for the operand stack. At runtime, the type checker reads the stackmaps for each such method and uses these maps to generate a proof of the type safety of the instructions in the `Code` attribute. This two-step procedure is completed in significantly less time with less static memory footprint than the conventional VM implementations used in Java Standard Edition. The `preverify` program is included in the `bin` directory of Nokia device SDKs. The following command takes in the compiled Java class files from the `tmp\tmpclasses` directory and outputs the preverified class files to the `tmp\pvclasses` directory.

```
\Nokia\Devices\Nokia_S40_DP20_SDK_1_0\bin\preverify
-classpath
C:\Nokia\Devices\Nokia_S40_DP20_SDK_1_0\lib\classes.zip
-d tmp\pvclasses tmp\tmpclasses
```

Copying Resource Files

The application JAR file contains not only the preverified Java class files but also application resource files. In our application, the photo image files are resource files. We have to copy the image files from the `res` directory into the `tmp\pvclasses` directory before packaging the application (see Figure 3–11).

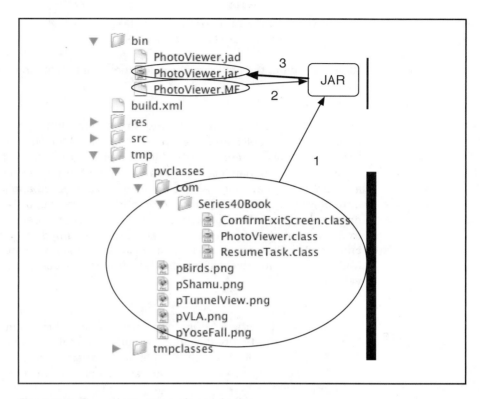

Figure 3–11 The project content after packaging.

Packaging

The MIDP specification requires the application JAR file to contain certain meta-information in its manifest file. You need to create a manifest file `bin\PhotoViewer.MF` as follows.

```
Manifest-Version: 1.0
MIDlet-1: PhotoViewer, ,com.Series40Book.PhotoViewer
MIDlet-Name: Photo Viewer
MIDlet-Version: 1.0.0
MIDlet-Vendor: The Nokia Series 40 Blueprints
MicroEdition-Configuration: CLDC-1.1
MicroEdition-Profile: MIDP-2.0
```

The `MIDlet-1` attribute specifies the MIDlet name, icon (empty), and the MIDlet class name for that MIDlet. Now, we can invoke the following `jar` command (all in one line) inside the `tmp\pvclasses` directory to build the archive in `bin\PhotoViewer.jar`.

```
jar cvfm ..\..\bin\PhotoViewer.jar
         ..\..\bin\PhotoViewer.MF.
```

After packaging, the final directory structure is illustrated in Figure 3–11.

The JAD File

The JAR file is only part of the story. A complete MIDP application requires a matching Java Application Descriptor (JAD) file. The AMS checks the JAD file before it installs or launches the MIDlet suite. The content of the JAD file is similar to the JAR manifest file with additional information such as the location and size of the matching JAR file. In addition to required application metadata attributes, we can also put custom attributes in the JAD file to provide name/value properties accessible to the `MIDlet.getAppProperty()` method from the runtime. In a trusted MIDlet, the same named properties in the JAD and manifest files must have matching values, or the AMS would not install the MIDlet. In an untrusted MIDlet, the JAD property values override the manifest values.

NOTE   A trusted MIDlet is a MIDlet that carries a verifiable digital signature from Nokia or a third-party developer. An untrusted MIDlet does not have a digital signature. All MIDP 1.0 MIDlets are untrusted. For more discussion on this topic, please refer to the later section on the "Security-Related MIDlet Attributes."

In our example, we put the photo file names and descriptions as custom attributes in the JAD file. The complete `bin\PhotoViewer.jad` file is as follows.

```
MIDlet-Name: Photo Viewer
MIDlet-Version: 1.0.0
MIDlet-Jar-Size: 58425
MIDlet-Jar-URL: PhotoViewer.jar
MIDlet-Vendor: The Nokia Series 40 Blueprints
NumberOfImages: 5
Image-1: pBirds.png, Flying off
Image-2: pVLA.png, The VLA telescopes
Image-3: pShamu.png, Shamu in Sea World
Image-4: pYoseFall.png, Yosemite Falls
Image-5: pTunnelView.png, Yosemite Tunnel View
```

The `NumberOfImages` and `Image-n` attributes are custom properties for the MIDlet to locate the image files and descriptions at runtime. The JAR manifest and JAD files can be generated from the NDS's Create Application Package screen (see Figure 3–12). We just need to specify the MIDlet attributes and what source code and resource files to include in the JAR. Using the NDS, the

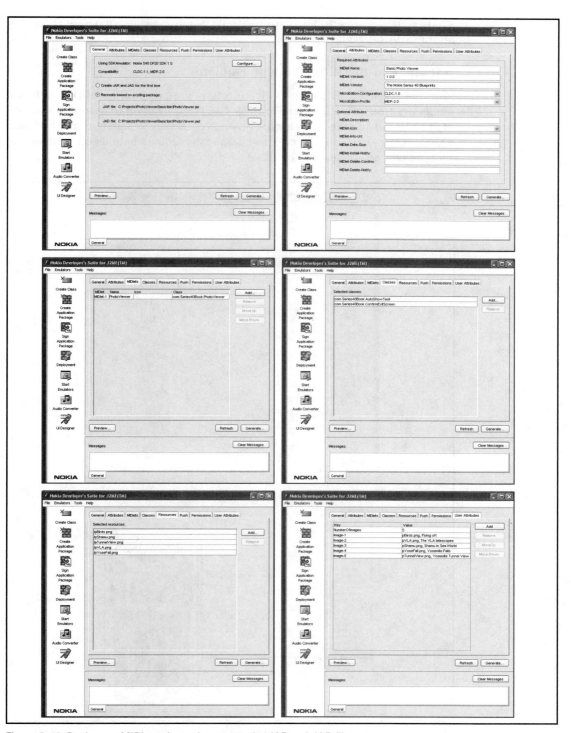

Figure 3–12 Package a MIDlet suite and generate the JAR and JAD files.

`MIDlet-JAR-Size` attribute in the JAD file is automatically generated correctly after the JAR is built.

Test and Run the MIDlet Suite in Emulator

With the correct JAR and JAD files in place, we can run the MIDlet in Nokia emulators from the NDS (see Figure 3–13). We only need to enter the location of the JAD file into the file selection box and click the Emulate button. The Nokia 6230 emulator provides a nice set of diagnostic tools to help us understand the runtime characteristics of the MIDlet.

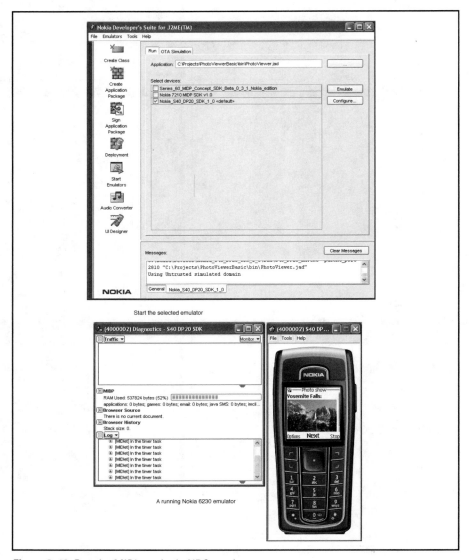

Figure 3–13 Run the MIDlet suite in NDS emulators.

Automated Build with Ant

To build Java applications entirely from the command line is tedious. For instance, if we have many Java packages in the source tree, we could have to build the matching tree in the tmp\tmpclasses directory and invoke the javac command for every package. Using Apache Ant, we can automate the above process and integrate the build workflow into Java IDEs. The following listing shows the Ant script build.xml we use for the Photo Viewer project.

```xml
<project name="PhotoViewer" default="all">

  <target name="init">
    <tstamp/>
    <property name="projname" value="PhotoViewer" />

    <property name="SDK"
      value="C:/Nokia/Devices/Nokia_S40_DP20_SDK_1_0" />
    <property name="midpclasses"
              value="${SDK}/lib/classes.zip" />
    <property name="preverify"
              value="${SDK}/bin/preverify" />

    <property name="tmp" value="tmp" />
    <property name="tmpclasses"
              value="${tmp}/tmpclasses" />
    <property name="pvclasses"
              value="${tmp}/pvclasses" />
  </target>

  <target name="clean" depends="init">
    <delete dir="${tmp}" />
    <delete file="bin/${projname}.jar" />
    <delete file="bin/*.sh" />
  </target>

  <target name="prepare" depends="clean">
    <mkdir dir="${tmp}" />
    <mkdir dir="${tmpclasses}" />
    <mkdir dir="${pvclasses}" />
  </target>

  <target name="compile" depends="prepare">
    <javac srcdir="src" destdir="${tmpclasses}"
           bootclasspath="${midpclasses}"
    >
      <classpath>
        <pathelement path="${tmpclasses}"/>
```

```
                  <pathelement path="${midpclasses}"/>
                </classpath>
              </javac>
            </target>

            <target name="preverify" depends="compile">
              <exec executable="${preverify}">
                <arg line="-classpath ${midpclasses}"/>
                <arg line="-d ${pvclasses}" />
                <arg line="${tmpclasses}" />
              </exec>
            </target>

            <target name="package" depends="preverify">
              <copy todir="${pvclasses}">
                <fileset dir="res" />
              </copy>
              <jar jarfile="bin/${projname}.jar"
                   basedir="${pvclasses}"
                   manifest="bin/${projname}.MF"
              />
            </target>

            <target name="all" depends="package" />

        </project>
```

NOTE   Different OSes uses different symbols as path directory separators. Windows OSes use the back-slash (\), while the Unix OSes use the forward slash (/). Ant is a crossplatform build system. We can use the forward slash as the directory separator in build.xml for all platforms. So, in this book, you will sometimes see us use the forward slash in Windows path names.

This Ant script defines six build targets:

1. The init target initializes the system variables used in the script.

2. The clean target cleans out the temporary directories and the JAR file from previous builds.

3. The prepare target prepares the directories.

4. The compile target compiles the source code.

5. The preverify target preverifies the class files.

6. The package target copies the image files and builds the JAR file.

When we run `ant` from the command line, all six targets are executed in the above order (see Figure 3–14).

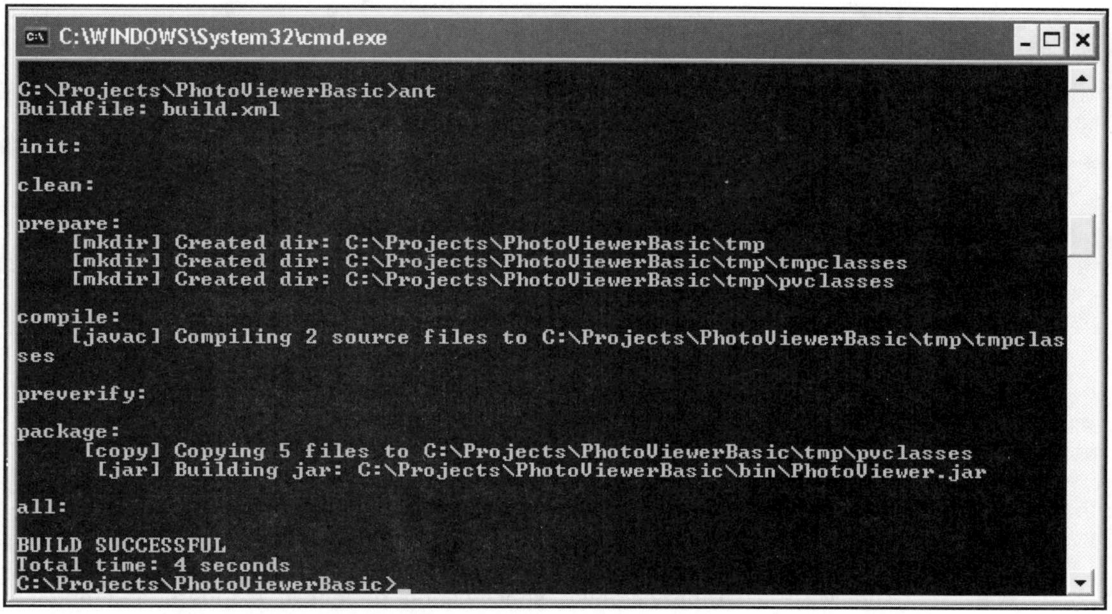

```
C:\WINDOWS\System32\cmd.exe

C:\Projects\PhotoViewerBasic>ant
Buildfile: build.xml

init:

clean:

prepare:
    [mkdir] Created dir: C:\Projects\PhotoViewerBasic\tmp
    [mkdir] Created dir: C:\Projects\PhotoViewerBasic\tmp\tmpclasses
    [mkdir] Created dir: C:\Projects\PhotoViewerBasic\tmp\pvclasses

compile:
    [javac] Compiling 2 source files to C:\Projects\PhotoViewerBasic\tmp\tmpclas
ses

preverify:

package:
    [copy] Copying 5 files to C:\Projects\PhotoViewerBasic\tmp\pvclasses
    [jar] Building jar: C:\Projects\PhotoViewerBasic\bin\PhotoViewer.jar

all:

BUILD SUCCESSFUL
Total time: 4 seconds
C:\Projects\PhotoViewerBasic>
```

Figure 3–14 Run the ANT build script from the command line.

WARNING

After using the ANT script to build the JAR file, we should manually check the JAR file size and update the corresponding attribute in the JAD file before running the application. Unmatched JAR size and JAD attribute would cause the emulator or device to reject the application.

It is not difficult to develop a custom ANT task that automatically updates the JAD attribute. For instance, the open source Antenna project has produced several such J2ME-specific ANT tasks. However, extending ANT is clearly beyond the scope of this book. We leave the readers to explore more on this topic.

The Ant script can be integrated into any IDE that supports Ant. Figure 3–15 shows the Ant control window for the Photo Viewer project in the IntelliJ IDEA. It instantly adds J2ME support to this popular IDE.

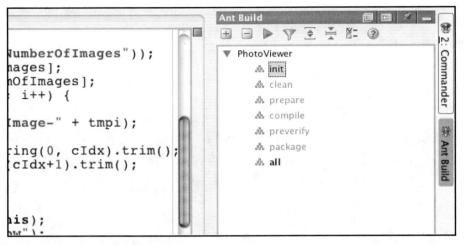

Figure 3–15 IDEA's Ant task window.

Now we have successfully built the MIDlet suite. The next challenge is to get into the millions of user devices.

Over-the-Air Provisioning

The MIDP OTA provisioning specification defines a standard and efficient mechanism to install MIDlet into Java devices using the existing wireless data infrastructure. We can use OTA to provision the MIDlet to one device for testing or to millions of devices for commercial deployment.

OTA Process Overview

From a user's point of view, the OTA provisioning process takes the following steps.

- **Discovery.** The user uses a phone Web browser or a specialized catalog browser to locate applications she wants to use. The application download page contains a link to the MIDP JAD file.

- **Download and verify the JAD file.** By following the above mentioned link, the phone browser downloads the JAD file and invokes the on-device AMS. The AMS takes over the installation from now on. The next several steps until "Execute the MIDlet suite" happens automatically without active user effort. The AMS verifies the JAD file and makes sure the device has the correct versions of system software and enough memory space to run the MIDlet suite. If anything fails in this step, the MIDlet suite is rejected.

- **Download the JAR file.** The AMS downloads the MIDlet suite JAR file following the URL specified in the JAD file.

- **Authenticate the MIDlet suite.** If the JAD file carries digital signatures, the MIDlet suite will be authenticated by the AMS. This feature is not available on MIDP 1.0 devices.

- **Authorize API usage.** A MIDP 2.0 application can request to use some restricted system APIs (e.g., network access) via attributes in the JAD file. The AMS grants permissions based on the authenticated developer or distributor digital signature.

- **Install the MIDlet suite.** If all the above steps succeed, the AMS installs the MIDlet suite on the device.

- **Execute the MIDlet suite.** The user can then launch the MIDlet from a menu item in the phone user interface.

- **Update the MIDlet suite.** When a new version of the MIDlet suite comes out, the user has the option to update it. All the persistent data associated with this MIDlet (e.g., RMS data, see Chapter 6) can be preserved.

- **Remove the MIDlet suite.** The user can request the AMS to remove any installed MIDlet suite from the device memory. All the persistent data storage space used by the MIDlet suite is freed.

We can use NDS to test the OTA process in an emulated environment. To access that functionality, select the OTA tab in the Start Emulator screen (see Figure 3–16). Now, let's look at the technical details from a developer's perspective.

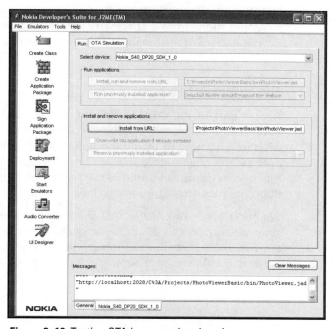

Figure 3–16 Testing OTA in an emulated environment.

The Server Setup

The first thing the developer needs to do is to make the JAD and JAR files available for download from a network server. The provisioning server has to support HTTP. In addition, in order for the WAP gateway and client device to recognize the JAD/JAR files and take appropriate actions, the server must associate those files with the following MIME types.

```
text/vnd.sun.j2me.app-descriptor    jad
application/java-archive             jar
```

For Apache Web servers, we can insert the above two lines into the `conf/mime.types` file. For Tomcat 4.*x* servers, the correct mappings are already in the `conf/web.xml` file. An OTA-compatible mobile device must have a WAP June 2000–compatible browser that supports HTTP authentication (i.e., server response code 401 and 407) and supports the HTTP POST operation. The reason for the authentication support requirement is that some provisioning servers may be routed via a proxy, which may request authentication details, or the provisioning servers themselves may wish to authenticate users before allowing the MIDlet downloads. The WAP browser invokes the AMS to process the downloaded JAD and JAR files when it detects the above two MIME types.

NOTE   Some wireless operators require developers to provision applications over their managed networks for better security and billing controls. In this case, you have to sign a service agreement with the operator, certify your application, and upload it to their servers. The users will download and buy applications from a special menu on their device. As a developer, you will get a share of the revenue from the operator according to your agreements.

The MIDlet Attributes

A core part of the OTA specification is the JAD file, which contains critical information about the application. The device uses the JAD file to decide whether and how to install the application. Similarly, the manifest file in the JAR also contains attributes of the MIDlet suite. Some of the attributes are required to appear in both the JAD and JAR manifest files. We can optionally duplicate manifest attributes in the JAD file.

We had a quick look at the JAD and manifest files for the Photo Viewer MIDlet suite already. In this section, we give a complete review of available MIDlet attributes. Most attributes, unless specifically mentioned, apply to both MIDP 1.0 and 2.0. As we have seen, the NDS's Create Application screen provides a template-based user interface to generate JAD and JAR files (see Figure 3–12).

Required MIDlet Attributes

The MIDlet attributes listed in Table 3–1 are required by all MIDP applications.

Table 3–1 Required MIDlet Attributes

Attribute	Description	Required in Files
MIDlet-Jar-URL	This is the URL of the JAR file location. Both relative and absolute URL paths are accepted. However, the length of the URL string in this attribute has to be below 256 characters.	JAD
MIDlet-Jar-Size	This specifies the size of the JAR file. The device would have a chance to reject a very large MIDlet suite before downloading it. The downloaded JAR is checked against this attribute. If they mismatch, the MIDlet suite installation is rejected.	JAD
MicroEdition-Configuration	This specifies the J2ME configuration upon which this MIDlet suite can run. The current available values on Nokia Series 40 devices are CLDC-1.0 and CLDC-1.1	Manifest
MicroEdition-Profile	This specifies the J2ME profile upon which this MIDlet suite can run. For example, the Nokia 6230 device is based on MIDP 2.0 and is backward-compatible with MIDP 1.0, so we can use either MIDP-1.0 or MIDP-2.0 for Nokia 6230 applications.	Manifest
MIDlet-Name	This is a descriptive name of the entire MIDlet suite application.	JAD and manifest
MIDlet-Version	This is the version of the MIDlet suite. The device AMS uses this information to update the installed MIDlet suite. We suggest using delimitated numerical values (e.g., x.y.z) for this attribute. If this attribute is missing, the Series 40 default value of 0.0.0 is used.	JAD and manifest
MIDlet-Vendor	This is the name of the MIDlet suite vendor.	JAD and manifest
MIDlet-n	This attribute takes a comma-delimited list of parameters that specify the name, icon, and class name for each MIDlet in the suite. The *n* starts from 1 for the first MIDlet in the suite and counts up. An example of this attribute could be something like this: MIDlet-2: Demo, /demo.png, example.demo.	Manifest

Optional Informational MIDlet Attributes

The JAD and JAR manifest files can also contain optional attributes that provide additional information about the suite (Table 3–2).

Table 3–2 Optional Informational MIDlet Attributes

Attribute	Description	Required in Files
MIDlet-Description	The description of the entire MIDlet suite.	JAD and/or manifest
MIDlet-Icon	The display icon of the MIDlet suite.	JAD and/or manifest
MIDlet-Info-URL	The URL for more information about the MIDlet suite.	JAD and/or manifest
MIDlet-Data-Size	Persistent storage size required by this MIDlet suite. The download may be aborted if a very large value is specified for this attribute.	JAD and/or manifest

NOTE
The `MIDlet-Description` and `MIDlet-Icon` attributes both apply to the entire MIDlet suite. Description and icon for each individual MIDlet are specified in the comma-delimited list of each `MIDlet-n` attribute.

Push-Related MIDlet Attribute

The `MIDlet-Push-n` attribute in the JAD file allows us to declaratively register types of incoming network connections with the AMS. It takes three parameters: an incoming connection URL, which typically specifies a protocol and an incoming data port (see Chapter 7 for incoming connections in MIDP Generic Connection Framework); a MIDlet class name; and a filter for allowed originating address of the connection. The AMS invokes the MIDlet when the device receives data from the specified incoming port. After it starts, the MIDlet can access the pushed data by opening a connection to the incoming URL. Example usages of the `MIDlet-Push-n` attribute are as follows.

```
MIDlet-Push-1: socket://:79, com.Series40Book.midlet, *
MIDlet-Push-2: datagram://:1234, com.Series40Book.midlet, *
```

Security-Related MIDlet Attributes

A MIDlet suite can be authenticated based on its digital signature. The Sign Application screen in the NDS provides tools to digitally sign applications. The

MIDlet suite with authenticated digital signature is trusted. For Nokia devices, the signing digital certificate must have a root of Verisign or Thawte. This feature is only available in MIDP 2.0. Table 3–3 lists the authentication related MIDlet attributes.

Table 3–3 Authentication MIDlet Attributes

Attribute	Description	Required in Files
MIDlet-Certificate-n-m	This attribute takes in a Base64 encoded digital certificate that officially identifies the application developer or distributor (the digital signer). The number n indicates the chain path, and the number m indicates the individual certificate in the chain. The idea is that multiple authentication chains for the signing certificate are allowed. The root certificate is not specified in the JAD file. The device stores valid root certificates in its native key store. At least one of these chains must be validated against at least one root certificate on the device before the AMS can install the MIDlet suite.	JAD
MIDlet-Jar-RSA-SHA1	This attribute takes in a Base64 encoded digital signature of the JAR file generated by digest algorithm SHA1 and public key algorithm RSA. The signature must be verified before the AMS can install the MIDlet suite.	JAD

The MIDP application security model allows devices to restrict access to certain APIs, such as the network connections, message sending, and camera operations, based on the MIDlet suite's digital signer. If the user installs a MIDlet from the Internet, she will always be informed about the signer's identity (or the lack of digital signature) and the security implications before she finishes the installation.

- On a Nokia device, a trusted MIDlet signed by one of Nokia's or the carrier's digital certificates would be allowed access to all APIs without explicit user confirmation. The factory- or carrier-installed MIDlets could come with such digital signatures.

- A trusted MIDlet signed by a third-party developer (i.e., not Nokia and not the carrier) prompts the user for approval before it accesses restricted APIs.

- An untrusted MIDlet suite (i.e., no digital signer) would also require explicit user approval before it accesses restricted APIs.

The difference between an untrusted MIDlet and a third-party trusted MIDlet is that the untrusted MIDlet typically needs to ask permission every time it accesses an API call, while the third-party trusted MIDlet often only needs to ask once (the first time) in a session. Table 3–4 shows the difference between the runtime behaviors of untrusted and third-party trusted MIDlets. The MIDlet can check whether a permission is granted to it by calling the `checkPermission()` method.

Table 3–4 Runtime Behaviors of Untrusted and Third-Party Trusted MIDlets When Asking for User Permission for Restricted APIs

Restricted API	Untrusted MIDlet	Third-Party Trusted MIDlet
Network access (see Chapter 7)	Ask every time.	Only ask the first time of the session.
Messaging (see Chapter 8)	Ask every time.	Ask every time.
Connectivity (IR and Bluetooth; see Chapters 7 and 10)	Only ask the first time of the session.	Only ask the first time of the session.
Multimedia (e.g., camera access; see Chapter 9)	Ask every time.	Only ask the first time of the session.
Read user data (PIM data from JSR 75)	Not allowed.	Ask every time.
Edit user data (PIM data from JSR 75)	Ask every time.	Ask every time.
Auto-start	Only ask the first time of the session.	Only ask the first time of the session.

TIP

Both Series 40 and Series 60 devices allow users to fine-tune the security policy applied to each MIDlet. For example, the user can suppress all Bluetooth connectivity confirmations for an untrusted or a trusted third-party MIDlet. On Nokia 6230 (Series 40), this is done via the Options menu for each MIDlet in the Applications menu. On Nokia 6600 (Series 60), this is done via the Options menu in the Application Manager. The trusted MIDlet has known origin and the trust makes it easier for the user to relax security policies.

NOTE The Read user data and Edit user data permissions listed in Table 3–4 refer to the permissions to access the native personal information manager (PIM) database (e.g., address book, calendar, and to-do list) via the J2ME PIM and File I/O Optional Package defined in JSR 75. In addition, as we will see in Chapter 4, the PHONENUMBER type TextField in the MIDP UI could prompt the user with a list of phone number choices read from the device's native PIM database.

A MIDlet suite could declare its requirement for accessing restricted APIs via its MIDlet attributes. The attributes listed in Table 3–5 allow the AMS to determine whether the device can run the MIDlet. For example, if the MIDlet's required permission does not exist on the device (e.g., camera snapshot permission on a device without camera) or is not available in the MIDlet's security domain, the MIDlet installation would be rejected.

Table 3–5 API Access Permission MIDlet Attributes

Attribute	Description	Required in Files
MIDlet-Permissions	This specifies APIs that are critical to the function of this MIDlet suite.	JAD and manifest
MIDlet-Permissions-Opt	This specifies noncritical APIs the MIDlet suite might use.	JAD and manifest

We can use the NDS to sign a MIDlet suite (see Figure 3–17). The NDS provides a default signing certificate, and we can import our own certificate as well.

Notification and Reporting MIDlet Installation Events

During installation, the device uses HTTP POST to send a "status report" to the notification URL. Each status report consists of a special code and a short message on the first line. The codes and messages are defined by the OTA specification. They are listed in Table 3–6. Most of the messages are self-explanatory.

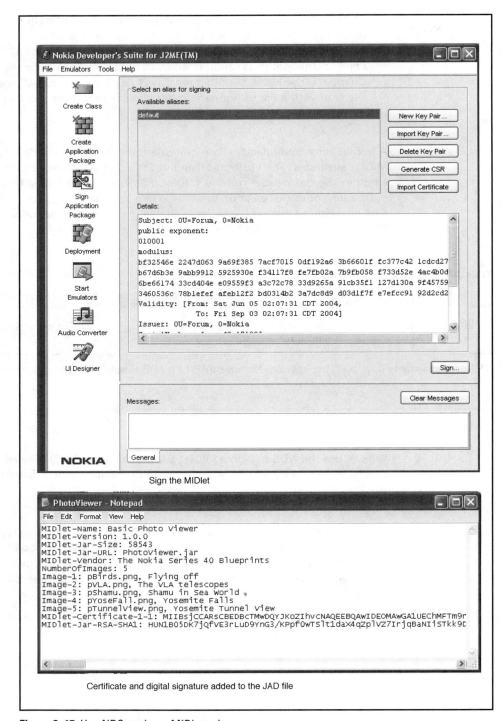

Figure 3–17 Use NDS to sign a MIDlet suite.

Table 3–6 Status Report Codes and Messages

Code	Message
900	Success
901	Insufficient memory
902	User cancelled
903	Loss of network service
904	JAR size mismatch
905	Attribute mismatch
906	Invalid descriptor
907	Invalid JAR
908	Incompatible configuration or profile
909	Application authentication failure
910	Application authorization failure
911	Push registration failure
912	Deletion notification

The notification server must reply to the POST message with "200 OK" to acknowledge the status report. Otherwise, the device will attempt to resend the report until it reaches a maximum retry limit determined by the device manufacturer.

In addition to the automatic reports, developers can instruct the MIDP device to report application installation and deletion status to any arbitrary Web site using the three MIDlet attributes listed in Table 3–7. That helps developers and carriers to track users and bill them accordingly.

Nokia Specific MIDlet Attribute

On a Nokia Series 40 device, a user-downloaded MIDlet suite is placed under the Applications | Collection menu by default. We can use a special JAD attribute to place it under the Applications | Games menu. A Settings menu is available under the Games menu but not under the Collection menu. Using the

Table 3–7 Notification and Reporting MIDlet Attributes

Attribute	Description	Required in Files
MIDlet-Install-Notify	Upon successful installation of the MIDlet suite, the device posts a notification message to the specified URL.	JAD
MIDlet-Delete-Notify	When the user deletes the MIDlet suite, the device posts a notification message to the specified URL.	JAD
MIDlet-Delete-Confirm	This attribute value is a text message that is displayed to the user when he chooses to delete a MIDlet.	JAD

Games | Settings menu, the user can define an overall policy on sounds, lights and vibrations for all games. For example, a user can turn off all game sound to avoid disturbing neighbors in a crowded environment.

```
Nokia-MIDlet-Category: Games
```

Other Provisioning Options for Nokia Phones

OTA provisioning is great for making mobile applications available to a large number of users. However, for developers, it is inconvenient and expensive to upload the application to an OTA server and then download it from the wireless network every time we recompile. Nokia supports alternative ways for developers to provision test applications onto devices without Internet connections.

Cables

Nokia phones can be connected to development PCs via serial or USB cables. We can transfer wallpapers, ringtones, and MIDP applications to the device via those cable connections. The NDS supports application provisioning through serial cables (see Figure 3–18). We should specify both the JAR and JAD files before clicking on the Deploy button.

NOTE   The NDS also allows us to deploy a MIDlet application to a remote OTA sever via FTP. Then, we can download and install the MIDlet directly from the phone browser (see Figure 3–18).

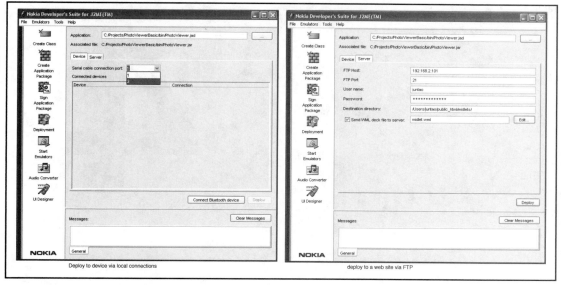

Figure 3–18 MIDlet suite deployment options in the NDS.

Bluetooth

Many new Nokia phone models support Bluetooth connectivity as a cable replacement technology. We can send a MIDlet JAR file to a device. The received JAR file shows up as an incoming message in the phone's message Inbox. When the user opens the message, the AMS is automatically invoked to install the MIDlet suite inside the JAR file. Since there is no JAD file, information in the JAR manifest is used for the installation.

Infrared Port

Most existing and future Nokia devices support infrared ports for short-range data communication. MIDlet installation over the infrared port is similar to an installation over Bluetooth.

Summary

In this chapter, we covered the entire process of developing and deploying a MIDlet application using Nokia tools. We also discussed the basic concepts, APIs, and techniques of MIDP programming. It lays the foundation for the next several chapters, where we look at more MIDP APIs and techniques to develop end-to-end applications.

chapter

4

MIDP User Interface

Develop rich mobile phone user interfaces using the MIDP UI.

A core feature of the MIDP technology is its support for developing mobile phone user interfaces. The MIDP provides a set of Java APIs known as the LCDUI, which has functionalities similar to the Java Abstract Windows Toolkit (AWT) and Swing APIs in the desktop world. This chapter covers mobile phone UI development using the MIDP APIs. Our focus is the MIDP 2.0 API, which is standard on all Nokia Developer Platform 2.0 devices. At the time of writing (late 2004), Developer Platform 1.0 devices, which are based on MIDP 1.0, still have a large installed base. Hence, the key differences between the MIDP 2.0 and MIDP 1.0 API are also briefly covered throughout the discussion. The topics in this chapter are as follows:

- **The design of the MIDP UI API:** covers the overall design of the LCDUI API, including the distinction between the high-level and low-level APIs. We introduce the common display and UI event models for all LCDUI `Screen` and `Canvas` classes.

- **The high-level API:** covers the `Form` and other standard UI components. We illustrate the API usage through examples with both Series 40 and Series 60 screenshots.

- **The low-level API:** covers the pixel-based API. We discuss how to draw on the `Canvas` and how to handle keypad events. A useful example illustrates how to add animation functionality to `Canvas` applications.

- **Advanced MIDP UI Concepts:** covers advanced UI topics not adequately addressed by the previous sections. This section is essentially a collection of MIDP UI tips and techniques. Examples of those topics include high-level item layout management and low-level pixel image manipulation.

- **The Nokia UI API:** covers Nokia's UI extension for MIDP. It is especially useful in Developer Platform 1.0 devices but not portable to non-Nokia devices. In Developer Platform 2.0 devices, the current version of Nokia UI API contains some deprecated API for backward compatibility.

After reading this chapter, you will understand the design characteristics and limitations of the MIDP UI. You will also learn to use the MIDP UI API effectively for business applications. Although we give a simple animation example in this chapter, we do not cover the MIDP 2.0 enhancements for action games. For game developers, Chapter 5, "Developing Action Games," has detailed discussions and tutorial examples on the game API.

The Design of the MIDP UI API

Existing Java developers can get started with the MIDP very quickly because it leverages some proven design patterns in standard Java UI APIs, such as the AWT and Swing. The MIDP LCDUI supports two programming models: the widget-based, high-level model and the pixel-based, low-level model.

The UI Models

The LCDUI high- and low-level APIs satisfy the needs of different developers. The high-level API is very easy to learn and to use. It aims to support fast development cycles, and it is easier to write portable code with the high-level API. The low-level API provides raw power and flexibility to developers who need to control every aspect of the user experience. In this section, we look at those two APIs from a bird's-eye view. Detailed programming tutorials are given in later sections in this chapter.

The High-Level API

The design goal of the high-level API is to support programming applications that are portable across devices. It provides a set of standard UI classes representing basic UI components at a high abstraction level. Devices implement the components, and therefore an application programmed with high-level APIs adopts the native look-and-feel of that device. For example, the Series 40 and Series 60 devices often render the same widget differently according to their own UI guidelines. We see more examples later in this chapter when we show side-by-side comparison screenshots of the same MIDP program running on Series 40 and Series 60 devices. The high-level API is mostly suitable for business applications, which do not differentiate themselves with UI innovations. Such applications offer "no surprise" UI to users and have minimal learning curves. Their value comes from the content and functionalities behind the user interface.

However, the drawback with the high-level UI approach is also obvious: the developer has little control over the drawing details and cannot go beyond the predefined set of widget components. For instance, it would be hard to develop an animation screen using the high-level API alone.

The Low-Level API

The low-level API gives developers complete control of the entire device display, including drawing on any pixel, rendering basic shapes, and drawing text with specific fonts. The low-level API also supports richer user interactions than the high-level API, which only captures the soft-key events. The low-level API provides mechanisms for developers to handle all keypad key events and pointer movements. Custom rendering and event handling are crucial to game developers.

A low-level UI application needs to render itself rather than delegating the task to the runtime library. Hence, low-level API applications usually require much more code than the high-level ones. Porting low-level UI applications to different devices can sometimes be a tedious task. For instance, it is hard to implement a native look-and-feel text input box using pixel-level tools. In addition, a text input box implemented with a low-level API would not have the same performance as the ready-to-use high-level API component, since we now need to do all the font calculation and rendering on the Java level instead of the optimized native level. So, we should use the high-level components whenever possible and leave only the parts that require custom rendering to low-level APIs.

Architecture of the LCDUI

Figure 4–1 shows important classes and interfaces in the MIDP UI package. In this section, we focus on the API design of the four important classes: `Display`, `Displayable`, `Command`, and `CommandListener`.

Display

The `Display` class provides access to the physical screen. To avoid complications in multi-thread applications, only one instance of the `Display` object is allowed for each MIDlet. For this reason, the `Display` class constructor is private, and the single instance policy (the Singleton pattern) is enforced by a factory method. We can obtain the instance of the `Display` class by passing the `MIDlet` object to the static `Display.getDisplay()` method.

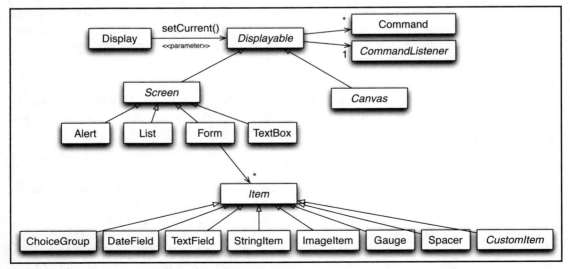

Figure 4–1 Important classes and interfaces of the MIDP UI.

```
public static Display getDisplay (MIDlet m)
```

The most important methods in the `Display` class display `Displayable` objects to the physical screen. The `Displayable` object represents a view of the screen, and it is discussed in the next section. In MIDP, there is only one `Displayable` object visible at any given time. It is different from the Windows programming model in which the forms display themselves and more than one window can be visible on the same screen. Hence, the `setCurrent()` method is used to switch the view.

```
public void setCurrent(Displayable d)
public void setCurrent(Alert a, Displayable d)
public void setCurrentItem(Item item)
public Displayable getCurrent()
```

The first method simply displays a `Displayable` instance, such as a `List` or a `Form`, to the screen. The second method pops up an `Alert` note. Upon dismissal, the specified `Displayable` object is shown. The third method displays the `Displayable` object that contains the specified UI component item (available on MIDP 2.0 devices only). The `Display` class makes sure that the item is properly focused and scrolled to be visible.

WARNING

The `setCurrent()` method call is asynchronous. That means the screen change may not take place immediately upon the application calling `setCurrent()`. The screen is only updated and rendered when the UI thread is idle. For example, if we call `setCurrent()` within a method running in the UI thread (e.g., a UI event callback method), the screen is not updated until the method returns. This problem is illustrated in the "Why Multi-threading?" section in Chapter 2 as well as in the splash screen example in the "Advanced MIDP UI Concepts" section later in this chapter. The `getCurrent()` method is hence a useful means of finding out whether the change has actually occurred.

Displayable

The `Displayable` class is an abstract representation of a full screen of display content. Despite being an abstract class, the `Displayable` does not contain any abstract method. It is abstract because the `Displayable` class does not contain any rendering logic and hence cannot be used directly. The abstract modifier and nonpublic constructor of the `Displayable` class force developers to use its concrete subclasses in the LCDUI, which do contain the rendering logic. We can query whether a `Displayable` object is shown on the LCD by calling its `isShown()` method. The `Displayable` class allows us to query the size of the screen display area. The returned values do not necessarily indicate the physical size of the LCD. Rather, it is the available screen area for the MIDlet, which is always smaller than the physical LCD size.

```
public int getWidth()
public int getHeight()
public boolean isShown()
```

The `Displayable` class also provides methods to add and manipulate the title and ticker of the display area. Figure 4–2 shows the title and ticker on Series 40 and Series 60 devices.

```
public void setTitle(String title)
public String getTitle()
public void setTicker (Ticker ticker)
public Ticker getTicker ()
```

 NOTE   A ticker is an optional line of text string scrolling across the top of the display area.

The most important functionality of the `Displayable` class is to provide the basic infrastructure for user interactions through the observer design pattern. A key interface in the infrastructure is `CommandListener`, which has only one method declared.

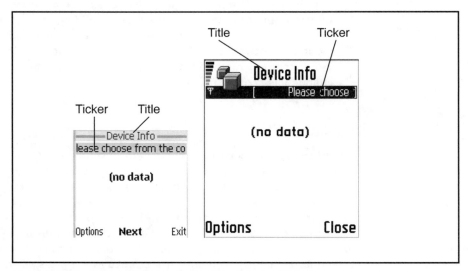

Figure 4–2 The title and ticker on Series 40 and Series 60 devices.

```
public interface CommandListener {
  void commandAction(Command command, Displayable
displayable);
}
```

The developer provides an implementation of the commandAction() method to specify what to do when a specific command is invoked by the user. Figure 4–3 illustrates this pattern.

The Command and CommandListener classes work together with the Displayable as follows.

1. We can associate Command objects with a Displayable screen.

2. Each Command object is mapped to a visual element, such as a soft key, on a Displayable screen.

3. When the user presses the soft key, a UI event is generated against the current Displayable object.

4. The Displayable object calls the commandAction() method in the registered CommandListener object and passes in the Command object mapped to the soft key. The listener object changes the display to the next screen by calling Display.setCurrent() from within the commandAction() method.

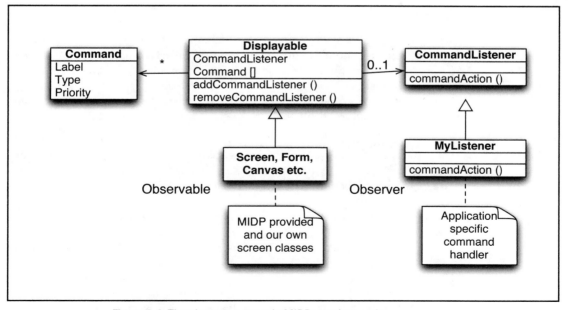

Figure 4–3 The observer pattern in MIDP user interaction.

WARNING

As we discussed in the "Why Multi-threading?" section in Chapter 3, "Getting Started", the `commandAction()` must return immediately to avoid blocking the user interface.

NOTE

The observer pattern is a behavior design pattern that describes how application components communicate with each other. Its purpose is to provide a way for a component to flexibly broadcast messages to interested receivers. In the MIDP UI model, the `Command` object is a broadcaster. It broadcasts UI event messages to `CommandListener` objects and invokes the appropriate callback methods. The `CommandListener` objects are registered with the container `Displayable` object that holds the `Command` objects.

The `Command`-related methods in the `Displayable` class are used in all the examples throughout this book. We can add a `Command`, remove a `Command`, or register a `CommandListener` in the `Displayable` object. The `Command`-related methods are as follows.

```
public void addCommand(Command cmd)
public void removeCommand(Command cmd)
public void setCommandListener(CommandListener l)
```

Command

When a `Command` object is added to a `Displayable` object, it is mapped to a soft key on the phone. If the `Displayable` object contains more than two commands, the menu label for one soft key automatically becomes "Options." If the user presses that key, the rest of the commands are displayed in a menu. Figure 4–4 shows how the `Command` objects are mapped. Notice that the Options menu automatically gets the native look-and-feel on different devices.

For each command, the MIDP API provides a mechanism for developers to specify its functional nature and priority. Based on that information, the Java runtime decides how to map the `Command` object to soft keys or Options menus. The `Command` class constructors are as follows.

```
Command (String label, int cmdType, int priority)
Command (String shortLabel, String longLabel,
          int cmdType, int priority)
```

Now, let's examine the second version of the constructor, which contains all the optional arguments. The first argument in the constructor is a short text label for the `Command`. It is displayed when the `Command` is mapped to a soft key. The second argument is a long text label for the `Command`. It is displayed when the `Command` is shown in an expanded menu. On Nokia devices, the long text label

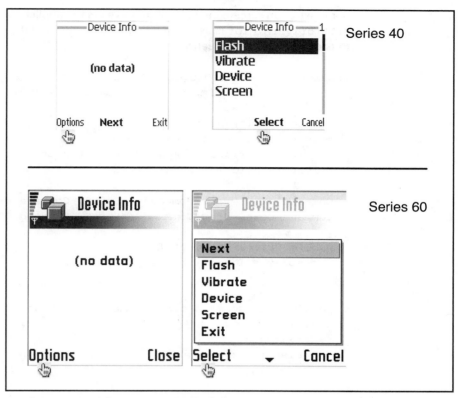

Figure 4–4 The mapping of Command objects.

is displayed in the expanded options menu only when it can fit into one line (typically three or four words). If it needs to be truncated, the short text label is used in the Options menu. The third argument is the type of the `Command`. It determines the mapping of the `Command` to soft keys. For example, on Nokia devices, the `EXIT` type `Commands` always map to a single soft key on the rightmost soft key or appear in the Options menu. The MIDP specification defines the following `Command` types: SCREEN, BACK, OK, CANCEL, HELP, STOP, EXIT, and ITEM. The last argument is the priority level of the `Command`. Higher priority corresponds to a smaller value here. Given the same type, a high-priority `Command` is displayed in a more accessible position.

A Sample Application

In this chapter, we use a sample application to display various demo screens and demonstrate the usage of the MIDP UI APIs. The entry MIDlet class `DriverMidlet` holds the `Display` object and provides two shared commands for each the 14 demonstration screens in the application. The Next command invokes the `DriverMidlet.next()` method to instantiate and display the next demonstration screen; the Exit command exits the application. The source code of the `DriverMidlet` is listed below. Notice that we add the shared commands to each of the demo screens.

```java
public class DriverMidlet extends MIDlet {
                    implements CommandListener {

  static Display display;
  private static Displayable demo;
  // static variable keeps track of the demo state
  private static int index = -1;

  Command exit = new Command ("Exit", Command.EXIT, 1);
  Command next = new Command ("Next", Command.OK, 1);

  public DriverMidlet () {
    display = Display.getDisplay(this);
  }

  public void commandAction (Command c, Displayable d) {
    if (c == exit) {
      exit ();
    } else if (c == next) {
      next ();
    }
  }

  protected void startApp () {
    next ();
  }

  protected void pauseApp () {
    // Do nothing
  }

  protected void destroyApp (boolean unconditional) {
    notifyDestroyed ();
  }

  public void next () {
    index++;
    if (index > 16) {
      index = 0;
    }

    switch (index) {
      case 0: demo  = new DeviceInfoDemo (this); break;
```

```
        case 1: demo    = new AlertDemo (this); break;
        case 2: demo    = new ListDemo (this); break;
        case 3: demo    = new MenuDemo (this); break;
        case 4: demo    = new TextBoxDemo (this); break;
        case 5: demo    = new TextDateDemo (this); break;
        case 6: demo    = new ChoiceGroupDemo (this); break;
        case 7: demo    = new PopupDemo (this); break;
        case 8: demo    = new GaugeDemo (this); break;
        case 9: demo    = new StringImageDemo (this); break;
        case 10: demo   = new LayoutDemo (this); break;
        case 11: demo   = new ItemCommandDemo (this); break;
        case 12: demo   = new CanvasDemo (this); break;
        case 13: demo = new AnimationDemo (this); break;
        case 14: demo = new ScrollCanvasDemo (this); break;
        case 15: demo = new WrapTextDemo (this); break;
        case 16: demo = new ImageButtonDemo (this); break;
    }
    // Add shared commands
    demo.addCommand (exit);
    demo.addCommand (next);

    display.setCurrent(demo);
  }

  public void exit () {
    destroyApp (true);
  }
}
```

The next listing shows how a generic demonstration class is structured. Notice that we pass the DriverMidlet reference to each demo class. In the demo class's commandAction() method, we always delegate to DriverMidlet.commandAction() to reuse the handler logic for the shared Next and Exit commands. We provide the source code of the demonstration classes throughout this chapter.

```
public class UIDemo extends Form
               implements CommandListener {

  // declare commands that are specific to this demo
  // ...

  // Handler for shared commands ("next" and "exit")
  private CommandListener comm;

  public UIDemo (CommandListener c) {
    super ("Title");
```

```
        comm = c;

        // instantiate and add demo specific commands
        this.setCommandListener(this);
    }

    public void commandAction (Command c, Displayable d) {
        // Handle demo specific commands ...

        // delegate "next" and exit" to DriverMidlet
        comm.commandAction(c, d);
    }

    // Other methods ...
}
```

NOTE   For more information on the design of screen navigation models, see the "Overall Architecture" section of Chapter 11, "End-to-End Design Patterns."

The High-Level API

The high-level API consists of easy-to-use widget classes that are rendered by the device. This API is divided into two parts in the inheritance tree: components that inherit from the Screen abstract class and those that inherit from the Item abstract class. The Item objects are displayed in a Form, which is special type of Screen object.

Screen

The Screen abstract class inherits from the Displayable class and represents high-level UI components that take up the entire display area. In MIDP 2.0, the Screen class does not add any methods or fields to the Displayable class. It is merely kept for backward compatibility with MIDP 1.0 applications. As is the case for Displayable, we use only Screen subclasses in our applications. Now let's look at the List, Alert, and TextBox classes.

List

The List class shows a list of choices. Its constructor takes the following forms.

```
List(String title, int listType)
List(String title, int listType,
     String[] choices, Image[] images)
```

The first constructor instantiates an empty list with a specified title and type. We can later change the choices in the list programmatically, using methods like insert(), append(), delete(), and deleteAll(). The second constructor instantiates a list with initial choices from the choices array. The images array contains icons for each listed choice. It must be the same size as the choices array or be null. The listType parameter takes one of the static constants defined in the Choice interface (see Table 4–1).

Table 4–1 Static Constants in the Choice Class for List and Choice Group Types

Constant	Description
EXCLUSIVE	This is equivalent to a radio button list. The user can select only one choice.
MULTIPLE	This is equivalent to a checked box list. The user can select multiple choices.
POPUP	This is equivalent to a combo selection box. This type is only available for ChoiceGroup components and is discussed later in this chapter.
IMPLICIT	This option mimics the behavior of a menu. The registered CommandListener is invoked as soon as the user chooses an option.

NOTE

As we discussed in Chapter 2, "Introducing Nokia Developer Platforms," list and menu screens constitute a key component in the Series 40 device UI. In MIDP, an implicit List has the exact same property and behavior as the menu screen in native Series 40 applications.

TIP

We can find the best icon image size to use in List items using methods from the Display class. Please refer to the "Advanced MIDP UI" section later in this chapter.

The user selects a choice item by pressing the select key on the device or through a special Command object provided by the device Java runtime itself. In exclusive and multiple lists, the user needs to press a soft-key mapped to a Command to proceed after she makes the choices; in an implicit list, the pre-defined SELECT_COMMAND is the default selection command. Or, on MIDP 2.0 devices, we can set an arbitrary Command as the default command via the setSelectCommand() method. On MIDP 1.0 devices, where the setSelectCommand() method is not available, we can simply add a Command with higher priority to override the default one. Once the user selects an implicit option, the default command event is passed to the `CommandListener`. In the `CommandListener`, we can retrieve the selected options using the following methods. The first method retrieves the index of the selected option in an exclusive or implicit list. The second method retrieves the selection flags for all options in an array. This is the best way to get results from multiple-choice type lists. The third method checks whether a certain item is selected.

```
public int getSelectedIndex ()
public void getSelectedFlags(boolean[]selected)
public boolean isSelected(int elementNum)
```

We can also set the selection flags for each choice option programmatically from the application.

```
public void setSelectedIndex(int elementNum,
                             boolean selected)
public void setSelectedFlags(boolean[] selected)
```

The following code illustrates an implicit list used as a menu (Figure 4–5).

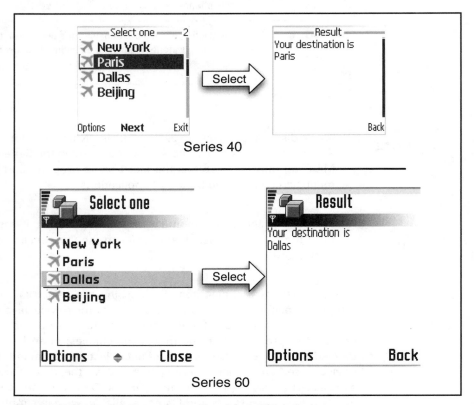

Figure 4–5 The Implicit List on Series 40 and Series 60 devices.

```java
public class MenuDemo extends List
        implements CommandListener {

  private Command go;
  private CommandListener comm;
  private Image icon;

  public MenuDemo (CommandListener c) {
    super ("Select one", Choice.IMPLICIT);
    comm = c;

    try {
      icon = Image.createImage("/" + "fly.png");
    } catch (Exception e) {
      icon = null;
    }

    append ("New York", icon);
    append ("Paris", icon);
    append ("Dallas", icon);
    append ("Beijing", icon);

    go = new Command ("Go", Command.SCREEN, 2);

    setSelectCommand(go);
    setCommandListener (this);
  }

  public void commandAction (Command c, Displayable d) {
    if (c == go) {
      int i = getSelectedIndex ();

      // The InfoForm class is a Form that displays a
      // text message and provides navigation back to
      // its previous screen. See the source code in the
      // download package
      Form form = new InfoForm ("Result", this);
      form.append ("Your destination is \n");
      form.append (getString(i) + "\n");

      DriverMidlet.display.setCurrent(form);
    }
    comm.commandAction(c, d);
  }
}
```

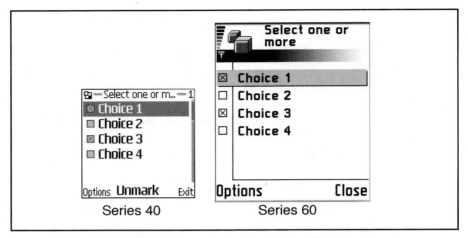

Series 40   Series 60

Figure 4–6 The multiple selection list on Series 40 and Series 60 devices.

The following code illustrates how to use the multiple selection list (Figure 4–6).

```
public class ListDemo extends List
           implements CommandListener{

  private Command report;
  private CommandListener comm;

  public ListDemo (CommandListener c) {
    super ("Select one or more", Choice.MULTIPLE);
    comm = c;

    append ("Choice 1", null);
    append ("Choice 2", null);
    append ("Choice 3", null);
    append ("Choice 4", null);
    // Flag item 3 as selected
    setSelectedIndex (2, true);

    report = new Command ("Report", Command.SCREEN, 2);

    addCommand (report);
    setCommandListener (this);
  }

  public void commandAction (Command c, Displayable d) {
    if (c == report) {
      boolean [] selections = new boolean [size()];
```

```
          getSelectedFlags (selections);

          Form form = new InfoForm ("Result", this);
          form.append ("Selected items: \n");

          for (int i = 0 ; i < selections.length; i++) {
             if (selections[i]) {
                form.append (getString(i) + "\n");
             }
          }
          DriverMidlet.display.setCurrent(form);
       }
       comm.commandAction(c, d);
    }
 }
```

Alert

The `Alert` class represents a screen informing the user of certain conditions in the application execution. It operates rather like an information or yes/no dialog box in a desktop windowing toolkit. An `Alert` note is typically displayed for a period of timeand then dismissed. There are two constructors in the `Alert` class.

```
Alert(String title)
Alert(String title, String alertText,
       Image alertImage, AlertType alertType)
```

The first constructor instantiates an `Alert` object with the given title. The second constructor allows us to put a message text and an image inside the `Alert` box of the given type. The alert type is represented by an `AlertType` class. The MIDP has five predefined `AlertType`s: ALARM, CONFIRMATION, ERROR, INFO, and WARNING. All of them are static final fields in the `AlertType` class. The `AlertType` mandates which default text or icon is shown in an alert if some of these parameters are null. If the `alertImage` and `alertType` arguments are both `null`, no image is presented in the `Alert` box, and the MIDlet has more space to fit the alert text into one screen.

Once an `Alert` object is instantiated, you can access and change its title, text, image, and type via standard `get` and `set` methods. A particularly important method in the `Alert` class is

```
public void setTimeout (int time)
```

It takes in an integer parameter indicating how long (in milliseconds) the alert should stay on the screen. If a special value FOREVER is passed, the alert screen stays until the user explicitly dismisses it. If the alert text is so long that it requires the user to scroll to read, the alert screen also requires explicit dismissal. In that case, the system would automatically add a DISMISS_COMMAND object and its default CommandListener to the alert screen. The default DISMISS_COMMAND object and its handler can be replaced by custom values so that we can control the timeout behavior of the Alert note.

NOTE   We can add Command objects to alert screens, but this feature is not available on MIDP 1.0 devices.

An Alert object is displayed to the device display via the setCurrent() method in the Display class.

```
public void setCurrent(Alert alert, Displayable next)
```

The second parameter (next) specifies the Displayable screen to show after the alert is dismissed or timed out. The following code demonstrates how to use the built-in ALARM type alert and how to develop a custom alert that vibrates the device. The ALARM alert is shown as a note that has to be dismissed explicitly, while the custom alert has a six-second timeout. Figure 4–7 shows the ALARM type alert screen.

```
public class AlertDemo extends Form
                implements CommandListener {

  private Command alarm;
  private Command confirm;
  private CommandListener comm;

  public AlertDemo (CommandListener c) {
    super ("Show Alert");
    append ("Use soft button menu to display alert");

    comm = c;
    alarm = new Command ("Alarm", Command.SCREEN, 2);
    confirm = new Command ("Confirm", Command.SCREEN, 2);

    addCommand (alarm);
    addCommand (confirm);
    setCommandListener (this);
  }

  public void commandAction (Command c, Displayable d) {
```

```
    if (c == alarm) {
      Display display = DriverMidlet.display;
      Alert alert = new Alert ("Alarm Demo",
              "Attention!", null,
              AlertType.ALARM);
      alert.setTimeout(Alert.FOREVER);
      display.setCurrent (alert, this);

    } else if (c == confirm) {
      Display display = DriverMidlet.display;
      Alert alert = new Alert ("Confirmation Demo",
              "Transaction finished", null,
              AlertType.CONFIRMATION);
      alert.setTimeout(6000);
      display.setCurrent (alert, this);
    }
    comm.commandAction(c, d);
  }
}
```

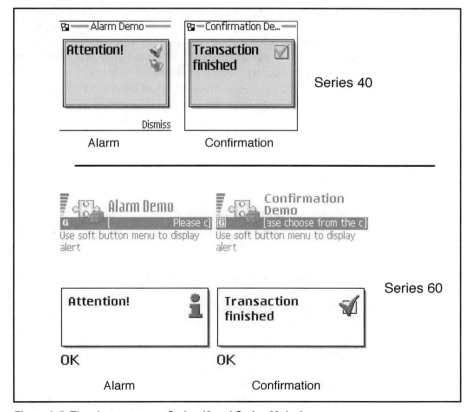

Figure 4–7 The alert screen on Series 40 and Series 60 devices.

For MIDP 2.0 devices, we can query the best image sizes to use in list and alert screens from related methods in the `Display` class. It is best to use images with transparent backgrounds to minimize interference with system-specific canvas colors.

TextBox

The `TextBox` class represents a text box that takes user input. Its constructor is as follows.

```
TextBox(String title, String text, int maxSize, int
constraints)
```

If the `title` is `null` and the `constraint` is `ANY`, the `TextBox` input area is displayed to occupy the full screen.

We can set a title, initial text, size, and input constraints for the box. The `constraints` argument takes one of the static constraint values defined in the `TextField` class. They specify what characters are allowed in the `TextBox` and how the `TextBox` responds to and interprets user inputs. The use of constraints is detailed when we cover the `TextField` component later. The text inside the box can be programmatically altered using the following methods. We can delete a substring between specified indices, insert a string at a specified position, and set the entire content of the `TextBox`.

```
public void delete(int offset, int length)
public void insert(String src, int position)
public void setString(String text)
```

We can retrieve information from the `TextBox` using the following methods.

```
public String getString ()
public int size ()
public int getCaretPosition()
```

Figure 4–8 shows the `TextBox` in action. It is the result of the following code.

```
public class TextBoxDemo extends TextBox
                implements CommandListener {

    private Command report;
    private Command clear;
    private Command notice;
    private CommandListener comm;
```

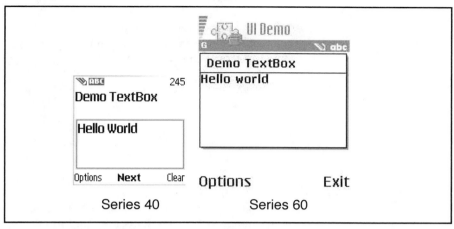

Figure 4–8 The TextBox screen on Series 40 and Series 60 devices.

```
public TextBoxDemo (CommandListener c) {
  super ("Demo TextBox", "", 256, TextField.ANY);
  comm = c;

  report = new Command ("Report", Command.SCREEN, 2);
  clear = new Command ("Clear", Command.SCREEN, 2);
  notice = new Command ("Notice", Command.SCREEN, 2);

  addCommand (report);
  addCommand (clear);
  addCommand (notice);
  setCommandListener (this);
}

public void commandAction (Command c, Displayable d) {
  if (c == report) {
    Form result = new InfoForm ("Result", this);
    result.append ("Text in the box is: " +
            this.getString());
    result.append("\n");
    result.append ("Text size: " + this.size());
    result.append("\n");
    result.append("Cursor position: " +
            this.getCaretPosition());

    DriverMidlet.display.setCurrent (result);

  } else if (c == clear) {
    this.delete(0, this.size());
```

```
    } else if (c == notice) {
      this.insert("Copyright, Michael Yuan.",
                   this.size());
    }
    comm.commandAction(c, d);
  }
}
```

Form

The most versatile `Screen` subclass is the `Form` class. A `Form` is a container holding any number of UI components inherited from the `Item` abstract class. Examples of an `Item` include a gauge or a text input field. The `Form` class has two constructors.

```
Form (String title)
Form (String title, Item[] items)
```

The first constructor instantiates an empty `Form` with the specified title. The second constructor allows us to specify the initial items in the `Form`. All the items in a `Form` are indexed from zero. We can use methods in the `Form` class to add and remove items. The `insert()` and `delete()` methods increase and shrink the items collection in the `Form` while keeping all the items in a continuous sequential order. We can also replace an existing item with the `set()` method.

```
public int append (Item item)
public int append (String s)
public int append (Image image)
public void insert (int itemNum, Item item)
public void delete (int itemNum)
public void deleteAll ()
public void set (int itemNum, Item item)
```

We do not specify the exact size and positions of items on a `Form` screen. The `Form` screen scrolls vertically but not horizontally to display all the `Items` in it. However, as we will see, we can influence the positioning using layout and spacers. In the next section, we look at the `Item` classes.

Item

The `Item` subclasses are visual components that can be added to a `Form`. They include `ChoiceGroup`, `DateField`, `Gauge`, `ImageItem`, `Spacer`, `StringItem`, and

TextField. In addition, the CustomItem, discussed in the "Advanced MIDP UI" section, can also be added to a Form. Each item can display (above the main content area) a text label of up to three lines above the main content area.

StringItem and ImageItem

The StringItem and ImageItem classes represent simple string and image objects on a Form. Their constructors are as follows.

```
StringItem(String label, String text)
StringItem(String label, String text, int mode) // MIDP 2
ImageItem(String label, Image img,
          int layout, String altText)
ImageItem(String label, Image img, int layout,
          String altText, int mode) // MIDP 2
```

On MIDP 2.0 devices, both classes can take an appearance mode argument in their constructors, which determines how the item should look. The mode argument takes values of Item.PLAIN, Item.BUTTON, and Item.HYPERLINK. For further description about the StringItem appearance mode, please refer to the "Item Commands" section later in this chapter. For now, we deal with only the PLAIN mode. The layout parameter in the ImageItem constructor takes value from the layout constant in the Item class (see the "Advanced MIDP UI" section later). The following code illustrates how to build a Form with StringItem and ImageItem objects. Figure 4–9 shows the code in action.

```
public class StringImageDemo extends Form
                implements CommandListener {

   private CommandListener comm;

   public StringImageDemo (CommandListener c) {
      super ("String and Image items");
      comm = c;

      // Will be displayed as PLAIN not BUTTON since
      // there is no associated item command
      StringItem title = new StringItem("Telescope",
             "VLA, New Mexico, USA", Item.BUTTON);
      // Font will be explained in the Graphics
      // section later
      title.setFont(Font.getFont(Font.FACE_MONOSPACE,
             Font.STYLE_ITALIC | Font.STYLE_UNDERLINED,
             Font.SIZE_MEDIUM));
      Image img;
      try {
```

```
        img = Image.createImage("/" + "telescope.png");
    } catch (Exception e) {
      e.printStackTrace ();
      img = null;
    }
    ImageItem imgItem =
            new ImageItem("VLA telescope", img,
                    ImageItem.LAYOUT_CENTER, "VLA");

    append (title);
    append (imgItem);

    setCommandListener (this);
  }

  public void commandAction (Command c, Displayable d) {
    comm.commandAction(c, d);
  }
}
```

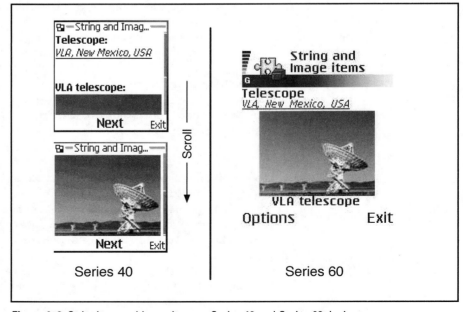

Figure 4–9 StringItem and ImageItem on Series 40 and Series 60 devices.

NOTE   The MIDP specification mandates that all devices must support the PNG image format. All Nokia devices also support the JPEG image format. Some Series 60 devices also support the GIF image format, including animated GIF images.

TextField and DateField

The `TextField` class shows the user a text input box in a `Form`. Its constructor has the following signature.

```
TextField(String label, String text, int maxSize,
          int constraints)
```

It has the same behavior as the `TextBox` class discussed earlier in this chapter. All the input constraints used in `TextField` and `TextBox` constructors are defined as static final fields in the `TextField` class (listed in Table 4–2). There are two types of input constraints.

- Restrictive constraints specify what characters are allowed in the input field. For example, if the input field has a `NUMERIC` constraint, it simply ignores any alphabetic keystroke.

- Modifier constraints specify the behavior of the `TextField` and `TextBox`. For example, we could flag an input field as `PASSWORD` and it would obscure the input characters with replacement characters. If we use the `INITIAL_CAPS_WORD` constraint, the input text mode automatically changes to uppercase after each space and switches back to lowercase from the second character of the word.

NOTE   On Series 40 devices, we need to select the Edit command (a system command) on a `TextField` to open the editor (see Figure 4–10). If the constraint is `ANY` and the label is `null`, a full-screen editor is shown. If the constraint is any other combination, a popup editor with a query title is displayed.

A restrictive constraint and a modifier constraint can be combined using the logic `OR` operator to form a single `constraints` parameter that can be passed to the `TextField` and `TextBox` constructors. In addition to input constraints, we can specify the initial input mode of an editor via the `setInitialInputMode()` method. For example, on a Chinese language device, we can set up the editor to start in the Pinyin input mode for Chinese characters so the user does not have to manually change the mode. Table 4–3 lists the available input mode constants for devices in different markets. The exact availability of input modes for each editor depends on the constraints.

Table 4–2 Static Constants in the TextField Class for Input Constraint Types

Constant	Description	Type
ANY	The user is allowed to enter anything. All input modes, including T9, are possible.	Restrictive
EMAILADDR	The user is allowed to enter an email address. No constraint on available characters is set, but the editor's auto-capitalization modes and T9 are disabled. Series 40 devices allow the user to choose from the native address book from this `TextField` or `TextBox`.	Restrictive
NUMERIC	The user is allowed to enter an integer number. An optional hyphen (-) at the beginning represents a negative number.	Restrictive
PHONENUMBER	The user is allowed to enter a phone number. Series 40 devices allow the user to choose from the native address book from this `TextField` or `TextBox`.	Restrictive
URL	The user is allowed to enter a URL. No constraint on available characters is set, but the editor's auto-capitalization modes and T9 are disabled.	Restrictive
DECIMAL	The user is allowed to enter numeric values with optional decimal fractions. The available characters for the decimal point are determined by the device locale.	Restrictive
PASSWORD	The text input is obscured on the screen. Suitable for a password entry field.	Modifier
UNEDITABLE	The content of this `TextField` or `TextBox` is not editable by users.	Modifier
SENSITIVE	The device should not cache sensitive text in the dictionary for autocompletion. T9 text input mode would be disabled. No effect on full-keyboard devices.	Modifier
NON_PREDICTIVE	This field should not contain words that are common in input completion dictionaries. The T9 text input mode would be disabled. No effect on full-keyboard devices.	Modifier
INITIAL_CAPS_WORD	The editor capitalizes the initial letter of each word. No effect on full-keyboard devices.	Modifier
INITIAL_CAPS_SENTENCE	The editor capitalizes the initial letter for each sentence. No effect on full-keyboard devices.	Modifier

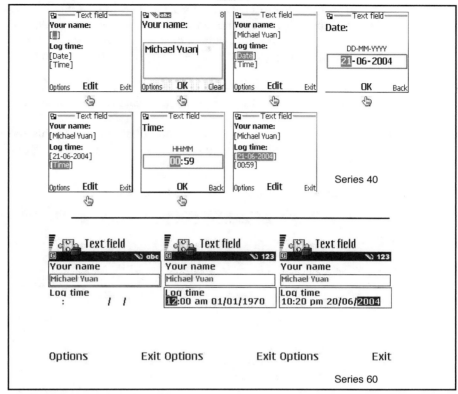

Figure 4–10 TextField and DateField on Series 40 and Series 60 devices. On Series 60 devices, the uninitialized DateField defaults to 01/01/1970.

Table 4–3 Text Input Modes

Device Market	Input Modes
All devices	MIDP_UPPERCASE_LATIN, MIDP_LOWERCASE_LATIN, IS_LATIN, IS_LATIN_DIGITS, IS_BASIC_LATIN
Indian languages	UCB_DEVANAGARI, UCB_BENGALI
Japanese	UCB_HIRAGANA, UCB_KATAKANA, IS_FULLWIDTH_DIGITS, IS_FULLWIDTH_LATIN, IS_HALFWIDTH_KATAKANA, IS_KANJI
Korean	IS_HANJA, UCB_HANGUL_SYLLABLES11
Chinese	IS_SIMPLIFIED_HANZI, IS_TRADITIONAL_HANZI, X_NOKIA_PINYIN, X_NOKIA_STROKE, X_NOKIA_ZHUYIN
Arabic	UCB_ARABIC, X_NOKIA_ARABIC_INDIC_DIGITS
Other languages	UCB_GREEK, UCB_CYRILLIC, UCB_ARMENIAN, UCB_HEBREW, UCB_THAI

The `DateField` class is very similar to the `TextField` class except that the former allows you choose a date from a calendar UI (see Figure 4–10). The display format of the date is determined by the device locale and systemwide region settings. The `DateField` constructors are as follows.

```
DateField(String label, int mode)
DateField(String label, int mode, TimeZone tz)
```

The `mode` argument specifies the editable fields in this `DateField` item. The available `mode` values are constants in the `DateField` class (see Table 4–4).

Table 4–4 Static Constants for th eDateField Modes

Constant	Description
DATE	Day, month, year
TIME	Hour, minute
DATE_TIME	Day, month, year and hour, minute

The following code shows the use of `TextField` and `DateField` classes. Figure 4–10 shows the code in action.

```
public class TextDateDemo extends Form
                implements CommandListener {

  private Command report;
  private CommandListener comm;
  private TextField name;
  private DateField logtime;

  public TextDateDemo (CommandListener c) {
    super ("Text field");
    comm = c;

    report = new Command ("Report", Command.SCREEN, 2);

    name = new TextField ("Your name", "", 20,
                    TextField.INITIAL_CAPS_WORD);
    append (name);

    logtime = new DateField ("Log time",
                    DateField.DATE_TIME);
    append (logtime);
```

```
      addCommand (report);
      setCommandListener (this);
   }

   public void commandAction (Command c, Displayable d) {
      if (c == report) {

         Form form = new InfoForm ("User profile", this);
         form.append ("Name: " + name.getString() + "\n");

         Calendar cal = Calendar.getInstance();
         cal.setTime (logtime.getDate());
         form.append ("Log time: " +
                          cal.toString() + "\n");

         name.delete(0, name.size());

         DriverMidlet.display.setCurrent(form);
      }
      comm.commandAction(c, d);
   }
}
```

ChoiceGroup

The ChoiceGroup class is very similar to the List class: both of them implement the Choice interface, which specifies most of the essential methods. The constructor signatures of the ChoiceGroup class are as follows.

```
ChoiceGroup(String label, int type)
ChoiceGroup(String label, int type,
              String[] choices, Image[] images)
```

The type argument has the same meaning as the type argument in the List class. Allowed types for a ChoiceGroup are MULTIPLE, EXPLICIT, and POPUP. A POPUP type ChoiceGroup is a lot like a combo box in the desktop UI world. On a Form, it only shows the current selection and some visual cue (i.e., a small triangle pointing downwards) to indicate that there are more options. Select or activate it, and the whole list of choices pops up, ready for a new selection. The following code shows how to implement a set of radio buttons using an exclusive ChoiceGroup item. Figure 4–11 and Figure 4–12 show the exclusive and popup ChoiceGroup components in action, respectively.

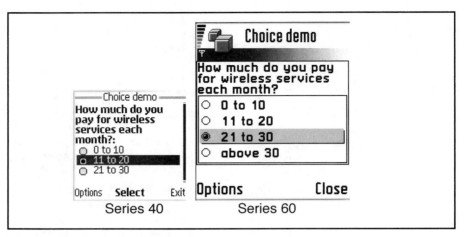

Figure 4–11 Exclusive ChoiceGroup on Series 40 and Series 60 devices.

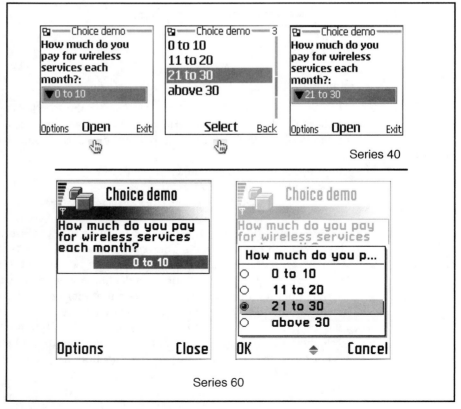

Figure 4–12 Popup ChoiceGroup on Series 40 and Series 60 devices.

```java
public class ChoiceGroupDemo extends Form
                implements CommandListener {

  private Command report;
  private ChoiceGroup choices;
  private CommandListener comm;

  public ChoiceGroupDemo (CommandListener c) {
    super ("Choice demo");
    comm = c;

    choices = new ChoiceGroup ("How much do you pay " +
            "for wireless services each month?",
            Choice.EXCLUSIVE);
    choices.append("0 to 10", null);
    choices.append("11 to 20", null);
    choices.append("21 to 30", null);
    choices.append("above 30", null);
    append (choices);

    report = new Command ("Report", Command.SCREEN, 2);

    addCommand (report);
    setCommandListener (this);
  }

  public void commandAction (Command c, Displayable d) {
    if (c == report) {
      int index = choices.getSelectedIndex();
      Form form = new InfoForm ("Result", this);
      form.append("You are paying ");
      form.append(choices.getString(index));
      form.append(" per month");
      DriverMidlet.display.setCurrent(form);
    }
    comm.commandAction(c, d);
  }
}
```

Gauge

A Gauge item is a graphical representation (e.g., a progress bar) of an integer value. A Gauge object can be instantiated as follows.

```java
Gauge(String label, boolean interactive,
      int maxValue, int initValue)
```

There are two types of gauges: interactive and noninteractive. An interactive gauge allows the user to change its value from the user interface. The application can retrieve the current value of an interactive Gauge or change it programmatically.

```
public int getValue()
public void setValue(int value)
public int getMaxValue()
public void setMaxValue()
public boolean isInteractive()
```

For noninteractive Gauge objects, the user is not allowed to change its value. There are two types of noninteractive gauges.

- A noninteractive gauge with a finite maximum value displays a graphic representation of its value. Although the gauge value cannot be changed by the user, it can be changed programmatically by the setValue() method. Such a gauge can be used as a dynamically updated progress indicator for users in a lengthy task with a known endpoint.

- A noninteractive gauge with an indefinite maximum value (Gauge.INDEFINITE) shows the user that the application is in a busy state with no known endpoint. The state of the gauge is indicated by an integer number passed in as the initValue argument. All the states are listed in Table 4–5.

Table 4–5 Static Constants in the Gauge Class for Gauge Types

Constant	Description
CONTINUOUS_IDLE, INCREMENTAL_IDLE	No gauge activity in idle states.
CONTINUOUS_RUNNING	Gauge updates itself continuously to indicate a generic busy state (animated).
INCREMENTAL_UPDATING	Gauge updates itself only incrementally when the setValue() method is called

The next code listing shows the use of an interactive gauge and a noninteractive, indefinite range gauge. The results are shown in Figure 4–13.

```
public class GaugeDemo extends Form
        implements CommandListener {

  private Command report;
```

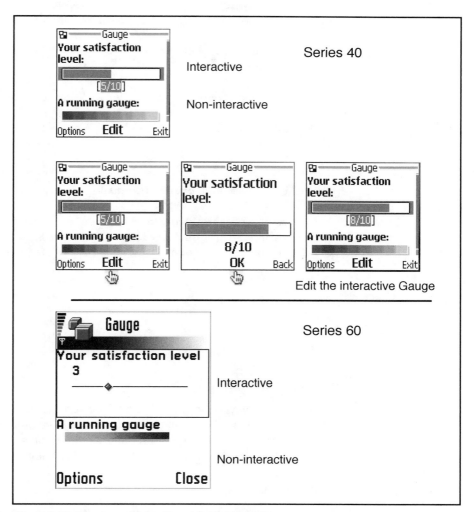

Figure 4–13 Gauges on Series 40 and Series 60 devices.

```
private Gauge interactiveGauge;
private Gauge autoGauge;
private CommandListener comm;

public GaugeDemo (CommandListener c) {
  super ("Gauge");
  comm = c;

  interactiveGauge =
          new Gauge ("Your satisfaction level",
                       true, 10, 5);
  autoGauge = new Gauge ("A running gauge", false,
```

```
                          Gauge.INDEFINITE, Gauge.CONTINUOUS_RUNNING);

        append (interactiveGauge);
        append (autoGauge);

        report = new Command ("Report", Command.SCREEN, 2);

        addCommand (report);
        setCommandListener (this);
    }

    public void commandAction (Command c, Displayable d) {
      if (c == report) {
        Form form = new InfoForm ("Result", this);
        form.append ("Your satisfaction level is \n");
        form.append (interactiveGauge.getValue() + "\n");

        DriverMidlet.display.setCurrent(form);
      }
      comm.commandAction(c, d);
    }
}
```

Customizing the Behavior of Items

So far, we have surveyed the ready-to-use Item subclasses defined by the MIDP specification. In this section, we discuss how to add custom behavior to Item objects via item commands and item state listeners. Most of the features we discuss in this section are available only on MIDP 2.0 devices.

Item Commands

On MIDP 2.0 devices, we can add context-sensitive Command objects to an item through the following methods. As we have mentioned, the Item commands are in fact displayed before the Displayable commands on the screen. The use of the ItemCommandListener interface is identical to that of the CommandListener interface.

```
public void addCommand (Command cmd)
public void removeCommand (Command cmd)
public void setDefaultCommand (Command cmd)
public void setItemCommandListener (ItemCommandListener l)
```

The following example (as shown in Figure 4–14) shows how to assign a Command to a StringItem on a form. The effect of the command is to echo the user input in the TextField. The PLAIN string text is automatically converted to HYPERLINK appearance mode in order to mimic the appearance of a Web

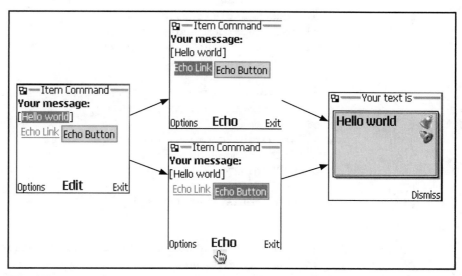

Figure 4–14 Item command for the StringItem on a Series 40 device.

page with action links. A `StringItem` with item commands can also have the `BUTTON` appearance mode.

```
public class ItemCommandDemo extends Form
                    implements CommandListener {

  private CommandListener comm;
  private TextField textField;
  private StringItem si;
  private Command echo;

  public ItemCommandDemo (CommandListener c) {
    super ("Item Command");
    comm = c;

    textField = new TextField("Your message",
            "", 20, TextField.ANY);

    echo = new Command ("Echo", Command.ITEM, 1);
    EchoListener el = new EchoListener ();

    // The PLAIN appearance mode will automatically
    // be converted to HYPERLINK if there is an
    // item Command associated with this item.
    si = new StringItem("", "Echo Link", Item.PLAIN);
    si.setLayout(Item.LAYOUT_CENTER);
```

```
      si.addCommand (echo);
      si.setDefaultCommand(echo);
      si.setItemCommandListener (el);
      append (si);

      si = new StringItem("", "Echo Button", Item.BUTTON);
      si.setLayout(Item.LAYOUT_CENTER);
      si.addCommand (echo);
      si.setDefaultCommand(echo);
      si.setItemCommandListener (el);
      append (si);

      setCommandListener (this);
    }

    public void commandAction (Command c, Displayable d) {
      comm.commandAction(c, d);
    }

    // Inner class as command handler.
    // It has access to private members
    class EchoListener implements ItemCommandListener {

      public void commandAction (Command c, Item i) {
        if (c == echo) {
          Display display = DriverMidlet.display;
          Alert alert = new Alert ("Your text is",
              textField.getString(),
              null, AlertType.ALARM);
          alert.setTimeout(Alert.FOREVER);
          display.setCurrent (alert);
        }
      }
    }

  }
```

Item State Changes

Item commands, even default ones, require explicit user actions to activate. An MIDP application can respond to item state changes passively via the `ItemStateListener` interface. Examples of UI item internal state changes include the following.

- Change of the selected options in a `ChoiceGroup` item

- Value change of an interactive `Gauge` item

- Changes of the text inside a `TextField`

- Entry of a new date in a `DateField`

- Method call to `notifyStateChanged()` on any `Item` object

The `Form` class has the ability to monitor its member items' states. The `Form.setItemListener()` method registers an `ItemListener` implementation with the `Form`. Every time an item is changed, the `ItemStateListener.itemStateChanged()` method is called.

```
public interface ItemStateListener {
   public void itemStateChanged(Item item);
}
```

The Low-Level API

The low-level UI API consists of four classes, the `Canvas` class, the `Graphics` class, the `Image` class, and the `Font` class. Additional classes to manipulate the low-level drawing are available in the MIDP Game API, discussed in Chapter 5, "Developing Action Games." Unlike widgets in the high-level API, which are drawn by the Java runtime, the `Canvas` object draws itself on the screen. It works as follows.

- The `Canvas` abstract class defines an abstract method `paint(Graphics g)`.

- Each concrete `Canvas` subclass must implement the `paint()` method to specify how to draw itself on the screen.

- When a `Canvas` object is displayed, the `paint()` method is automatically invoked. The `Graphics` object is passed in by the Java runtime. Developers do not invoke the `paint()` method directly.

- When the screen needs updating, the application calls `repaint()`, which schedules the runtime to call the `paint()` method. Note that the `repaint()` method is asynchronous. The `paint()` method might not be called immediately after the `repaint()` method returns. In addition, the `Canvas` class provides a second version of the `repaint()` method, which takes in four integer arguments (`x, y, width, height`), to repaint only the specified rectangle region of the screen.

- The `serviceRepaints()` method forces the runtime to service all pending `repaint()` requests. We have to use it with caution, since it compromises the automaticity built into the platform and could cause deadlock. For example, we should never call `serviceRepaints()` from within a `paint()` method.

Inside the paint() method, all the actual drawing work is done with methods in the Graphics object.

WARNING   The paint() method is not invoked when the Display.setCurrent() method is called. It is invoked when the screen is actually rendered by the UI thread.

Graphics

The Graphics class provides methods to do the actual drawing on a Canvas. It is usually passed into the Canvas.paint() method. We never call the paint() method or instantiate the Graphics object in our applications. They are jobs for the Java runtime.. The following methods in the Graphics class set the drawing mode such as the current color, font, and stroke style. Two stroke-style constants are defined in the Graphics class: SOLID and DOTTED. The corresponding get methods are also available.

```
public void setColor(int red, int green, int blue)
public void setColor(int RGB)
public void setGrayScale(int value)
public void setStrokeStyle(int style)
public void setFont(Font font)
```

The drawing methods can draw the following objects and shapes at the specified location.

- Lines

- Outline of geometric objects such as arcs and rectangles

- Filled geometric objects

- Text strings

- Images

```
public void drawChar(char c, int x, int y, int anchor)
public void drawChars(char[] data, int x, int y, int anchor)
public void drawString(string str, int x, int y, int anchor)
public void drawSubstring(String str, int offset, int len,
                          int x, int y, int anchor)
public void drawImage(Image img, int x, int y, int anchor)

public void drawLine(int x1, int y1, int x2, int y2)
```

```
public void drawArc(int x, int y, int width, int height,
                    int startAngle, int arcAngle)
public void fillArc(int x, int y, int width, int height,
                    int startAngle, int arcAngle)
public void drawRect(int x, int y, int width, int height)
public void fillRect(int x, int y, int width, int height)
public void drawRoundRect(int x, int y, int width,
                    int height, int arcWidth, int arcHeight)
public void fillRoundRect(int x, int y, int width,
                    int height, int arcWidth, int arcHeight)
public void fillTriangle(int x1, int y1,
                    int x2, int y2, int x3, int y3)
```

The text- and image-drawing method takes in an anchor argument, which specifies where the object should be drawn relative to the specified location. The available anchor values are static final fields defined in the Graphics class. The available anchors are listed in Table 4–6.

Table 4–6 Static Constants for Anchors

Constant	Description
BASELINE	Baseline of the text
BOTTOM	Bottom of the text or image
TOP	Top of the text or image
LEFT	Left of the text or image
RIGHT	Right of the text or image
VCENTER	Vertical center of the text or image
HCENTER	Horizontal center of the text or image

We can limit the effect of any rendering method by specifying a rectangular clipping area via the setClip(int x, int y, int width, int height) method. Only the screen area within the clip would be affected by any subsequent rendering method.

Fonts

The MIDP specification defines a `Font` class, which represents available text fonts we can use in the `StringItem` component or the `Graphics.drawString()` method. The most important method is the `getFont()` method.

```
Font getFont (int face, int style, int size)
Font getFont (int fontSpecifier)
```

In the first version of the `getFont()` method, the available `face` values are `FACE_MONOSPACE`, `FACE_PROPORTIONAL` and `FACE_SYSTEM`; the available `style` values are `STYLE_PLAIN`, `STYLE_BOLD`, `STYLE_ITALIC`, and `STYLE_UNDERLINED`; the available `size` values are `SIZE_SMALL`, `SIZE_MEDIUM`, and `SIZE_LARGE`. Considerable design effort has been made to make sure that Nokia fonts are easy to read on Series 40 devices. All Series 40 fonts are proportional. In the second version of the `getFont()` method, the `fontSpecifier` takes either of the following two values:

- `FONT_INPUT_TEXT`: the returned font must be the same as used in `TextField` in `Form`.

- `FONT_STATIC_TEXT`: the return font must be the same as used in `StringItem` body (not in the label) in `Form`.

In addition, the `Font` class provides methods, such as `getHeight()` and `getWidth()`, to measure the width and height of any given string in any supported font. Those methods are very handy when we need to manually control text layout on a `Canvas`. Please see the wrap-text code sample in the "Advanced MIDP UI Concepts" section for an example.

NOTE   The standard Latin font sizes for Series 40 Developer Platform 2.0 devices are 9/12/16 for `SIZE_SMALL`, `SIZE_MEDIUM`, and `SIZE_LARGE` respectively. Most old S40 products used 9/16/23, but some (i.e., 3510i) with 96 x 65 displays used 8/11/13, and new products with much higher resolutions and much larger fonts will be released within the life of Developer Platform 2.0. Because there are so many different combinations of fonts used in Series 40 alone, it is bad practice to hardcode the height of a font into your application. When drawing text with the low-level interface, it is important to always check the size of the fonts using the `Font.getHeight()` method and to adjust the line spacing accordingly.

Key-Event Model

A concrete `Canvas` subclass not only draws itself on the screen but also handles events from the keypad and touch screen. For example, when the user presses a key, the MIDP runtime calls the `Canvas.keyPressed()` method and passes the key code. By default, the `keyPressed()` method does nothing. It just ignores the event. The `Canvas` subclass overrides it to respond to the event. The `Canvas` class has multiple event-handler methods mapped to different types of events. The following key-event handlers are called when the user presses, releases, or holds a key.

```
public void keyPressed(int keyCode)
public void keyReleased(int keyCode)
public void keyRepeated(int keyCode)
```

The `keyCode` argument passed into the handler methods is an integer value representing the event key. For simple keys, the `keyCode` value corresponds directly to static final fields in the `Canvas` class. Nokia devices may deliver key codes other than the MIDP defined ones to the MIDlet. Some Nokia devices (e.g., Nokia 6800) support full keyboards and can deliver a large number of key codes. All MIDP standard and Nokia-specific key codes are listed in Table 4–7.

Table 4–7 MIDP Standard and Nokia-Specific Key Codes

Constant	Description
`KEY_NUM0`, `KEY_NUM1`, `KEY_NUM2`, `KEY_NUM3`, `KEY_NUM4`, `KEY_NUM5`, `KEY_NUM6`, `KEY_NUM7`, `KEY_NUM8`, `KEY_NUM9`	The number keys from 0 to 9 on the keypad
`KEY_STAR`	The * key
`KEY_POUND`	The # key
−1	The scroll-up key
−2	The scroll-down key
−3	The scroll-left key
−4	The scroll-right key
−5	The Select key or the middle soft key
−6	The left soft key (available on `Canvas` with no Command)
−7	The right soft key (available on `Canvas` with no Command)

Table 4–7 MIDP Standard and Nokia-Specific Key Codes (continued)

Constant	Description
-8	The Clear key
-50	The Shift or Edit key
-10	The Send key
-11	The End key (may not be available if it causes the MIDlet to exit)
-12	The Voice key
10	The Enter key in full keyboard
32	The Space key in full keyboard
8	The Backspace key in full keyboard
27	The Escape key in full keyboard
9	The Tab key in full keyboard
127	The Delete key in full keyboard
Character Unicode	Alphabetic keys on full keyboard. For example, the A key maps to Unicode 0x0061, or 0x0041 if the shift key is held down.

For game action keys, the keyCode value must be mapped to game action constants via the getGameAction() method. The mapping is necessary because multiple keys might correspond to the same game action. For example, the numeric key 4 and the scroll-left key are often both mapped to the move-left action in a game. For more portable applications, you are strongly encouraged to use game action values rather than raw key codes whenever possible. Table 4–8 lists the game action constants in Canvas class. Figure 4–15 shows those keys on a device.

For devices with touch screen and pointer (e.g., the Nokia 7710 in Series 90), the MIDP runtime can also capture pointer events when the user presses, releases, or drags the pointer across the screen. The arguments passed into these methods are the pixel coordinate of the pointer position on the screen.

Table 4–8 Static Constants in the Canvas Class for Game Action Code Mapped by the getGameAction() Method (on an ITU-T Numeric Keypad)

Constant	Description
UP	The scroll-up key or the number 2 key on the keypad; the R key on a full keyboard
DOWN	The scroll-down key or the number 8 key on the keypad; the V key on a full keyboard
LEFT	The scroll-left key or the number 4 key on the keypad; the D key on a full keyboard
RIGHT	The scroll-right key or the number 6 key on the keypad; the G key on a full keyboard
FIRE	The selection key (at the middle of the scroll keys) or the number 5 key on the keypad; the Send key or the K key on a full keyboard
GAME_A, GAME_B, GAME_C, GAME_D	These are general-purpose game actions. On Series 40 devices, these game actions are mapped to numeric keys 9, #, 7, and * respectively. On full keyboards, actions are mapped to M, J, H, and U keys.

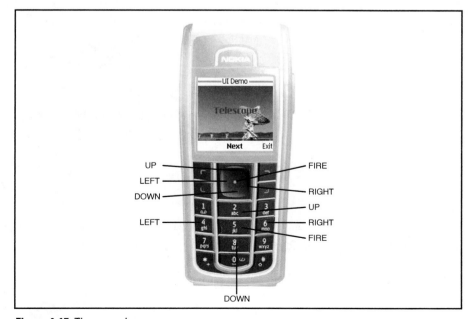

Figure 4-15 The game keys.

```
public void pointerPressed(int x, int y)
public void pointerReleased(int x, int y)
public void pointerDragged(int x, int y)
```

Canvas in Action

In this section, we demonstrate the use of the Canvas class via three examples.

The Movable Text

The following example shows how to draw an image on a Canvas and a string of text on top of it. When the user presses the scroll keys, the key-event handler changes the location of the string accordingly and calls the repaint() method to update the display. Hence, we appear to move the string around on the screen using scroll keys. Figure 4–16 shows the application in action.

```
public class CanvasDemo extends Canvas
                implements CommandListener {

    private CommandListener comm;
    private Image img;
    private Font font;
    public int currentPosX, currentPosY;
    public int width, height;

    public CanvasDemo (CommandListener c) {
        comm = c;
        width = getWidth ();
        height = getHeight ();
        // The current cursor position for the text
        currentPosX = width / 2;
        currentPosY = height / 2;
        // The text font
        font = Font.getFont(Font.FACE_PROPORTIONAL,
                    Font.STYLE_BOLD, Font.SIZE_LARGE);

        // setFullScreenMode (true);
        setCommandListener (this);

        try {
            img = Image.createImage("/" + "telescope.png");
        } catch (Exception e) {
            e.printStackTrace ();
            img = null;
```

```
    }
  }

  public void commandAction (Command c, Displayable d) {
    comm.commandAction(c, d);
  }

  public void paint (Graphics g) {
    // Fill a white background
    g.setColor(0xffffff);
    g.fillRect(0,  0, width, height);
    // Set text color
    g.setColor(0x000000);
    g.drawImage (img, width / 2, height / 2,
             Graphics.HCENTER | Graphics.VCENTER);
    g.setFont (font);
    g.setColor (255, 0, 0);
    g.drawString ("Telescope", currentPosX, currentPosY,
             Graphics.BASELINE | Graphics.HCENTER);
  }

  // Move the text around when the game keys are pressed
  public void keyPressed (int keyCode) {
    int gameCode = getGameAction (keyCode);
    if (gameCode == UP) {
      currentPosY -= 10;
      repaint ();
    } else if (gameCode == DOWN) {
      currentPosY += 10;
      repaint ();
    } else if (gameCode == LEFT) {
      currentPosX -= 10;
      repaint ();
    } else if (gameCode == RIGHT) {
      currentPosX += 10;
      repaint ();
    } else {
      super.keyPressed(keyCode);
    }
  }
}
```

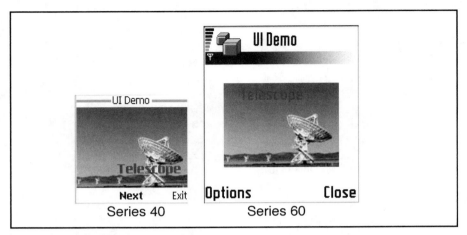

Series 40   Series 60

Figure 4–16 A key handler example.

We instantiate the `font` object and retrieve screen width and height values from outside the `paint()` method. Since the `paint()` method is called every time the screen refreshes, we should avoid expensive method calls and/or object instantiation/garbage collection in `paint()`.

Animation

The above `Canvas` example can be expanded to illustrate the basic technique of animation. In the code below, the handler for the `Start` command starts a new thread. The thread keeps updating the position of the text and calling the `repaint()` method. That causes the text to scroll up and down on the screen automatically.

WARNING

Do not try to run the animation loop inside the `commandAction()` method. As we discussed, the `commandAction()` method runs in the main UI thread and it blocks the device UI until it returns.

```
public class AnimationDemo extends Canvas
           implements CommandListener {

    private Command start, stop;
    private Animator animator;
    private CommandListener comm;
    private Image img;
    private Font font;
    public int currentPosX, currentPosY;
```

```java
public int width, height;

public AnimationDemo (CommandListener c) {
  comm = c;
  width = getWidth ();
  height = getHeight ();
  // position of the text
  currentPosX = width / 2;
  currentPosY = 10;
  // text font
  font = Font.getFont(Font.FACE_SYSTEM,
           Font.STYLE_ITALIC, Font.SIZE_LARGE);
  animator = new Animator (this);

  // setFullScreenMode (true);
  start = new Command ("Start", Command.SCREEN, 2);
  stop = new Command ("Stop", Command.SCREEN, 2);

  addCommand (start);
  addCommand (stop);
  setCommandListener (this);

  try {
    img = Image.createImage("/" + "telescope.png");
  } catch (Exception e) {
    e.printStackTrace ();
    img = null;
  }
}


public void commandAction (Command c, Displayable d) {
  if (c == start) {
    Thread t = new Thread (animator);
    t.start ();
  } else if (c == stop) {
    animator.stopped = true;
  }
  comm.commandAction(c, d);
}

public void paint (Graphics g) {
  g.setColor(0xffffff);
  g.fillRect(0,  0, width, height);

  g.setColor(0x000000);
  g.drawImage (img, width / 2, height / 2,
```

```
                    Graphics.HCENTER | Graphics.VCENTER);
      g.setFont (font);
      g.setColor (255, 0, 0);
      g.drawString ("Telescope", currentPosX, currentPosY,
            Graphics.BASELINE | Graphics.HCENTER);
    }
  }

class Animator implements Runnable {

  AnimationDemo demo;
  public boolean stopped;

  public Animator (AnimationDemo demo) {
    this.demo = demo;
    stopped = false;
  }

  public void run () {
    while (!stopped) {
      demo.currentPosY += 5;
      if (demo.currentPosY > demo.height) {
        demo.currentPosY = 0;
      }
      demo.repaint ();
    }
  }
}
```

Figure 4–17 shows the animated example in action.

Advanced MIDP UI Concepts

Now, we have seen the basics of the MIDP UI, but we skipped some advanced topics that might prove overwhelming or difficult to beginners. However, they are often crucial for developing professional-looking UI applications. In this section, we cover those advanced topics.

Advanced Device Controls

Although the Display class is primarily used to switch the display screen (via the setCurrent() method), it can also be used to control other device hardware and query device UI characteristics. We can use the following methods in the Display class to flash the screen backlight or vibrate the phone (MIDP 2.0 devices only). The duration argument specifies the duration of the requested operation in milliseconds.

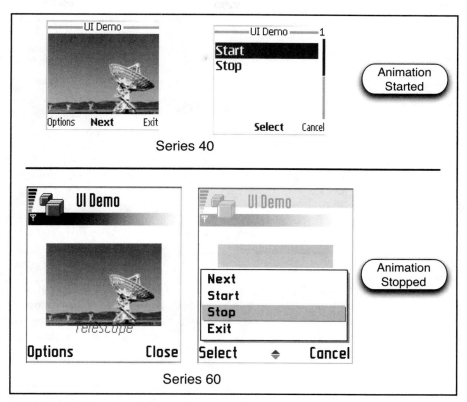

Figure 4–17 An animation example.

```
public boolean flashBacklight(int duration)
public boolean vibrate(int duration)
```

We can query the physical characteristics of the physical screen from the Display object. The following methods query whether the phone has a color LCD, how many colors (or gray tones) and alpha transparency levels it supports, and the color scheme. The alpha transparency and color scheme support are available only in MIDP 2.0 devices.

```
public boolean isColor ()
public int numColors ()
public int numAlphaLevels ()
public int getColor (int colorSpecifier)
```

The getColor() method takes a colorSpecifier argument that specifies the requested color scheme and returns the color in 0x00RRGGBB format. The available `colorSpecifier` values are static constants in the `Display` class (Table 4–9).

Table 4–9 Static Constants in the Display Class for Color Schemes

Constant	Description
`COLOR_BACKGROUND,` `COLOR_HIGHLIGHTED_BACKGROUND`	The background color in normal and highlighted states
`COLOR_FOREGROUND,` `COLOR_HIGHLIGHTED_FOREGROUND`	The foreground color in normal and highlighted states
`COLOR_BORDER,` `COLOR_HIGHLIGHTED_BORDER`	The color for boxes and borders in normal and highlighted states

On MIDP 2.0 devices, we can query the best image sizes for different screen elements used in this handset through the `Display` object. These methods give more specific information than the `getWidth()` and `getHeight()` methods in the `Displayable` class. They are very useful in optimizing the application for multiple devices.

```
public int getBestImageWidth(int imageType)
public int getBestImageHeight(int imageType)
```

The `imageType` argument is from static constants in the `Display` class (see Table 4–10).

Table 4–10 Static Constants in the Display Class for Image Types

Constant	Description
`ALERT`	Image in an `Alert` box
`CHOICE_GROUP_ELEMENT`	Image associated with a `ChoiceGroup` element
`LIST_ELEMENT`	Image associated with a `List` element

Command Placement

The `Command` class supports user interaction with the UI via soft keys and the Options menus. The device normally makes an intelligent guess about where to display the command labels based on the command type and priority as well the device-specific convention. However, if you want to control exactly where your commands are mapped on a Nokia device, you have to learn the exact algorithm Nokia uses to map the Command objects.

On Nokia devices, each Command type has a default label in case the MIDlet does not provide one. The Command objects are first mapped to device soft keys according to the rules listed in Table 4–11. The Select soft key corresponds to the middle soft key on three-key devices and the left soft key on two-key devices.

Table 4–11 Command Types on Nokia Devices (see text for the Select soft key)

Command Type	Function	Placement	Default Label
BACK	Returns to the logical previous display.	Right soft key	Back
OK	Standard positive response to a dialog on the current display.	Select soft key	OK
CANCEL	Standard negative response to a dialog on the current display.	Right soft key	Cancel
HELP	Requests help information about the current MIDlet or current display screen.	Select soft key	Help
STOP	Stops a running operation.	Right soft key	Stop
EXIT	Exits the MIDlet.	Right soft key	Close
ITEM	Generic command that relates to the focused or selected item on the display screen.	Select soft key	Select
SCREEN	Generic command that relates to the current display screen.	Select soft key	Select

If two or more commands are mapped to the same physical soft key, an Options menu is necessary to present the extra commands. The rules for allocating soft keys for the Options menu are as follows.

- On a standard Series 40 Developer Platform 2.0 device with three soft keys (e.g., Nokia 6230), the left soft key is always reserved to bring up the Options menu. If there is no Options menu for this screen (i.e., all commands are mapped to the remaining two soft keys), the left soft key has an empty label and does not respond to user actions.

- On an older device (or a Series 60 device) with two soft keys (e.g., Nokia 7210 and 6600), the left soft key is mapped to bring up the Options menu if there is one. If there is no Options menu, the left soft key could be mapped to a command or an empty label.

All Nokia devices use the following set of rules to determine the display order of the commands. The highest ordered command is mapped to the soft key, and the remaining commands appear in the options menu ordered from top to bottom.

- If the item currently in focus has associated item commands, the item commands have the highest order.

- The `Displayable` commands are ordered by the command type (1) STOP, (2) OK, (3) CANCEL, (4) ITEM, (5) SCREEN, (6) HELP, (7) BACK, (8) EXIT.

- The priorities are used to order commands of the same type only.

- Finally, commands of the same type and priority appear in the order in which they were added to the `Displayable`, oldest first.

Please check out the code examples throughout this chapter for the actual command placement in action.

Item Layout Management

The `Item` objects are placed on a `Form` based on rows. In a western language device, the items are placed from left to right and from top to bottom. Once the right edge of the screen is reached or one of the Series 40 row-break conditions (discussed later) is met, the next item is placed in the next row. The first row is on the top of the screen, the next row is below it, and so on. A `Form` screen can have an unlimited number of rows. Vertical scrolling is automatically provided if the rows exceed the screen height.

On MIDP 1.0 devices, we can specify the vertical and horizontal alignment of an `ImageItem` in a row using its layout attribute. On MIDP 2.0 devices, each `Item` object can have a `layout` attribute, and the concept of layout is extended beyond simple alignment. The `Item` abstract class defines static constants for each layout option (see Table 4–12). We can combine those options with the logical OR operator. The `Item.setLayout()` method is used to set the item's `layout` attribute. We can use the `layout` attribute to specify how items in a row are aligned:

- The `LAYOUT_LEFT`, `LAYOUT_CENTER`, and `LAYOUT_RIGHT` options horizontally align items in the same row.

- The `LAYOUT_BOTTOM`, `LAYOUT_CENTER`, and `LAYOUT_TOP` options vertically align items in the same row.

Table 4–12 Static Constants for the Layout Options in the Item Class

Constant	Description
LAYOUT_2	Apply MIDP 2.0 layout rules.
LAYOUT_BOTTOM, LAYOUT_TOP	Top or bottom aligned.
LAYOUT_CENTER, LAYOUT_VCENTER	Horizontally or vertically centered.
LAYOUT_LEFT, LAYOUT_RIGHT	Left or right aligned.
LAYOUT_NEWLINE_AFTER, LAYOUT_NEWLINE_BEFORE	Last or first item in a row.
LAYOUT_EXPAND, LAYOUT_VEXPAND	Fill the width or the height of the screen.
LAYOUT_SHRINK, LAYOUT_VSHRINK	Use the minimum width or height.
LAYOUT_DEFAULT	The factory default layout. On western language devices, it is the same as LAYOUT_LEFT. On right-to-left language devices, it is the same as LAYOUT_RIGHT.

Each item has a preferred size and a minimum size. Both of them are specified by the implementation of the Item subclass. The preferred size is returned from the getPreferredHeight() and getPreferredWidth() methods. We can change the preferred size using the setPreferredSize() method. The minimum size is returned from the getMinimumHeight() and getMinimumWidth() methods. Combined with the layout attributes, the device determines how much space to allocate to each item in a row and the row itself.

- When packing items into a row, we use each item's preferred width unless the LAYOUT_SHRINK option is set, in which case the minimum width is used. If a row has extra space left but not enough room for the next item, the space is evenly distributed to all items with the LAYOUT_EXPAND option.

- Given the set of items on a particular row, the height of the row is calculated from the tallest item's preferred size (or minimum size if the LAYOUT_VSHRINK option is set). Then, items with the LAYOUT_VEXPAND option are expanded to the height of the row.

Now, we have seen how to lay out items in a row. But, how do we determine where to break a row? Here are the conditions of row breaks on Series 40 devices.

- Since there is no horizontal scroll bar, the row breaks when the next item cannot be fit into the screen width in the current row.

- The row breaks after an item with the `LAYOUT_NEWLINE_AFTER` option or before an item with the `LAYOUT_NEWLINE_BEFORE` option.

- A `StringItem` whose contents starts or ends with `\n` has a row break before or after it, respectively.

- If the next item has a different horizontal layout alignment option (`LAYOUT_LEFT, LAYOUT_CENTER, LAYOUT_RIGHT`), it is placed in a new row.

- A `Gauge, ChoiceGroup, DateField,` or `TextField` item is always placed in its own row.

The following code shows how to use the layout options, and the results are shown in Figure 4–18.

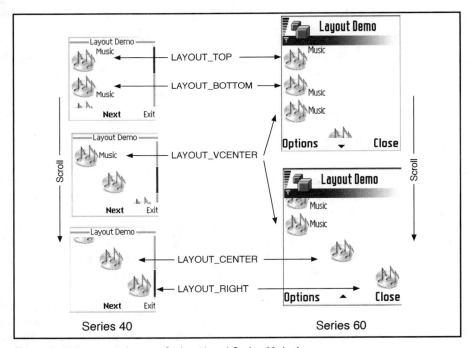

Figure 4–18 Layout options on Series 40 and Series 60 devices.

```
public class LayoutDemo extends Form
          implements CommandListener {
  private CommandListener comm;
  private Image img;

  public LayoutDemo (CommandListener c) {
    super ("Layout Demo");
    comm = c;
    try {
```

```
      img = Image.createImage("/music.png");
    } catch (Exception e) {
      e.printStackTrace ();
      img = null;
    }

    int layout = Item.LAYOUT_2 | Item.LAYOUT_TOP |
        Item.LAYOUT_LEFT;
    ImageItem ii = new ImageItem ("", img, layout, "");
    append (ii);
    StringItem si = new StringItem ("", "Music");
    si.setLayout (layout | Item.LAYOUT_NEWLINE_AFTER);
    append (si);

    layout = Item.LAYOUT_2 | Item.LAYOUT_BOTTOM |
        Item.LAYOUT_LEFT;
    ii = new ImageItem ("", img, layout, "");
    append (ii);
    si = new StringItem ("", "Music\n");
    si.setLayout (layout);
    append (si);

    layout = Item.LAYOUT_2 | Item.LAYOUT_VCENTER |
        Item.LAYOUT_LEFT;
    ii = new ImageItem ("", img, layout, "");
    append (ii);
    si = new StringItem ("", "Music\n");
    si.setLayout (layout);
    append (si);

    layout = Item.LAYOUT_2 | Item.LAYOUT_CENTER;
    ii = new ImageItem ("", img, layout, "");
    append (ii);

    layout = Item.LAYOUT_2 | Item.LAYOUT_RIGHT;
    ii = new ImageItem ("", img, layout, "");
    append (ii);

    // setFullScreenMode (true);
    setCommandListener (this);
  }

  public void commandAction (Command c, Displayable d) {
    comm.commandAction(c, d);
  }
}
```

Transparency and Pixel-Level Image Manipulation

Transparency is a key concept in game and other graphics-intensive applications. By drawing images with various levels of transparency on top of each other, we can create very sophisticated visual effects at runtime while using a minimum amount of memory for image raw data. The trade-off, however, is that transparency manipulation can sometimes be computationally intensive. All Nokia MIDP devices support transparency in image drawing.

ARGB Image Data Format

A typical raster image can be represented by an array of integer values. Each value has a format of `0xAARRGGBB`, which represents the transparency and RGB (red, green, and blue) color of a pixel. Using different combinations of the RGB color values, we can describe more than 16 million different colors with this format. For each pixel color, there are also 256 levels of transparency (the alpha channel). Of course, the actual color and transparency display capability differs for each device. A typical Series 40 Developer Platform 2.0 device can display 65,536 colors and process 16 levels of alpha transparency values. When a transparent image is drawn on top of a background image, the result depends on the transparency level of each pixel. Figure 4–19 shows the effects of opaque, transparent, and partially transparent foreground images.

- If a pixel value has leading bits of `0xff`, it means the pixel is completely opaque. The new RGB color replaces whatever color the background pixel had before.

- If a pixel has leading bits of `0x00`, it means the pixel is completely transparent. The background pixel color is visibly unchanged.

- If a pixel has transparency between `0x00` (0) and `0xff` (256), it is partially transparent. The new pixel color is a combination of the foreground and background colors. For example, if the foreground pixel has value `0x7fff0000`, the resultant pixel would look like the background color behind a red glass.

TIP

In terms of CPU power consumption, supporting the basic transparency with binary alpha levels (i.e., either completely opaque or transparent) is much cheaper than supporting full alpha blending of partially transparent images. So, we recommend MIDlets use transparent PNG image files in preference to full alpha blending whenever possible.

Transparent images are especially important in game applications, which require irregularly shaped moving foreground figures (e.g., a person or a bullet). Since we can only draw images in rectangles, it is important to fill the pixels outside of the object boundary but within the rectangle boundary with transparent ARGB values.

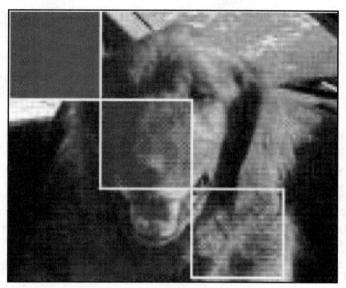

Figure 4–19 Red squares with different levels of transparency laid on top of a background image.

Convert Image to or from ARGB Array

In MIDP 2.0, the `Image` class provides a static factory method to assemble an `Image` object from an ARGB data array.

```
Image createRGBImage (int [] argb, // ARGB data array
                      int width,    // Image width
                      int height,   // Image height
                      boolean processAlpha)
```

The `processAlpha` argument determines whether to process the transparency information in the array. If it is false, the constructed image will have every pixel opaque. Using the MIDP 2.0 version of the `Image` class, we can also convert an `Image` object to an ARGB array.

```
void getRGB (int [] argb, // Returned ARGB data array
             int offset,  // Start offset in array
             int scanlen, // Offset to a new row
             int x,       // Left corner of sampling area
             int y,       // Upper corner of sampling area
             int width,   // Width of sampling area
             int height)  // Height of sampling area
```

The `scanlen` argument must be equal to or larger than `width` to avoid data overlapping between rows. Once we have the image data in an ARGB array, we

can resize it, rotate it, change its transparency, and do any other manipulation
we want to.

The ARGB data array contains the raw image with no compression. It could
take up a much larger heap-memory space than the original Image object.
Extensive image manipulation is very computationally intensive and it
should be avoided on small devices.

The Graphics.drawRGB() Method

In MIDP 2.0, the Graphics class provides a convenience method, drawRGB(),
to draw an ARGB array to a specified position on the Canvas directly without
going through the intermediary Image object. The signature of the method is
listed below. The arguments are self-explanatory.

```
void drawRGB (int [] argb, int offset, int scanlen,
              int x, int y, int width, int height,
              boolean processAlpha)
```

The drawRGB() method allows us to directly manipulate individual pixels on
the screen.

Using Part of an Image for Drawing

Since reading out an Image to an ARGB array consumes a lot of memory and
CPU resources, the MIDP 2.0 Graphics.drawRegion() method allows us to
draw part of an existing Image to a specified region on the screen with a
predefined transformation.

```
void drawRegion (Image src, int x_src, int y_src,
                 int width, int height, int transform,
                 int x_dest, int y_dest, int anchor)
```

It copies a region of the specified source image (x_src, y_src, width,
height) to a location within the destination (x_dest, y_dest) using the
specified anchor. The transform argument is a constant value from the
Sprite class (see Chapter 5), and it specifies how the source image should be
rotated and reflected before drawing. In addition, the Graphics.copyArea()
method allows us to copy a rectangle area of the screen (x_src, y_src,
width, height) and paste it to another part specified by the location (x_dest,
y_dest) and an anchor.

```
void copyArea (int x_src, int y_src, int width, int height,
               int x_dest, int y_dest, int anchor)
```

The CustomItem

Although the low-level MIDP UI API gives developers complete control over the Canvas, it is not flexible enough for many applications. One key limitation is that it requires the developer to paint the entire screen and handle all user events. In many cases, the application developer wants only low-level control over part of the Canvas. For example, if we wish to build an input screen with text input boxes and a custom-looking button, we only want to paint the button. Using the Canvas alone, we have to manually draw the text box and update its content at every user keystroke. The CustomItem class introduced in MIDP 2.0 allows us to develop a customized item and then use it along with other high-level items, such as the TextField. In fact, since CustomItem objects are reusable, we might even see a marketplace for MIDP UI components in the future.

The CustomItem class inherits from the Item class and hence has all properties of an Item.

- We can add a CustomItem to a Form container along with any other Item objects.

- We can specify the layout property of a CustomItem object.

- We can add Commands and CommandListeners to a CustomItem.

The CustomItem class represents any Form-compatible UI widget that paints itself and handles its own events. To develop a concrete widget with a specific look and behavior, we extend the CustomItem abstract class and implement its abstract methods. The following four methods are used to provide the item's minimum required and preferred size to the Form container.

```
protected abstract int getMinContentHeight ()
protected abstract int getMinContentWidth ()
protected abstract int getPrefContentHeight ()
protected abstract int getPrefContentWidth ()
```

The paint() method allows us to specify how to paint the CustomItem within its boundary. Like the paint() method in Canvas, it is invoked when the system redraws the screen or when the repaint() method of this CustomItem is called explicitly. The paint() method takes in the Graphics object as well as the dimensions of the item, which are determined and passed in by the Form object at runtime. The dimensions are width and height in number of pixels.

```
protected abstract void paint (Graphics g, int w, int h)
```

The CustomItem object could handle its own UI events by overriding the following key and pointer-event-handler methods. The coordinate information passed into the pointer handler methods is the current position of the pointer relative to the origin of the item.

```
protected void keyPressed (int keyCode)
protected void keyReleased (int keyCode)
protected void keyRepeated (int keyCode)
protected void pointerPressed (int x, int y)
protected void pointerReleased (int x, int y)
protected void pointerDragged (int x, int y)
```

In addition to those simple UI events, the `CustomItem` class allows us to respond to UI events specific to items inside a `Form`. For example, we can respond to the change of the item size by overriding the `sizeChanged()` method; we can respond to the focus in and out of the item by overriding the `traverse()` and `traverseOut()` methods.

The next example shows how to write a `CustomItem` subclass, `ImageButtonItem`, which renders an image button. The button can be associated with a `TextField`. If the user presses the game action key when the focus is on the button, an alert with the content of the `TextField` is shown. The button displays different images when it is in and out of focus. We cannot do this with button-style `ImageItems`.

```
public class ImageButtonItem extends CustomItem {

  private Image img;
  public TextField textField;

  public ImageButtonItem () {
    super ("");

    try {
      img = Image.createImage("/echo1.png");
    } catch (Exception e) {
      e.printStackTrace ();
      img = null;
    }
  }

  public int getMinContentWidth () {
    return 108;
  }

  public int getMinContentHeight () {
    return 33;
  }

  public int getPrefContentWidth (int width) {
    return getMinContentWidth ();
  }
```

```java
public int getPrefContentHeight (int height) {
  return getMinContentHeight ();
}

// Called when the cursor moves in focus
protected boolean traverse (int dir, int w, int h,
                            int [] visRect_inout) {
  try {
    img = Image.createImage("/echo2.png");
  } catch (Exception e) {
    e.printStackTrace ();
    // do nothing
  }
  repaint ();
  return false;
}

// Called when the cursor moves out of focus
protected void traverseOut () {
  try {
    img = Image.createImage("/echo1.png");
  } catch (Exception e) {
    e.printStackTrace ();
    // do nothing
  }
  repaint ();
}

public void paint (Graphics g, int w, int h) {
  g.drawImage (img, w / 2, h / 2,
          Graphics.HCENTER | Graphics.VCENTER);
}

public void keyPressed (int keyCode) {
  int gameCode = getGameAction (keyCode);

  if (gameCode == Canvas.FIRE) {

    Display display = DriverMidlet.display;
    Alert alert = new Alert ("Your text is",
            textField.getString(),
            null, AlertType.ALARM);

    alert.setTimeout(Alert.FOREVER);
    display.setCurrent (alert);
```

```
    } else {
      super.keyPressed(keyCode);
    }
  }
}
```

The following code shows how to use the `ImageButtonItem` class. Figure 4–20 demonstrates the `ImageButtonItem` class in action.

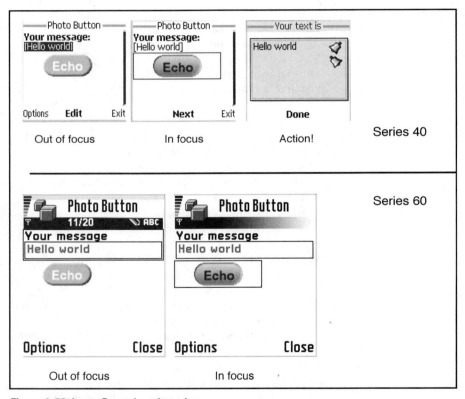

Figure 4–20 ImageButtonItem in action.

```
public class ImageButtonDemo extends Form
              implements CommandListener {

  private CommandListener comm;
  private TextField textField;
  private ImageButtonItem imageButton;

  public ImageButtonDemo (CommandListener c) {
    super ("Photo Button");
```

```
      comm = c;

      textField = new TextField("Your message",
              "", 20, TextField.ANY);
      imageButton = new ImageButtonItem ();
      imageButton.setLayout(Item.LAYOUT_CENTER);
      imageButton.textField = textField;

      append (textField);
      append (imageButton);

      setCommandListener (this);
    }

    public void commandAction (Command c, Displayable d) {
      comm.commandAction(c, d);
    }
  }
```

Use a Splash Screen

The splash screen is a screen that is displayed at the MIDlet start time. It typically presents the developer's logo and gives the MIDlet a professional look-and-feel. For applications that require lengthy initialization (e.g., to verify user credentials at the remote server or to download the multimedia content needed in the application), the splash screen improves user experience by cutting the perceived start-up time. For novice developers, a common mistake is to put the code for the splash screen directly in the `MIDlet.startApp()` method (see pseudocode below).

```
// The following code does not work
public class myMidlet extends MIDlet {

  // ... ...
  Display display;

  public void startApp () {
    Displayable splash = new SplashScreen ();
    display.setCurrent (splash);

    // Do the length initialization work
    // or wait for a while

    Displayable d = new AppScreen ();
    display.setCurrent (d);
  }
}
```

The problem with this approach is that the `startApp()` method runs in the MIDlet's UI thread. As we discussed in the "Why Multi-threading?" section in Chapter 3 "Getting Started", the display change is not rendered by the UI thread until it finishes executing the `startApp()` method. Hence, the splash screen never shows.

The correct way to display a splash screen is to put the screen-switch code in a separate, non-UI thread and start the thread from the `startApp()` method. The separate worker thread keeps the UI thread idle and hence allows it to render the `setCurrent()` requests. The following listing shows the `startApp()` method for the `DriverMidlet`, which displays a splash screen.

```
public class DriverMidlet extends MIDlet
                implements CommandListener {

  // ... ...

  protected void startApp () {
    Thread t = new SplashScreenThread (this);
    t.start();
  }
}
```

The `SplashScreenThread` class is a Java `Thread` class. Its `run()` method displays the splash screen first, counts down to zero, and then displays the first screen of the application. The `SplashScreen` class represents the splash screen with a welcome logo and an integer for the countdown value. The countdown value can be changed from outside by invoking the `SplashScreen.show(i)` method.

```
  public void run () {
      // Instantiate a splash screen and display it
      SplashScreen s = new SplashScreen (driver);
      DriverMidlet.display.setCurrent(s);

      // Do the startup work
      // and/or animate the splash screen
      // Here, we just have a simple count down
      for (int i = 10; i > 0; i--) {
        try {
          s.show (i);
          Thread.sleep (1000);
        } catch (InterruptedException ie) {
          // do nothing
        }
      }
```

Virtual Canvas Space

The MIDP Canvas allows us to draw on a virtual screen that is larger than the physical boundary of the display screen. We could construct a big virtual scene and expose only part of it by clipping the display screen on top of it at any given moment in the application workflow. This technique reduces the developer's work to dynamically reconstruct the display content for every screen update.

As an example, if the phone's LCD screen is 128 by 128, the display screen contains all the pixels inside the square (or a rectangle if X and Y dimensions of pixels are different) between [0,0] and [127,127]. However, when we draw on a canvas, we can draw at any coordinate position. For instance, we could draw content to fill a 512 by 512 virtual screen. Things outside the 128 by 128 display screen boundary just would not be visible. Clipping is used to position the coordinate of the upper-left corner of the virtual screen so that the [0,0] to [127,127] box contains just what we want to display. That is equivalent to moving a large piece of canvas behind a small open widow so that a person standing in front of the widow sees different content exposed at different times. This concept is shown in Figure 4–21.

In this section, we demonstrate the virtual screen and clipping technique through the example of a generic scrollable Canvas. The ScrollCanvas abstract class allows the user to scroll a Canvas against a large virtual screen using the navigation or game keys. The scrollX and scrollY variables are the coordinates of the upper-left corner of the virtual screen. The ScrollCanvas class overrides the keyPressed( ) method to change those values when the user presses game keys, and repaints the screen to realize scrolling.

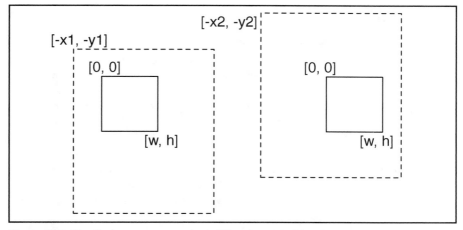

Figure 4–21 The display screen can show different parts of the virtual screen.

The ScrollCanvas demonstrates the most generic way to add scroll support to Canvas. In the case of mobile games, this is often not an efficient way to implement scrolling. Please refer to Chapter 5 for more scrolling techniques from the MIDP Game API.

```java
public abstract class ScrollCanvas extends Canvas
        implements CommandListener {

  // The upper left corner coord of the virtual canvas
  // They are typically both negative values
  protected int startX, startY;
  protected int w, h;

  // The displayed part of the virtual canvas is
  // always the area between [0,0] to [w,h]

  public ScrollCanvas () {
    startX = 0;
    startY = 0;

    w = getWidth ();
    h = getHeight ();
  }

  public void commandAction(Command c, Displayable s) {

    // Handle commands that are common to
    // every ScrollCanvas.
    // By default, there is none.
  }

  protected void keyReleased (int keyCode) {
    switch (getGameAction(keyCode)) {
      case UP:    startY += h / 2; break;
      case DOWN:  startY -= h / 2; break;
      case LEFT:  startX += w / 2; break;
      case RIGHT: startX -= w / 2; break;
      default: break;
    }
    // Do not scroll beyond the top
    if (startY > 0) startY = 0;
    // Do not scroll beyond the left edge
    if (startX > 0) startX = 0;
    repaint ();
  }
}
```

To use the `ScrollCanvas` class, we must first extend it and implement the `paint()` method to draw the entire virtual screen at the given upper-left coordinate (`startX` and `startY`). We can also override and delegate the `commandAction()` and `keyPressed()` methods in the subclass to handle commands and key events specific to the subclass. Below is an example that shows how to implement a scrollable text screen. Figure 4–22 shows it in action. The example also shows how to use the `Font` class to manipulate the appearance of the text.

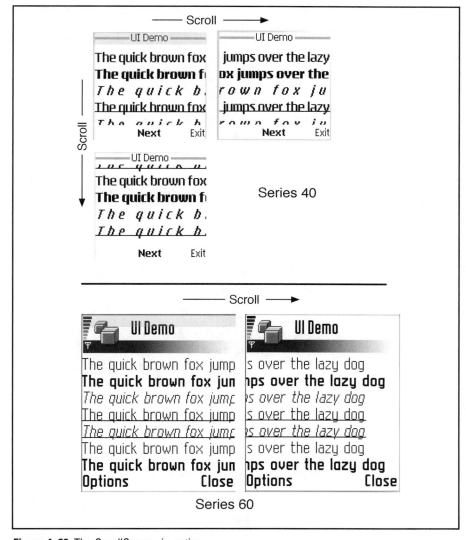

Figure 4–22 The ScrollCanvas in action.

```java
public class ScrollCanvasDemo extends ScrollCanvas {

    private CommandListener comm;

    private String sample =
            "The quick brown fox jumps over " +
            "the lazy dog";

    private Font font01 =
        Font.getFont(Font.FACE_PROPORTIONAL,
                Font.STYLE_PLAIN, Font.SIZE_LARGE);
    private Font font02 =
        Font.getFont(Font.FACE_PROPORTIONAL,
                Font.STYLE_BOLD, Font.SIZE_LARGE);
    // ... ...


    public ScrollCanvasDemo (CommandListener c) {
      comm = c;
      setCommandListener (this);
    }

    protected void paint (Graphics g) {
      g.setColor(0xffffff);
      g.fillRect(0,   0, w, h);
      g.setColor(0x000000);

      int x = startX;
      int y = startY;

      g.setFont (font01);
      y += font01.getHeight() + 5;
      g.drawString (sample, x, y,
              Graphics.BASELINE | Graphics.LEFT);

      g.setFont (font02);
      y += font02.getHeight() + 5;
      g.drawString (sample, x, y,
              Graphics.BASELINE | Graphics.LEFT);

      // ... ...
    }

    protected void keyReleased (int keyCode) {
      // Screen specific logic goes here
```

```
        super.keyReleased (keyCode);
    }

    public void commandAction(Command c, Displayable d) {
        comm.commandAction(c, d);
        super.commandAction(c, d);
    }
}
```

Wrap Text on Canvas

When we draw a text string on a Canvas, it comes out in one line. If the screen were not wide enough, the text would just flow out of the display screen. Although we can still use the ScrollCanvas to see the whole text, it is much better if we can make the text automatically wrap as string items do in the high-level forms. The following class shows the static utilities methods that are used to calculate the size of the string and break it into properly wrapped multiline formats. The getHeight() and substringWidth() methods in the Font class are heavily used to automatically lay out the text so that the code is portable across different screen sizes and font sizes. The wrap() method breaks a long line of text into a Vector of strings. It only breaks between words. Each String object contains characters that just fill the given width. The drawMultilineString() method draws a wrapped long string to the screen with our specified font, position, anchor, and column width. If your target language is not English, you might need to come up with a different algorithm. But this example should serve to illustrate how this might be done.

```
public class TextWrapUtil {

    static Vector wrap (String text,
                        Font font, int width) {
        Vector result = new Vector ();
        if (text == null) return result;

        boolean hasMore = true;
        // The current index of the cursor
        int current = 0;
        // The next line break index
        int lineBreak = -1;
        // The space after line break
        int nextSpace = -1;

        while (hasMore) {
            // Find the line break
            while (true) {
```

```
      lineBreak = nextSpace;
      if (lineBreak == text.length() - 1) {
        // We have reached the last line
        hasMore = false;
        break;
      } else {
        nextSpace = text.indexOf(' ', lineBreak+1);
        if (nextSpace == -1)
          nextSpace = text.length() -1;
        int linewidth = font.substringWidth(text,
                         current, nextSpace-current);
        // If too long, break out of the find loop
        if (linewidth > width) break;
      }
    }
    String line = text.substring(current,
                                 lineBreak + 1);
    result.addElement(line);
    current = lineBreak + 1;
  }
  return result;
}


// Returns the next line y value
static public int drawMultilineString (Graphics g,
            Font font, String str, int x, int y,
                        int anchor, int width) {

  g.setFont (font);
  Vector lines = wrap(str, font, width);
  for (int i = 0; i < lines.size(); i++) {
    int liney = y + (i * font.getHeight());
    g.drawString((String)lines.elementAt(i), x,
                 liney, anchor);
  }
  return y + (lines.size() * font.getHeight());
}
}
```

The next code snippet illustrates how to use the wrap functions and Figure 4–23 shows the resultant Canvas.

```
public class WrapTextDemo extends ScrollCanvas {

  private CommandListener comm;
```

```
private String sample =
        "The quick brown fox jumps over " +
        "the lazy dog";

private Font font01 =
    Font.getFont(Font.FACE_PROPORTIONAL,
            Font.STYLE_PLAIN, Font.SIZE_LARGE);
// ... ...

public WrapTextDemo (CommandListener c) {
  comm = c;
  setCommandListener (this);
}

protected void paint (Graphics g) {
  g.setColor(0xffffff);
  g.fillRect(0,   0, w, h);
  g.setColor(0x000000);

  int x = startX;
  int y = startY;

  y = TextWrapUtil.drawMultilineString(g, font01,
          sample, x, y + font01.getHeight(),
          Graphics.BASELINE | Graphics.LEFT, w);

  y = TextWrapUtil.drawMultilineString(g, font02,
          sample, x, y + font02.getHeight(),
          Graphics.BASELINE | Graphics.LEFT, w);

  // ... ...
}

protected void keyReleased (int keyCode) {
  // Screen specific logic goes here
  super.keyReleased (keyCode);
}

public void commandAction(Command c, Displayable d) {
  comm.commandAction(c, d);
  super.commandAction(c, d);
}
}
```

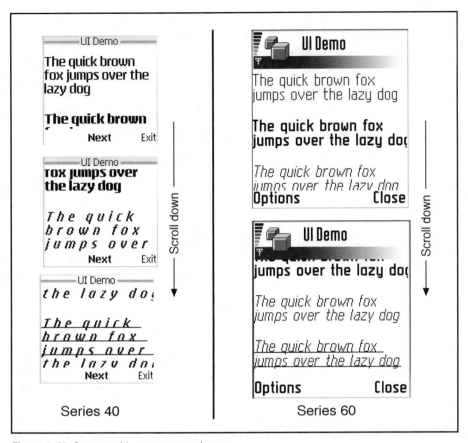

Figure 4–23 Canvas with auto-wrapped text.

Background MIDlet on Series 60 Devices

As we discussed in Chapter 3, "Getting Started," Nokia devices do not support the paused MIDlet state. On Series 60 devices, the user can put the MIDlet UI into background by pressing the End key. The MIDlet can also put itself into the background by calling the `Display.setCurrent(null)` method. The background MIDlet is still running. It just ceases to respond to any user events. The user can bring a background MIDlet back to the front at any time using the Menu key on Series 60 devices. Or the MIDlet can bring itself to the front by invoking the `Display.setCurrent()` method with a valid `Displayable` object.

If the MIDlet is displaying a `Canvas` screen when it enters the background state, the `Canvas.hideNotify()` method is called by the application management software (AMS). For a MIDlet that primarily displays a single `Canvas` screen (e.g., an animated game), we can override this method to stop threads, cancel timers, save important values, and so on, to reduce energy and resource consumption caused by background MIDlets. Similarly, when the MIDlet is brought back to front, the `Canvas.showNotify()` method is called.

```
protected void hideNotify() {
   remainingTime = endTime — System.currentTimeMillis();
   myThread.stop();
   autoPaused = true;
   repaint();
}

// A pause test in paint() method to check if paused.
// Paint a pause message on screen if autoPaused true.
protected void paint(Graphics g) {
   // paint game screen here
   if (autoPaused == true) {
     // paint pause message
   }
}
```

WARNING

Using the `Canvas.hideNotify()` method to pause the MIDlet works great for most games, where the user spends most play time on only one Canvas screen. It may not work for MIDlets that switch among several different screens.

MIDP UI Designer in Nokia Developer's Suite

The Nokia Developer's Suite (NDS) for J2ME 2.1 and above provides a visual UI designer to help us assemble MIDP UI code quickly. The designer features a drawing-canvas area that represents the phone screen, a tool bar consisting of UI elements that can be displayed on the screen, and a properties editor to control the look and behavior of the UI element (Figure 4–24). The designer canvas has the same width as the target device but can have an unlimited height to support horizontal scrolling in MIDP `Forms`. In MIDP terms, the canvas area is a `Displayable` (both `Form` and `Canvas` are supported), and the UI elements are `Items`, `Commands`, and images.

To assemble a screen, we can drag and drop UI elements from the tool bar to the canvas area. We can then move the items around using the mouse and adjust their attributes visually through the properties editor. Figure 4–25 shows how various MIDP `Items` can be arranged and customized on a `Form` designer.

When we are satisfied with the look, we can instruct the NDS to generate the source code for a `Displayable` class, which would render the exact view on the designer. The developer can then edit the source code and fill in appropriate

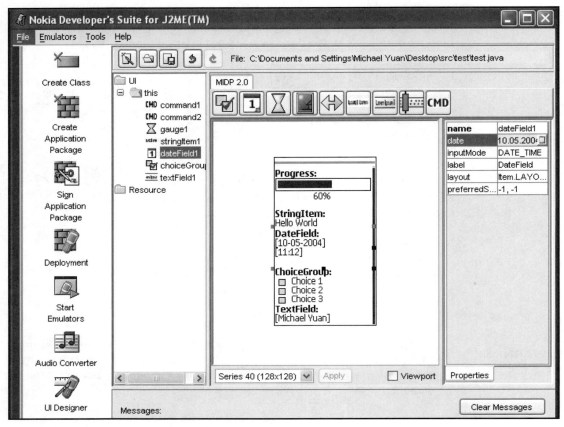

Figure 4–24 The NDS MIDP UI designer.

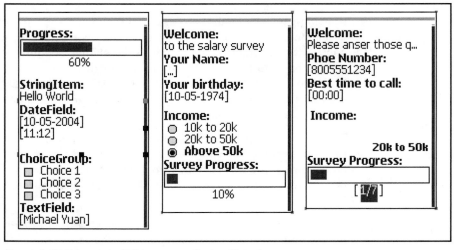

Figure 4–25 Examples of UI items on a Series 40 designer canvas.

command handlers and so forth. The visual UI designer proves to boost developer productivity by reducing the manual coding time for user interfaces.

The designer canvas can be shaped to emulate a Series 40, Series 60, or Series 90 device screen. Since the canvas can be higher than the real device screen to accommodate horizontal scroll, it is sometimes hard to tell exactly what is visible on a screen at any given scroll position. To solve this problem, the NDS introduces the concept of *viewport*. A viewport is a highlighted window that can be slid up and down along the designer canvas. It has the same height as the real screen. Everything outside of the viewport is grayed if this option is on (see Figure 4–26).

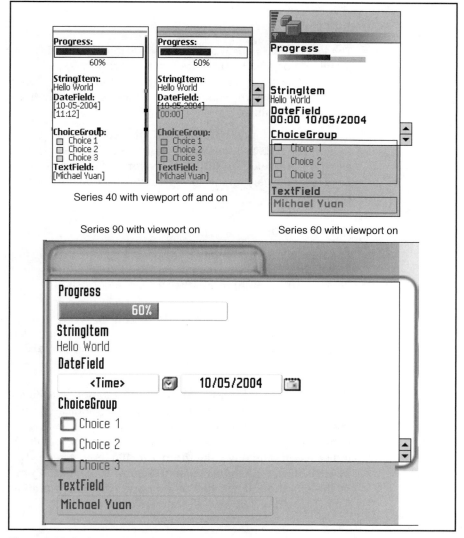

Figure 4–26 Series 40, 60, and 90 designer canvas and the viewport.

Nokia UI API Extensions

In addition to the standard MIDP UI, all Nokia Java devices support the Nokia UI API package. The Nokia UI API was originally designed to address some shortcomings in the MIDP 1.0. For Developer Platform 2.0 devices, MIDP 2.0 UI supports many features in Nokia UI API. Hence, some classes in the Nokia UI are deprecated and only kept for backward compatibility.

There are two Java packages in the Nokia UI API: com.nokia.mid.ui and com.nokia.mid.sound. We cover the ui package in this section. The sound package is being replaced by MIDP 2.0's javax.microedition.media package, which is covered in Chapter 5 and in Chapter 9, "Multimedia."

FullCanvas

The FullCanvas abstract class extends the Canvas class to support full-screen drawing. For MIDP 1.0 devices, we can simply extend the FullCanvas class and use it as a Canvas instance. However, the FullCanvas class does not allow Commands. Calls to addCommand() and setCommandListener() methods result in exceptions.

In MIDP 2.0, any Canvas can be set to full screen mode via the Canvas.setFullScreenMode(true) method call. Hence, the FullCanvas class is not useful in MIDP 2.0 devices. A full-screen mode Canvas can have Command objects, and the command labels appear when the user clicks the soft key.

DeviceControl

The DeviceControl utility class contains static methods to control the screen backlight and vibrator on the device. As we have seen, these methods are deprecated by methods in MIDP 2.0's Display class.

```
static void flashLights (long duration)
static void setLights (int num, int level)
static void startVibra (int freq, long duration)
static void stopVibra ()
```

The num argument in the setLights() method specifies the light to control. Currently, only value 0 is supported, which indicates the LCD backlight. The level argument takes in a value from 0 to 100 indicating the brightness of the light. But for most devices, the light is either on or off. In this case, value 0 indicates off, and any value from 1 to 100 indicates on. The freq argument in startVibra() takes in a value from 0 to 100 indicating the relative frequency of the vibration. If the device supports only one vibration frequency, values from 1 to 100 would have the same effect.

DirectUtils

The `DirectUtils` utility class contains static methods to convert standard MIDP image array and `Graphics` objects to their enhanced Nokia UI API counterparts.

```
Image createImage (byte [] data, int offset, int length)
Image createImage (int width, int height, int color)
DirectGraphics getDirectGraphics (Graphics g)
```

The `Image` objects created here are mutable and have alpha transparency channels. They are suitable for use in `DirectGraphics` objects. Now, let's look at the `DirectGraphics` object in more detail.

DirectGraphics

The `DirectGraphics` class offers several enhancements over the `Graphics` class. Like the latter, it is called inside the `Canvas.paint()` method. Using `DirectGraphics`, we can transform an image when drawing it. We can also use MIDP 2.0's `Graphics.drawRegion()` method to manipulate images.

```
void drawImage (Image img, int x, int y,
                int anchor, int manipulation)
```

Using the `manipulation` argument, we can flip and rotate the image. For example, the argument `FLIP_VERTICAL | ROTATE_90` instructs the `DirectGraphics` object to flip the image vertically and then rotate it 90 degrees counterclockwise. The `manipulation` argument is also available in the `drawPixels()` methods, which draw a pixel array to the screen. Minus the manipulation feature, the Nokia UI API's `drawPixels()` method is equivalent to the `Canvas.drawRGB()` method in MIDP 2.0.

The Nokia UI API's `getPixels()` method supports reading part of the screen into a pixel array for later use. In contrast, the `copyArea()` method in MIDP 2.0 supports copying and pasting only within one screen.

Another important feature of the Nokia UI API is the support for `drawPolygon()` and `fillPolygon()` methods to draw and fill arbitrary polygon shapes.

```
void drawPolygon (int [] xPoints, int xOffset,
   int [] yPoints, int yOffset, int nPoints, int argbColor)
void fillPolygon (int [] xPoints, int xOffset,
   int [] yPoints, int yOffset, int nPoints, int argbColor)
```

Summary

MIDP offers an impressive set of rich APIs to build GUI applications on mobile phones. In this chapter, we focused on the MIDP 2.0 API, which is standard on Nokia Developer Platform 2.0 devices.

The high-level API is easy to use and produces portable applications, since it relies on the device runtime to render UI components with the native look-and-feel. The low-level API gives the developer the ultimate control of the screen area. It is great for mobile games and other applications that need custom UIs. We covered the API basics with examples as well as advanced topics and useful techniques. Near the end of this chapter, we discussed the Nokia UI API extension, which provides UI enhancement for earlier Nokia MIDP 1.0 devices.

chapter

5

Developing Action Games

Using the MIDP 2.0 game and media APIs to create games.

Games are among the most popular applications for mobile devices. MIDP 1.0 allowed developers to create games, but contained no APIs or other explicit support for game development. MIDP 2.0 contains a Game API (the `javax.microedition.lcdui.game` package) that provides several classes that are highly useful in games. Topics covered in this chapter include:

- **Game design concepts**: discusses an architecture that updates and displays the game world continuously while monitoring for user input.
- **Managing player input**: covers techniques for maximum code portability.
- **Sprites and animation**: includes collision detection, backgrounds, layers, and trade-offs between processing power and JAR file size.
- **Frame rate regulation**: techniques for smooth animation and predictable game response.

Basic Game Concepts

Most applications spend most of their time idle. That is, they wait for the user to input something, then do whatever processing is necessary in response to that command, display the results to the user, and wait until the next action by the user.

Most games work differently. They perform processing and update the display continually—and listen for user input at any time. When the user does something, the game does whatever processing is required, which usually means changing some data that is used to update the display, and the display continues being updated in real time.

In other words, during the play of the game itself, the user is inside a continuous loop that checks for user input, modifies game state data, displays the new game state in visual form, and repeats. The loop continues until the game ends, the player quits or pauses the application, or the application is forced to pause or end for some reason (e.g., the player takes an incoming call). As we discussed before, in order to avoid blocking the display rendering and user input events in the main UI thread, the game loop must run in its own thread. You can see how this is done in the example in this chapter.

Since so much of what happens during gameplay itself involves modifying the display, the main game loop is almost always implemented inside Canvas—or, in MIDP 2.0, inside GameCanvas. GameCanvas is a subclass of Canvas and includes all of Canvas's methods and objects as well as features, like double-buffering and improved user input handling, that are very useful for games.

A complete MIDlet for a game consists of more than this loop, however, even though the player spends most of his time in the loop. Typically, there is a splash screen; a high-level menu that lets the player set options, load a saved game, start a new game, or quit; a page that reports the player's score and whether he won or loss; and possibly a number of other pages as well, such as a high-score list, help pages, and so on.

The Game MIDlet

At a very high level, you'd expect a game MIDlet's startApp() method to begin by displaying a splash screen and loading things in the background as needed, then passing off to standard event-handling code to guide the user through the high-level menus, then using GameCanvas for the main game processing. The following list shows the skeleton code of a game MIDlet.

```
import javax.microedition.lcdui.*;
import javax.microedition.lcdui.game.*;
//add other imports as necessary

public class MyGameMIDlet extends MIDlet
                        implements CommandListener {

    private MyGameCanvas myGameCanvas;
    private Display display;
    private boolean gameStarted = false;
    private Command play;
    // More Commands or menu options for events
    // outside of the game loop ...

    public MyGameMIDlet() {
        play = new Command ("Play", Command.OK, 2);
        // Initialize other Commands ...
    }

    public void startApp() {
        display = Display.getDisplay (this);

        // Start the thread for splash screen and
        // initialization (see chapter 4). At the end
        // of the start up thread, display the main
        // game menu with the "Play" Command.
    }
```

```
// The UI event handler for events
// outside of the game loop
public void commandAction (Command c, Displayable d) {
  if (c == play) {
    display.setCurrent (myGameCanvas);
    myGameCanvas.start ();
    gameStarted = true;
  } // Handle other Commands
}

// does not have effect on Nokia devices — see Chap 3
public void pauseApp() {
}

public void destroyApp(boolean unconditional) {
  if (gameStarted) {
    myGameCanvas.stop();    // stop game loop
  }
}
//add other methods needed for the
// main MIDlet class here
}
```

To explain this a little bit, at the beginning, we declare myGameCanvas as an instance of MyGameCanvas, which is a GameCanvas implementation defined later in this chapter. We also declare a boolean variable gameStarted, to track whether or not we've started the main game loop.

TIP   Think of it this way: starting the MIDlet starts the "stuff around the game," but the actual game doesn't start until the user selects Play on the main game menu. The gameStarted variable tracks whether or not this has happened.

The startApp() method is called when the MIDlet is started. It just delegates the splash screen and initialization work to a worker thread as suggested in Chapter 4, "MIDP User Interface." After the initialization is done, the worker thread displays the main menu screen and assigns the MIDlet class itself as the command listener. The user might change options, look at help, or make other menu selections, but eventually he or she will start the game by pressing the Play command. The Play command handler sets the display to be painted by myGameCanvas, and starts myGameCanvas.

Thread for the Game Loop

But what of the GameCanvas itself? Since it contains the main game loop, it needs to run in its own thread and implement the Runnable interface. Below is an example implementation of the GameCanvas class. The code for the main loop is enclosed in the run() method.

```
class MyGameCanvas extends GameCanvas
                      implements Runnable {
  private Thread gameThread = null;
  private final Graphics g;
  private Boolean playing;

  public MyGameCanvas() {
    super(true);

    // Include this in constructor instead of loop
    // because a new instance is created every time
    // you call getGraphics()
    g = getGraphics();
  }

  // start() just starts a Thread that, when started
  // itself, invokes run()
  public void start() {
    gameThread = new Thread(this);
    gameThread.start();
    playing = true;
  }

  public void stop() {
    playing = false; // ask the thread to stop
    try {
      gameThread.join(); // wait until it has stopped
    } catch (InterruptedException ie) { }
    gameThread = null;
  }

  public void run() {
    while (playing == true) {
      readInput();
      simulateWorld();
      draw();

      //this is instead of repaint(),
      // and puts g on the display
      flushGraphics();
```

```
            delayUntilNextFrame();
        }
    }

    private void readInput() {
        // read user input here
    }

    private void simulateWorld() {
        // update game data here
    }

    private void draw() {
        //draw whatever we need to on g, our Graphics object

    }

    private void delayUntilNextFrame() {
        //implement code to handle animation frame delay
    }
}
```

NOTE The GameCanvas class complements the Canvas's paint() and repaint() methods with getGraphics() and flushGraphics() methods, as discussed in more detail later.

The start() method is invoked from our main MIDlet class's commandAction() method when the user presses the Play button. Inside the start() method, we start a thread, gameThread, to perform the processing we need. The stop() method is also defined here and gets called when the MIDlet is destroyed. The run() method is invoked when gameThread is started and it runs the game loop. Let's now focus on its implementation.

Inside the run() method, boolean variable, playing, controls whether the loop continues. We do three basic things each time through the loop. We check for user input; we update game data; and we draw the next frame of animation. Unlike the Form and Canvas applications we discussed in Chapter 4, where the main UI thread is interrupted by callbacks every time the user presses a key, the game loop thread should run continuously. Instead of being interrupted at random times, the game loop pulls in the user input for processing when the program is ready. We will see how it gets implemented later in this chapter.

In the code above, we have three separate method calls, one for each of these actions. These aren't standard MIDP methods—these methods are part of our implementation of MyGameCanvas and are added later.

TIP

It's generally a good idea to keep code that checks for user input, code that updates the model, and code that displays to the device separate. Among other things, this makes modifying your code to deal with different device characteristics (screen size, key layout, etc.) easier.

Next, we use `flushGraphics()`, a standard method defined as part of `GameCanvas`. `GameCanvas` is double-buffered; there is a back buffer, which you render into, and `flushGraphics()` then flushes it to the LCDUI.

There's one final method invocation in the loop—`delayUntilNextFrame()`. Note that the display is being updated each time through the loop. If the time spent updating the world, responding to user input, or drawing varies from iteration to iteration, the animation will be jerky. Alternatively, if only a little processing is required each time through the loop, animation might be too fast. Therefore, we need to control how often the loop iterates, to ensure smooth and reasonably paced animation. The `delayUntilNextFrame()` method calculates a dynamic delay to regulate the loop.

Finally, we need to define the four methods invoked in the `run()` method—`readInput()`, `simulateWorld()`, `draw()`, and `delayUntilNextFrame()`. In this example, we just include them as "stubs," without any real code.

The Game API Package

So far, we have a generic game skeleton that doesn't require any real use of the MIDP 2.0 Game API (although we've mentioned, but not really talked about, `GameCanvas`). It's possible, in fact, to implement a game without using the Game API—it didn't exist in MIDP 1.0, and many games were developed using that—but its features are extremely useful for game development.

Let's look at each class in the API—and show how we can use that class to implement some of the methods that are just stubs in our current skeleton. In the process, we'll flesh the skeleton out to produce a little game that allows you to control the motion of an on-screen fish. See Figure 5–1.

GameCanvas

The `GameCanvas` extends `Canvas` by adding an off-screen `Graphics` buffer and allowing efficient polling of the keys. As an extension of `Canvas`, all of the fields and methods available in `Canvas` are also available in `GameCanvas`, while some new fields and methods are defined.

The GameCanvas Graphics Buffer

MIDP 2.0 allows us to synchronously update the screen via the off-screen `Graphics` buffer. The `getGraphics()` method returns the off-screen buffer. An off-screen buffer can be drawn on like any other `Graphics` object. At the end of

Figure 5–1 A fish game.

all the drawing operations, call flushGraphics() to paint the off-screen graphics onto the screen. The flushGraphics() routine is not intended to be called more than once per frame.

```
protected Graphics getGraphics()
public void flushGraphics()
public void flushGraphics(int x, int y, int width, int
height)
```

The second version of flushGraphics()—the one with four parameters—paints only part of the buffer to the screen. The x and y parameters indicate the upper-left corner of the part of the buffer that is to appear on the screen; the width and height parameters indicate the width and height of the region. To put it another way, flushGraphics() is the same as flushGraphics(0,0,g.getWidth(), g.getHeight()), assuming g is the Graphics object we're using for the buffer.

Full-Screen Mode

One more feature added with MIDP 2.0 is full-screen mode. In MIDP 1.0, there wasn't a way to take over the full screen, including the areas used by soft key labels; MIDP 2.0 does allow this, with the setFullScreenMode(Boolean) method. (This method is actually part of Canvas, not GameCanvas, so you can use it even if not using GameCanvas, but it's new with MIDP 2.0 and worth mentioning here.)

If you do use full-screen mode, however, be cautious about how you use soft keys. Generally, in full-screen mode, you should use soft keys only to exit the game or go to a menu from the game screen. If soft keys do have some game function, you should probably place text above the soft keys indicating their function. Otherwise, players may be puzzled about how to use them and what they do.

```
public void setFullScreenMode(boolean mode)
```

Reading Player Input

In MIDP, you can either detect the use of literal keys on the device or of "game actions." Game actions include things like Left, Right, Up, Down, and Fire. The manufacturer decides which keys correspond to which action and sometimes map multiple keys to the same action (for instance, pressing Up on a direction rocker and pressing 2 might both map to the game action Up). In general, game developers are advised to use game actions rather than literal key presses, because keypad layouts vary, and in this way, the code will be more transportable among different devices.

In Chapter 4, we saw that the Canvas has event handlers called keyPressed() and keyReleased() that receive control when a key event occurs. These events can occur at any time during our game loop, but we need our readInput() method to retrieve the key information when it is called. One way to do this is to use the event handlers to store key information in public variables, and then have readInput() look at those variables to check on current key status. In fact, that is the only way to do it on MIDP 1.0 devices. On MIDP 2.0 devices, the getKeyStates() method defined in GameCanvas is specially designed to handle this situation. We will take advantage of this new MIDP 2.0 feature in our examples.

```
public int getKeyStates()
```

The getKeyStates() method returns an integer indicating the combination of game actions that has been pressed since the last time it is called. Different bits in the integer value correspond to different game actions. So, by using an AND operation (&), you can check a particular bit—and if it is set, you know that game action has been requested since the last loop. You don't even need to know *which* bit corresponds to which action, because GameCanvas also defines a set of fields you can use to perform the AND operation (Table 5–1).

Table 5–1 Static Constants in the GameCanvas Class for Game Key States

Constant	Description
UP_PRESSED DOWN_PRESSED LEFT_PRESSED RIGHT_PRESSED	Bitmask for the UP, DOWN, LEFT, RIGHT game action keys
FIRE_PRESSED	Bitmask for the FIRE game action key
GAME_A_PRESSED GAME_B_PRESSED GAME_C_PRESSED GAME_D_PRESSED	Bitmask for the GAME_A, GAME_B, GAME_C, GAME_D game action keys.

TIP

The Game_A through Game_D buttons are not required for all devices, and we won't use them here.

Please note a couple of things here, though. First, not all keys on a standard mobile phone's keypad are captured by getKeyStates()—for example, no game action may be mapped to the 1 key, and if you want to allow diagonal movement, you might want that to mean "move up and left." If you want to be able to capture presses on literal keys, you still need to use the keyPressed() and keyReleased() methods. But for most games, including our fish game, the game actions are enough, and getKeyStates() is all we need.

The readInput() Method Implementation

Here's how we implement readInput():

```
private Fish myFish;

private void readInput() {
  int keyStates = getKeyStates();
  if ((keyStates & UP_PRESSED) != 0) {
    myFish.swim(Fish.UP);
  } else if ((keyStates & DOWN_PRESSED) != 0) {
    myFish.swim(Fish.DOWN);
  }
  if ((keyStates & LEFT_PRESSED) != 0) {
    myFish.swim(FISH.LEFT);
  } else if ((keyStates & RIGHT_PRESSED) != 0) {
    myFish.swim(Fish.RIGHT);
  }
}
```

All we're doing here is checking the four directional keys and then invoking the swim() method in a class called Fish that we haven't defined yet. The Fish class is responsible for actually making whatever changes are required to the game world. That is, we're only handling input here, actual changes to the game state will happen later on.

Note that because we have one if…else if construct for Up and Down, and a separate one for Left and Right, it is possible for someone to move diagonally by holding one of the Up-Down keys down at the same time as a Left-Right key. But a caution is in order here. MIDP 2.0 does not *require* all devices to detect simultaneous key presses, so on a particular device, you might only capture the most recently pressed key. (This is a big problem for games that require you to move and fire at the same time.) However, all Nokia devices that support MIDP 2.0 *will* detect simultaneous key presses. (Not all earlier MIDP 1.0 devices do so.)

Suppress Unnecessary Callbacks

If we want to use the getKeyStates() method, there's something else we need to do, however. We don't want the MIDlet to make calls to keyPressed() and keyReleased() unnecessarily—even if we just leave those methods empty, it still takes system resources and processing power to make those calls. Luckily, the GameCanvas specification allows us to suppress calls to those methods, at least when a game action is invoked—they still get called when keys that do not map to game actions are pressed. The way to suppress these calls is to construct your GameCanvas object by passing a true argument to its super class's constructor as we did with the MyGameCanvas class earlier in this chapter. If you do *not* want to suppress the key events, you must include the code super(false); in the class constructor.

Layer

The `Layer` class is a new class introduced with the Game API package. There are two `Layer` subclasses: `Sprite` and `TiledLayer`. The `Layer` class itself is rarely instantiated or extended, but the class provides a set of methods that are inherited and used by both `Sprite` and `TiledLayer` classes.

In a game, there are typically two or more graphical layers. For example, there might be a background layer with terrain and obstacles, and a foreground layer where characters, enemies, and other sprites are painted. Developers need to ensure that objects are painted in the correct order so that the background doesn't get painted over a sprite, for instance.

In MIDP 2.0, each sprite is considered its own "layer" so that a layer can be assigned a position. This frees us from having to define variables to hold the x and y coordinates of every object in the game, because a layer tracks its own position.

Layers keep track of their own size and position and can be moved, hidden, and set visible. The following is a list of the methods exposed by `Layer`, and thus also by `Sprite` and `TiledLayer`.

```
public void setPosition(int x, int y)
public void setVisible(boolean visible)
public final boolean isVisible()
public void move(int dx, int dy)
public final int getHeight()
public final int getWidth()
public final int getX()
public final int getY()

abstract void paint(Graphics g)
```

The `setPosition()` method is used to set a layer to a specific `x,y` coordinate in its graphics context (e.g., the `Graphics` object on which it is to be painted). The upper left-hand corner of the `Layer`'s image will appear at this position when it is painted.

A layer is initially assumed to be "visible," meaning that it will be painted when its `paint()` method is called (or when a `LayerManager` is appended to paints). `setVisible(false)` sets it to invisible, meaning it will not paint. `setVisible(true)` makes it visible again. Similarly, `isVisible()` can be used to determine whether or not a layer is visible at the moment.

The `move()` method moves a layer from its current position, incrementing its current x and y coordinates by the parameters you pass. (You can of course pass negative parameters.) The `getHeight()` method returns the height, in pixels, of the layer; `getWidth()` returns the width. Similarly `getX()` and getY() return the x and y coordinates where it is displayed—or rather, the x,y coordinates of the upper-left corner of the layer.

Finally, a layer's paint() method paints it to the specified Graphics object at its current coordinates relative to the object.

The Fish Class

In readInput(), we invoked a method in some class called Fish to store the player's orders for her fish in the game. Our fish is, of course, a Sprite, which is a subclass of Layer—but moving it only requires the use of one of Layer's method, specifically move(). Let's see how this works.

Here's what the Fish class looks like:

```
public class Fish extends Sprite {

    public static final int UP = 1;
    public static final int DOWN = 2;
  public static final int LEFT = 3;
  public static final int RIGHT = 4;

    private static final int MOVE_X = 4;
    private static final int MOVE_Y = 3;
    // these are values rather than hard-coded later,
    // so if we want the fish to move slower or faster,
    // we can just recompile with different values

    //used to store the player's input
    public int dx, dy;

    //method used to store player's orders in dx and dy
  public void swim(int direction) {
    switch (direction) {
      case UP:    dy = -MOVE_Y; break;
      case DOWN:  dy = MOVE_Y; break;
      case LEFT:  dx = -MOVE_X; break;
      case RIGHT: dx = MOVE_X; break;
      default: break;
    }
  }

  public void moveCompleted() {
    dx = 0;
    dy = 0;
  }
}
```

We're extending `Sprite`, a subclass of `Layer`. A constructor for the `Fish` class is missing—we describe how to write that when we get to the `Sprite` class.

The `swim()` method hides the amount of movement it makes in a each direction from the caller, but the class member variables are public. Adding accessors and mutators for all the member variables would bloat the size of the class slightly. As you add more and more features and graphics to a game, you need all the space you can get. MIDlet JAR packages are restricted in size by the handset and the phone service operators, so we need to limit the size of the MIDlet as much as possible.

The `moveCompleted()` method simply resets the variables that track movement components to zero to await further player input.

How does the fish actually get moved? That happens in the `simulateWorld()` method, which we explore in a bit, but the code it uses, where `myFish` is an instance of the `Fish` class, is very simple:

```
myFish.move (myFish.dx, myFish.dy);
```

Sprite

The MIDP 2.0 `Sprite` class extends `Layer` to support animation, collision detection, and image transformation.

`Sprites` are created from images. A sprite can be animated or nonanimated, depending on which constructor is used. A nonanimated `Sprite` uses the whole image.

```
Sprite(Image image)
Sprite(Image image, int frameWidth, int frameHeight)
Sprite(Sprite s)
```

There are three constructors for a `Sprite`. The first is used to create a nonanimated `Sprite` by specifying an `Image` object to contain the `Sprite`'s image (which might be created with `Graphics` methods or loaded from a file packaged with the JAR). The third is used to copy a `Sprite`. The middle one is the one you use for animated `Sprites`.

Essentially, for an animated sprite, you supply a single image graphic that contains all possible frames of animation for this sprite. All the frames must have the same height and width, which are specified in the `Sprite` constructor. The number of frames in the image is determined by dividing the full image into equally sized cells (see Figure 5–2). If the image can't be evenly divided into cells of the given width and height, the constructor throws an exception.

The `Sprite` class has a large number of methods; we discuss a few at a time.

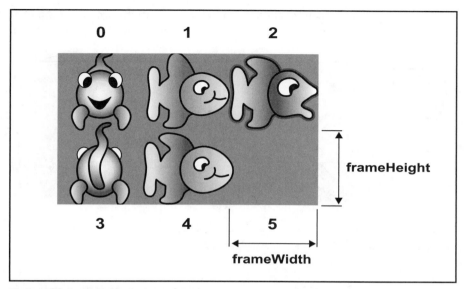

Figure 5–2 Sprite image frame numbers.

Collision Detection

```
collidesWith(Image image, int x, int y,
                            boolean pixelLevel)
collidesWith(Sprite s, boolean pixelLevel)
collidesWith(TiledLayer t, boolean pixelLevel)
defineCollisionRectangle(int x, int y, int width,
                                      int height)
```

The collidesWith() method, in its various forms, is used to determine whether any part of the Sprite intersects with something else. This is quite useful in many games, since game sprites often bounce off, blow up, or do other things to each other when they collide.

All three versions have a boolean, pixelLevel, as one of the passed parameters. Layers (and other images) can contain transparent pixels. If you pass a value of false, the method just checks to see if any part of the rectangle containing the Sprite intersects any part of the rectangle defined by the other object. If you pass a value of true, the method instead checks for pixel-level collision—that is, no collision is reported if only transparent portions of the two objects' images overlie one another. Figure 5–3 is an example: In the first case, no collision is reported. In the second case, the bounding rectangles intersect, but only transparent pixels overlie one another—even though the fish and the rock don't look as if they are colliding, this is still reported as a collision unless pixelLevel is true. The third case is always a collision.

WARNING   Pixel-level collision detection is more processor-intensive than regular collision detection—so be careful to use it only when it's really necessary.

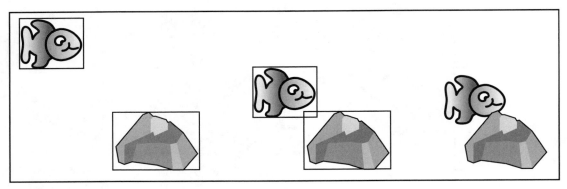

Figure 5–3 Rectangle collision versus pixel-level collision.

The collidesWith() method for use with other Sprites is simplest; you just pass that Sprite. You can also pass a non-Sprite image, but images do not inherently have x and y coordinates the way Sprites do, so you need to pass x and y coordinates, too. The method basically says, "If I plop this image down at these coordinates, will the Sprite intersect it?"

Finally, you can also check for collision with a TiledLayer—the other subclass of Layer, which we describe later.

Normally, collidesWith() uses the Sprite's own size and location to determine collisions. However, if you wish, you can define a rectangle that is larger or smaller than the literal Sprite image, or offset from its upper left-hand corner. You do that with the defineCollisionRectangle() method. The x and y parameters are measured from the Sprite's upper left-hand corner, and the height and width parameters are the height and width you want for the collision rectangle.

Using Collision Detection

Before we go on to Sprite's other methods, let's use collision detection. During simulateWorld() in our main game loop, the game system needs to calculate where all the game objects will move and what they will do. As previously discussed, we don't do any drawing or player input here—we just take care of things that affect the game state, such as actually resolving the effects of player input, physics, artificial intelligence if any, and so on.

In our fish demo, the "world" is very sparse. It has no other objects for our fish to interact with. We can add more objects later, but for now let's say the fish is not allowed to swim past the edges of the screen, so the screen edges act as barriers. This means the physics simulation consists of fish movement and obstacle collision. We can use collidesWith() to handle this.

```
public class Obstacle extends Sprite {

  public Obstacle(int width, int height) {
    super(MyGameMIDlet.createImage(width,height));
  }
}
```

All this does is create a sprite with the passed height and width. Obstacle is an extension of Sprite; the Sprite constructor requires an image, thus just as we had to pass a boolean to GameCanvas via super(), here we have to pass the image to Sprite via super(). Initially, the image is white, but we can change that later if desired.

To create the walls, we need to call some code during the game's initialization, before entering the game loop. We place this in the MyGameCanvas constructor:

```
layerManager = new LayerManager;

private static final int WALL_TOP=0;
private static final int WALL_BOTTOM=1;
private static final int WALL_LEFT=2;
private static final int WALL_RIGHT=3;
private static final int WALL_COUNT=4;
private static Obstacle walls[] =
                new Obstacle[WALL_COUNT];

public void initWalls(int screenWidth,
                      int screenHeight)
                      throws NullPointerException {

  walls[WALL_TOP] = new Obstacle(screenWidth,1);
  layerManager.append(walls[WALL_TOP]);
  walls[WALL_TOP].setPosition(0,0);

  walls[WALL_BOTTOM] = new Obstacle(screenWidth,1);
  layerManager.append(walls[WALL_BOTTOM]);
  walls[WALL_BOTTOM].setPosition(0,screenHeight-1);

  walls[WALL_LEFT] = new Obstacle(1,screenHeight);
  layerManager.append(walls[WALL_LEFT]);
  walls[WALL_LEFT].setPosition(0,0);

  walls[WALL_RIGHT] = new Obstacle(1,screenHeight);
  layerManager.append(walls[WALL_RIGHT]);
  walls[WALL_RIGHT].setPosition(screenWidth-1,0);
  }
```

Note that we're using another Game API object here, `LayerManager`, and one of its methods, `append()`. We discuss those later, but here's a brief explanation: The `LayerManager` object exists to manage a bunch of layers. Essentially, you can `append()` objects to a `LayerManager`, then tell it to `paint()`, and it paints all the objects on the relevant graphics context. This is a lot easier than drawing or painting each object independently.

So, at the beginning of this code, we create a new `LayerManager` object. We also define some constants we can use to remember which wall we're talking about, and an array of `Obstacle` objects to hold the walls.

We then define a method, `initWalls()`, that is called from the `MyGameCanvas` constructor before entering the main game loop. For each wall, `initWalls()` creates the `Obstacle` object for that wall, appends it to `LayerManager`, and sets its position on the screen.

Remember that `Obstacle` just creates an image with width and height; so for the top and bottom walls, we want an image that is as wide as the screen (`screenWidth`), and just 1 pixel high. For the left and right walls, we want an image that is as high as the screen (`screenHeight`), and just 1 pixel wide.

The `setPosition()` method is one of `Layer`'s methods and sets the image's upper left-hand corner at the specified coordinates. For the top and left walls, the upper left-hand corner is also the upper left-hand corner of the screen—0,0. For the right wall, it's at the top and right of the screen (we subtract 1 because the image is 1 pixel thick), and for the bottom, it's at the lower left-hand corner.

To detect a collision between the fish and a wall, we need to define the fish's `Sprite`—which we do in a little bit, to show how animated sprites work. For now, assume that we have already instantiated a `Sprite` for the fish, called `myFish`.

We can now write our `simulateWorld()` routine. We'll get the fish's tentative new position and see if it collides with the walls. If so, then the fish's movement component in that wall's direction is reversed. At the end of the routine, we set the movement component variables back to zero by calling `myFish`'s `moveCompleted()` method to await further player input.

This is fairly unsophisticated physics. It doesn't bounce the fish off the wall using a physics equation, such as "angle of reflection equals angle of incidence." It doesn't even always let the fish move right up against the wall. But in this game architecture, this method is where you would put this sort of physics simulation.

```
private void simulateWorld() {
  myFish.move(myFish.dx, myFish.dy);
  //move fish
  //then check for collision with walls
  for (int idx=WALL_COUNT-1; idx>=0; —idx) {
    if (!mFish.collidesWith(walls[idx],false)) {
```

```
      continue;
    }
    //fish collided with wall, so erase movement component
    switch(idx) {
      case WALL_LEFT:
      case WALL_RIGHT:
        //back out x-component of move
        myFish.move(-myFish.dx,0);
        break;
      case WALL_TOP:
      case WALL_BOTTOM:
        //back out y-component of move
        myFish.move(0,-myFish.dy);
        break;
    }
  }
  myFish.moveCompleted();
}
```

This code moves the `myFish` sprite to the location it will move to, assuming no collision takes place. Then, we enter a loop that checks for collisions with each of the four walls. If a collision occurs, we reverse the movement of the fish's appropriate component. We then call `moveCompleted()` to zero out the movement component variables in preparation for the player's next input.

When we add more game objects into the world, we determine their movement and behavior here in the `simulateWorld()` method as well.

NOTE   While this code demonstrates how we can use `collidesWith()` in a straightforward way, this probably isn't the way you'd want to implement walls in a real game. Creating images takes a fair bit of system overhead, and memory space is at a premium in most MIDP applications. It would actually be better practice just to use math to detect whether the sprite is close to the screen edge.

Sprite Animation

We used the `Sprite` constructor for a static image. We want to animate our fish, however, and for this we need the second `Sprite` constructor:

```
Sprite(Image image, int frameWidth, int frameHeight)
```

When constructing an animated sprite, the frames in the image are numbered starting from the upper left, first across the top row and then down to the next row below. For example, if we supplied the images for a fish as shown in Figure 5–4, we'd get six animation frames, three drawn from left to right across the top

Figure 5–4 Frame sequence {1, 4, 4, 0, 1, 4, 4}.

and three from left to right across the bottom. This is actually somewhat wasteful, because the sixth frame is blank.

It is better to store these images stacked vertically like a film strip.

```
public void setFrameSequence(int[] sequence)
public int getFrameSequenceLength()
public int getRawFrameCount()
```

The Sprite class maintains a frame sequence for its animation. Initially, this sequence is the same in length and order as the frames in the image supplied in the Sprite constructor.

However, you can change the length of this sequence by skipping, repeating, and reusing the image frames by calling the Sprite method setFrameSequence(). It accepts an array of integers that represents the new sequence. For example, using the source image pictured in Figure 5–4, we could set a sequence array like this: {1, 4, 4, 0, 1, 4, 4}. This sequence would show the fish swimming a stroke to the right, turning to look out the screen, then swimming to the right a bit more, as shown.

The method getFrameSequenceLength() reports the current length of the frame sequence—in our example, this would be 7. The method getRawFrameCount(), by contrast, reports the total number of frames that exist in the image originally supplied in the Sprite constructor. Thus, in our example, it would return 6, not 7 (there were six frames in our original image, as shown in Figure 5–4).

```
public void setFrame(int sequenceIndex)
public void nextFrame()
public void prevFrame()
public int getFrame()
public final void paint(Graphics g)
```

Once you have set your desired animation sequence, you can animate the sprite by switching the currently active frame before painting the sprite. There are three ways to switch the frame: setFrame(), nextFrame(), and prevFrame().

When calling `setFrame()`, be sure to pass the index of the frame in the *sequence*, not the number of the frame from the source *image*. For example, after setting the example {1, 4, 4, 0, 1, 4, 4} sequence, you would call `setFrame(0)`, then `setFrame(1)`, and so on until `setFrame(7)`.

In this situation, where your animation follows the frame sequence, it is easier to call `nextFrame()` instead of `setFrame()`. The `nextFrame()` method automatically cycles the frames, which is useful for continuous loops like an idle animation. You can determine which frame is currently shown with `getFrame()`.

Positioning and the Reference Pixel

The sprite's paint method displays it on the screen at its current position. The methods concerning the sprite's location on the screen, such as `setPosition()`, `getX()`, and `getY()`, all refer to the upper-left corner of the sprite.

However, a sprite has another special anchor point that can be used to position it on the screen and is also used to rotate or flip the image. This point is called the *reference pixel*, and it can be redefined to any point relative to the sprite, even outside of the sprite's bounds. By default, it's set to the sprite's upper-left corner. The reference pixel is set using `defineReferencePixel()`. The values given are the coordinates relative to the sprite's upper-left corner. This relative location can be retrieved later using `getRefPixelX()` and `getRefPixelY()`.

If you prefer to specify where the sprite will be painted by referring to its reference pixel rather than to its upper-left corner, you can do so with `setRefPixelPosition()`. This moves the sprite to the screen coordinate you pass—that is, locates it on the screen with the reference pixel at this location.

```
public void defineReferencePixel(int sprite_x,
                                 int sprite_y)
public int getRefPixelX()
public int getRefPixelY()
public void setRefPixelPosition(int screen_x,
                                int screen_y)
```

Sprite Transforms

The more common use of the reference pixel is in rotating and flipping the image. You rotate and/or flip images with the `setTransform()` method. When you do so, however, the image rotates or flips *around the current reference pixel*. Since this is by default at the upper left, if you don't change the reference pixel, the image will appear to rotate about one corner of the image's bouncing rectangle. In most cases, you will prefer to have the image rotate in place, as it were, in which case you should set the reference pixel to the image's midpoint.

Why would you want to flip or rotate a `Sprite`? Consider the sprite source image in Figure 5–4; it does not show the fish facing left. Obviously, we do want the fish to be able to swim to the left as well as to the right. We can flip the image to have the fish swim to the left.

Similarly, in a game in which an object could move in four directions, we could rotate and/or flip a single set of animations to produce animations for any of the four directions. This results in a considerable memory savings, because we need to supply only one set instead of four sets of animations for a game object. Since memory limitations are often severe on mobile devices, this is important.

Caution should be taken with this technique, however; image transformations are quite costly in terms of processing power. In essence, you're trading off processing power for memory. If you are doing many transforms, and processing power proves to be a bottleneck for your game, you might be better off making the reverse trade-off—that is, supplying prerotated or preflipped animations, consuming more memory but using less processing power.

How do you use the `setTransform()` method? You pass it one of the special `Field` values defined for the `Sprite` class, listed in Table 5–2.

Animating the Fish

Here's how the `Fish` constructor will look:

```
private static final String IMAGE_FILENAME =
"/res/fishsprite.png";
private static final int FRAME_WIDTH=20;
private static final int FRAME_HEIGHT=18;

public Fish() throws java.io.IOException {
   super(Image.createImage(IMAGE_FILENAME),
         FRAME_WIDTH,
         FRAME_HEIGHT);
}
```

Again, we need to use `super()` to pass the image to the `Sprite` constructor. When we created our walls, we created blank images; here, we're loading the image from a file and also passing the frame width and height, indicating that the file contains multiple animation frames and that we intend to animate this sprite.

The call to `super()` must be the first call in the constructor. Before calling `super()`, the fish object instance doesn't exist yet, so the constructor can't do any operations on the object until later. This creates the question of where to load the sprite's source image.

Table 5–2 Sprite Transforms

Transform	Effect	Example
TRANS_NONE	The sprite is unchanged.	
TRANS_ROT90	Rotates the sprite clockwise by 90 degrees.	
TRANS_ROT180	Rotates the sprite clockwise by 180 degrees.	
TRANS_ROT270	Rotates the sprite clockwise by 270 degrees.	
TRANS_MIRROR	Mirrors the sprite about its vertical axis (flipped right to left).	
TRANS_MIRROR_ROT90	Mirrors the sprite, then rotates it clockwise 90 degrees.	
TRANS_MIRROR_ROT180	Mirrors the sprite, then rotates it clockwise 180 degrees. This is the same as flipping it vertically about its horizontal axis.	
TRANS_MIRROR_ROT27	Mirrors the sprite, then rotates it clockwise 270 degrees.	

We could move the image-loading code out of the fish constructor into the `GameCanvas`, and then during fish instantiation, the canvas would pass the image to the fish constructor. However, in the interest of keeping it object-oriented, we should load the fish image in the `Fish` class.

The technique used above is to load the image inside the call to `super()`. However, `Image.createImage()` can throw an exception (the file might be missing), so the `Fish` constructor is required to handle this. We just use a standard IO error above.

Now let's animate the fish. We start with the earlier image, but arrange the frames linearly (Figure 5–5).

Figure 5–5 Fish source image.

The following definitions now go in the `Fish` class:

```
private static final int IMAGE_COLUMNS = 5;
private static final int IMAGE_ROWS = 1;

private static final int ANIM_FACE = 0;
private static final int ANIM_TAIL = 1;
private static final int ANIM_RIGHT = 2;
private static final int ANIM_HIT = 3;
private static final int myanimations[][] = {
    {0},
    {1},
    {2,2,3,3,3},
    {4}
};
```

Note that the `ANIM` constants are used to determine the animation sequence; that is, `ANIM_FACE`, used as an index in `myanimations[][]`, points to the animation we'll use when the fish is facing the player, and so on.

The animation sequences are stored in the `myanimations[][]` array. The first index defines the animation sequence; the second defines the sequence of frames. You'll note that only the ANIM_RIGHT sequence is really animated; when the fish is facing toward us, away, or is hit, the sequence consists of a single frame. The sideways swim animation shows the fish swimming by setting the frame sequence and then, on every loop, calling nextFrame() and paint().

This source image only has frames for the fish swimming toward the right, so we have to mirror the sprite when the fish is swimming left. As discussed earlier, we need to set the reference pixel to the center of the sprite if it will stay in place when it gets mirrored.

```
defineReferencePixel(getWidth()/2, getHeight()/2);

// If direction changed, set left/right sequence
// and transform
if (dxPrevious != dx) {
  dxPrevious = dx;
  if (dx < 0) {
    setTransform(TRANS_MIRROR);
    setFrameSequence(myanimations[ANIM_RIGHT]);
  } else if (dx > 0) {
    setTransform(TRANS_NONE);
    setFrameSequence(myanimations[ANIM_RIGHT]);
  }
} else {
  nextFrame();
}
```

This would need to be in the Fish class. This isn't much code to add, but it is all that's needed to animate the fish.

TiledLayer

Our next major class is TiledLayer. One very common technique in games is to construct a background image out of image tiles. That is, imagine the screen divided into squares or rectangles and a set of images of the same size as these squares or rectangles. One image might represent grass, another pavement, and so on. You could then build an array to represent the location of different tiles and paint tiles as specified by the array on the screen.

The Game API provides a class called TiledLayer to do precisely this. As with Sprite, it's a subclass of Layer and inherits Layer's methods.

Like Sprites, TiledLayers are created from a source image. However, a very important difference is that the tiles in the source image are ordered starting with the number 1 (see Figure 5–6). Although we refer to the tiles by their index, this is not like the Sprite frame numbers, which are numbered starting at zero.

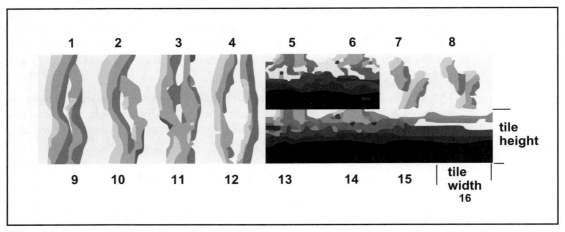

Figure 5–6 Background source image.

```
public TiledLayer(int columns, int rows,
             Image image, int tileWidth, int tileHeight)
public void setStaticTileSet(Image image,
                          int tileWidth, int tileHeight)
public void fillCells(int col, int row,
                    int numCols, int numRows,
                    int tileIndex)
public void setCell(int col, int row,
                  int tileIndex)
```

The TiledLayer() method is the constructor for a TiledLayer. The first two parameters determine how many cell columns and cell rows there are in the TiledLayer—or to think of it another way, the size of the array used to map the tiles to the display. Note that you might want the TiledLayer to be bigger, physically, than the screen of the device if the game world is larger than a single screen.

The Image parameter is the image from which tiles are constructed for use in the TiledLayer. The tileWidth and tileHeight parameters specify the width and height of each tile. Just as the image supplied for an animated sprite is automatically divided into frames of a specified width and height, the image you supply for a TiledLayer is automatically divided into tiles of the specified width and height.

Initially, however, each "cell" in the TiledLayer is empty—that is, all cells start with an index of zero, and if the TiledLayer is painted in this state, nothing gets painted. To think of it another way, constructing a TiledLayer creates a tile set from the image you supply and separately creates an array you can use to specify which tile goes in each cell of the `TiledLayer`—but you haven't specified where tiles go yet.

To specify where tiles go, you use the `setCell()` and `fillCell()` methods. `setCell()` is used to specify what tile goes in a particular cell. For example, `setCell(0,0,9)` is used to say "when we paint the upper-left cell of the tiled layer [that is, the cell at 0,0], use tile # 9" (in our example image, that would be the tile at the lower left in Figure 5–6). A tile value of zero (the initial value for all cells) means that the cell is transparent.

The `fillCell()` method, by contrast, is used to fill a rectangular block of cells with the same tile. The first two parameters specify the upper-left cell that gets filled; the second two indicate how many cells across and how many down we fill; and the final parameter specifies what tile we want in all of those cells.

The `setStaticTileSet()` method replaces a `TiledLayer`'s current set of tiles with a new set of tiles, constructed from the image passed as a parameter. If the new tile set contains at least as many tiles as the old one, the cell values (and animations) are retained; if there are fewer tiles in the new tile set, all cell values are set back to zero again.

Figure 5–7 is an example of a painted `TiledLayer` we could construct from the image in Figure 5–6.

Figure 5–7 TiledLayer background built from the source image.

In this case, we have specified in Table 5–3 the tile values for each of the cells in the `TiledLayer`.

Table 5–3 TiledLayer Cell Values

Row/Column	0	1	2	3	4	5	6	7
0	0	0	0	0	0	0	0	0
1	0	0	8	0	0	0	0	0
2	7	0	10	8	0	0	7	0
3	2	0	1	4	0	0	1	0
4	10	0	9	12	0	0	9	0
5	1	0	4	3	0	0	3	0
6	9	0	12	11	0	0	9	0
7	14	15	14	13	16	15	13	15

Note that *tiles* are indexed from 1, while *cells* are indexed from 0, like an array.

Animated Tiles

`TiledLayer` cells can be animated, like sprites. However, doing this is rather more complicated than for sprites.

```
public int createAnimatedTile(int staticTileIndex)
public void setAnimatedTile(int animatedTileIndex,
                            int staticTileIndex)
public int getAnimatedTile(int animatedTileIndex)
```

To tell `TiledLayer` that a particular cell is animated, we use `setCell()` to place a *negative* number at that cell—for example, `setCell(0,0,-1)`. A negative number means that the cell is animated; the *value* of the negative number indicates what animation sequence is used for this cell. That is, all cells with a value of –1 are animated in the same way at the same time; all cells with a value of –2 follow the second animation sequence, and so on.

However, before you start assigning negative numbers to cells, you must use `createAnimatedTile()`. The first time you do so, you create the animation indexed by –1; the second time, the animation indexed by –2; and so on. In fact, the createAnimatedTile() method returns the newly created index, which is helpful. (If you try to assign a negative index to a TiledLayer cell before you create the associated animated tile, you'll throw an exception.)

When you call createAnimatedTile(), you may pass a (nonnegative) tile index (if you don't, it defaults to zero). Initially, when the TiledLayer paints, every time it encounters a cell with the new negative index value, it will paint the tile with the (positive) index value in that cell. For example, if you pass 3 when you call the method for the first time, then all cells with the value of –1 will be painted with the third tile in your tile set.

So far, this doesn't sound very animated, right? You've just established that 1 is the same as 3, as far as TiledLayer is concerned. This is where setAnimatedTile() comes in. You use it to *change* the association between the (negative) animated tile index and the (positive) tile index it points to. Thus, setAnimatedTile(-1, 4) means that the next time TiledLayer repaints, all cells containing the value –1 will be painted with the 4 tile. So, if you had a two-stage animation represented by tiles 3 and 4, you would simply swap back and forth between the two tiles (calling setAnimatedTile() to do so) each time you go through the main game loop, before painting.

Note that there is no equivalent to Sprite's nextFrame() method; you have to define the animation sequence explicitly in your code, and there is no automatic "wrap-around" to restart from frame zero when you come to the end of the sequence. Thus, implementing animated tiles is a bit more work.

The getAnimatedTile() method is used to determine what (positive) tile index is currently associated with a (negative) animated tile index. You pass the animated tile index, and the positive tile index currently associated with that animated tile is returned.

Animating the Background

Let's provide an animated TiledLayer background of seaweed for some additional visual interest:

```
public class Background extends TiledLayer {
  private static final String IMAGE_FILENAME =
                                    "/res/background.png";
    private static final int IMAGE_COLUMNS = 8;
    private static final int IMAGE_ROWS = 2;

    private static final int MAP_COLUMNS = 8;
    private static final int MAP_ROWS = 8;
    private static final int mymap[][] = {
        { 0,   0,   8,   0,   0,   0,   0,   0 },
        { 0,   0,   2,   0,   0,   0,   0,   0 },
        { 7,   0,  10,   8,   0,   0,   7,   0 },
        { 3,   0,   1,   4,   0,   0,   4,   0 },
```

```
      {11,   0,   9,  12,   0,   0,  12,   0 },
      { 1,   0,   4,   3,   0,   0,   2,   0 },
      { 9,   0,  12,  11,   0,   0,  10,   0 },
      { 5,  15,  14,  13,  16,  15,   6,  16 }
  };

  public Background() {
      super(MAP_COLUMNS, MAP_ROWS, getImage(),
              myimage.getWidth() / IMAGE_COLUMNS,
              myimage.getHeight() / IMAGE_ROWS);

      for (int row=MAP_ROWS-1; row>=0; —row) {
        for(int column=MAP_COLUMNS-1; column>=0; —column) {
          setCell(column, row, mymap[row][column]);
        }
      }
    }
  }
```

This is an example `Background` class. A map array holds the static tile numbers, and the constructor assigns those values to the `Background` cells. The `MyGameCanvas` class simply instantiates a `Background` object.

To animate the seaweed in the background, we give negative index numbers to the seaweed tiles and make animation sequences for them. Note that the base of the seaweed and the ocean floor is not animated, so those tiles have positive index numbers.

```
private static final int mymap[][] = {
      {  0,   0,  -8,   0,   0,   0,   0,   0 },
      {  0,   0,  -2,   0,   0,   0,   0,   0 },
      { -7,   0, -10,  -8,   0,   0,  -7,   0 },
      { -3,   0,  -1,  -4,   0,   0,  -4,   0 },
      {-11,   0,  -9, -12,   0,   0, -12,   0 },
      { -1,   0,  -4,  -3,   0,   0,  -2,   0 },
      { -9,   0, -12, -11,   0,   0, -10,   0 },
      {  5,  15,  14,  13,  16,  15,   6,  16 }
};
private static final int myanims[][] = {
      { 1,   2,   3,   4},
      { 2,   3,   4,   1},
      { 3,   4,   1,   2},
      { 4,   1,   2,   3},
      { 5,  13},
      { 6,  14},
      { 7,   8},
      { 8,   7},
```

```
        { 9,  10,  11, 12},
        {10,  11,  12,  9},
        {11,  12,   9, 10},
        {12,   9,  10, 11}
};
private static final int ANIM_COUNT = 12;
private static int myframeindex[] = new int[ANIM_COUNT];
private static int myanim_trigger = 7;
```

The animations do not have the same length, so we need to keep track of which frame in the animation is shown. The myframeindex array holds this value for each animation.

The Background constructor is the same as before, but now we need to instantiate the animated tiles before assigning the cell index. If the animated tile doesn't exist before calling setCell() for that negative tile index, then it will throw an exception.

We'll also add an animate() method that advances the background animations by one frame. This can be called from the game loop during the simulation phase.

```
public Background() {
  super(...);

  for (int idx=0; idx<ANIM_COUNT; ++idx) {
    createAnimatedTile(myanims[idx][0]);
  }
  for (int row=MAP_ROWS-1; row>=0; −row) {
    for (int column=MAP_COLUMNS-1; column>=0; −column) {
      setCell(column, row, mymap[row][column]);
    }
  }
}


public void animate() {
  if (−myanim_trigger == 0) {
    myanim_trigger = 7;

    for (int idx=ANIM_COUNT-1; idx>=0; −idx) {
      setAnimatedTile(-idx-1,
                          myanims[idx][myframeindex[idx]]);
      if (++myframeindex[idx] >= myanims[idx].length) {
        myframeindex[idx] = 0;
      }
    }
  }
}
```

The seaweed should have a somewhat languid movement. We could do this by adding extra frames in the animation sequences, but it takes less space if we just don't animate as often. The myanim_trigger variable causes the animation to advance only once every 7 frames.

The loop runs through every animated tile and advances it by one frame. If the animation is finished, it resets to the first frame index.

As you can see, having to call setAnimatedTile() to animate a tile is a little more complicated than calling nextFrame() to animate a sprite, but it only requires a few more lines of code.

LayerManager

After creating all the sprites and backgrounds for your game, you have to place and paint them on the display. Each Layer class has its own paint method—but it's generally more convenient to use the LayerManager class to paint everything in the game at once with a single line of code.

The LayerManager maintains all the layers in an ordered list. The order corresponds to the drawing order on the screen, which is referred to as the *z-order*. You can think of it as drawing the layers from front to back, where the frontmost layer is at list index 0, and the other layers are behind it. Objects in layer 0 are painted over those in layer 1, which are painted over those in layer 2, and so on.

```
public void append(Layer l)
public void insert(Layer l, int index)
public int getSize()
public void remove(Layer l)
public void setViewWindow(int x, int y,
                             int width, int height)
public void paint(Graphics g, int x, int y)
public Layer getLayerAt(int index)
```

The append() method adds layers to the LayerManager (we used this with our walls). It literally appends them—that is, the first layer appended is the frontmost layer, the second added is the second layer, and so on. The insert() method inserts a layer at the index you specify—that is, if you want to insert a layer between layers 3 and 4, you insert it at 4 (4 gets pushed back to 5, and so on). The insert() method can also be used to change the z-order of a layer already in the LayerManager. A layer can only be in the LayerManager list once, so if you insert or append a layer that is already in the list, it is moved to the new position.

The getSize() method returns the number of layers in the LayerManager. If there's only one, it returns 1—but remember that the layers are indexed from zero. The remove() method removes a specified layer from the

LayerManager. Note that the parameter is the layer itself, not an index—to remove a sprite named mySprite at index 2, you'd use remove(mySprite).

The setViewWindow() method is most useful when the game world is larger than the device's display. Imagine that you have a game world that is twice as high and twice as wide as the display. The LayerManager tracks all layers (sprites, backgrounds, etc.) in the game world, but you only want to paint the part of the world immediately around the player's character You would use this method to set the view window to the area around the character. The first two parameters are the x and y coordinates, in the LayerManager's pixel coordinate system, where we will start to paint (that is, this pixel will be painted in the upper left-hand corner of the display). The width and height parameters specify how many pixels across and down we paint.

Notice that the paint() method also allows us to specify an x and y coordinate. In this case, the coordinate is in the display's coordinate system, that is, measuring from the upper left-hand corner of the display. Many games use "clipping," meaning that they only repaint the part of the display that changes from frame to frame, to save on processor cycles. You can implement a clipping system by using setViewWindow() and the x and y coordinates of paint() together; set the view window to paint only the area you want, then use paint()'s coordinates to ensure that this area is painted to the right part of the screen.

Finally, the getLayerAt() method returns the layer at the index specified by the parameter.

Drawing the Game World to the Display

So far, our game consists of six layers: four wall obstacles, the fish sprite, and a TiledLayer background. If we attach them all to a LayerManager, we can use the LayerManager's paint() method to show them all on the screen. We must be careful with the order in which they're attached to LayerManager, however; the fish sprite has to be at index 0, the TiledLayer at the very back, and the walls in between. One way to do that is to create the wall obstacles first and append() them; then the background, and append() it; and instead of appending the fish, make sure it's at the front with:

```
layerManager.insert(myFish,0);
```

Now that the positions of all the game objects are resolved, we need to place them on the screen. The draw() method simply paints to the GameCanvas; flushGraphics() is then used to place it on the display. (Note again that GameCanvas is inherently double-buffered—painting always occurs off screen, then flushGraphics() puts it on-screen.)

```
private void draw() {
  int width = getWidth();
```

```
    int height = getHeight();

    // clear screen to blue
    g.setColor(0x0000FF);
    g.fillRect(0, 0, width, height);

    layerManager.paint(g,0,0);
}
```

This is delightfully simple. We fill our Graphics object, g (defined in MyGameCanvas), with a blue background to represent water (and to ensure that TiledLayer cells with index of zero appear empty and blue). We then use LayerManager's paint() method, which paints everything we've appended to LayerManager to the Graphics object we pass it—g. When draw() returns, MyGameCanvas's run() method uses flushGraphics() to show it on the screen.

A caution is in order, however. What we're doing here is painting the whole canvas every frame. Because not all that much happens in our Fish game (so far, at least), this is probably not a problem. However, if a lot of processing happens between each frame, the frame rate may slow unacceptably because painting takes a fair bit of time. Many games use clipping; that is, they only repaint to the parts of the display that have changed since the last update. This minimizes the amount of time spent painting.

Improving the Fish Game

Now, we have used the Fish game to provide a tour through the MIDP 2.0 Game APIs. There are a number of optimizations we can still do to make this game better.

Regulating the Animation Speed

Remember that our main game loop looked like this:

```
public void run() {
  while (playing == true) {
    readInput();
    simulateWorld();
    draw();
    flushGraphics();
    // this is instead of repaint(),
    // and puts g on the display
    delayUntilNextFrame();
  }
}
```

The one method here we haven't discussed is `delayUntilNextFrame()`. Humans visually blend images together into an animation when they are shown at a rate as slow as five frames per second. We want our game loop to run at least that fast. But on LCD screens, it's best not to update the screen faster than its pixel refresh rate, or else the screen looks washed out and hazy. Modern computer LCD screens have a refresh rate of less than 13 milliseconds, which is a rate of well over 70 frames per second, but most mobile phone screens do not refresh nearly as quickly. While phone screens are improving rapidly, it's a good idea to limit the animation speed to 15 frames per second or less.

Another aspect to consider is how smooth the animation runs. Game players rely on the consistent behavior of a game in order to play it. They assume that animation occurs at a consistent speed—that, for example, in a driving game, the game will not suddenly speed up, making their anticipated timing in steering around a curve wrong and slamming them into a wall. In other words, it is better to have a slow but consistent rate of animation than animation that speeds up and slows down as other demands on the processor's time wax and wane. Thus, you want and need to control the frame rate.

Another issue that can cause timing fluctuations is garbage collection. Obviously, the best way to avoid this is not to churn objects through the game loop. That isn't always possible because some MIDP APIs (the SMS API, for example) create objects outside the MIDlet's control. If a game does churn a lot of objects, it is sometimes good practice to call `System.gc()` on a regular basis—perhaps as part of the frame delay.

We can ensure consistent timing by inserting a delay in the game loop with the `delayUntilNextFrame()` method. This limits the maximum frame rate of the game, but ensures a *consistent* frame rate.

```
private static final int MILLISECS_PER_FRAME = 70;
private Thread thread;
private long startTime;

public void start() {
  thread = new Thread(this);
  thread.start();
  startTime = System.currentTimeMillis();
}

private void delayUntilNextFrame() {
  long elapsed = startTime;
  startTime = System.currentTimeMillis();
  elapsed = startTime - elapsed;
  if (elapsed < MILLISECS_PER_FRAME) {
    try {
      thread.sleep(MILLISECS_PER_FRAME - elapsed);
    } catch (Exception e) { }
```

```
    } else {
      // We consumed all our allotted time so don't sleep,
      // but before exiting, yield to allow other threads
      // a chance to process.
      thread.yield();
    }
}
```

Sleeping inside an animation thread is a good way to delay between frames of the animation, but we could use timers to regulate the loop instead. If you know the task will complete within the interval time, then a timer simplifies the code. If the task might run longer than one frame interval, then using a thread is more graceful because it explicitly handles the delays.

A Further Discussion of Frame Rate Issues

This note is not important to understanding the Game API, but important for developers of sophisticated mobile games.

In our method, we delay the loop in order to ensure a consistent frame rate. It is possible that you might have the reverse problem: that if your game-update code (e.g., simulateWorld()) takes a long time because you are simulating many objects or doing complicated physics calculations or the like, your animation would wind up being jittery because completing the main game loop would sometimes (or often) take *longer* than the desired frame rate. Thus, the animation would sometimes seem to hang momentarily—and again, we need to ensure a consistent, smooth animation.

There is a workaround for this problem. Remember that it's possible to drop to as few as 5 frames per second and still fool the human eye into thinking that it is seeing continuous motion. Thus, we could drop a frame every once in a while, reducing the effective frame rate below 15, so long as game objects continue to move the same distance each real-time second—that is, motion appears continuous to the player and does not speed up or slow down.

How would this work? At the end of simulateWorld(), you check the time. If at that moment, it appears that painting to the display would exceed 1/15 second (or whatever frame rate we're trying to maintain), you skip over the draw() method and begin the next iteration of the loop. So long as you don't drop more than half the frames in the course of a second, the results should not be bothersome to the player; you may want to insert code to force display refreshes if too many frames are being dropped—although, if this is the case, your game may just be too much for this device, and you might be better off optimizing it and/or dropping some game features to allow it to run more efficiently.

Multiple Game Loops

Since the game loop is performing simulation and display in the same loop, simulation and animation happen at the same rate. However, it is possible to make two loops that run simultaneously to simulate the world at a different rate than the animation.

High Frequency Sampling

There are valid reasons for simulating at a different rate, frame rate issues being only one. For example, suppose a game has very high-speed balls bouncing around. In this situation, it becomes difficult to determine collisions between the balls because they are moving so fast. In Figure 5–8, two balls are traveling toward each other. In the first frame, they are on a collision course, but in the next frame, they have already passed each other.

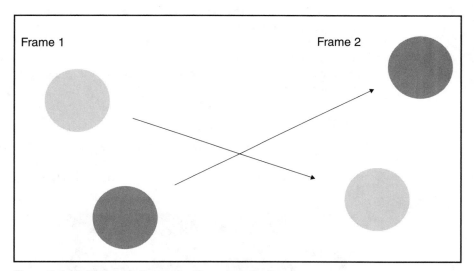

Figure 5–8 High-speed balls passing through each other.

This means that these balls won't collide, because we only check for collisions at Frame 1 and Frame 2. The only way the balls will collide is if the simulation processing occurs by chance, just as the balls are overlapping.

One solution is to run the simulation in a loop at a higher rate so it has a higher chance of catching the balls intersecting. To save some computation time, the display will run in a different loop that runs at its normal rate. It is still expensive to run collision detection on all of the objects at a high frequency, so this is not an ideal solution.

Discrete Event Simulation

In this contrived example, all we care about is when the balls collide. The rest of the time, we just need to move the balls into the proper position. Another method, called discrete-event simulation, requires us to predictively calculate when an event of interest will occur. Then the simulation can sleep and schedule itself to wake up when that event is predicted to happen. Predictive calculations are also expensive, but they can be more intelligent and more efficient than the brute-force approach of sampling the system at a higher rate. For example, it is fairly easy to calculate at what time and location a ball is going to hit a wall. When the simulation thread wakes itself to handle the collision and update that ball, it does not have to scan all of the game objects in the world and update them. Instead, it can defer the processing of other objects until they are handled. Thus, these predictive calculations can be run at an adaptive rate according to how often they are needed.

One nice aspect of games is that we can change the design of the game to fit our technical limitations. If it requires too much processing time to run high-frequency simulation or discrete-event simulation, the game can be redesigned to rely on a slower simulation. Whether it is necessary to run the simulation at a different rate than the display depends on the balance of game design and technical design.

Starfish

Let's add another game object for the fish to interact with. The following class is for the starfish (see Figure 5–9). The stars will fall down from the top of the screen, and the player must try to collect them before they reach the bottom.

Figure 5–9 Starfish source image.

```
import javax.microedition.lcdui.*;
import javax.microedition.lcdui.game.*;
import java.util.*;

public class Star extends Sprite {
    private static final String IMAGE_FILENAME =
                            "/res/starsprite.png";
    private static final int IMAGE_COLUMNS = 3;
```

```
  private static final int IMAGE_ROWS = 1;

  private int fallY;

  private static Image image;
  static {
    try {
      image = Image.createImage(IMAGE_FILENAME);
    } catch (Exception e) {
      // ...
    }
  }

  public Star(Random rand, int screenwidth, int y) {
    super(getImage,
          image.getWidth() / IMAGE_COLUMNS,
          image.getHeight() / IMAGE_ROWS);
  }

    if (Math.abs(rand.nextInt()) % 3 == 0) {
      fallY = 2;
    } else {
      fallY = 1;
    }
    int x = Math.abs(rand.nextInt()) %
               (screenwidth - getWidth());
    setPosition(x, y);
  }

  public void fall() {
    move(0, fallY);
    nextFrame();
  }
}
```

The constructor places the starfish at a random position across the top of the screen and sets the speed at which it falls. This isn't much code to add, because we're taking advantage of the Sprite base class.

As with the fish earlier, we must set the position of the sprites before determining collisions. We should modify the Fish class a bit. For one thing, we previously moved the fish in simulateWorld(), but it would be better and more object-oriented to have simulateWorld() call a method to perform the move. Also, we were sloppy about not checking positions that would place the fish outside the bounds of the Graphics object. Finally, we need to include our code for flipping the fish animation when it switches its left-right heading.

We'll make a `Fish` method, `beginMove()`, to move the fish at the beginning of the simulation phase. In this routine, we force the fish to stay on the screen, and we also set up the fish animation as was shown earlier in the animation code snippet. Because `beginMove()` handles the fish movement due to user input, it doesn't need its `moveCompleted()` method anymore.

```
public void beginMove() {
    int x = getX() + dx;
    int y = getY() + dy;

    //Check boundaries
    if (x < minX) {
      x = maxX; //wrap around to right
    } else if (x > maxX) {
      x = minX; //wrap around to left
    }
    if (y < minY) {
      y = minY;
    } else if (y > maxY) {
      y = maxY;
    }

    setPosition(x, y);

    // If direction changed, set left/right sequence
    // and transform
    if (dxPrevious != m_dx) {
      dxPrevious = m_dx;
      if (dx < 0) {
        setTransform(TRANS_MIRROR);
        setFrameSequence(myanimations[ANIM_RIGHT]);
      } else if (dx > 0) {
        setTransform(TRANS_NONE);
        setFrameSequence(myanimations[ANIM_RIGHT]);
      }
    } else {
      nextFrame();
    }

    dx = 0;
    dy = 0;
}
```

In the `MyGameCanvas` class, the `simulateWorld()` method randomly creates stars and checks whether they collide with the fish. We append the stars to our `LayerManager`, keeping track of the starting and ending star layers so we can iterate through them to move the stars.

```
public static final Random RANDOM = new Random();

private static final int SCORE_STAR = 10;
public static int score;

public static int num_star_layers = 0;

private static final int MAX_STARS = 6;

private void simulateWorld() {
  myFish.beginMove();

  //randomly add stars
  Star star;
  if ((RANDOM.nextInt() % 20 == 0) &&
      (num_star_layers < MAX_STARS)) {
    star = new Star(RANDOM, width, 0);
    layerManager.insert(star, 0);
    num_star_layers++;
  }
  // we insert rather than append to layerManager
  // because the TiledLayer background must remain
  // the final layer. It's okay to insert at 0, as
  // we check for collisions with myfish and remove
  // the star before painting if so, thus neither
  // will paint over the other

  //check for collision with falling stars
  for (int idx=num_star_layers-1; idx>=0; —idx) {
    star = layerManager.getLayerAt(idx);
    star.fall();
    if (myFish.collidesWith(star, false)) {
      layerManager.remove(idx);
      score += SCORE_STAR;
      num_star_layers—;
    }
    if (star.getY() > height) {
      layerManager.remove(first_star_layer+idx);
      score -= SCORE_STAR;
      num_star_layers—;
    }
  }
}
```

Because we added the Stars to layerManager, when our draw() method paints it, the stars get painted too, and we need do nothing further.

Adding Manta Rays

Before wrapping up, we also add another game creature that will compete with our fish to catch the falling starfish. The manta ray (Figure 5–10) will appear randomly at the sides of the screen and will glide across, catching any starfish in its path. It's bigger than our fish, so if they collide, the manta ray will push our fish aside.

Figure 5–10 Manta ray sprite.

```java
public class MyGameCanvas extends GameCanvas
                                  implements Runnable {

  public static final Random RANDOM = new Random();
  private static final int MILLISECS_PER_FRAME = 70;
  private Thread thread;
  private long startTime;

  public boolean isStopped;
  public boolean isPaused;

  public int width, height;
  private Graphics g;

  private static final int MANTA_BUMP = 2;
  private static final int MANTA_MARGIN = 20;
  private static final int MAX_STARS = 6;
  private Fish myFish;
  private Manta myManta;
  private Background myBackground;
  private LayerManager layerManager;

  public MyGameCanvas() {
    //Suppress events for game action keys
    super(true);

    setFullScreenMode(true);

    width = getWidth();
    height = getHeight();
    g = getGraphics();

    try {
      myFish = new Fish (width, height);
```

```
        myManta = new Manta(width);
        myBackground = new Background();
        layerManager = new LayerManager();
    } catch (Exception e) {
        System.err.println("ERROR creating game object.");
    }
    layerManager.append(myFish);
    layerManager.append(myManta);
    layerManager.append(myBackground);
    }
}
```

The `MyGameCanvas` constructor creates the manta ray, the background, and the `LayerManager`. It appends all starting layers. The `start()` method is called by the MIDlet, and we launch the game loop from there.

```
public boolean start() {
    if (layerManager == null) {
        return false;
    }
    setCommandListener (MyGameMidlet.mymidlet);

    //launch the game loop thread
    thread = new Thread(this);
    thread.start();
    startTime = System.currentTimeMillis();
    return true;
}
public void stop() {
    isStopped = true;
    thread = null;
}
```

The `run()` and `readInput()` methods have not changed much at all, so they are not shown here again, but you can download the full source code from the book's Web site.

Next, we need to give life to the manta ray and check for collisions. The manta ray will randomly choose when to appear and which side to appear from. However, if our fish is too close to one side, the manta ray will start on the other side. Here's the full `simulateWorld()` to give you a sense of how everything works together:

```
private void simulateWorld() {
    myBackground.animate();
    myFish.move();
```

```
//add starfish
Star star;
if ((RANDOM.nextInt() % 20 == 0) &&
    (num_star_layers < MAX_STARS)) {
  star = new Star(RANDOM, mywidth, 0);
  layerManager.insert(star,0);
  num_star_layers++;
}
//add manta ray
if (!myManta.isVisible() && RANDOM.nextInt()%50 == 0) {
  myManta.setVisible(true);
  int dir, x, y;
  if (RANDOM.nextInt() > 0 &&
      myFish.getX() > width/8) {
    dir = Manta.RIGHT;
    x = -myManta.getWidth()/2;
  } else {
    dir = Manta.LEFT;
    x = width - myManta.getWidth()/2;
  }
  y = MANTA_MARGIN +
     (Math.abs(RANDOM.nextInt()) %
     (height - myManta.getHeight() - 2*MANTA_MARGIN));
  myManta.init(x, y, dir);
}

//check for collision with manta ray
if (myManta.isVisible()) {
  myManta.swim();
  if (myFish.collidesWith(myManta, false)) {
    int x = myFish.getX();
    int y = myFish.getY();
    //bump fish if it's near front of manta
    if (myManta.direction == Manta.LEFT) {
      if (x < myManta.getX() + myFish.getWidth()) {
        x = myManta.getX() - myFish.getWidth();
      }
    } else {
      int mantaXR = myManta.getX() + myManta.getWidth();
      if (x > mantaXR - myFish.getWidth()) {
        x = mantaXR;
      }
    }
    if (myFish.getRefPixelY() < myManta.getRefPixelY()) {
      y -= myFish.getHeight();
    } else {
      y -= myManta.getHeight();
```

```
      }
      myFish.setPosition(x, y);
   }
}

//check for collision with falling stars
for (int idx=num_star_layers-1; idx>=0; --idx) {
   star = layerManager.getLayerAt(idx);
   star.fall();
   if (myFish.collidesWith(star, false) ||
       myManta.collidesWith(star, false) ||
       star.getY() > height) {

     layerManager.remove(idx);
     num_star_layers--;
   }
}
}
```

The Manta class is just like the Fish and Star sprite classes. As you can see, it's easy to add more creatures to the game with only a little extra code.

```
public class Manta extends Sprite {
   public static final int LEFT = 1;
   public static final int RIGHT = 2;

   private static final String IMAGE_FILENAME =
                                    "/res/mantasprite.png";
   private static final int IMAGE_COLUMNS = 4;
   private static final int IMAGE_ROWS = 1;
   private static final int myanim[] = {0,0,1,1,2,2,3,3};

   private static final int MANTA_MOVE = 2;

   public int direction;
   private int moveX;
   private int minX, maxX;

   private static Image image;
   private static final Image getImage() {
      try {
       image = Image.createImage(IMAGE_FILENAME);
      }
      catch (Exception e) {
       System.err.println("Error loading manta image");
       return null;
```

```java
        }
        return image;
    }

    public Manta(int screenwidth) {
        super(getImage(),
            image.getWidth() / IMAGE_COLUMNS,
            image.getHeight() / IMAGE_ROWS);

        minX = 0 - getWidth();
        maxX = screenwidth;

        setVisible(false);
        defineReferencePixel(getWidth()/2, getHeight()/2);
        setFrameSequence(myanim);
    }

    public void init(int x, int y, int passed_direction) {
        setPosition(x, y);
        direction = passed_direction;

        if (direction == RIGHT) {
         setTransform(TRANS_NONE);
         moveX = MANTA_MOVE;
        }
        else {
         setTransform(TRANS_MIRROR);
         moveX = -MANTA_MOVE;
        }

        setVisible(true);
    }

    public void swim() {
        nextFrame();
        move(moveX, 0);
        int x = getX();
        if (x < minX || x > maxX) {
         setVisible(false);
        }
    }
}
```

Additional MIDP 2.0 Enhancements

While these features are covered in Chapter 4 "MIDP User Interface," it is worthwhile mentioning how they apply specifically to games.

Transparency and Pixel Arrays

In MIDP 2.0, the Image class is required to support simple PNG transparency, which was optional in MIDP 1.0. All loaded images are rectangles; without transparency, "blank" areas of a rectangle (e.g., the area about our fish) will paint over other sprites, making it difficult to achieve a clean graphical look in a game. Nokia devices have always supported transparency, so this is not a big change, but it is nice to have it standardized on this issue. Note that this is not the same as alpha blending; while Nokia phones support alpha blending, it is much more processor-intensive than transparency, and should be avoided unless really needed.

One addition to the Image class that is potentially very useful is the createRGBImage() method. This creates an Image instance from an array of color values. This means we can now write arbitrary pixels into an array to compose a scene or graphic, then convert it to an image that can be written to the screen. The 32-bit color values must be in the form 0xAARRGGBB, where AA represents the alpha channel byte, and the rest of the integer is a standard 24-bit RGB value.

Backlight

One feature that all game developers contend with is the backlight. It often seems to turn itself off at the exact moment that you are intently watching the screen but not pressing any buttons.

The Display class flashBacklight() method causes the light to strobe on and off, which you might want to do at some point, but it doesn't help you keep it on.

When coding for Nokia Series 40 devices, you can use the setLights() method in com.nokia.mid.ui.DeviceControl. This is part of the Nokia UI API, meaning it will not work on non-Nokia devices.

Summary

The core game framework was presented here and should lay the foundation for more elaborate game development. Most games have a progression of advancement through levels or other challenges. While this chapter presented only a very basic game, it should be clear that more game characters and enemies can be added by extending the Sprite class. All the game objects can be displayed in a scene with the `LayerManager`. Each step in the game loop has a specific place for your game objects' functionality. More gameplay can be added with character skills, attribute points and levels, power-ups, bosses, and other typical game mechanisms.

Already, games are a popular pastime on mobile phones. The MIDP 2.0 Game API is a boon to mobile gaming and will contribute to better games. The next generation of phones promises to have significantly more powerful processors, more memory, and better displays and media capabilities. It is an exciting time to be developing mobile games.

chapter

6

Handling Application Data

Understand serialization and persistent storage for application data.

Data and code are the two most important defining aspects of modern computer programs. Smart clients distinguish themselves from thin clients (i.e., Web browsers) by storing and processing data on the device itself. Local persistent data storage allows the mobile device to access application data even when the wireless network is temporarily unavailable. However, persistent storage also poses two big challenges to developers: we first need to convert object-oriented memory data to a linear format that is suitable for storage and transportation; then we have to manage storage resources efficiently, since they are very limited on mobile devices. The MIDP Record Management System is an easy-to-use storage system available on all Java phones. The RMS has core features of both the traditional file system and database storage systems. It provides a good compromise among functionality, performance, and footprint on resource-constrained small devices. The following topics are covered in this chapter.

- **Introduction to data persistence:** covers the basics of data persistence. We also introduce the sample application used in this chapter.

- **Java objects serialization:** discusses how to serialize or deserialize in-memory Java objects to or from linear byte arrays. Byte arrays are the basis for most mobile data storage and network solutions.

- **RecordStore:** covers the usage of the `RecordStore` class, which is the basis of the RMS.

- **Browsing and searching the RecordStore:** covers how to retrieve and browse data in a record store using the `RecordEnumeration`, `RecordFilter`, and `RecordComparator` interfaces.

In this chapter, we cover object serialization and MIDP RMS programming in detail. A complete sample application is used to illustrate key points and real-world API usage. The sample application enhances the photo viewer application in Chapter 3, "Getting Started," to support user comments, search, and rating.

Introduction to Data Persistence

At its core, the key functionality of any computer program is to manipulate data and present the data to users. The invention of dedicated data storage marks a cornerstone in modern computer science. There are three types of data storage: volatile memory, local persistent storage. and remote storage.

The Volatile RAM

Random Access Memory (RAM) provides fast random access to application data, such as objects created by the application. However, the RAM is volatile. The data is lost when the device is powered off or the application exits. For Java developers, the RAM is managed by the virtual machine and is largely transparent. When we instantiate a new object, the required memory space is automatically allocated from the RAM heap space. The Java garbage collector automatically frees memory space occupied by destroyed or out-of-scope objects without explicit intervention from the programmer.

TIP
We can call `System.gc()` from within Java applications to manually run the garbage collector when necessary. However, since the garbage collector can take a long time to run, it is best to call the above method when the system is idle or in a separate thread.

Local Persistent Memory

Unlike the RAM, persistent storage such as the flash memory card and hard drive can retain information between application restarts. However, persistent storage must be managed explicitly by the developer. On a Java mobile phone, several local persistent storage facilities are available.

For starters, we can include read-only attribute values in the JAD and JAR manifest files. We can read those attribute values using the following method in the MIDlet class. This is a great way to store default configuration data.

```
// "key" is the attribute key in the JAD or manifest file
public String getAppProperty(String key)
```

We can also bundle multiple read-only files and directories in the JAR archive file. Those bundled files can be accessed as Java standard input streams via the following method in the Class class (see Chapter 3 for more details).

```
// "name" is the absolute path to the bundled file
public InputStream getResourceAsStream(String name)
```

However, for most applications, the read-only storage is not sufficient. We need to store data generated by the application during its execution. A traditional PC application would save the persistent data into the file system on a local hard disk. If the persistent data is highly structured and must be frequently searched, the application might utilize a local SQL database. On mobile phones, local file systems and SQL databases are luxury items. They are only available on the highest end of smart phones. The MIDP specification requires all Java phones to support a new type of local read-write persistent storage system called the Record Management System (RMS). The RMS combines the key features of both the file system and searchable database in a very compact package.

- A record store contains a collection of records. Each record is a byte array of data and is identified by a unique ID. Records can be accessed and updated at any time using their IDs.

- We can add listener objects to monitor changes in the record store. When the content of the record store is changed, a registered callback is automatically invoked.

- We can enumerate the records, search the record store, and order the search results using APIs provided by the MIDP RMS package. Searching and ordering are two of the most popular features in SQL databases.

- In addition, we can limit access to a record store to a specific set of MIDlets. Access control is a crucial security feature borrowed from modern file systems and databases.

We cover the RMS API in detail in later sections.

Remote Storage

For networked MIDlets, it is possible to access data storage on remote servers (e.g., a database server) via network connections. In complex applications, we probably need a combination of local and remote storages. The local storage can act as a cache of the remote data to enable smooth offline operations. Careful data model design is needed to use the device and network resources most efficiently. MIDlet networking and remote server access are discussed in detail in Chapter 7, "Data Connectivity," and beyond.

TIP

Byte array is the basis for mobile storage solutions. The storage unit for an RMS store and the basic transport supported by a network connection are both byte arrays. However, Java objects in the RAM are not represented as byte arrays. So, the first step for any practical storage solution is to design a scheme to convert Java objects to and from byte arrays (i.e., object serialization and deserialization). We cover this topic in detail in this chapter. The object serialization techniques are extensively used in network applications in future chapters.

Photo Viewer with Comments

The example application in this chapter is a photo viewer MIDlet that supports user ratings and comments. It adds features to the basic photo viewer MIDlet we discussed in Chapter 3. For each photo, the user can give a rating and a comment (Figure 6–1). Both the rating and the comment are persisted to a local record store and hence are available the next time we run the MIDlet.

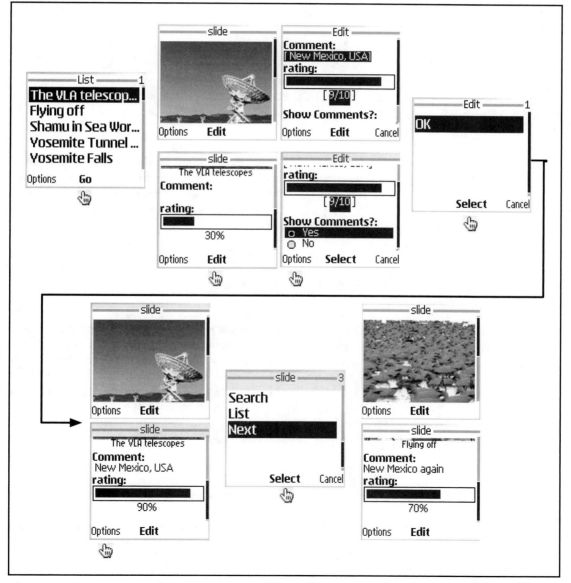

Figure 6–1 Rate and comment on the photo.

The user can also search the comments for keywords. All matched photos are returned in the order of their ratings. The user can then browse the returned list to view individual photos (Figure 6–2).

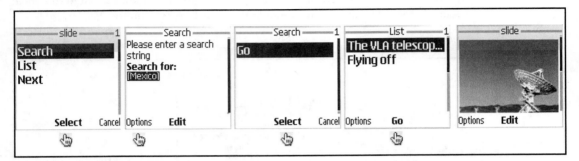

Figure 6–2 Search photo comments.

Now, let's discuss how the example application is designed and implemented. We first cover how to serialize Java objects (e.g., photo attributes) in the RAM to byte arrays that are suitable for RMS storage and then discuss how to manage the RMS itself. In the RMS management API, we frequently use the object serialization techniques.

Java Objects Serialization

When data is stored in RMS records and files or transmitted via network data connections, it is simply a stream of bytes. However, inside the application, data is always stored in structured Java objects. Our first challenge is to serialize Java objects into a byte array for storage and then deserialize the array into in-memory objects when we need the data. In MIDP, the standard Java object serialization facility in J2SE is not supported. We must serialize objects by hand. However, that also gives us the opportunity to optimize the serialized format for the storage space and network bandwidth. The key utility classes in MIDP data serialization are from the `java.io` package.

Communication Classes

Most classes in the `java.io` package represent data streams.

- The `InputStream` and `OutputStream` classes are abstract representations of data streams. They define basic methods to read and write bytes from or to generic streams.

- The `ByteArrayInputStream` and `ByteArrayOutputStream` are concrete subclasses of `InputStream` and `OutputStream`. They support read and write from or to byte arrays using the stream API.

- The `DataInputStream` and `DataOutputStream` objects wrap around existing `InputStream` and `OutputStream` objects. They provide methods to read or write Java primitive type variables and the `String` type objects from or to data streams in a device-independent way.

A variable or object written by the `writeXXX()` method in a `DataOutputStream` object can be retrieved by the corresponding `readXXX()` method in a `DataInputStream` object. For example, when we use the `DataOutputStream` class's `writeUTF()` method to write out a `String` object, it first writes two bytes indicating the number of bytes to follow and then writes each character in the string in sequence using the UTF-8 encoding. The corresponding `readUTF()` method in the `DataInputStream` class first reads out the two bytes and constructs a `String` object with the appropriate length. It then reads the characters one by one to populate the `String` object. The key `readXXX()` and `writeXXX()` methods in the `DataInputStream` and `DataOutputStream` classes are as follows.

```
// readXXX() methods in DataInputStream
int read (byte [] buf)
int readFully (byte [] buf)
boolean readBoolean ()
byte readByte ()
short readShort ()
char readChar ()
int readInt ()
long readLong ()
String readUTF ()
```

```
// writeXXX() methods in DataOutputStream
void write (byte [] buf, int start, int length)
void writeBoolean (boolean b)
void writeByte (byte b)
void writeShort (short s)
void writeChar (char c)
void writeInt (int i)
void writeLong (long l)
void writeUTF (String s)
```

The `InputStreamReader` and `OutputStreamWriter` classes are also included in the MIDP version of `java.io` package. The `Reader/Writer` classes convert byte-based streams into char-based streams, which allows us to read and write internationalized text strings over the streams.

Now, let's look at a concrete example on how different stream classes work together to serialize and deserialize Java data objects.

Serialize the Photo Attributes

In the photo viewer application, each photo has a number of attributes. We need an internal data model to represent the photo metadata. The `ImageAttribute` class has several public fields for the attributes. The `serialize()` method writes the attribute fields into a byte array using `OutputStream`, `ByteArrayOutputStream`, and `DataOutputStream` classes. The static `deserialize()` method does just the opposite of the `serialize()` method. It reads values from the `InputStream` object and assembles a new `ImageAttribute` object.

```
public class ImageAttribute {
  public String fileName;
  public String title;
  public String comment;
  public int rating;
  public boolean showComment;

  public ImageAttribute (String fileName) {
    this.fileName = fileName;
    title = " ";
    comment = " ";
    rating = 3;
    showComment = true;
  }

  protected ImageAttribute () { }

  public byte [] serialize () throws Exception {
    ByteArrayOutputStream bos =
              new ByteArrayOutputStream ();
    DataOutputStream dbos = new DataOutputStream (bos);
    dbos.writeUTF (fileName);
    dbos.writeUTF (title);
    dbos.writeUTF (comment);
    dbos.writeInt (rating);
    dbos.writeBoolean (showComment);
    return bos.toByteArray ();
  }

  public static ImageAttribute deserialize (
                  byte [] record) throws Exception {
    ImageAttribute attr = new ImageAttribute ();
```

```
        ByteArrayInputStream bis =
                new ByteArrayInputStream (record);
        DataInputStream dbis = new DataInputStream (bis);

        attr.fileName = dbis.readUTF ();
        attr.title = dbis.readUTF ();
        attr.comment = dbis.readUTF ();
        attr.rating = dbis.readInt ();
        attr.showComment = dbis.readBoolean ();
        return attr;
    }
}
```

RecordStore

Now, we can serialize an `ImageAttribute` object to a byte array and read it back into memory as needed. The next task is to actually store the byte array to the persistent memory space so that we can maintain the information across restarts. The MIDP RMS API provides access to the persistent storage on the device. The `RecordStore` class is the only concrete class in the `javax.microedition.rms` package.

NOTE

Different devices have different size limits for RMS storage. On a Series 40 device, the Java runtime can only manage 1MB of total RMS storage space. However, the physical memory space is often less than 1MB on older Series 40 devices. For more information on the total storage on each device, please refer to the Nokia device specifications on Forum Nokia. Since the RMS shares the same storage space with other native application data, such as contact lists, ringtones, and pictures, the actual available space for RMS could be reduced even more. Moreover, the size of each individual record store is limited to 32KB. That might prove to be a greater constraint for applications. Series 60 devices can support larger RMS record stores. The MIDlet suite can specify the amount of RMS storage space it requires to run in the `MIDlet-Data-Size` attribute in the JAD file. If the device were unable to provide the required storage space, the AMS would not install the MIDlet.

Manipulate the RecordStore

`RecordStore` instances are instantiated by static factory methods. The factory method contains the logic to ensure that there is only one `RecordStore` instance for each physical record store in the system. The simplest factory method takes in two arguments: the `name` argument specifies the unique identification name of the record store; the create parameter indicates whether to create a new record store if the named one does not exist. Inside the Nokia MIDP implementation, a record store is uniquely identified by its name and the combination of the MIDlet-Vendor and MIDlet-Name attributes in the JAD file. In another words, different record stores owned by different MIDlets can have the same name.

```
static RecordStore openRecordStore (String name,
                                          boolean create)
```

The record store created by the above method is only accessible to its creator MIDlet suite for security reasons. To create a shared record store, we can use an overloaded version of the openRecordStore() method. If the authMode argument is the AUTHMODE_ANY constant, the created record store is shared. The writable argument specifies whether a MIDlet outside of the current MIDlet suite can write to the shared record store. The authMode and writable arguments are ignored if the named record store already exists. Please note that record store sharing and the following version of the openRecordStore() method are only supported in MIDP 2.0 and above.

```
static RecordStore openRecordStore (String name,
      boolean create, int authMode, boolean writable)
```

To access a shared record store created by another MIDlet suite, we need to specify the vendorName and the suiteName of the owner MIDlet suite in the openRecordStore() method. Again, the following version of the method is only available in MIDP 2.0 and above.

```
static RecordStore openRecordStore (String name,
             String vendorName, String suiteName)
```

We can get a list of names of record stores owned by the current MIDlet suite using the listRecordStores() static method.

```
static String [] listRecordStores ()
```

After we finish using a record store, we have to manually release the resources it uses by calling the closeRecordStore() method. We can also remove a record store altogether from the physical media. When the user removes a MIDlet from the device, all of its record stores are removed, but the device alerts the user to possible data loss before proceeding. On the other hand, if the user updates a MIDlet, the old record store stays intact and becomes accessible to the new MIDlet.

```
void closeRecordStore ()
static void deleteRecordStore (String name)
```

The `RecordStore` provides methods to query the size, version, and last modified date of the record store. The version of a record store is changed every time its content is changed. This feature is very useful when we need to synchronize the record store with another data source (e.g., a backend server). The `RecordStore` also allows us to query the available storage space on this device.

```
int getSize ()
int getSizeAvailable ()
int getVersion ()
long getLastModified ()
String getName ()
```

WARNING The record store is not actually closed until `closeRecordStore()` is called as many times as `openRecordStore()` was called. It is up to the developers to balance the open and close method calls.

Manipulate Records

Each record inside a record store is a byte array. We can add a new record into the record store using the `addRecord()` method. The return value of this method is a unique integer identifier (i.e., record ID) of the record. The first record in the store has a record ID equal to 1. The value increases by one every time we add a record to the store but never decreases even if we delete records. The record ID could theoretically go up to the maximum value allowed by an integer type value. We can find out the next available record ID and the number of records in the store using the methods below.

```
int addRecord (byte [] record)
int getNextRecordID ()
int getNumRecords ()
```

Like primary keys in databases, the record IDs in the record store allow us to access, change, or delete specific records. Those record store modification methods do not return until their tasks are completed.

```
byte [] getRecord (int recordId)
int getRecord (int recordId, byte [] buffer, int offset);
int getRecordSize (int recordId)
void setRecord (int recordId, byte [] newRecord,
                int offset, int length);
void deleteRecord (int recordId)
```

WARNING   In multithread applications, we should not assume that we can always get the "next" record ID via the `getNextRecordID()` method. Another thread might have advanced it first. For applications that require deterministic behavior, we should synchronize all code blocks that call the `getNextRecordID()` method.

Store ImageAttribute Data

In the photo viewer application, we use a record store to save user comments and ratings data. The record store is opened in the `startApp()` method and closed in the `destroyApp()` method.

```java
public class PhotoViewer extends MIDlet {

  // ... ...
  private static RecordStore imageAttrStore;

  protected void startApp () {
    try {
      imageAttrStore =
          RecordStore.openRecordStore("Attr", true);
      if (imageAttrStore.getNumRecords() == 0) {
        initRMS ();
      }
    } catch (Exception e) {
      e.printStackTrace();
      notifyDestroyed ();
    }
    // ... ...
  }

  protected void destroyApp (boolean unconditional)
                   throws MIDletStateChangeException {
    if (!unconditional) {
      if (!exitConfirmed) {
        throw new MIDletStateChangeException ();
      }
    } else {
      try {
        imageAttrStore.closeRecordStore ();
      } catch (Exception e) {
        e.printStackTrace ();
      }
    }
  }
  // ... ...
```

```
}
```

The initRMS() method reads the initial attribute data from the manifest and adds them into the record store.

```
private void initRMS () throws Exception {
  int numOfImages = Integer.parseInt(
      controller.getAppProperty("NumberOfImages"));

  for (int i = 0; i < numOfImages; i++) {
    int tmpi = i + 1;
    String tmp =
        controller.getAppProperty("Image-" + tmpi);
    int cIdx = tmp.indexOf(",");
    ImageAttribute attr = new ImageAttribute (
            tmp.substring(0, cIdx).trim());
    attr.title = tmp.substring(cIdx+1).trim();

    byte [] record = attr.serialize ();
    imageAttrStore.addRecord(record, 0, record.length);
  }
}
```

RecordStore Listeners

The RecordStore class allows applications to monitor the records passively and receive callbacks when the record store changes. The RecordListener interface declares the following callback methods, which are invoked by the record store when a new record is added or an existing record is changed or deleted. The RecordStore caller object passes its own reference and the changed record's ID to the callback method.

```
void recordAdded (RecordStore rs, int recordId)
void recordChanged (RecordStore rs, int recordId)
void recordDeleted (RecordStore rs, int recordId)
```

We register or remove a RecordListener object to a RecordStore using the following methods in the RecordStore class.

```
void addRecordListener (RecordListener rl)
void removeRecordListener (RecordListener rl)
```

In Nokia J2ME implementations, there are several points about RecordListener that deserve special attention.

- The implementation commits all modifications to the record store before calling any of the listeners. However, the record modification methods (e.g., addRecord( ), setRecord( ), and deleteRecord( ), etc.) do not return until all the listeners are called and returned.

- If the application sets several listeners for a record store, they are called in the same order as they were added, and in a serialized fashion so that the next is called after the previous one has returned.

- Although the implementation blocks the thread that modifies the record store (as implied in the above point), it does not block other threads accessing the record store.

Browsing and Searching the RecordStore

To use the RecordStore class to access the records directly, we need to know the record IDs. The RecordEnumeration API supports a simple mechanism to filter, sort, and browse record IDs from any store using user-defined algorithms.

WARNING   Some developers use a for loop to iterate record IDs from ID 1 to getNumRecords( ) to browse the record store. But if a record is deleted, you would have an invalid record in the loop. For example, a record store containing three records does not necessarily contain records with ID 1, 2, and 3. The IDs can be 4, 200, and 4711 as well. So, the best way to browse a record store is to use the RecordEnumeration object.

RecordEnumeration

The RecordEnumeration supports bidirectional browsing of a set of record IDs from a record store. We can obtain a RecordEnumeration instance via method call RecordStore.enumerateRecords( ). The call takes three arguments. The filter argument is a RecordFilter object that determines the inclusion criteria of the enumeration; the comparator argument is a RecordComparator object that determines the order of the record IDs in the enumeration; the keepUpdated argument determines whether the enumeration should be kept updated to the record store. If the keepUpdated argument is false, we might have invalid record IDs when the record store changes.

```
RecordEnumeration enumerateRecords (RecordFilter filter,
        RecordComparator comparator, boolean keepUpdated)
```

If we pass null values to both the filter and comparator arguments, we get a complete list of record IDs in the store in an undetermined order. The following code snippet illustrates how to go through the record IDs in the enumeration. The destroy( ) method releases any resources that are held by the enumeration object.

```
RecordStore rs;
// Open the record store etc.

RecordEnumeration re =
    rs.enumerateRecords(null, null, false);

while ( re.hasNextElement() ) {
  int recordId = re.nextRecordId ();
  // Do something about recordId in rs
}

re.destroy ();
```

The above example demonstrates forward browsing using the hasNextElement() method. We can also browse backwards using hasPreviousElement() and previousRecordId() methods. The related methods are listed below.

```
boolean hasNextElement ()
boolean hasPreviousElement ()
int nextRecordId ()
int previousRecordId ()
byte [] nextRecord ()
byte [] previousRecord ()
int numRecords ()
```

NOTE

The keepUpdated argument in the RecordStore.enumerateRecords() method determines whether the enumeration is automatically updated as the record store changes. After a RecordEnumeration object is instantiated, we can use the keepUpdated() method to change its sync status programmatically. The keep-updated enumeration feature is a convenient way to monitor the RecordStore without manually developing a RecordListener. However, for large and frequently changing record stores, maintaining the enumeration up to date has a large performance penalty.

RecordFilter

The filter object passed into the enumerateRecords() method implements the RecordFilter interface. The interface declares only one method.

```
boolean matches (byte [] candidate)
```

That method is called against all records in the store. Only the ones that return true are filtered into the enumeration. For example, in the photo view application, we need a search filter that returns only those records that contain the search string in its title or comment attributes. To do that, we first deserialize the record into an `ImageAttribute` object and then match the search string against the `title` and `comment` fields. Listed below is the source code of the `SearchFilter` class.

```
public class SearchFilter implements RecordFilter {

    private String searchStr;

    public SearchFilter (String s) {
        searchStr = s;
    }

    public boolean matches (byte [] record) {
        ImageAttribute attr;

        try {
            attr = ImageAttribute.deserialize (record);
        } catch (Exception e) {
            e.printStackTrace ();
            return false;
        }

        if (attr.comment.indexOf (searchStr) != -1 ||
            attr.title.indexOf (searchStr) != -1) {
            return true;
        } else {
            return false;
        }
    }
}
```

RecordComparator

The `RecordComparator` interface declares a `compare()` method, which compares the relative order of any two records.

```
int compare (byte [] rec1, byte [] rec2)
```

The method returns the value FOLLOWS if the first argument follows the second argument in the sort order; it returns PRECEDES if the first argument precedes the second argument; it returns EQUIVALENT if the sort order of the two arguments are the same. The RecordStore.enumerateRecords() method takes in a RecordComparator object to sort the filtered results of the records in the enumeration object. In the photo view example, we use the photo ratings to sort the order. In the RatingComparator class, we first retrieve the rating from both records and then compare them.

```java
public class RatingComparator
            implements RecordComparator {

  public RatingComparator () { }

  public int compare (byte [] r1, byte [] r2) {
    ImageAttribute attr1, attr2;

    try {
      attr1 = ImageAttribute.deserialize (r1);
      attr2 = ImageAttribute.deserialize (r2);
    } catch (Exception e) {
      e.printStackTrace ();
      return EQUIVALENT;
    }

    if (attr1.rating > attr2.rating) {
      return PRECEDES;
    } else if (attr1.rating < attr2.rating) {
      return FOLLOWS;
    } else {
      return EQUIVALENT;
    }
  }
}
```

Search and Sort in Photo Viewer

Using the filter and comparator classes discussed above, we can easily implement the search feature in the photo viewer MIDlet (refer to the earlier Figure 6–2 to see it in action): After the user enters the search keywords and hits the Search soft key, the PhotoViewer.doSearch() method is invoked. It filters the records for the keywords and sorts the results according to the photo's rating. Then, the search results are enumerated to fill a new List screen. The code snippet is as follows.

```java
public class PhotoViewer extends MIDlet {

  // ... ...
  ratingComp = new RatingComparator ();

  public static void doSearch (String s) {

    SearchFilter searchFilter = new SearchFilter (s);
    try {
      imageAttrEnum =
          imageAttrStore.enumerateRecords(searchFilter,
                                    ratingComp, false);
    } catch (Exception e) {
      e.printStackTrace ();
    }

    showList ();
  }

  public static void showList () {
    String [] titles = null;
    try {
      int n = imageAttrEnum.numRecords();
      titles = new String [n];
      for (int i = 0; i < n; i++) {
        current = ImageAttribute.deserialize (
                          imageAttrEnum.nextRecord());
        titles[i] = current.title;
      }
    } catch (Exception e) {
      e.printStackTrace();
    }

    listslides = new ListSlides (titles);
    display.setCurrent (listslides);
  }

  // ... ...
}
```

Summary

In this section, we introduced the MIDP Record Management System (RMS). We discussed how to serialize Java objects in MIDP applications. The RMS supports a simple but very useful set of features commonly found in file systems and SQL databases. It is an excellent persistent storage solution for limited smart phone devices. But for more complex data persistence tasks, we should probably rely on more powerful backend servers. In the next chapter, we introduce how MIDlets communicate with servers via the MIDP networking API.

chapter

7

Data Connectivity

Use MIDP connectivity API to integrate mobile applications with Internet servers.

Connectivity has been a key feature of mobile devices since the early days of analog mobile phones. Today, mobile devices often need to be connected to the Internet or its peer devices in order to deliver valuable information to users. Network connectivity also helps mobile devices to move beyond their hardware limitations by enabling them delegate computational and data-intensive tasks to powerful Internet servers and databases. MIDP devices can access the wireless Internet via the Generic Connection Framework (GCF) API, which supports multiple network protocols. The following topics are covered in this chapter:

- **Introduction to the Generic Connection Framework:** covers the structure and API of the GCF. In particular, we discuss usage of the HTTP API.

- **Networked photo viewer:** illustrates how to design and implement communication protocols between mobile smart clients and Internet servers using the familiar photo viewer example. This time, the photo viewer MIDlet displays photos fetched from the server. We also show how to use worker threads to handle blocking operations such as network data retrieval.

- **Nonblocking UI design:** covers how to design and implement the transit screen when the device is waiting for the slow network data transfer to complete. Informative transit UI is crucial to improving the usability of networked mobile applications.

- **Stateful network operations:** shows how to add support for HTTP cookies to transparently maintain states (sessions) in network applications. Shared states enable better integration between the client and server. Sessions also allow a server to remember and serve many clients and hence make the best use of the network resources.

- **The HttpClient utility:** introduces an extendible framework to handle HTTP headers. Examples of how to use HTTP cookies, basic authentication, and digest authentication headers are given.

- **HTTPS:** covers the secure HTTP protocol. This is a new API introduced by MIDP 2.0.

In this chapter, we not only illustrate how to use the standard MIDP network APIs, but also show how to enhance them for real-world, end-to-end applications. More client-server design patterns are discussed in Chapter 11, "End-to-End Design Patterns."

Introduction to the Generic Connection Framework

The standard Java platform for PCs and servers (J2SE) has an extensive set of networking APIs with multiple abstraction layers designed for maximum flexibility. However, for mobile devices, the J2SE networking API is unnecessarily complex. In order to reduce the footprint and programming complexity, the MIDP defines its own lightweight connectivity API, known as the GCF, in the `javax.microedition.io` package. The GCF supports most popular data protocols on wide area networks, including the IP network and wireless messaging network. It also supports local connectivity protocols such as Bluetooth (see Chapter 10, "The Bluetooth API") and the infrared port. The GCF has been so successful that it is now also available under J2SE as an optional package (JSR 197).

Connector

A very prominent design pattern in the GCF is the use of static factory methods. All network connections and data streams in the GCF are represented as Java interfaces. Device vendors can develop the most efficient implementation of those interfaces in their J2ME runtime. From the developer's perspective, we instantiate connection and stream objects using factory methods in the `Connector` class. The `Connector.open()` static method takes in a URL string and returns a `Connection` object. It can take optional arguments to determine the read/write mode of the connection and whether to throw an exception if the connection cannot be established after a certain amount of time.

```
static Connection open (String url)
static Connection open (String url, int mode)
static Connection open (String url, int mode,
                                    boolean timeout)
```

The format of the URL string is `{scheme}:[{target}][{params}]`, where the scheme is the type of the connection protocol, `target` is a network address, and `params` is a list of connection parameters in the `;key=value` form. The MIDP specification defines URL schemes listed Table 7–1.

NOTE

The connection URL schemes listed in Table 7-1 are defined in the MIDP 2.0 specification. MIDP optional packages define their own URL schemes to leverage the generic factory class in the GCF for other types data connections. For example, the Wireless Messaging API defines connection schemes to send and receive SMS and MMS messages (see chapter 8); the Mobile Multimedia API defines connection schemes to get data from the built-in digital camera or voice recorder (see chapter 9); the Bluetooth API defines connection schemes to access or serve peer devices in a Bluetooth network (see chapter 10). If a device supports these optional packages, its

Table 7-1 URL Schemes in the GCF

Supported URLs in the GCF	Description	Series 40 Support
`http://host:port`	Make an HTTP connection to a remote server.	Supported on all devices.
`https://host:port`	Make an HTTPS connection to a remote server.	Supported on Developer Platform 2.0 devices.
`socket://host:port`	Make a socket connection to a remote server.	Supported on Developer Platform 2.0 devices and some later Developer Platform 1.0 devices (e.g., Nokia 6800).
`ssl://host:port`	Make a secure socket connection to a remote server.	Supported on Developer Platform 2.0 devices.
`socket://:port`	Listen for incoming socket connections at a local port.	Supported on Developer Platform 2.0 devices and some later Developer Platform 1.0 devices (e.g., Nokia 6800).
`comm://IR#` or `nokiacomm://IR#` or `comm://COM#`	Connect to the device's IR or serial port.	Connection string `nokiacomm://IR0` is supported on Nokia 5140 (see more discussion later).
`datagram://host:port`	Send or receive UDP datagrams.	Supported on Developer Platform 2.0 devices and some later Developer Platform 1.0 devices (e.g., Nokia 6800).

GCF implementation must be able to instantiate the correct `Connection` objects for those optionally defined URLs.

The returned `Connection` interface is a very generic representation of the physical connection. In fact, it only declares one method, `close()`, to close the connection. In applications, we always need to cast the returned `Connection` object to a more specific subclass, which is determined by the scheme parameter in the URL. The `Connection` subclass contains methods that are unique to the protocol it represents. For example, we can obtain HTTP, HTTPS, and socket connection objects using the following code:

```
HttpConnection hc =
  (HttpConnection) Connector.open("http://host.com/");
HttpsConnection hsc =
  (HttpsConnection) Connector.open("https://host.com");
SocketConnection sc =
  (SocketConnection) Connector.open("socket://host.com:79");
```

The standard MIDP API supports the HTTP, HTTPS, socket, server socket, secure socket, UDP, and serial communication port protocols. A hierarchy of interfaces is used to represent those protocols (see Figure 7–1). However, not all these interfaces are implemented on Nokia devices, as we saw in Table 7–1. In the next several sections, we cover the interfaces for those protocols.

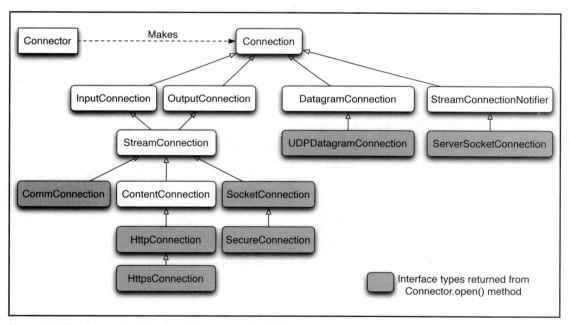

Figure 7–1 The Connection interface hierarchy in the GCF.

WARNING

The factory method `Connector.open()` takes in a URL string and returns an object based on the scheme of the URL. A major drawback of this method is that there is no compile-time safeguard for developers. We have to research the documentation to find out the supported URL schemes and manually cast the returned `Connection` objects. If we make any mistake here, a runtime exception is thrown.

HttpConnection

HTTP is the most popular data protocol of the Internet. Most wireless data networks support HTTP on top of their native wireless data carrier layers. The MIDP specification mandates support for HTTP version 1.1 on all Java handsets. We can use HTTP connections to pass both text and binary data between clients and servers. The `HttpConnection` interface represents a HTTP connection. It is instantiated by a `http://` scheme URL string in the `Connector.open()` method.

HTTP data is transferred over continuous streams. Hence, the `HttpConnection` inherits from the `StreamConnection` interface. The two most important methods in `HttpConnection` open data streams to and from the server.

```
DataInputStream getDataInputStream ()
DataOutputStream getDataOutputStream ()
```

The `HttpConnection` interface supports both HTTP `GET` or `POST` operations.

- In a `GET` operation, data is retrieved from the specified URL. We can customize the URL to pass request arguments. In this case, we only need to call the `openDataInputStream()` method to make the physical connection and read the data from the `DataInputStream`.

- In a `POST` operation, we have to open a `DataOutputStream` to the specified URL first and write the request parameters to the stream. A connection is made, and the request is submitted when we close the `DataOutputStream`. Then we open a `DataInputStream` to retrieve the server response.

We can set the operation mode using the `setRequestMethod()` method. The argument to this method is the `GET` and `POST` constant defined in the `HttpConnection` interface. The following code illustrates how to use HTTP `GET` to retrieve the HTML home page from `www.w3c.org` Web site. Notice how we use the buffer to read in the data. More examples are shown later in the chapter.

```
HttpConnection conn =
  (HttpConnection) Connector.open("http://www.w3c.org");
conn.setRequestMethod(HttpConnection.GET);

DataInputStream din = conn.openDataInputStream();
ByteArrayOutputStream bos = new ByteArrayOutputStream();

byte[] buf = new byte[256];
while (true) {
  int rd = din.read(buf, 0, 256);
  if (rd == -1) break;
```

```
        bos.write(buf, 0, rd);
    }
    bos.flush();
    buf = bos.toByteArray();

    // Convert the byte array to string using the
    // character encoding format of the remote site
    String content = new String (buf, "UTF-8");
```

NOTE

In the www.w3c.org example, we converted the downloaded byte array to a string using the UTF-8 character encoding format. Not all Web sites use UTF-8 to encode their text. For example, Japanese language sites often use the iso-2022-jp character encoding and Simplified Chinese language sites often use the gb2312 character encoding. To find out the encoding type a Web page uses, you can check the HTTP Content-type header of the page.

Since an HTTP connection can carry text or encoded content, the HttpConnection also inherits from the ContentConnection interface, which declares the following methods to query the properties of the content.

```
String getType ()
String getEncoding () // Content not character encoding
long getLength ()
```

Each HTTP response has an associated status code. Most of the HTTP status codes are defined as constants in the HttpConnection interface. For example, code 200 (HTTP_OK) indicates a successful response; code 404 (HTTP_NOT_FOUND) indicates that the URL does not point to a valid resource on the server; code 501 (HTTP_NOT_IMPLEMENTED) indicates that the server cannot fulfill the request. We can use the getResponseCode() method to retrieve the HTTP response status code.

TIP

If the HTTP response code is 301, 302, 303, or 307, the content you are looking for has been moved to a new URL location. In this case, the client MIDlet could retrieve the new URL from the returned Location header.

A key feature of the HTTP protocol is its ability to associate metadata with each connection. The metadata is stored as key and value pairs in the HTTP header. We can query the header values in the response using the header's numeric index or key name. We can also set key/value property pairs to the request.

```
String getHeaderField (int n)
String getHeaderField (String name)
void setRequestProperty (String key, String value)
```

HTTP headers can be extremely useful in a wide variety of applications. We discuss them in detail in later sections of this chapter.

HttpsConnection

An `HttpsConnection` object represents a secure HTTP (HTTPS) connection. HTTPS support is mandated in MIDP 2.0 but not supported in any Series 40 Developer Platform 1.0 devices. It supports both user authentication and data encryption. The URL scheme for `HttpsConnection` is `https://`. We cover HTTPS in more detail later in this chapter.

SocketConnection

A socket connection allows the client to communicate to specific socket ports. On the Internet, the HTTP infrastructure is built on top of the TCP/IP based socket connections. But on the wireless network, those protocols are implemented differently. Not all wireless data networks support sockets. Even if socket connections are available, they are not necessarily faster than HTTP.

The URL string of `SocketConnection` objects takes the format of `socket://host:port`. The most important methods in the `SocketConnection` interface are `openDataInputStream()` and `openDataOutputStream()`, which open data streams for the client to communicate with the remote socket.

We can also specify the operation mode of the `SocketConnection` using the `setSocketOption()` method.

```
void setSocketOption (byte option, int value)
int getSocketOption (byte option)
```

The `option` parameter is from the constants defined in the `SocketConnection` interface. For example, setting the `KEEPALIVE` option to a nonzero value would cause the socket to be connected all the time; the `RCVBUF` and `SNDBUF` options can be used to specify the sizes of receiving and sending buffers.

WARNING   Sending and receiving data in small pieces (i.e., several bytes a time) is not an efficient way to use network and device resources. The TCP connection works better when it is at full speed.

SecureConnection

A `SecureConnection` interface extends the `SocketConnection` interface to add support for the Secure Socket Layer (SSL). Its URL string takes the form `ssl://host:port`. We discuss it in more detail with HTTPS near the end of this chapter.

ServerSocketConnection

The `ServerSocketConnection` allows us to listen for incoming connections on a socket port and essentially turns the device into a server (not available in MIDP 1.0). Its URL string has the format of `socket://:port`, where the `port` parameter is the port number to listen to. An external device or application can now connect to the server device using the `socket://host:port` connection string, where `host` is the IP address of the server device. To make this work, the wireless network operator must expose the server device's IP address. This typically requires special service contracts with the operator. Once a `ServerSocketConnection` object is instantiated, we can call the `acceptAndOpen()` method in a loop to listen for incoming connections. The `getLocalAddress()` method retrieves the IP address of the device assigned by the network operator. When it detects an incoming connection, the method returns a `SocketConnection` object. The following snippet illustrates the basic use of the `ServerSocketConnection`.

```
// Create the server listening socket for port 79
ServerSocketConnection scn =
   (ServerSocketConnection) Connector.open("socket://:79");

while (true) {
  // Wait for a connection
  SocketConnection sc =
     (SocketConnection) scn.acceptAndOpen();

  sc.setSocketOption(RCVBUF, 128);
  sc.setSocketOption(SNDBUF, 128);

  // do something with sc
  sc.close ();
}
scn.close ();
```

WARNING   The `acceptAndOpen()` method in `ServerSocketConnection` blocks its execution thread until an incoming connection is detected. We should put the loop in a separate thread to avoid hanging the main application thread. We discuss worker threads extensively later in this chapter.

CommConnection

The CommConnection interface supports access to the device's serial port or logical serial port (e.g., the IrDA port). The URL scheme takes the form comm:port_id;params. The port_id is COM# for RS232 serial ports and IR# for IrDA ports. For example, the URL string comm:IR0;baudrate=19200 opens a connection to the first infrared port with a 19,200 bit per second data rate. As of June 2004, no Series 40 device supports the COM# ports, but this may change soon.

Like every other connection interface we have covered so far, the CommConnection interface inherits from the StreamConnection interface. It supports the openDataInputStream() and openDataOutputStream() methods to open data streams from and to the serial port.

WARNING

Nokia 5140, a Series 40 Developer Platform 2.0 device, supports the nokiacomm://IR0 connection string instead of comm://IR0. This does not conform to the MIDP specification and is listed as a Java known issue for Nokia Series 40 devices.

TIP

The MIDP specification allows us to retrieve a list of logical serial ports supported on a particular device by calling the System.getProperty ("microedition.commports") method. The method returns a list of logical serial port IDs separated by commas.

UDPDatagramConnection

Unlike stream-based connection protocols, the datagram protocol directly passes data packets between endpoints without trying to assemble them to match their originating order or recover lost data. The datagram arrival order or even the delivery itself is not guaranteed. It is, however, often faster and more suitable for real-time applications. In UDP, there is no concept of request and response. All data goes one way from sender to receiver.

The UDPDatagramConnection interface inherits from the DatagramConnection interface. The URL string is datagram://host:port. It cannot open data streams but has methods to support composing, sending, and receiving datagrams.

```
Datagram newDatagram(int i)
Datagram newDatagram(int i, String s)
Datagram newDatagram(byte[] bytes, int i)
Datagram newDatagram(byte[] bytes, int i, String s)
void send(Datagram datagram)
void receive(Datagram datagram)
```

TIP

Although Nokia devices support the UDP protocol, the underlying network may not necessarily support it. So, there is no guarantee that the Datagram classes would work in real-world applications.

Now, we have covered all the connection protocols supported by a standard MIDP implementation. The HTTP protocol is by far the most important one. In the rest of this chapter, we drill down to study patterns, techniques, and tools for effective mobile networking applications.

Networked Photo Viewer

In our previous photo viewer examples, the MIDlets display photos that are bundled inside the JAR file. That not only increases the JAR file size but also requires us to deploy new JARs every time the photos are updated. A much better approach is to separate the application from the data: We could distribute a small MIDlet viewer application and have it fetch photos from a Web site at runtime. We can update the photos from the server side and have them instantly available to all clients. In this section, we demonstrate a networked photo viewer application that does so. The application has two parts: a Java servlet that serves the photos and a MIDlet that fetches and displays the photos on demand. The communication between the servlet and MIDlet is via the HTTP protocol. It works as follows:

- The MIDlet client sends an integer code to the servlet via HTTP POST.

- The servlet executes the required operation specified by the integer code and returns the resultant data in the HTTP response.

- The client reads the response from an input stream, parses it, and displays relevant data to the user.

We can immediately identify two design choices in the above scenario.

1. We use the HTTP protocol to pass binary data. On the Internet, TCP/IP sockets are generally considered more efficient for binary data. HTTP is primarily used for text data. However, as we mentioned before, HTTP is much more widely supported than sockets in the wireless world. Using HTTP, we can leverage the server response code and headers to pass application specific metadata (e.g., session states and authentication tokens, as we discuss later in this chapter). Finally, an HTTP servlet is easy to program.

2. The client and server are tightly coupled. The server must know exactly what parameters to expect from the client; and the client must know how to parse the server response using the correct DataInputStream I/O methods in the correct order. If we change any communication code on the server

side, the corresponding component on the client must change too. Tight coupling makes application maintenance more difficult but improves network efficiency. Loosely coupled integration schemes, such as XML Web Services, are discussed later in this book.

Now, let's walk through the implementation of the application.

PhotoServlet

The PhotoServlet class is a servlet that runs on a Java Web server (e.g., Apache Tomcat). It holds reference arrays of photo image files, their titles, and their descriptions. When an HTTP POST request is received, the servlet's doPost() method is invoked by the server. The doPost() method analyzes the request (i.e., retrieves the opcode) and dispatches to the getPhoto() and getNext() methods. For the moment, let's focus on the getPhoto() method, which writes the data of the first photo in the array to the HTTP response data stream. The response data starts with the photo title, followed by the description, followed by the file size of the photo, and at last followed by the actual binary data of the photo.

```java
public class PhotoServlet extends HttpServlet {

    // The opcodes
    private static int GET_PHOTO = 1;
    private static int GET_NEXT = 2;

    private String [] titles =
        {"Birds", "Shamu", "VLA Telescope",
         "Tunnel View", "Yosemite Fall"};

    private String [] descriptions =
        {"Birds at Bosque, New Mexico",
         "Shamu at SeaWorld, Texas",
         "The VLA radio telescopes, New Mexico",
         "Tunnel View, Yosemite Valley, CA",
         "Yosemite Falls, CA"};

    private String [] filenames =
        {"/pBirds.png", "/pShamu.png", "/pVLA.png",
         "/pTunnelView.png", "/pYoseFall.png"};

    public void init() throws ServletException {
      // Do nothing
    }
```

```
public void doPost(HttpServletRequest request,
                   HttpServletResponse response)
    throws ServletException, IOException {

  response.setContentType("application/binary");
  try {
    InputStream in = request.getInputStream();
    OutputStream out = response.getOutputStream();
    DataInputStream din = new DataInputStream(in);
    DataOutputStream dout = new DataOutputStream(out);

    int opcode = din.readInt();
    if (opcode == GET_PHOTO) {
      getPhoto (din, dout);
    } else if (opcode == GET_NEXT) {
      getNext (din, dout, request);
    } else {
      throw new Exception("wrong op code");
    }
    din.close();
    dout.close();
    in.close();
    out.close();

  } catch (Exception e) {
    e.printStackTrace();
  }
}

private void getPhoto(DataInputStream din,
          DataOutputStream dout) throws Exception {

  byte [] buf = readFromFile (filenames[0]);

  dout.writeUTF(titles[0]);
  dout.writeUTF(descriptions[0]);
  dout.writeInt(buf.length);
  dout.write(buf, 0, buf.length);
}

// The getNext() method is discussed later

private byte [] readFromFile (String name)
                                    throws Exception {
```

```
        InputStream in =
            this.getClass().getResourceAsStream(name);
        ByteArrayOutputStream baos =
                            new ByteArrayOutputStream ();
        byte [] buf = new byte [256];
        int i = 0;
        while ( (i = in.read(buf)) != -1 ) {
          baos.write(buf, 0, i);
        }
        baos.flush();
        byte [] result = baos.toByteArray();
        baos.close();
        in.close();
        return result;
    }
}
```

The servlet is mapped to URL `http://host/PhotoServer/servlet/PhotoServlet` by its deployment descriptor file (`web.xml`). The photo viewer MIDlet posts HTTP requests to the above URL.

TIP   The image files are placed inside the server application's classpath (`WEB-INF/classes`). We can access them directly using the method `Class.getResourceAsStream()` rather than specifying nonportable absolute file paths in file I/O methods.

PhotoViewer

The `PhotoViewer` class is the MIDlet. It serves as the client-side UI controller and defines static methods to manage state transitions inside the client application. We will refactor the `PhotoViewer` class multiple times throughout this chapter. This first simple example is located in the `SimpleViewer` package in the accompanying source code. The MIDlet displays contents via the `View` class.

```
class View extends Form
        implements CommandListener {

  private Command fetch, exit;

  public View (String title) {
    super (title);
```

```
      fetch = new Command ("Fetch", Command.SCREEN, 1);
      exit = new Command ("Exit", Command.EXIT, 1);
      addCommand (fetch);
      addCommand (exit);
      setCommandListener (this);
   }

   public void commandAction (Command c, Displayable d) {
      if (c == exit) {
         PhotoViewer.exit ();
      } else if (c == fetch) {
         PhotoViewer.getPhoto ();
      }
   }
}
```

When the user presses the `Fetch` soft key, the `PhotoView.getPhoto()` static method is invoked to retrieve the photo over the network and display it to a new `View` screen.

FetchWorker

Since the `PhotoViewer.getPhoto()` method is called inside a `commandAction()` method, the MIDP specification requires it to return immediately to avoid blocking the user interface thread (see discussion in Chapter 4, "MIDP User Interface"). However, the network operation to retrieve the photo might take a while to complete. The correct way to do it is to put network-related operations in a separate thread (see Figure 7–2).

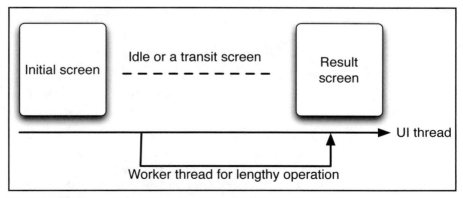

Figure 7–2 Using worker thread to avoid blocking the user interface.

The code snippet below shows the `PhotoViewer` class. The server URL is obtained from the `PhotoServerURL` property in the JAD file.

```
public class PhotoViewer extends MIDlet {

  public static String url;

  protected void startApp () {

    url = getAppProperty ("PhotoServerURL");

    Form view = new View ("Photo Viewer");
    view.append ("Select Fetch to start");
    display.setCurrent (view);
  }

  // ... ...

  public static void getPhoto () {
    Thread t = new Thread (new FetchWorker(url));
    t.start ();
  }
}
```

The `FetchWorker` class implements the `Runnable` interface, which allows us to execute its `run()` method in a separate thread.

```
class FetchWorker extends Fetch implements Runnable {

  public FetchWorker (String url) {
    super (url);
  }

  public void run () {
    getPhoto ();
    PhotoViewer.showPhoto (
        title, description, img, isSuccessful);
  }
}
```

The network-related work is delegated to the `Fetch.getPhoto()` method. Please note that `Fetch.getPhoto()` is different from `PhotoViewer.getPhoto()`. The former does all the network heavy lifting and the latter is used to start the `FetchWorker` thread. The `Fetch` class is separated from the `FetchWorker` class to give the `FetchWorker` class more implementation flexibility. We see this point in the animated Wait-screen example later in this chapter. The `Fetch` class defines several methods, but let's focus on the `getPhoto()` method at this moment.

```
public class Fetch {

  private String url;
  private int GET_PHOTO = 1;
  private int GET_NEXT = 2;

  protected String title;
  protected String description;
  protected Image img;
  protected boolean isSuccessful;

  public Fetch (String url) {
    this.url = url;
    title = "error";
    description = "error";
    img = null;
    isSuccessful = false;
  }

  // This is a template method
  // Ignore it for now
  protected void updateWaitStatus () { }


  protected void getPhoto () {

    HttpConnection conn = null;
    DataInputStream din = null;
    DataOutputStream dout = null;

    try {
      conn = (HttpConnection) Connector.open(url);
      conn.setRequestMethod(HttpConnection.POST);

      dout = conn.openDataOutputStream ();
      dout.writeInt (GET_PHOTO);
      dout.flush ();
      dout.close ();
      updateWaitStatus ();
```

```
        din = conn.openDataInputStream();
        title = din.readUTF ();
        updateWaitStatus ();
        description = din.readUTF ();
        updateWaitStatus ();
        int size = din.readInt ();
        updateWaitStatus ();
        byte [] buf = new byte [size];
        din.readFully(buf);
        updateWaitStatus ();
        img = Image.createImage (buf, 0, buf.length);
        updateWaitStatus ();

        isSuccessful = true;

    } catch (Exception exp) {
        exp.printStackTrace ();
        isSuccessful = false;
    } finally {
        try {
            if (dout != null) dout.close ();
            if (din != null) din.close();
            if (conn != null) conn.close();
        } catch (Exception exp) {}
    }
}

// ... ...
}
```

When the `Fetch.getPhoto()` method returns, the data fields in the `Fetch` object are populated with the photo data retrieved from the servlet. The `FetchWorker.run()` method then invokes the `PhotoViewer.showPhoto()` method to display the photo and other data in a new `View` screen.

```
public class PhotoViewer extends MIDlet {

    public static Display display;

    // ... ...

    public static void showPhoto (String title,
                String description, Image img,
                boolean isSuccessful) {
```

```
Form view = new View (title);
if (isSuccessful) {
  view.append (
      new ImageItem (description, img,
          ImageItem.LAYOUT_CENTER, ""));
} else {
  view.append (new StringItem("Status",
          "The network is NOT available"));
}

display.setCurrent(view);
  }
}
```

Figure 7–3 shows the simple networked photo viewer application in action.

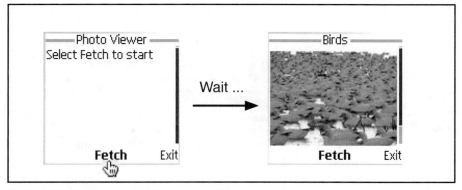

Figure 7–3 Simple networked photo viewer.

NOTE Network applications can be hard to test and debug. The Nokia Series 40 Developer Platform 2.0 SDK includes a network traffic monitor that records all data coming in and out of the device emulator. The data is presented in a structured log in the diagnostics window (see Figure 7–4). That allows developers to see exactly what's going on over the network at real time. It is an invaluable tool for network application developers.

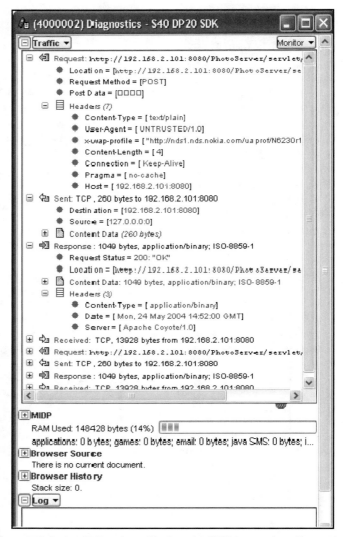

Figure 7–4 Series 40 Developer Platform 2.0 SDK's network traffic monitor.

Nonblocking UI Designs

The photo viewer example in our example has the basic functionalities, but the user experience is poor. When the background thread fetches content from the remote server, the foreground UI thread sits idle. It does not give the user any feedback on what the application is doing and provides no means for the user to cancel the lengthy operation. That is especially a problem for mobile applications, where the user's attention span is short and multitasking is a key feature. Numerous mobile usability studies have shown that the act of immediate acknowledgment, not the absolute speed, makes the biggest difference in user perception of application performance. In this section, we explore ways to display an interactive transit screen when the background thread is working.

In a GUI client application, the device is idle when it is waiting for user input. If we can somehow predict the user's next move, we could use the background worker thread to get a head start. For example, in a photo slide show application, we know that the user would probably go to the next photo after viewing the current one. So, we can preemptively start a background thread to fetch the next photo while the user is still viewing the current one. Of course, we still have to inform the user and obtain explicit permission for network access that might cost money.

Noninteractive Gauge

The simplest way to inform users about the busy state is to display the transit screen before we start the thread. At the end of the thread's run() method, the result screen is set to the current display to replace the transit screen via the PhotoViewer.showPhoto() static method. The source code of this example is located in the GaugeWaitViewer package.

```
public class PhotoViewer extends MIDlet {
  // ... ...

  public static void getPhoto () {
    Form screen = new GaugeWait ();
    display.setCurrent (screen);

    Thread t = new Thread (new FetchWorker(url));
    t.start ();
  }
}
```

A simple transit screen (GaugeWait) is a form with a continuously running, noninteractive gauge. It has an exit command, which allows the user to interrupt the download process by exiting the MIDlet.

```
class GaugeWait extends Form
       implements CommandListener {

  private Command exit;

  public GaugeWait() {
    super("Please wait ...");
```

```
    Gauge g = new Gauge ("In progress", false,
          Gauge.INDEFINITE, Gauge.CONTINUOUS_RUNNING);
    append (g);

    exit = new Command("Exit", Command.EXIT, 1);
    addCommand(exit);
    setCommandListener(this);
  }

  public void commandAction(Command c, Displayable d) {
    if (c == exit) {
      PhotoViewer.exit();
    }
  }
}
```

Figure 7–5 shows the transit gauge in action.

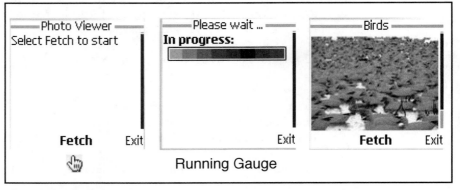

Figure 7—5 Photo viewer with a gauge transit screen.

Still-Image Transit Screen

A problem with the above moving gauge approach is that the animated noninteractive gauge is only available in MIDP 2.0 and above devices. For earlier MIDP 1.0 phones (i.e., Series 40 Developer Platform 1.0 and 60 Developer Platform 1.0 devices), we must settle for a simpler solution. We can display a transit screen with custom graphics. The source code for this solution is in the `ImageWaitViewer` package. Key code segments are shown in the following.

```java
public class PhotoViewer extends MIDlet {

  // ... ...

  public static void getPhoto () {
    Canvas screen = new ImageWait ();
    display.setCurrent (screen);

    Thread t = new Thread (new FetchWorker(url));
    t.start ();
  }
}

class ImageWait extends Canvas
              implements CommandListener {

  private Image img;
  private Command exit;

  public ImageWait () {

    try {
      img = Image.createImage("/" + "wait.png");
    } catch (Exception e) {
      e.printStackTrace ();
      img = null;
    }
    exit = new Command ("Exit", Command.EXIT, 1);
    addCommand (exit);
    setCommandListener (this);
  }

  public void commandAction (Command c, Displayable d) {
    if (c == exit) {
      PhotoViewer.exit ();
    }
  }

  public void paint (Graphics g) {

    int width = getWidth ();
    int height = getHeight ();

    g.setColor(0xffffff);
```

```
    g.fillRect(0,   0, width, height);
    g.setColor(0x000000);

    g.drawImage (img, width / 2, height / 2,
            Graphics.HCENTER | Graphics.VCENTER);
    return;
  }
}
```

Figure 7–6 shows the image transit screen in action.

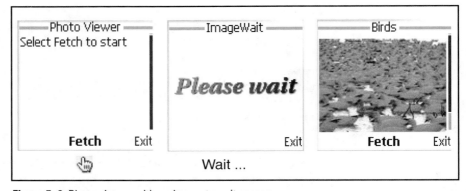

Figure 7–6 Photo viewer with an image transit screen.

A More Reliable Image Transit Screen

Unfortunately, the above two solutions do not always work as expected. The reason is that the `Display.setCurrent()` method only asynchronously requests the system to change the display screen (see Chapter 4). There is no guarantee that the change would take effect immediately even if we call it from a non-UI thread. On some devices, such as the Nokia 7210 and several other Series 40 Developer Platform 1.0 phones, the worker thread takes priority. The AMS waits until the end of the thread to display the transit screen and result screen in rapid succession. If this happens, the user does not see the transit screen at all. To work around this problem, we should make sure that the worker thread only starts after the transit screen is rendered. The solution is available in the `ImageWaitViewer2` package. We do not explicitly start the thread in the controller. Instead, we only request the system to show the wait screen, and the wait screen starts the thread when it is actually displayed.

```
public class PhotoViewer extends MIDlet {

    // ... ...
```

```
public static void getPhoto() {
  Canvas screen = new ImageWait2(url);
  display.setCurrent(screen);
}
}
```

The `ImageWait2` class starts the worker thread in its `paint()` method, which is called when the UI thread renders the canvas. This guarantees that the worker thread is always started after the wait screen is displayed.

```
class ImageWait2 extends Canvas
            implements CommandListener {

  private String url;
  private Image img;
  private Command exit;

  public ImageWait2 (String url) {
    this.url = url;
    try {
      img = Image.createImage("/" + "wait.png");
    } catch (Exception e) {
      e.printStackTrace ();
      img = null;
    }
    exit = new Command ("Exit", Command.EXIT, 1);
    addCommand (exit);
    setCommandListener (this);
  }

  public void commandAction (Command c, Displayable d) {
    if (c == exit) {
      PhotoViewer.exit ();
    }
  }

  public void paint (Graphics g) {

    int width = getWidth ();
    int height = getHeight ();

    g.setColor(0xffffff);
    g.fillRect(0,  0, width, height);
    g.setColor(0x000000);

    g.drawImage (img, width / 2, height / 2,
```

```
                        Graphics.HCENTER | Graphics.VCENTER);

        Thread t = new Thread (new FetchWorker(url));
        t.start ();

        return;
    }
}
```

Animated Transit Screen

A significant problem with the static transit screen is that the user cannot tell how the background process is progressing. For a long process, the phone might still look as if it is hanging. Our solution is to have the worker thread update the display of the transit screen. The solution is available in the AnimatedWaitViewer package. The controller code is almost identical to the previous example.

```
public class PhotoViewer extends MIDlet {

    // ... ...

    public static void getPhoto () {
        Canvas screen = new AnimatedWait (url);
        display.setCurrent (screen);
    }
}
```

The AnimatedWait class has a setCount() method that updates and repaints the progress bar. As before, we start the worker thread in the paint() method. However, as the paint() method is called multiple times for the AnimatedWait object (every time the progress bar is updated), we take the precaution to make sure that the worker thread is started only once when the screen is initially rendered.

```
class AnimatedWait extends Canvas
                implements CommandListener {

    private int maxCount = 10;
    private int count = 0;
    private Command exit;

    private Image img;
    private String url;
    private FetchWorker worker;

    public AnimatedWait (String url) {
```

```
    this.url = url;
    worker = null;

    try {
      img = Image.createImage("/" + "wait.png");
    } catch (Exception e) {
      e.printStackTrace ();
      img = null;
    }
    exit = new Command ("Exit", Command.EXIT, 1);
    addCommand (exit);
    setCommandListener (this);
}

public void setCount (int value) {
    count = value % maxCount;
    repaint ();
    serviceRepaints ();
}

public void commandAction (Command c, Displayable d) {
    if (c == exit) {
      PhotoViewer.exit ();
    }
}

public void paint (Graphics g) {

    int width = getWidth ();
    int height = getHeight ();

    g.setColor(0xffffff);
    g.fillRect(0,  0, width, height);
    g.setColor(0x000000);

    g.drawImage (img, width / 2, height / 2,
            Graphics.HCENTER | Graphics.VCENTER);

    int buffer = 10; // Pixels at both ends of the bar

    int endX = buffer +
          ((width - (2 * buffer)) * count / maxCount);
    g.setColor(0, 0, 255);
    int startY = height * 2 / 3;
    g.fillRect(buffer, startY,
                endX-buffer, 15);
```

```
        if (worker == null) {
          worker = new FetchWorker(url);
          // The worker updates the current screen
          worker.wait = this;
          Thread t = new Thread(worker);
          t.start();
        }
        return;
    }
}
```

The worker thread object (FetchWorker) holds a reference to the AnimatedWait screen (the wait data member). FetchWorker calls wait.setCount() to update the progress bar of the transit screen. We recall that the Fetch.getPhoto() method calls the updateWaitStatus() method at different stages of the progress. In this example, we implement the updateWaitStatus() template method in FetchWorker to update the progress bar at those stages. The separation between the Fetch and FetchWorker classes allows us to have multiple FetchWorker implementations while reusing the same Fetch class.

```
class FetchWorker extends Fetch implements Runnable {

  public AnimatedWait wait;
  private int count = 0;

  public FetchWorker (String url) {
    super (url);
  }

  protected void updateWaitStatus () {
    count++;
    wait.setCount(count);
  }

  public void run () {
    getPhoto ();

    PhotoViewer.showPhoto(title, description,
                          img, isSuccessful);
  }
}
```

Figure 7–7 shows the animated transit screen in action.

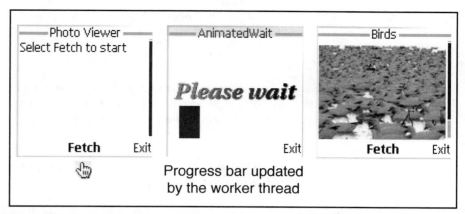

Figure 7–7 Photo viewer with an animated transit screen.

NOTE In the example in this chapter, the FetchWorker and AnimatedWait classes are tightly coupled. While this allows us to explain the interaction
between the classes clearly, it is not the best design. In the real world, we
do not want to write a separate (and very similar) AnimatedWait class for
each worker task. In Chapter 11, we introduce a better, "loosely coupled"
design to approach this problem and reduce code duplication.

Stateful Network Operations

All of our networked photo viewer examples so far utilize stateless HTTP
connections. Each HTTP request is independent. Hence, from the servlet's point
of view, each request is a new request, and it would always serve the first photo
in the array. To develop a realistic network photo viewer, we would like the
server to remember the connection history for each client and serve the next
photo in the array when a new request from the same client comes in. The
client source code of this example is available in the SessionViewer package.
The server groups the HTTP requests from the same client during the same visit
into a session. We can associate data objects indicating the application state
with each session. It usually works as follows.

- When the client makes its first request, the server creates a session object
  and an ID. The ID is returned to the client.

- The client stores the ID and puts it in all subsequent requests to the same
  server.

- The server then has a way to identify and link the request with session
  objects.

The key is to exchange and keep track of session IDs. The HTTP `cookie` headers can be used to pass the state information.

HTTP Cookies

Cookies are pieces of session identification strings embedded in HTTP headers. They take the format of `Name=Value` pairs. When the client makes its first connection, a session ID is created and returned to the client via the HTTP `set-cookie` header.

```
set-cookie: SESSIONID=value; expires=Date; path=Path
domain=Domain; secure
```

The first `SESSIONID=value` pair is the cookie itself. All the following attributes, such as the expiration date, domain, and path, are optional. When the client makes subsequent HTTP requests, it sends the cookies in the cookies header to identify itself. The client decides which cookies to send back based on the server domain, expiration date, and so forth.

```
cookie: Name1=Value1; Name2=Value2; ...
```

TIP

The server can send out multiple cookies in one HTTP response using multiple `set-cookie` headers. The client can send back multiple cookies in one request header by separating the `name=value` pairs using semicolons.

PhotoServlet

In the `PhotoServlet` class, the `getNext()` method is triggered by the `GET_NEXT` opcode in the HTTP request. It gets an `HttpSession` object associated with the current request from the servlet container. The `HttpSession` object can take in arbitrary objects as attributes. Those attributes are accessible via all `request` objects in the same session. In our example, we store the next photo index in the `HttpSession` object. The index increases by one for each successful response and starts over when it reaches the end of the array.

```
public class PhotoServlet extends HttpServlet {

    // ... ...

    private void getNext(DataInputStream din,
        DataOutputStream dout,
        HttpServletRequest request) throws Exception {

      int i; // The current index
```

```
HttpSession sess = request.getSession (true);
Integer index =
    (Integer) sess.getAttribute ("Index");

if (index == null) {
  i = 0;
} else {
  i = index.intValue();
  if (i >= titles.length) {
    i = 0;
  }
}
sess.setAttribute("Index", new Integer(i+1));

byte [] buf = readFromFile (filenames[i]);

dout.writeUTF(titles[i]);
dout.writeUTF(descriptions[i]);
dout.writeInt(buf.length);
dout.write(buf, 0, buf.length);
}
```

The Java servlet container manages requests and sessions using HTTP cookies. The process is completely transparent to server-side developers. However, on the MIDP client side, cookie management is a lot more explicit.

SessionConnector

The MIDP's standard `HttpConnection` implementation class does not support cookies by default. But it does provide the functionalities to read and write the `set-cookie` and `cookie` headers. We can easily extend the GCF to support cookies and HTTP session tracking on the client side. The first step is to extend the `Connector` factory class so that the `open()` method returns a cookie-aware `HttpConnection` implementation when we pass in the `http://` URL scheme.

TIP

In the `SessionConnector` class, we set the `Content-Language` header to be the locale of the device. On devices with multiple language support, the user can select the locale from a system menu. The server could detect the locale and then respond with the correct language content.

```
public class SessionConnector {

  private SessionConnector() {
  }
```

```
private static String cookie;

public static HttpConnection open (String url)
                                throws IOException {
  HttpConnection c =
      (HttpConnection) Connector.open(url);
  addCookie(c);
  c.setRequestProperty("User-Agent",
      "Series 40 Session Connector");
  c.setRequestProperty("Content-Language",
      System.getProperty("microedition.locale"));
  HttpSessionConnection sc =
      new HttpSessionConnection(c);
  return sc;
}

public static HttpConnection open (String url,
                String command) throws IOException {
  HttpConnection conn = open(url);
  conn.setRequestMethod(HttpConnection.POST);
  DataOutputStream os = null;
  command = command + '\n';
  try {
    os = conn.openDataOutputStream();
    os.write(command.getBytes());
  } finally {
    if (os != null) {
      os.close();
    }
  }
  return conn;
}

public static void close(HttpConnection conn,
                         InputStream is,
                         OutputStream os) {
  if (is != null) {
    try {
      is.close();
    } catch (IOException ignore) {
      // ignore
    }
  }

  if (os != null) {
    try {
      os.close();
```

```
        } catch (IOException ignore) {
          // ignore
        }
      }

    if (conn != null) {
      try {
        conn.close();
      } catch (IOException ignore) {
        // ignore
      }
    }
  }
}

  static void addCookie(HttpConnection c)
                          throws IOException {
    if (cookie != null) {
      c.setRequestProperty("cookie", cookie);
    }
  }

  static void getCookie(HttpConnection c)
                          throws IOException {
    int k = 0;
    while (c.getHeaderFieldKey(k) != null) {
      String key = c.getHeaderFieldKey(k);
      String value = c.getHeaderField(k);
      if (key.equals("set-cookie")) {
        int j = value.indexOf(";");
        String cValue = value.substring(0, j);
        cookie = cValue;
      }
      k++;
    }
  }
}
```

The addCookie() and getCookie() methods are static utility methods that are used in both the SessionConnector class as well as the HttpSessionConnection class. The HttpSessionConnection class is a cookie-aware implementation of the HttpConnection interface. It is a decorator of the device runtime's default HttpConnection implementation class, and it delegates most method calls to the latter. HttpSessionConnection retrieves and saves cookies from the HTTP response when the openInputStream() and openDataInputStream() methods are called. After the cookies are saved, they are automatically added to the HTTP headers when the SessionConnector opens a new connection in the future.

```
class HttpSessionConnection implements HttpConnection {
  private HttpConnection c;

  public HttpSessionConnection(HttpConnection c) {
    this.c = c;
  }

  public String getURL() {
    return c.getURL();
  }

  public String getProtocol() {
    return c.getProtocol();
  }

  // Other delegate methods

  public InputStream openInputStream()
                        throws IOException {
    checkResponseCode();
    SessionConnector.getCookie(c);
    return c.openInputStream();
  }

  public DataInputStream openDataInputStream()
                              throws IOException {
    checkResponseCode();
    SessionConnector.getCookie(c);
    return c.openDataInputStream();
  }
}
```

NOTE   The SessionConnector and HttpSessionConnection classes are originally implemented by Sun Microsystems as a part of the Sun Java Smart
Ticket sample application v1.0.

FetchWorker

The Fetch.getNext() method posts the GET_NEXT opcode to the servlet. It
shows how to use the SessionConnector class. As we can see, cookie
handling is now transparent from the application developer's point of view.

```
public class Fetch {

  private String url;
```

```
private int GET_PHOTO = 1;
private int GET_NEXT = 2;

protected String title;
protected String description;
protected Image img;
protected boolean isSuccessful;

protected void getNext () {

  HttpConnection conn = null;
  DataInputStream din = null;
  DataOutputStream dout = null;

  try {

    conn =
        (HttpConnection) SessionConnector.open(url);
    conn.setRequestMethod(HttpConnection.POST);

    dout = conn.openDataOutputStream ();
    dout.writeInt (GET_NEXT);
    dout.flush ();
    dout.close ();
    updateWaitStatus ();

    din = conn.openDataInputStream();
    title = din.readUTF ();
    updateWaitStatus ();
    description = din.readUTF ();
    updateWaitStatus ();
    int size = din.readInt ();
    updateWaitStatus ();
    byte [] buf = new byte [size];
    din.readFully(buf);
    updateWaitStatus ();
    img = Image.createImage (buf, 0, buf.length);
    updateWaitStatus ();

    isSuccessful = true;
  } catch (Exception exp) {
    exp.printStackTrace ();
    isSuccessful = false;
  } finally {
    try {
      if (dout != null) dout.close ();
      if (din != null) din.close();
```

```
            if (conn != null) conn.close();
        } catch (Exception exp) {}
    }
}

// ... ...
}
```

The `FetchWorker` class in the `SessionViewer` package inherits from `Fetch` and calls the `getNext()` method to interact with the server.

```
class FetchWorker extends Fetch implements Runnable {

    public AnimatedWait wait;
    private int count = 0;

    public FetchWorker (String url) {
        super (url);
    }

    protected void updateWaitStatus () {
        count++;
        wait.setCount(count);
    }

    public void run () {
        getNext ();
        PhotoViewer.showPhoto (
            title, description, img, isSuccessful);
    }
}
```

Figure 7–8 shows the session viewer in action.

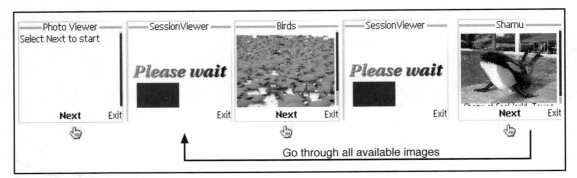

Figure 7–8 Session based photo viewer.

The HttpClient Utility

In the previous section, we saw the power of HTTP cookie headers. HTTP headers can be used to pass any application-specific metadata transparently. Its application goes beyond session tracking. For example, the HTTP authentication protocol utilizes headers to authenticate clients and provide access control to server resources. In this section, we introduce an HTTP framework to transparently handle any HTTP headers. For simplicity, the new transport class treats all requests and responses as byte arrays rather than streams. If your application requires direct stream I/O access (e.g., an object deserializer), you can easily wrap a `ByteArrayInputStream` or `ByteArrayOutputStream` around those arrays.

The Framework

The two key components in the framework are the `Handler` interface and `HttpClient` class. Each concrete implementation of the `Handler` interface processes a specific type of HTTP header. The `Handler` interface declares only two methods. The `prepareHeaders()` method sets headers for the HTTP request; the `processHeaders()` method processes headers from the HTTP response. The `processHeaders()` method returns a `boolean` value indicating whether the `HttpClient` object needs to repost its request after this round of header processing. For example, in order to complete HTTP digest authentication, the client first posts a request, the server sends back a random number (known as the salt), and the client must repost with the digest of the salt mixed with the correct password. The `Handler` interface source code is as follows.

```
public interface Handler {

  public void prepareHeaders (HttpConnection c)
                                throws Exception;

  public boolean processHeaders (HttpConnection c)
                                throws Exception;
}
```

In the `HttpClient` class, the key method is `query()`. It takes in the request byte array and returns the response byte array. Class `HttpClient` contains a chain of HTTP header handlers. The source code of the `HttpClient` class is listed below. Notice how we walk through the handlers chain twice to process both the request and response headers in the `query()` method. The `maxIteration` property is used to prevent infinite loops in case of failed challenge-response cycles.

The chain of responsibility pattern is to establish a chain within a system to process and redirect messages. In `HttpClient`, we can have multiple handlers in a `Vector`. The HTTP request and response are both processed through the chain.

```
public class HttpClient {

    private String url;
    private String requestMethod;
    private Vector handlers = new Vector ();
    // Max number of challenge/response cycles.
    private int maxIteration = 3;

    public HttpClient() {}

    public void setUrl (String url) {
        this.url = url;
    }

    public void setRequestMethod (String method) {
        this.requestMethod = method;
    }

    public void setMaxIteration (int n) {
        maxIteration = n;
    }

    public void addHandler (Handler h) throws Exception {
        handlers.addElement(h);
    }

    public void removeAllHandlers () throws Exception {
        handlers = new Vector ();
    }

    public byte [] query (byte [] req) throws Exception {
        boolean needConnect = true;
        HttpConnection c = null;
        InputStream is = null;
        OutputStream os = null;
        ByteArrayOutputStream bos = null;
        byte [] buf = null;

        try {
            int currentIteration = 0;
            while (needConnect) {
                currentIteration++;
```

```
        if (currentIteration > maxIteration)
          throw new Exception("Too many Iterations");

        needConnect = false;

        if (c != null) c.close();
        if (os != null) os.close();
        c = (HttpConnection) Connector.open (url);
        c.setRequestMethod( requestMethod );

        for (int i = 0; i < handlers.size(); i++) {
((Handler) handlers.elementAt(i)).prepareHeaders(c);
        }
        c.setRequestProperty("User-Agent",
                             "HttpClient");
        c.setRequestProperty("Content-Language",
          System.getProperty("microedition.locale"));

        if ( req != null ) {
          os = c.openOutputStream ();
          os.write(req);
        }

        for (int i = 0; i < handlers.size(); i++) {
          needConnect =
((Handler) handlers.elementAt(i)).processHeaders(c)
                     || needConnect;
        }
      }
      is = c.openInputStream ();
      bos = new ByteArrayOutputStream();
      buf = new byte[256];
      while (true) {
        int rd = is.read(buf, 0, 256);
        if (rd == -1) break;
        bos.write(buf, 0, rd);
      }
      buf = bos.toByteArray();
    } finally {
      if (c != null) c.close();
      if (is != null) is.close();
      if (os != null) os.close();
      if (bos != null) bos.close();
    }
    return buf;
  }
}
```

Use HttpClient and Handlers

To use `HttpClient`, we have to first implement the HTTP header handlers. In the companion source code bundle, the `HttpClient` package has the following `Handler` implementations (see Figure 7–9).

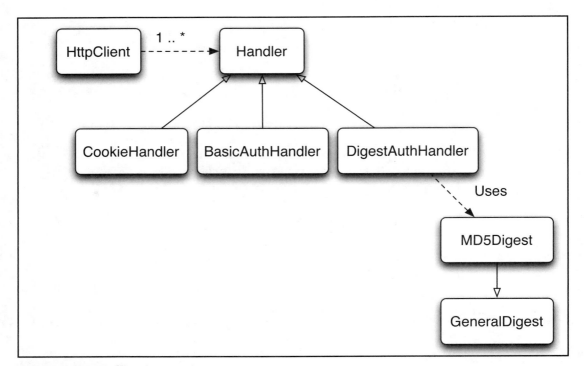

Figure 7–9 The HttpClient framework.

- The `CookieHandler` class processes HTTP cookie–related headers to help track sessions. The implementation is similar to the `SessionConnector` class we discussed earlier.

- The `BasicAuthHandler` class processes the HTTP basic authentication headers.

- The `DigestAuthHandler` class processes the HTTP digest authentication headers. It utilizes the `MD5Digest` class to generate the digests.

A version of the `Fetch.getNext()` method uses `HttpClient` and `CookieHandler` to retrieve the next photo from the server in an HTTP session. The `SessionView2` package in the sample code shows how to use it in our photo view MIDlet. As we mentioned, we can put several handlers in the chain. For example, the following code snippet demonstrates how to use HTTP Digest authentication in a session.

```
HttpClient client = new HttpClient ();
Handler h1 = new CookieHandler ();
Handler h2 = new DigestAuthHandler (username, password);

client.addHandler (h1);
client.addHandler (h2);

client.setUrl(url);
client.setRequestMethod (HttpConnection.POST);

byte [] reqData; // populate it
byte [] respData = client.query (reqData);
```

As an example of a concrete `Handler` class, we show the source code for the `BasicAuthHandler` class below.

```
public class BasicAuthHandler implements Handler {

  private String username;
  private String password;

  public BasicAuthHandler (String u, String p) {
    username = u;
    password = p;
  }

  public void prepareHeaders(HttpConnection c)
                                    throws Exception {
    String s = encode(username + ":" + password);
    c.setRequestProperty("Authorization", "Basic " + s);
  }

  public boolean processHeaders (HttpConnection c)
                                      throws Exception {
    // Do nothing. Do not respond to the challenge
    return false;
  }

  // Base64 encoding.
  //
  // This implementation is adopted from Kenneth
  // Ballard's HttpClient package. Released under LGPL.
  private String encode(String d) {
    String c = "ABCDEFGHIJKLMNOPQRSTUVWXYZ" +
               "abcdefghijklmnopqrstuvwxyz" +
               "0123456789+/";
```

```
byte [] code = c.getBytes();
byte [] s = d.getBytes();

int x;
int y = d.length() - (d.length() % 3);
byte [] coded = new byte[4];
String dest = "";

for(x = 0; x < y; x += 3) {
   coded[3] = code[s[x + 2] % 64];
   coded[0] = code[s[x] >> 2];

   coded[1] =
        new Integer((s[x] % 4) << 4).byteValue();
   coded[1] += s[x + 1] >> 4;
   coded[1] = code[coded[1]];
   coded[2] =
        new Integer((s[x + 1] % 16) << 2).byteValue();
   coded[2] += s[x + 2] / 64;
   coded[2] = code[coded[2]];
   dest += new String(coded);
}
x = y;

if(s.length % 3 == 0) return dest;

if(s.length % 3 == 1) {
   coded[2] = '=';
   coded[3] = '=';
   coded[0] = code[s[x] >> 2];
   coded[1] =
     code[new Integer((s[x] % 4) << 4).byteValue()];
   dest += new String(coded);
}

if(s.length % 3 == 2) {
   coded[3] = '=';
   coded[0] = code[s[x] >> 2];
   coded[1] =
        new Integer((s[x] % 4) << 4).byteValue();
   coded[1] += s[x + 1] >> 4;
   coded[1] = code[coded[1]];

   coded[2] =
        code[new Integer(
            (s[x + 1] % 16) << 2).byteValue()];
   dest += new String(coded);
```

```
    }
    return dest;
  }
}
```

HTTPS and Secure Connections

Wireless data is transported through radio waves in the air. No firewall can prevent crackers from listening in using a radio receiver nearby. In addition, the Internet itself is an insecure network: anyone can intercept packets as they traverse the Internet. Therefore, mobile Internet applications must use strong encryption to protect sensitive communication data (e.g., financial transactions or privacy data). HTTPS, built on top of the ubiquitous HTTP, is the most widely used secure protocol to transport sensitive information. In MIDP 2.0, support for HTTPS is mandatory.

How HTTPS Works

The HTTPS protocol utilizes the public key infrastructure to authenticate communication parties and ensure data confidentiality once the connection is established. It works as follows.

1. The two communicating parties first use digital certificates to establish each other's identity. Digital certificates are public keys issues by Internet identity authorities. On mobile devices, certificates can be stored on the user changeable SIM card. On Nokia devices, the certificate is stored in the device software and cannot be changed by the user.

2. Using public key algorithms, the two parties exchange a small symmetric encryption key, the *session key*, which is known only between themselves.

3. The two parties use symmetric encryption algorithms to encrypt all future network traffic until the session key expires.

The reason we use a public key algorithm to exchange the key and then use a symmetric algorithm to encrypt real communication data is that symmetric algorithms are about 1,000 times faster than public key algorithms.

NOTE   Series 40 devices can only make HTTPS connections to servers that have valid root certificates issued from Verisign or Thawte. If the server has a self-issued or unknown certificate, a `CertificateException` is thrown. Series 60 devices can make HTTPS connections to servers with unknown certificates.

HttpsConnection and SecureConnection

In addition to HTTPS, MIDP 2.0 devices also support secure socket connections based on TLS and SSL. The usage is as follows.

- If we pass a `https://host` connection string to the `Connector.open()` method, a `HttpsConnection` object is returned.

- If we pass a `ssl://host` string to `Connector.open()`, a `SecureConnection` object is returned.

`HttpsConnection` and `SecureConnection` extend `HttpConnection` and `SocketConnection`, respectively. The secure version of the connection interface only adds the `getSecurityInfo()` method.

```
SecurityInfo getSecurityInfo ()
```

Now, let's look at the `SecurityInfo` interface.

SecurityInfo and Certificate

The `SecurityInfo` interface declares methods to retrieve security metadata such as the cipher suite, protocol name, protocol version, and the digital certificate of the remote server.

```
String getCipherSuite ()
String getProtocolName ()
String getProtocolVersion ()
Certificate getServerCertificate ()
```

The `Certificate` interface is defined in the `javax.microedition.pki` package. It abstracts the issuer (certificate authority), effective date, serial number, signature algorithm, subject, type, and version of the certificate.

```
String getIssuer ()
long getNotAfter ()
long getNotBefore ()
String getSerialNumber ()
String getSigAlgName ()
String getSubject ()
String getType ()
String getVersion ()
```

Summary

In this chapter, we covered the use of the GCF in MIDP and discussed how to build effective communication channels using the ubiquitous HTTP. UI design and implementation considerations for networked mobile clients were discussed. A big feature of HTTP is the ability to pass meta-information (e.g., session and authentication tokens) in headers. We demonstrated ways to transparently handle HTTP headers using decorator classes (e.g., the `HttpSessionConnection` class) and a process chain framework (e.g., the `HttpClient` framework). At the end, the HTTPS and secure connection APIs from MIDP 2.0 were covered. They provide strong identity authentication and data encryption for sensitive information.

chapter 8

Wireless Messaging

Take advantage of reliable and asynchronous peer-to-peer communication channels in the mobile network infrastructure.

During the 2004 spring festival season, mobile phone users in China sent out more than 15 billion short messages in a one-month period. Mobile messaging has become a killer application and significant revenue source for wireless network operators. For developers, the combination of the ubiquitous and reliable mobile messaging services and the powerful smart clients enables new breeds of mobile applications. The Wireless Messaging API (WMA) is a J2ME optional package available on many Nokia devices (including but not limited to all Series 40 Developer Platform 2.0 devices). In this chapter, we discuss how to use WMA in smart client applications. The following topics are covered in this chapter:

- **Messaging in smart clients**: explains the synergy between mobile messaging and smart clients.
- **Wireless Messaging API (WMA)**: covers WMA components, limitations, operation modes, and security settings. We also show how to invoke MIDlets on a remote handset via an SMS message and the MIDP Push Registry.
- **A mobile chat example**: shows how to use the WMA to develop a complete application.
- **New features in WMA 2.0**: discusses the new features in the WMA 2.0 specification. Future Nokia Series 40 phones will support this API.

After reading this chapter, you should be able to develop peer-to-peer or messaging-based mobile applications with Nokia devices.

Messaging in Smart Clients

In Chapter 7, "Data Connectivity," we discussed how to use HTTP and socket connections to pass data from mobile clients and backend servers. While it is a proven model in the desktop world, the direct data connection is not always available in older wireless networks. Even when HTTP is available, it is often inefficient and has many constraints, since the device is behind layers of proxies and firewalls. When the direct data connections are not sufficient, the wireless native communication protocols can help us develop better and more flexible applications. Short Messaging Service (SMS) is a very popular wireless communication protocol. Key advantages of mobile messaging are as follows.

- **Mobile messaging is ubiquitous.** SMS is practically available on any mobile network and any mobile phone deployed today. The wide coverage area and high availability make it an excellent data transport for always-on applications.

- **Mobile messaging is reliable.** A key feature in messaging-based applications is the reliability. Messages are delivered by messaging middleware servers. If the recipient is not available, the message can be scheduled to deliver later or result in a failure notice. With a dedicated messaging middleware server, the sender could know exactly what's happening and can respond accordingly. Even the relatively simple SMS is considered one of the most reliable data communication mechanisms on today's wireless data networks. By contrast, in a HTTP network scenario, if the connection is dropped in the middle of a transaction, the application might be left in an uncertain state.

- **Mobile messaging is asynchronous.** The application does not sit idle waiting for a server response, but instead, a message is pushed to it. Messaging-based applications can be more responsive to user requests and improve the overall experience. The asynchronous model also allows high-volume peers or servers to schedule tasks more efficiently and avoid peak traffic hours.

- **Mobile messaging enables flexible end-to-end architecture.** Unlike tightly coupled one-to-one connections, messages can be forwarded around and processed by multiple intermediaries. We can develop compartmented and loosely coupled services in a messaging architecture.

- **Mobile messaging makes it easy to develop push-based or peer-to-peer applications.** While it is possible to open server sockets on some MIDP 2.0 devices, it is a major challenge to figure out the server device's IP address and access it from outside the carrier's firewall. Mobile messaging is built into the wireless infrastructure and uses phone numbers to identify devices. That allows us to push data to devices (or server peers) at any time. Also, the built-in security measures in cellular networks make it impossible to spoof phone numbers and hence automatically authenticates the devices.

NOTE

Asynchronous messaging is very popular in enterprise backend applications. Enterprise messaging middleware servers support service-level guarantee and enable loosely coupled Service-Oriented Architecture (SOA) solutions. Several enterprise messaging middleware products (e.g., IBM WMQe and iBus//Mobile) support mobile integration via SMS gateways or special MIDP client libraries.

In smart mobile clients, we can use SMS to pass data between mobile peers. We can add peer-to-peer features in our applications. For example, in the Mobile Multimedia Trivia example application (in Chapter 11, "End-to-End Design Patterns"), we use SMS to build private chat channels between players. Other examples of mobile peer-to-peer applications include machine-to-machine applications such as a remote device control. We can also use SMS to pass information from devices and backend servers. For example, we can use a backend server to send messages to a device (see Chapter 14, "Multimedia Messaging Service") and trigger some actions on the device (e.g., to launch a MIDlet, covered later in this chapter).

Compared with native SMS clients that handle only standard formatted messages, smart clients allow us to expand the use of SMS via custom protocols. Java smart clients can use SMS to reliably transport human–readable short text messages, machine-to-machine commands, or even binary content of arbitrary length. For example, we can use binary SMS messages to transport image messages between smart clients.

Wireless Messaging API

The WMA is an MIDP optional package developed by JSR 120. It provides Java interfaces to interact with SMS messages. There are currently two versions of the WMA available on Nokia phones.

- WMA 1.0 provides basic APIs to compose, send, and receive messages. It is available on all Series 60 Developer Platform 1.0 smart phones except for Nokia 7650. Some Series 40 Developer Platform 1.0 devices (e.g., the Nokia 3300 phone) support WMA 1.0 as well.

- In addition to the features in the WMA 1.0, WMA 1.1 supports MIDP 2.0 related security features and Push Registry to WMA. It is supported by all Series 40, 60, 80, and 90 Developer Platform 2.0 devices.

The WMA 2.0, which includes support for Multimedia Messaging Service (MMS), is currently being developed by JSR 205. We will cover the key features of WMA 2.0 at the end of this chapter.

TextMessage and BinaryMessage

The WMA abstracts two message interfaces: `TextMessage` and `BinaryMessage`. Both interfaces inherit from the `Message` interface, which declares common methods to access the recipient address and message timestamp. Please note that we cannot change the address via the `setAddress()` method after the connection is opened.

```
String getAddress()
void setAddress(String addr)
Date getTimestamp ()
```

The `TextMessage` interface represents a text message and adds methods to access the body text.

```
String getPayloadText ()
void setPayloadText (String body)
```

The `BinaryMessage` interface represents a binary message and adds methods to access the binary content.

```
byte [] getPayloadData ()
void setPayloadData (byte [] content)
```

NOTE
An SMS message in a GSM network can carry only 160 characters (or the equivalent length of binary data depending on encoding). The native SMS editors in most of the Nokia devices can concatenate up to three SMS messages together with a total number of characters up to 450. The WMA implementation can automatically break up a long message into segments according to the GSM concatenation specification to get around the size limit. The receiving WMA device must assemble the segments transparently into a `Message` object even if the segment order is disturbed during the network transmission.

MessageConnection

The core of the WMA is the `MessageConnection` interface, which represents a network connection for sending and receiving messages via the SMS infrastructure. As a network API, the WMA is fully integrated into the MIDP's Generic Connection Framework (GCF). We can obtain a `MessageConnection` instance by passing a specially formatted URL string to the `Connector.open()` factory method. The valid WMA URL schemes are as follows. The first two connection types discussed below are in the client mode, and the last two are in the server mode.

- The `sms://phone_number` scheme: `MessageConnection` supports sending SMS messages to the specified phone number. The message is delivered to the SMS inbox controlled by the device's native messaging application (native SMS inbox).

- The `sms://phone_number:port` scheme: `MessageConnection` supports sending SMS messages to a specific port at a phone number. The message is delivered to a MIDlet on the recipient device that listens at the port (i.e., the MIDlet SMS inbox). It does not appear in the native SMS inbox. If you run multiple SMS applications on a device, precaution must be taken to avoid conflicting port numbers.

- The sms://:port scheme: MessageConnection listens at the specific port. Under this scheme, the MIDlet SMS client acts as a server on that particular port, so this connection is also called *server mode connection*. It can receive messages sent to that port but cannot receive portless messages directed to the native SMS client. We can also use this server connection to send out SMS messages.

- The cbs://:port scheme: MessageConnection listens at the specific port for inbound Cell Broadcast Service (CBS) messages. It cannot send any messages. This scheme is not supported on current Series 40 devices.

The MessageConnection interface declares several methods to compose, send, and receive messages.

```
Message newMessage(String type, String addr)
int numberOfSegments (Message msg)
Message receive ()
void send (Message msg)
void setMessageListener (MessageListener l)
```

The type argument in the newMessage() factory method is either TEXT_MESSAGE or BINARY_MESSAGE. A MessageConnection object can contain a MessageListener object. The MessageListener interface declares one method notifyIncomingMessage(), which is invoked when the host MessageConnection receives an incoming SMS message. Figure 8–1 shows the interfaces in the WMA optional package.

Sending and Receiving Messages

In this section, we illustrate how to use client and server mode MessageConnection objects to send and receive SMS messages. The following code snippet shows how to send a simple message to phone number 123456789 using a client mode MessageConnection.

```
String addr = "sms://+123456789";
MessageConnection conn =
    (MessageConnection) Connector.open(addr);
TextMessage msg = (TextMessage) conn.newMessage (
                    MessageConnection.TEXT_MESSAGE);
msg.setPayloadText ("Hello world");
conn.send (msg);
```

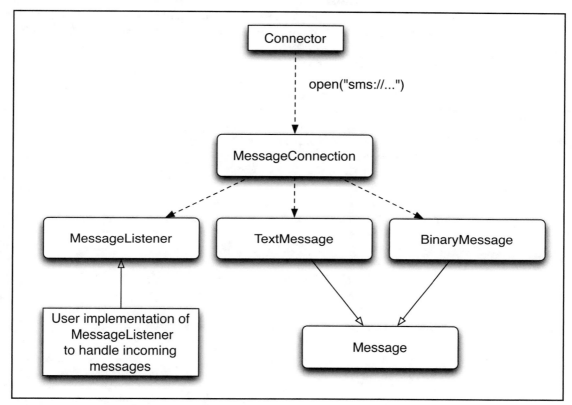

Figure 8–1 Connection interfaces in the WMA.

If we wish to reuse the same `MessageConnection` object to send messages to multiple recipients, we should use a server mode connection. In this case, the recipient address is embedded inside the message itself rather than in the connection object. An added bonus of a server mode connection is that it provides the correct return phone number and port number for the recipient to reply to. In this section's examples, we assume that all server mode connections listen at SMS port 3333.

```
MessageConnection sconn =
  (MessageConnection) Connector.open("sms://3333");
TextMessage msg = (TextMessage) sconn.newMessage (
                    MessageConnection.TEXT_MESSAGE);
// Send the message to port 3333 of the remote phone number
msg.setAddress ("sms://+123456789:3333");
msg.setPayloadText ("Hello world");
sconn.send (msg);
```

To receive a message using a server mode connection is very easy. We could call the `receive()` method directly, which blocks until it receives a message.

```
MessageConnection sconn =
    (MessageConnection) Connector.open("sms://3333");
Message msg = sconn.receive ();
if (msg instanceof TextMessage) {
   TextMessage tmsg = (TextMessage) msg;
   String text = tmsg.getPayloadText ();
   // do something with the message
}
```

A better way to receive incoming messages without blocking is to use the asynchronous `MessageListener`. We demonstrate its use in the WMA Chat example in the next section.

NOTE   The exact format of the phone number to use depends on the wireless network the device operates in. In most cases, a safe choice is to use the + sign followed by the international area code and then the phone number. On Series 40 devices, the prefix 00 is normalized to +.

Security

Sending and receiving mobile short messages costs money. The outgoing messages also carry the user's phone number and hence have privacy implications. In order to protect the user, access to the WMA is restricted by the Java Application Management Software (AMS) security manager. The restricted methods are `Connector.open()`, `MessageConnection.send()`, `MessageConnection.receive()`, and `MessageConnection.setMessage Listener()`. If the application does not have sufficient permission, a `SecurityException` is thrown.

All MIDP 1.0 and unsigned MIDlet suites are treated as untrusted by the AMS. In this case, the user must explicitly approve access to the restricted methods by confirming a popup system screen (Figure 8–2). If the user fails to grant access privileges, the AMS treats the MIDlet as not having sufficient permissions and throws the `SecurityException`. Signed MIDlet suites can declare requirement to access certain WMA APIs via the `MIDlet-Permissions` and `MIDlet-Permissions-Opt` MIDlet attributes (see Chapter 3, "Getting Started"). Depending on the MIDlet suite's security domain, which is determined by the signer's identity and a local device security policy, the AMS might allow or deny the MIDlet to have unlimited access to the WMA without user interruption. JAD permissions related to the WMA are listed in Table 8–1.

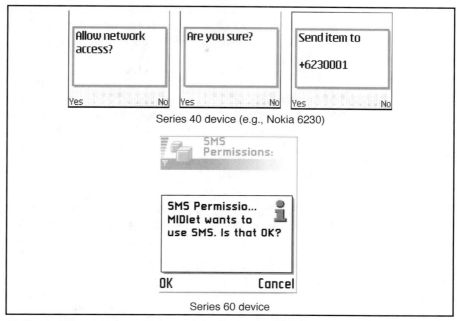

Series 40 device (e.g., Nokia 6230)

Series 60 device

Figure 8–2 The system screen asking for user permission to send SMS messages (the Series 40 prompt message applies to the Nokia 6230 phone and may be subject to change

Table 8–1 WMA Access Permissions

Attribute	Description
`javax.microedition.io.Connector.sms`	Require permission to call `Connector.open()` to open an SMS connection.
`javax.microedition.io.Connector.cbs`	Require permission to call `Connector.open()` to open a CBS connection. It is not supported on Nokia devices.
`javax.wireless.messaging.sms.send`	Require permission to call `MessageConnection.send()` to send SMS messages.
`javax.wireless.messaging.sms.receive`	Require permission to call `MessageConnection.receive()` or `MessageConnection.setMessageListener()` to listen for incoming SMS messages.
`javax.wireless.messaging.cbs.receive`	Require permission to call `MessageConnection.receive()` to listen for incoming CBS messages. It is not supported on Nokia devices.

For security reasons, Java applications cannot send messages to SMS ports that are reserved for other applications. Table 8–2 lists those restricted ports. If you try to send messages to those ports, a `SecurityException` is thrown.

Message Listener in Push Registry

It is possible to register a server mode `MessageConnection` to listen for incoming messages even when the MIDlet is not running. The following MIDlet attributes request the AMS to listen at the 3333 and 2222 ports for incoming SMS messages. If an SMS message from phone number 123456789 is received from port 3333, the SmsMidlet1 is started. If an SMS message from a phone number that starts from 512563 is received from port 2222, the SmsMidlet2 is started.

```
MIDlet-Push-1: sms://:3333, SmsMidlet1, 123456789
MIDlet-Push-2: sms://:2222, SmsMidlet2, 512563*
```

Inside the MIDlet, we can open a server mode connection to the listening port and retrieve the pushed message. For example, the SmsMidlet1 class could look like the following.

Table 8–2 Restricted SMS Ports

Portt	Description
2805	WAP WTA secure connectionless session service
2923	WAP WTA secure session service
2948	WAP Push connectionless session service (client side)
2949	WAP Push secure connectionless session service (client side)
5502	Service card reader
5503	Internet access configuration reader
5508	Dynamic Menu Control Protocol
5511	Message Access Protocol
5512	Simple Email Notification
9200	WAP connectionless session service
9201	WAP session service
9202	WAP secure connectionless session service
9203	WAP secure session service
9207	WAP vCal Secure
49996	SyncML OTA configuration
49999	WAP OTA configuration

```
public class SmsMidlet1 extends MIDlet {

  // ... ...

  protected void startApp () {
    MessageConnection sconn =
      (MessageConnection) Connector.open("sms://3333");
    // Retrieve the pushed SMS message
    Message msg = sconn.receive ();

    // process the message ...
  }

  // ... ...
}
```

The Chat Example Application

To illustrate the use of the WMA, we developed a sample chat application that allows Java handsets to exchange text messages using MIDlets instead of the native SMS client. Why do we do that? Well, it gives us a potentially more flexible messaging subsystem. The behavior of the native SMS client is not customizable. For example, it is impossible to program the native inbox to send automatic replies during certain times of a day or give new message alerts in alternative ways. But with the chat MIDlet suite, we can easily add custom message-processing logic. In this chapter, we focus on the core functionalities of a chat application (i.e., to send, receive, and store messages) and leave it to you to add cool features that are specific to real-world application needs.

Run the Example

To test and run WMA applications, we need at least two messaging endpoints with different phone numbers. This is easy to do with real phones, but how do we test WMA applications on emulators? Nokia device emulators can have pseudo phone numbers to support WMA testing. Instances of emulators on the same computer can send messages to each other using the "fake" phone numbers. To enable the SMS emulation functionality, you have to start the Nokia Connectivity Framework first. The Nokia Connectivity Framework is installed when you install the Nokia Series 40 Developer Platform 2.0 SDK. You can start the connectivity service via the following menu items on a Windows machine: Start | Programs | Nokia Developer Tools | Nokia Connectivity Framework | Nokia Connectivity Framework Lite.

TIP
The Nokia Connectivity Framework enables Nokia device emulator instances to communicate with each other via SMS, MMS and Bluetooth connections emulated inside the host PC. It is also possible to link physical devices into the emulated network environment via special hardware cards.

We can start multiple instances of the Nokia Series 40 Developer Platform 2.0 SDK (Nokia 6230 phone) emulator from the Nokia Developer's Suite (NDS) Start Emulator window by pressing the Emulate button multiple times. Each instance of the emulator is assigned a sequential phone number from 6230000 and up. Figure 8–3 shows the first two instances of the Nokia 6230 emulator. The assigned phone numbers are on the window title bar.

TIP
The Series 40 Developer Platform 2.0 SDK emulator permits us to change the prefix of the emulated phone numbers. For example, if we change the default prefix 6230 to 9999, the emulator phone numbers start from 9999000.

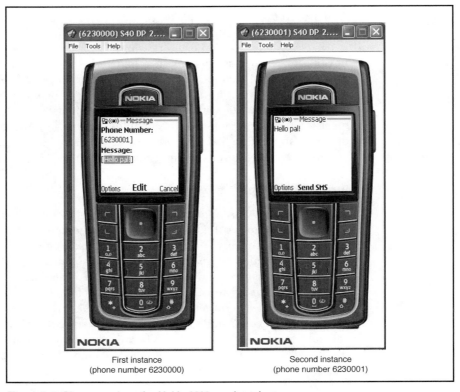

First instance
(phone number 6230000)

Second instance
(phone number 6230001)

Figure 8–3 Phone numbers for Nokia 6230 emulator instances.

NOTE Among Series 40 Developer Platform 1.0 SDKs, the Nokia 3300 SDK provides emulator support for the WMA. It works the same way as the Nokia 6230 emulator, and the emulated phone numbers start from `3300000`.

Send Messages

Following the Send SMS menu option, we can send messages from one device (or emulator) to another. If the message is sent successfully, the sender will receive a notification alert. The process is shown in Figure 8–4.

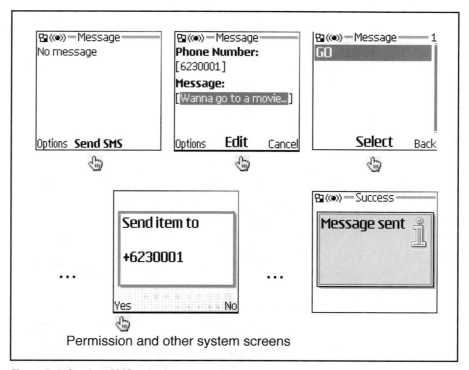

Figure 8–4 Send an SMS message.

TIP In order to input telephone numbers in a text field for outgoing SMS messages, we can specify the text field to have the PHONENUMBER constraint. On some Nokia devices, it allows us to select phone numbers from the device's native address book application (see Chapter 4).

The chat application defines a `Sender` interface. The abstract `Sender` interface enables us to have multiple implementations of the message sender object and keeps them decoupled from the rest of the program code. This is useful, since in legacy Series 40 devices, the Nokia SMS package is supported instead of the newer WMA. The `Sender` interface and its WMA implementation `SenderImpl` is shown below.

```
public interface Sender {
  public void setPort (String port);
  public void send (String addr, String mesg)
                                 throws Exception;
}

public class SenderImpl implements Sender {

  public String port;

  public SenderImpl () {
  }

  public void setPort (String port) {
    this.port = port;
  }

  public void send (String addr, String mesg)
                                 throws Exception {

    if (port == null) {
      addr = "sms://" + addr;
    } else {
      addr = "sms://+" + addr + ":" + port;
    }

    MessageConnection conn =
          (MessageConnection) Connector.open(addr);
    TextMessage msg =
          (TextMessage) conn.newMessage(
              MessageConnection.TEXT_MESSAGE);
    msg.setPayloadText( mesg );
    conn.send( msg );
    conn.close ();
  }
}
```

In the Chat MIDlet, we first instantiate a `Sender` object and then use it to send messages. If you choose another `Sender` implementation, you can simply change that one line of code in the `startApp()` method. Since sending a message is a time-consuming task, the `Chat.sendMessage()` method delegates the real work to a background thread—the `SenderWorker`.

```
public class Chat extends MIDlet {

  public static Display display;
  public static Sender sender;
  public static Inbox inbox;
  public static InboxViewer viewer;
  private static Chat controller;

  // ... ...

  protected void startApp () {

    sender = new SenderImpl ();
    sender.setPort (
              controller.getAppProperty("smsPort"));

    // ... ...
  }

  // ... ...

  public static void sendMessage (String addr,
                                    String mesg) {
    SendWorker worker = new SendWorker (addr, mesg);
    Thread t = new Thread (worker);
    t.start ();
  }
}

class SendWorker implements Runnable {

  private String addr, mesg;

  public SendWorker (String a, String m) {
    addr = a;
    mesg = m;
  }

  public void run () {
    try {
      Chat.sender.send(addr, mesg);
      Alert a = new Alert ("Success",
                            "Message sent",
                            null, AlertType.INFO);
      Chat.display.setCurrent (a);

    } catch (Exception e) {
```

```
        e.printStackTrace ();
        Alert a = new Alert ("Error",
                                    "Message failed",
                                    null, AlertType.ERROR);
        Chat.display.setCurrent (a);
      }
    }
}
```

Receive Messages

Once running, the chat MIDlet listens for incoming messages at the SMS port specified in the JAD file. When a new message arrives, it alerts the user and quietly saves it to the MIDlet inbox (Figure 8–5). The user can use the navigation menus to move to other messages and delete existing messages in the inbox (Figure 8–6).

Figure 8–5 Receive an SMS message.

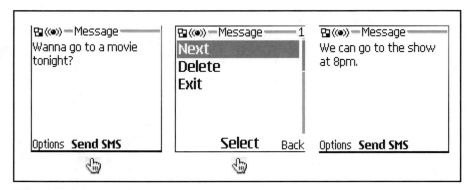

Figure 8–6 Browse the inbox.

Like Sender, Inbox is also defined as an interface to allow multiple implementations.

```
public interface Inbox {

  public boolean isBoxEmpty ();

  public void setupListener (String port) throws Exception;
  public String firstMessage () throws Exception;
  public String nextMessage () throws Exception;
  public void deleteMessage () throws Exception;
  public void cleanUp () throws Exception;
}
```

In the Inbox interface, most methods help navigate messages that are already saved in the inbox. Their implementations are typically based on the RMS store that stores the messages. RMS is discussed in Chapter 6, "Handling Application Data." A particularly interesting method in Inbox is setupListener(), which sets up an asynchronous listener at the specific port to process incoming messages.

```
public class InboxAsyncImpl
      implements Inbox, MessageListener {

  public void setupListener (String port)
                                    throws Exception {
    MessageConnection sconn =
 (MessageConnection) Connector.open("sms://:" + port);
    sconn.setMessageListener (this);
  }

  // ... ...
}
```

The registered MessageListener is the InboxAsyncImpl class itself. When a new message arrives, the MessageConnection object invokes the MessageListener.notifyIncomingMessage() method and passes in the connection object. In the notifyIncomingMessage() method, we launch a new thread to process the received message. The separate thread frees up the user interface and allows the MIDlet to receive messages without interruption. The relevant code is shown below.

```
public class InboxAsyncImpl
      implements Inbox, MessageListener {

  // ... ...
```

```
public void notifyIncomingMessage(MessageConnection c) {
  new Thread(new IncomingHandler(c)).start();
}

}

class IncomingHandler implements Runnable {

  private MessageConnection sconn;

  public IncomingHandler (MessageConnection c) {
    sconn = c;
  }

  public synchronized void run () {
    try {
      Message msg = sconn.receive();
      if (msg instanceof TextMessage) {
        String msgText =
            ((TextMessage) msg).getPayloadText();
        RecordStore inbox =
               RecordStore.openRecordStore(
                     InboxAsyncImpl.rmsName, true);
        inbox.addRecord(msgText.getBytes(), 0,
                            msgText.length());
        inbox.closeRecordStore ();

        Alert a = new Alert ("Success",
              "New message received",
                  null, AlertType.INFO);
        Chat.display.setCurrent (a);

        Chat.processNewMessage();

      } else {
        // Discard non-text messages
        Alert a =
            new Alert ("Discarded",
                "Non-text message discarded",
                null, AlertType.WARNING);
        Chat.display.setCurrent (a);
      }
    } catch (Exception e) {
      e.printStackTrace ();
      Alert a = new Alert ("Error",
          "Message receiving error",
          null, AlertType.ERROR);
```

```
            Chat.display.setCurrent (a);
        }
    }
}
```

New Features in WMA 2.0

The WMA 2.0 specification developed by the JSR 205 Expert Group adds MMS capabilities to the Java environment on handsets. For more information about MMS, please refer to Chapter 14. In a nutshell, MMS messages are SMS messages with multimedia file attachments. They greatly enhance the user's experience with mobile messaging services. As we discussed in Chapter 2, "Introducing Nokia Developer Platforms," all Nokia Series 40 Developer Platform devices support the MMS natively. Nokia is committed to support the WMA 2.0 on future Series 40 and Series 60 devices. For now, you can play with the API and generic device emulators using the Sun J2ME WTK 2.2 (see Chapter 3).

The WMA 2.0 is completely backward compatible with the WMA 1.0. In this section, we highlight the new APIs added by the WMA 2.0 to support MMS.

The Connection URL String

In addition to all connection URL formats supported in WMA 1.0, WMA 2.0 adds support for the mms:// scheme. For sending MMS messages, the recipient address in the URL can be a phone number or an email address. In order for the MMS to be delivered to a phone number, the device must support MMS and subscribe to MMS data service from the carrier. We can optionally append an application ID at the end of the recipient phone number. The application ID specifies a handler application other than the native MMS Inbox, which this MMS message should be delivered to. The application ID must be shorter than 32 characters, and it is typically the full Java class name of the MIDlet.

```
mms://+123456789
mms://email@host.com
mms://+123456789:com.domain.MMSmidlet
```

A MIDlet must register its application ID with the device AMS in order to receive MMS messages. A running MIDlet can establish a server mode Connection object using the application ID. An example server mode connection URL string is shown as follows. We can receive messages synchronously or asynchronously using the same API as the WMA 1.0.

```
mms://:com.domain.MMSmidlet
```

Or, we can link the application ID and its handling MIDlet in the Push Registry for automatic invocation upon the message arrival.

```
MIDlet-Push-3: mms://:com.domain.MMSmidlet, MMSmidlet, *
```

 NOTE   The application ID for MMS messages is functionally equivalent to the port number for SMS messages.

MultipartMessage and MessagePart

The `MultipartMessage` class is a new subclass of the `Message` interface in WMA 2.0. It represents an MMS message. Media components in the MMS message are represented by the `MessagePart` class. The `MultipartMessage` class has an internal array to store its `MessagePart` objects and provides methods to access those `MessagePart` objects. The `MessagePart` class has a byte array to store the media data and numerous attributes of the component (e.g., the media file name, the component ID, etc.). The following snippet shows how to assemble and send a `MultipartMessage` object with an image component, an audio component, and a text component. The data for the media components are already in the byte array format—probably downloaded from the Web or captured from the on-device camera or recorder (see Chapter 9, "Multimedia").

```
byte [] image;
byte [] audio;
byte [] text;

// Populate data into the byte arrays ...

// MessagePart constructor parameters:
// 1. The content array;
// 2. The MIME type of the content;
// 3. The component ID (must be unique in the message);
// 4. The media file name for this component;
// 5. The text encoding.
MessagePart imagePart =
  new MessagePart (image, "image/jpeg",
                      "<C01>", "img.jpg", null);
MessagePart audioPart =
  new MessagePart (audio, "audio/midi",
                      "<C02>", "sound.mid", null);
MessagePart testPart =
  new MessagePart (test, "text/plain",
                      "<C03>", "mesg.txt", "UTF-8");

MessageConnection conn =
```

```
    Connector.open ("mms://+123456789:com.domain.MMSmidlet");

MultipartMessage mesg =
    conn.newMessage (Message.MULTIPART_MESSAGE);
mesg.setSubject ("Picture and audio!");
mesg.setStartContentId ("<C03>");
mesg.addMessagePart (imagePart);
mesg.addMessagePart (audioPart);
mesg.addMessagePart (textPart);

conn.send (mesg);
conn.close ();
```

The following code snippet shows how to receive the above MMS message and recover the media data.

```
MessageConnection conn =
    Connector.opem("mms://:com.domain.MMSmidlet");
MultipartMessage mesg =
    (MultipartMessage) conn.receive ();

byte [] image =
    mesg.getMessagePart("<C01>").getContent();
byte [] audio =
    mesg.getMessagePart("<C02>").getContent();
byte [] text =
    mesg.getMessagePart("<C03>").getContent();

// Process the media data ...
```

Summary

In this chapter, we discussed how to send and receive SMS messages from MIDlets using the WMA optional package. We also covered the next version of the WMA that adds MMS functionalities. The WMA enables us to build peer-to-peer functionalities or a messaging-based communication layer in our MIDlets.

chapter

9

Multimedia

Support multimedia playback and capturing in J2ME smart clients.

The successes of portable MP3 players and camera phones have proven the value of multimedia in mobile applications. Mobile users not only play back media contents on the go, but also share daily experiences via audio and video capturing. The J2ME Mobile Media API (MMAPI) enables multimedia applications on Java devices. It is supported on all Developer Platform 2.0 devices and many Developer Platform 1.0 devices. In this chapter, we cover the following topics:

- **Introduction to the MMAPI:** covers the basics of the API and supported media formats.

- **Simple audio playback:** uses a MIDI player example to show how to play back simple audio content from a local file or over the network. We discuss various player controls available on Series 40 devices.

- **Advanced media playback:** goes beyond MIDI and tones to show how to play back media files with more complex audio and video formats.

- **Media capturing:** uses a multimedia blog example to illustrate the use of the audio and video capturing API and how to share the captured data over the network.

The second half of this chapter ("Advanced Playback" and "Media Capturing") uses examples running on today's Series 60 devices rather than Series 40 devices. That helps the Series 40 developers to keep up with coming advances, since the MMAPI support is fast evolving with each new device release. It also helps developers to scale existing Series 40 applications up to higher end Series 60 devices. This chapter shows you the capabilities and programming techniques of the MMAPI on Nokia Series 40 and Series 60 Developer Platform devices.

Introduction to the MMAPI

The MMAPI is designed to support multiple media content types and data capturing mechanisms. It bears a lot of resemblance to the Generic Connection Framework (GCF) discussed in Chapter 7, "Data Connectivity." A subset of the MMAPI for simple audio playback is included in the MIDP 2.0 specification. All

Nokia MIDP 2.0 devices, however, also implement the full MMAPI v1.1 (JSR 135) specification. The MMAPI features a generic factory class that instantiates media player objects from URI locator strings, `InputStream` objects, or `DataSource` objects. The device MMAPI implementation provides the concrete player classes for supported media formats. A player exposes some of its application-specific features via the `Control` interface. For example, a tone player has `ToneControl`, and a video capture player has `VideoControl` and `RecordControl`. We can interact with a player via its controls. Figure 9–1 shows the overall architecture of the MMAPI.

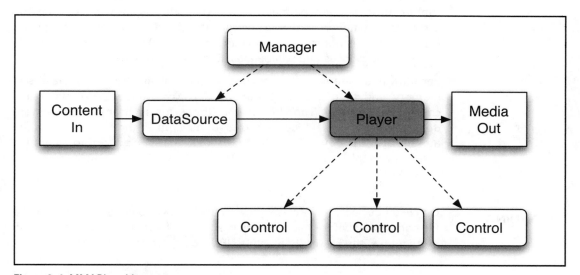

Figure 9–1 MMAPI architecture.

The Manager Class

The `Manager` class is the static factory class in the MMAPI. The `createPlayer()` method is the factory method used to create `Player` instances.

Create Player from URI Locators

The most versatile version of the `createPlayer()` method takes in a URI locator string to specify the network location of the media file, or the data capturing mode, or the in-memory empty device type.

```
static Player createPlayer (String locator)
```

In the MMAPI, three types of URI locator strings are supported.

- For media playback, the URI could point to a media file available on a remote HTTP server. The server must return the correct MIME type in the HTTP header for the `createPlayer()` method to determine which player instance to instantiate. For example, the URI locator string `http://host/sample.mid` is typically associated with the audio/midi MIME type on HTTP servers, and it would result in an audio MIDI file player instance. The supported MIME types in Series 40 and Series 60 Developer Platform 2.0 devices are listed in Table 9–1.

- For media capture, the URL string takes the special format `capture://audio` for audio capture or `capture://video` for still-image capture on a camera phone. The video mode displays video from the camera's viewfinder until you instruct the program to take a snapshot. Media capture is not supported in current Series 40 devices but is available on Series 60 devices and will be available on future Series 40 devices.

- For MIDI and tone sequence players, we can instantiate empty players in memory and then use `MIDIControl` and `ToneControl` objects to set content dynamically. The URI locator strings for such empty players are `device://midi`, which corresponds to the static value `Manager.MIDI_DEVICE_LOCATOR`, and `device://tone`, which corresponds to `Manager.TONE_DEVICE_LOCATOR`.

WARNING   On Nokia devices, the MMAPI player always downloads the remote media file completely before the playback is started. The real-time data streaming protocol (i.e, the `rtp://host` style URL locator) is not supported.

Create Player from Data Stream and MIME Type

The URI locator–based approach is simple and powerful. However, this approach relies on the server to provide the correct MIME types. If the server is configured incorrectly, or if the network protocol does not support MIME metadata (e.g., Unix socket), we cannor create the correct player. More importantly, not all media data is available over the network. We might need to play back locally stored media data, such as files bundled in the JAR file or data arrays stored in the RMS store. To address the above issues, we need a way to assign any MIME type programmatically to any data input stream available on the device. The second version of the `createPlayer()` method allows us to do just that.

```
static Player createPlayer (InputStream is, String type)
```

Refer to Table 9–1 for the list of supported MIME types. Please note that each individual device supports only a subset of those types. For example, most current Series 40 devices support only the `audio/x-tone-seq`, `audio/midi`, and `audio/sp-midi` MIME types. More detailed information is available in the Mobile Media API Technical Note published on the Forum Nokia Web site. If a `null` value is passed as the MIME `type` parameter, the implementation should try to figure out the media type based on its content. If the actual data in the `InputStream` is not encoded in the specified MIME format, or if the implementation cannot determine the media format when a `null` type parameter is passed, a `MediaException` may be thrown at runtime. We cannot instantiate data capture players with this method.

Table 9–1 MIME Types in the Nokia MMAPI Implementation (varies among devices)

MIME Types	Description
audio/x-tone-seq	tone sequence
audio/wav	wav audio format, but player cannot be created from `InputStream` using this MIME type
audio/x-wav	wav audio format
audio/au	au audio format
audio/x-au	au audio format, but player cannot be created from `InputStream` using this MIME type
audio/basic	raw audi format
audio/amr	amr audio format
audio/amr-wb	amr wb audio format
audio/midi	midi audio format
audio/sp-midi	extended midi format
video/mp4	Mpeg4 video format
video/mpeg4	mpeg4 video format, but player cannot be created from `InputStream` using this MIME type
video/3gpp	3gpp video format
application/vnd.rn-realmedia	real media video format

Create Player from DataSource

The third version of the `createPlayer()` method takes in a `DataSource` object to create a player. The `DataSource` class defines several abstract life cycle methods, which allow the users to specify how to connect to a custom data source and start or stop data transfer. A `DataSource` instance contains one or multiple `SourceStream` objects, which manage the actual media data. The `SourceStream` is different from the `InputStream` in the following aspects.

- `SourceStream` supports an API for random seeking that is required by some custom media data protocols.
- `SourceStream` defines abstract methods to support the concept of transfer size that is more suited for frame-delimited data (e.g., video).

Both the `DataSource` and `SourceStream` classes are abstract. They provide a framework for users to extend the MMAPI to support custom media data protocols. They are rarely used. We do not cover them in detail in this chapter.

Other Manager Methods

In addition to creating new player instances, we can use the `Manager` class to query the supported media types and protocols in this MMAPI implementation. Check out the `MediaPlayer` example later in this chapter to see those methods in action.

```
// Returns the supported media types for a given protocol
static String [] getSupportedContentTypes (String protocol)
// Returns the supported protocols for a given media type
static String [] getSupportedProtocols (String type)
```

The `Manager` class can also play tones directly to the device's speaker. This call does not block.

```
static void playTone (int tone, int duration, int vol)
```

The `duration` argument is the duration of the sound in milliseconds; the `vol` argument is the playback volume from 0 to 100; the `tone` argument takes a value from 0 to 127. The relationship between the `tone` value and the resultant frequency is as follows:

```
tone = 12 * log2 (freq/220) + 57
```

For example, the MIDI `tone` value 69 corresponds to the frequency of 440 Hz, which is the musical note A4. Table 9–2 shows musical notes and their corresponding frequencies and MIDI `tone` values. To get notes that are one octave higher or lower, we can add or subtract 12 from the MIDI `tone` values. Or, we can double or half the frequencies.

Table 9–2 Musical Notes and Their Corresponding Frequencies and MIDI Tone Values

Note	Frequency (Hz)	MIDI Tone
A4	440.00	69
A#	466.16	70
B	493.88	71
C	523.25	72
C#	554.36	73
D	587.33	74
D#	622.25	75
E	659.25	76
F	698.45	77
F#	739.98	78
G	783.99	79
G#	830.60	80

System Properties

The MMAPI specification leaves a lot of flexibility to implementers. For example, Nokia can decide what features and encoding types to support on each MMAPI-compatible device. As we have discussed, the `Manager.get SupportedContentTypes()` and `Manager.getSupportedProtocols()` static methods help us to determine the capabilities of the MMAPI implementation. In addition, the MMAPI implementation provides a number of system properties that can be retrieved via the `System.getProperty()` static method. Those properties give us information about the MMAPI implementation. Table 9–3 describes those properties and their values on Nokia 6230 (Series 40) and Nokia 6600 (Series 60) devices. The `MediaPlayer` example later in this chapter provides a utility to query MMAPI implementation capabilities based on the above methods and system properties.

Table 9–3 System Properties in the Nokia MMAPI Implementation

System Properties	Description	Nokia 6230	Nokia 6600
supports.mixing	Query for whether audio mixing is supported.	false	false
supports.audio.capture	Query for whether audio capture is supported.	false	true
supports.video.capture	Query for whether video capture is supported.	false	true
supports.recording	Query for whether recording is supported.	false	true
audio.encodngs	The string returned specifies the supported capture audio formats.		encoding = pcm encoding = ulaw encoding = alaw encoding = wav
video.encodings	The string returned specifies the supported capture video formats (video recording).		
video.snapshot.encodings	Supported video snapshot formats for the `VideoControl.getSnapshot()` method.		encoding = jpeg encoding = bmp encoding = png
microedition.media.version	Returns 1.1 for an implementation that is compliant with MMAPI v1.1.	1.1	1.0
streamable.contents	Returns formats that can be streamed. No streaming format is supported at this time.		

Player

The MMAPI specification declares the Player interface, which specifies the common behavior of all Player implementation classes provided by MMAPI implementers (e.g., Nokia) to handle different media types. The most important attribute of a Player is its life cycle states.

TIP

The state of the player has a big impact on its resource consumption. For example, an unclosed video capture player would prevent other applications from accessing the camera. It is essential that we open the player only when needed and close it as soon as we are done.

Player Life Cycle

A `Player` object can have the following states. Figure 9–2 illustrates the state transitions.

- CLOSED: The player has released most of its resources, and it can never be used again. We can change the player from any other state to the closed state by calling the `Player.close()` method.

- UNREALIZED: The player object has just been instantiated in the heap memory. It has not allocated any resources.

- REALIZED: If the `Player.realize()` method is called in a unrealized state, the player acquires required media resources and moves itself to the realized state. For example, if the player plays a remote media file over the HTTP network, the entire file is downloaded during the realizing process.

- PREFETCHED: If the `Player.prefetch()` method is called, the player performs a number of potentially time-consuming startup tasks and moves itself to the prefetched state. For example, during the prefetching process, the player acquires controls over the camera, the speaker, or other exclusive resources. The prefetching could fail if another program is already using some of those recourses. If the failure happens, we can call `prefetch()` later again on the same player. Once the player is prefetched, it can be started without further delay. Theoretically, we should move a prefetched player back to realized state by calling `Player.deallocate()`, but this method has not been implemented in Nokia devices.

- STARTED: By calling the `Player.start()` method, we can start the player, which starts the media playback or starts the capture player. Once the player is started, we can also call the `Player.stop()` method to stop it and return it to the prefetched state. A stopped player can be started again, and it will resume playing from the point at which it was stopped.

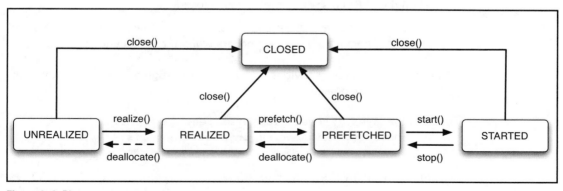

Figure 9–2 Player states.

To make life easier for developers, a `Player.start()` call to an unrealized player automatically triggers the `realize()` and `prefetch()` methods to be called. These implicit state changes cover all bypassed states.

PlayerListener

We can listen for the player's events by registering `PlayerListener` objects to a player instance. The `PlayerListener` interface declares only one method, `playerUpdate()`, which is invoked every time the registered player receives an event. The caller `Player` object passes the event and any application-specific data. Developers decide how to respond to the event by implementing this method.

```
void playerUpdate (Player player,
                   String event, Object data)
```

The event strings are defined as static variables in the `PlayerListener` interface. Most of them are self-explanatory: BUFFERING_STARTED, BUFFERING_STOPPED, CLOSED, DEVICE_AVAILABLE, DEVICE_UNAVAILABLE, DURATION_UPDATED, END_OF_MEDIA, ERROR, RECORD_ERROR, RECORD_STARTED, RECORD_STOPPED, SIZE_CHANGED, STARTED, STOPPED, STOPPED_AT_TIME, and VOLUME_CHANGED. Following are a couple of points to notice:

- Player state changes have their corresponding events, such as CLOSED, STARTED, and STOPPED. The player life cycle method always returns immediately, and we can process state changes asynchronously.

- A player could be stopped under several conditions. The END_OF_MEDIA event occurs when the entire media content is played back. The STOPPED_AT_TIME event occurs when the player is stopped at a preset time in a `StopTimeControl` (discussed later). The STOPPED event occurs only when the player's `stop()` method is invoked.

- The DEVICE_UNAVAILABLE event occurs when there is an incoming call. The DEVICE_AVAILABLE event occurs when the call is ended.

The `Player` class provides methods to register and remove the `PlayerListener` objects.

```
void addPlayerListener (PlayerListener listener)
void removePlayerListener (PlayerListener listener)
```

Other Methods in the Player Interface

The `Player` class supports methods to query the status of the current media file.

```
String getContentType ()
long getDuration ()
long getMediaTime ()
int getState ()
TimeBase getTimeBase ()
```

The following methods set how many times the player will loop and play the content, the media time of the current play position, and a new `TimeBase` to synchronize this player with another one. Please note that the current Series 40 devices only support the system time base.

```
void setLoopCount (int count)
long setMediaTime (long now)
void setTimeBase (TimeBase master)
```

NOTE   In MMAPI specification, *media time* refers to the play time in a media stream. All the media time values in the API are in the unit of microseconds (note, not milliseconds).

Control

The `Control` interfaces in MMAPI allow developers to control aspects of media-specific players programmatically. The same class can implement multiple `Control` interfaces for maximum API flexibility. Since the `Player` interface inherits from the `Controllable` interface, every `Player` class implements the following methods, which return the `Control` objects supported by this particular `Player` class.

```
Control getControl (String type)
Control [] getControls ()
```

`Control` objects are identified by the `type` strings. For example, the following code retrieves a `VolumeControl` object from an audio player and then adjusts the volume level.

```
VolumeControl vc = player.getControl ("VolumeControl");
vc.setLevel (50);
player.start ();
```

The MMAPI defines many player controls. However, only a subset of them is supported on the current Nokia devices. Table 9–4 lists the controls supported by different types of players on Nokia devices. Now we have covered the basics of the MMAPI; in the next two sections, we give concrete examples to show how to use the API.

Table 9–4 Players and Controls on Nokia MMAPI Implementation

MIME Types	Series 40 Controls	Series 60 Controls
audio/x-tone-seq	`ToneControl, TempoControl, RateControl, PitchControl, VolumeControl, StopTimeControl`	`VolumeControl, StopTimeControl, ToneControl`
audio/wav, audio/au, audio/amr	n/a	`VolumeControl, StopTimeControl, RecordControl`
audio/x-wav, audio/basic, audio/x-au, audio/amr-wb	n/a	`VolumeControl, StopTimeControl`
audio/midi, audio/sp-midi	`MIDIControl, TempoControl, RateControl, PitchControl, VolumeControl, StopTimeControl`	
video/mp4, video/mpeg4, video/3gpp, application/vnd_rn-realmedia	n/a	`VolumeControl, StopTimeControl, VideoControl`
Video Capture	n/a	`VideoControl, StopTimeControl`

NOTE The `Control` interface does not declare any method. It is a "tag" interface that identifies all subclasses as player controls. That simplifies the API design, since we can use the `Control` type as a placeholder for any player control objects.

Simple Audio Playback

The MMAPI implementation on standard Series 40 Developer Platform (e.g., the Nokia 6230 device) supports MIDI and tones playback. In this section, we walk through the source code of a MIDI player MIDlet. We cover MIDI player `Controls` that are supported on the Series 40 Developer Platform. This example MIDlet is tested on a Nokia 6230 device. When the `MidiPlayer` MIDlet is started, it shows a screen of playback options (Figure 9–3). Each UI component corresponds to an option in a player `Control`. When the MIDI file playback is started, the MIDlet displays a status page showing the playback volume of each MIDI channel (Figure 9–4).

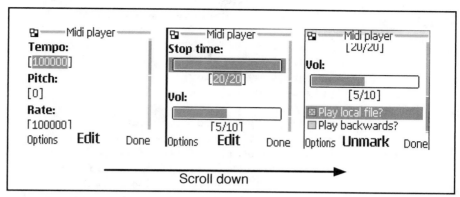

Figure 9–3 Playback options in the MidiPlayer MIDlet UI.

Figure 9–4 The MIDI channel volumes.

The current Series 60 devices do not support the various MIDI playback controls used in the MidiPlayer example (Table 9–4). So, do not try it on Nokia 3650 or 6600 devices.

The MidiPlayer MIDlet

The MidiPlayer class extends the MIDlet class and implements the CommandAction interface. It manages two Form objects: the playerOptions is for the option screen, and the playerStates is for the MIDI channel volume screen. The MidiPlayer class source code is shown below. The constructor retrieves the paths to the local and remote MIDI files from the JAD attributes. The startApp() method builds and displays the UI for the playback options screen.

```
public class MidiPlayer extends MIDlet
```

```
                  implements CommandListener {

    private Display display;
    private Command exit;
    private Command play;
    private Command back;

    private TempoControl tempoControl;
    private MIDIControl midiControl;
    private RateControl rateControl;
    private PitchControl pitchControl;
    private VolumeControl volumeControl;
    private StopTimeControl stopControl;

    private TextField tempoField;
    private TextField pitchField;
    private TextField rateField;
    private Gauge volumeGauge;
    private Gauge stopGauge;
    private ChoiceGroup config;

    private Form playerOptions = null;
    private Form playerStates = null;

    // media file location
    public static String mediaMidi;
    public static String remotePrefix;
    public static String localPrefix;

    public MidiPlayer () {
      display = Display.getDisplay(this);
      mediaMidi = getAppProperty ("MediaMidi");
      remotePrefix = getAppProperty ("RemotePrefix");
      localPrefix = getAppProperty ("LocalPrefix");

      exit = new Command ("Done", Command.EXIT, 1);
      play = new Command ("Play", Command.OK, 1);
      back = new Command ("Back", Command.BACK, 1);
    }

    protected void startApp () {
      playerOptions = new Form ("Midi player");
      playerOptions.addCommand (exit);
      playerOptions.addCommand (play);
      playerOptions.setCommandListener (this);

      tempoField = new TextField (
```

```
        "Tempo", "100000", 7, TextField.NUMERIC);
    pitchField = new TextField (
        "Pitch", "0", 7, TextField.NUMERIC);
    rateField = new TextField (
        "Rate", "100000", 7, TextField.NUMERIC);

    volumeGauge = new Gauge ("Vol", true, 10, 5);
    stopGauge = new Gauge ("Stop time", true, 20, 20);

    config = new ChoiceGroup ("", Choice.MULTIPLE);
    config.append ("Play local file?", null);
    config.append ("Play backwards?", null);

    playerOptions.append (tempoField);
    playerOptions.append (pitchField);
    playerOptions.append (rateField);
    playerOptions.append (stopGauge);
    playerOptions.append (volumeGauge);
    playerOptions.append (config);

    display.setCurrent (playerOptions);
}

protected void pauseApp () {
    // Do nothing
}

protected void destroyApp (boolean unconditional) {
    // Do nothing
}

public void commandAction (Command c, Displayable d) {
    if (c == exit) {
        destroyApp (true);
        notifyDestroyed ();

    } else if (c == play) {
        try {
            playMidi ();
            showStates ();
        } catch (Exception e) {
            e.printStackTrace ();
        }

    } else if (c == back) {
        display.setCurrent (playerOptions);
    }
```

```
    }

    // playMidi() and showStates() methods ... ...
}
```

The `playMidi()` and `showStates()` methods, which are left out of the above code listing, did the real work related to the MMAPI. Now, let's look at those methods more carefully.

Create the Player

The `playMidi()` method first creates a media player for the MIDI file. Recall that the first checkbox (index zero) in the `config` component on the playback options screen is "Play local file?" If it is checked, we create a player from a MIDI file bundled in the MIDlet JAR file and manually pass the audio/midi MIME type string to the `createPlayer()` method. If it is not checked, we create a player from the remote URL. In that case, the MIME type is returned from the server. After the player is created, we realize it, instantiate the controls, set control values, and start the player.

```
public void playMidi () throws Exception {
    Player player;

    // Check if the first check box in config is selected
    if (config.isSelected(0)) {
      InputStream is =
          this.getClass().getResourceAsStream (
              localPrefix + mediaMidi);
      player = Manager.createPlayer(is, "audio/midi");
    } else {
      player = Manager.createPlayer(
          remotePrefix + mediaMidi);
    }
    player.addPlayerListener(new StopListener ());
    player.realize();

    // Fix the controls ... ...

    player.start ();
}
```

WARNING   If the player is created from a remote MIDI file, the MIDlet needs permission to access the network and download the file. Since the downloading process might take some time, a more user-friendly approach is to put the entire player initialization process in a separate thread. We use the thread approach in the next example. But in the `MidiPlayer` example, since the remote file is small, we avoid the thread and focus on the code that is directly related to the MMAPI.

Player Events

In the `playMidi()` method, the `player.start()` statement returns after the playback begins, and the MIDI file plays in the background. In our application, we would like to be notified when the playback process is actually finished so that we can free up the player resources. It is critically important that we close players as soon as we are finished using them. It frees up system resources for other applications and reduces power consumption. Also, we want to pause the playback when the MIDI device is being interrupted by a high-priority system event such as an incoming phone call. The `PlayerListener` interface provides mechanisms for such notifications and callbacks.

In the `playMidi()` method code, we added a `PlayerListener` object to listen for any events in the audio player. The `StopListener` object's `playerUpdate()` method is called whenever a player event or an exception occurs. The `StopListener` object captures the events that correspond to the player-stopping event and puts the player back to closed state.

```
public class StopListener implements PlayerListener {

    public void playerUpdate (Player player,
                    String event, Object eventData) {
        try {
            if (event.equals (STOPPED) ||
                event.equals (STOPPED_AT_TIME) ||
                event.equals (ERROR) ||
                event.equals (END_OF_MEDIA)) {
                // Playback is finished
                player.deallocate ();
                player.close ();
                player = null;

            } else if (event.equals(DEVICE_UNAVAILABLE)) {
                // Incoming phone call
                player.stop();

            } else if (event.equals(DEVICE_AVAILABLE)) {
                // Finished phone call.
                // Start from where we left off
                player.start();
            }
            System.out.println(event);

        } catch (Exception e) {
```

```
                    e.printStackTrace ();
                }
            }
        }
```

Player Controls

In the `playMidi()` method, we set up the player controls before starting it. The standard controls supported in Series 40 Developer Platform are `VolumeControl`, `StopTimeControl`, `TempoControl`, `PitchControl`, `RateControl`, and `MIDIControl`. The code is listed as follows.

```java
public void playMidi () throws Exception {

    // ... ...
    player.realize();

    volumeControl = (VolumeControl) player.getControl(
        "VolumeControl");
    // The volume is from 0 to 100
    volumeControl.setLevel (
        volumeGauge.getValue() * 10);

    stopControl = (StopTimeControl) player.getControl(
        "StopTimeControl");
    // The argument microsecond NOT millisecond!
    stopControl.setStopTime (
        stopGauge.getValue() * 1000000);

    tempoControl = (TempoControl) player.getControl (
        "TempoControl");
    int t = Integer.parseInt (tempoField.getString());
    tempoControl.setTempo(t);

    pitchControl = (PitchControl) player.getControl (
        "PitchControl");
    int p = Integer.parseInt (pitchField.getString());
    pitchControl.setPitch(p);

    rateControl = (RateControl) player.getControl (
        "RateControl");
    int r = Integer.parseInt (rateField.getString());
    // Check whether to reverse playback direction
    if (config.isSelected(1)) {
        r = -1 * r;
    }
    rateControl.setRate(r);
```

```
    midiControl = (MIDIControl) player.getControl (
        "MIDIControl" );

    player.start ();
}
```

Now, let's check out those controls one by one.

VolumeControl

The `VolumeControl` object controls the sound volume of the player. We can mute the player via the `setMute()` method and set the volume using a linear scale from 1 to 100 via `setLevel()` method. In the `MidiPlayer` example, each step in the `stopGauge` gauge corresponds to a volume level change of 10. If the volume changes during the playback, a VOLUME_CHANGED event is delivered to the registered `PlayerListener`.

StopTimeControl

The `StopTimeControl` object allows us to preset a stop time for the player. The argument for the `setStopTime()` time is a long value for microseconds. In the `MidiPlayer` example, each step in the `stopGauge` gauge is one second in media play time.

TempoControl

The `TempoControl` object controls the tempo, which is often specified by beats per second, of a song. To allow fractional beats per minute, the `setTempo()` method takes in the milli-beat value, which is the beat per minute value multiplied by 1,000.

RateControl

Specifying the absolute tempo of a song is not always a good idea, since the absolute tempo is often overridden by the MIDI file. The `RateControl` object is used to set a relative tempo multiplier for all absolute tempo settings in this player. The rate, defined as a milli-percentage, is the ratio of the player's media time and the actual `TimeBase`. For example, a rate of 200,000 (2 × 100 percent × 1,000 milli) indicates that for every 1 second of `TimeBase` time (the real time), the player needs to play 2 seconds worth of media content. That makes the playback go faster. If the rate is a negative value, the playback would be backwards. The default playback rate is 100,000, which means that there is no change to the absolute tempo. Custom rate factors can be set via the `setRate()` method. The `getMaxRate()` and `getMinRate()` methods return the maximum and minimum rates supported by this device.

PitchControl

The `PitchControl` object raises or lowers the playback pitch without changing the playback speed. The argument for the `setPitch()` method is for milli-semitones. For example, a pitch value of 12,000 raises the pitch by 12 semitones and increases the frequency of perceived sound by a factor of 2.

MIDIControl

The `MIDIControl` object provides advanced access to the MIDI device. It gets or sets the volumes and assigned programs of each of the 16 MIDI channels. The `showStates()` method shows the volumes of the MIDI channels in the current player.

```
public void showStates () {
    playerStates = new Form ("Channel Vols");
    playerStates.addCommand (back);
    playerStates.setCommandListener (this);

    for (int i = 0; i <= 15; i++) {
      playerStates.append ("\n " + i + ": " +
          Integer.toString(
              midiControl.getChannelVolume(i)));
    }

    display.setCurrent(playerStates);
}
```

The `MIDIControl` object can also be used to send MIDI events to the device. MIDI events support is currently only available on the Nokia 3300, 6230, and 7600 devices. It is planned for future Series 40 devices.

Advanced Media Playback

In the previous section, we showed how to play MIDI files on Series 40 devices. Although most other media formats in the MMAPI are not yet supported on current Series 40 devices, Nokia plans to gradually support them in the future as the Series 40 hardware grows more powerful. On the other hand, today's Series 60 devices already support audio and video media formats beyond simple MIDI and tone files. For developers who are interested in writing scalable applications across Series 40 and Series 60 devices, it is important to understand those advanced MMAPI features. So, in this section and the next, we use Series 60–based examples to explain upcoming and advanced features of the MMAPI to Series 40 developers.

The `MediaPlayer` MIDlet is tested on Nokia 6600 and 3650 devices. Once it is started, you can select from a list of playback actions (Figure 9–5). Besides MIDI playback, `MediaPlayer` shows how to play wav format audio files. However, what's more interesting is that the `MediaPlayer` MIDlet demonstrates how to play back video files (3gpp format is supported on current devices).

Figure 9–5 The MediaPlayer MIDlet.

The `menu` object in the `MediaPlayer` MIDlet is the `List` object that represents the main menu (Figure 9–5). The MIDlet class itself acts as `menu` object's `CommandListener`. Hence, all user-initiated media playback actions are processed in the `MediaPlayer.commandAction()` method. The worker thread technique is widely used in the `MediaPlayer.commandAction()` method. So, let's briefly review why we need to use background threads for media playback.

NOTE The 3gpp format is a MPEG-4-based video compression and encoding format defined by the Third Generation Partnership Project. All Nokia video devices support the 3gpp format.

NOTE The `MediaPlayer` MIDlet provides a System Properties menu action. This action returns a screen with values of the MMAPI system properties (Table 9–3) and the `Manager.getSupportedContentTypes("http")` return values.

Initializing Players in a Thread

As we discussed in Chapter 7, we ought to avoid executing time-consuming blocking methods in the `CommandListener`, since they would temporarily freeze the user interface and result in a bad user experience. In media playback, especially when playing a remote media file, we need to perform several lengthy tasks before the player can be started. They include the following:

- When we create the player from a remote URL, the `Manager.createPlayer()` method makes the server connection and checks the MIME type. It might take a couple of seconds to make an HTTP connection on wireless networks.

- The `Player.realize()` method can take a long time to complete, since it must download the entire remote media file.

- The `Player.prefetch()` method gains control over exclusive resources and fills the buffer. On Nokia devices, it normally returns quickly but could possibly take a long time.

In the `MediaPlayer` MIDlet example, we use a background worker thread to do the above tasks for both remote and local media file playbacks.

Play Back wav Audio Files

When the user selects "Play local Wav" or "Play remote Wav" from the main menu, the following code snippet in the `MediaPlayer.commandAction()` method is triggered. Depending on whether the file is local or remote, the program first constructs a URL pointing to the file. Then, it constructs an `AudioPlayer` object with three arguments: the first argument is a `boolean` value indicating whether the URL is for a local file; the second argument is the URL string itself; the third argument is the MIME type of the media file pointed to by this URL. The `AudioPlayer` object is a `Thread` object that can be started in a separate thread. After the thread is started, the `commandAction()` method returns and frees up the main UI thread. At this point, the `wait` screen is displayed to the user.

```
public class MediaPlayer extends MIDlet
                implements CommandListener {

  public void commandAction(Command c, Displayable s) {

      // ... ...

          } else if (menu.getSelectedIndex() == 3) {
            display.setCurrent (wait);
            String url = localPrefix + mediaWav;
            String mime = "audio/x-wav";
            Thread t = new AudioPlayer(true, url, mime);
```

```
            t.start ();

        } else if (menu.getSelectedIndex() == 4) {
            display.setCurrent (wait);
            String url = remotePrefix + mediaWav;
            String mime = "audio/x-wav";
            Thread t = new AudioPlayer(false, url, mime);
            t.start ();

    // ... ...
    }
    // ... ...
}
```

The worker thread started by the above `t.start()` statement executes the `AudioPlayer` object's `run()` method. It creates a new `Player` instance based on the URL and whether or not the media file is local. After the worker thread initializes the `Player` object, it switches the display to the `AudioForm` screen and starts playing the audio.

```
class AudioPlayer extends Thread {

  private boolean local;
  private String url;
  private String mime;

  public AudioPlayer (boolean l, String u, String m) {
    local = l;
    url = u;
    mime = m;
  }

  public void run () {
    try {
      if (local) {
        InputStream is =
            getClass().getResourceAsStream (url);
        MediaPlayer.player =
            Manager.createPlayer(is, mime);
      } else {
        MediaPlayer.player = Manager.createPlayer(url);
      }

      MediaPlayer.player.addPlayerListener(
                            new StopListener ());
      MediaPlayer.player.realize();
```

```
            MediaPlayer.player.prefetch ();

            AudioForm form = new AudioForm ();
            MediaPlayer.display.setCurrent (form);

            MediaPlayer.player.start ();
        } catch (Exception e) {
            e.printStackTrace ();
        }
    }
}
```

The `AudioForm` screen provides a Done command to stop the playback. The Done command listener invokes the static method `stopPlayer()` in the `MediaPlayer` class.

```
public class MediaPlayer extends MIDlet
            implements CommandListener {

  // ... ...

  public static void stopPlayer () {
    try {
      player.stop ();
    } catch (Exception e) {
      e.printStackTrace ();
    }
  }

  // ... ...
}
```

Play Back Video Files

Code for video playback in the `MediaPlayer` MIDlet is very similar to that for audio playback. The following snippet shows the relevant parts in the `MediaPlayer.commandAction()` method. It starts the `VideoPlayer` thread with the required file URL and MIME type information.

```
public class MediaPlayer extends MIDlet
            implements CommandListener {

  public void commandAction(Command c, Displayable s) {

      // ... ...

        } else if (menu.getSelectedIndex() == 5) {
```

```
            display.setCurrent (wait);
            String url = localPrefix + media3gpp;
            String mime = "video/3gpp";
            Thread t = new VideoPlayer(true, url, mime);
            t.start ();

        } else if (menu.getSelectedIndex() == 6) {
            display.setCurrent (wait);
            String url = remotePrefix + media3gpp;
            String mime = "video/3gpp";
            Thread t = new VideoPlayer(false, url, mime);
            t.start ();


        }
    // ... ...
}
// ... ...
}
```

The VideoPlayer class is similar to the AudioPlayer class with one crucial difference. Since the video player needs access to the device's display, we need to set up the communication between the video playback screen and the player before starting the player. Hence, the VideoPlayer.run() method does not directly start the Player object. Instead, the VideoPlayer object delegates the player.start() call to the video playback screen's startPlayer() method, which handles the communication setup logic.

```
class VideoPlayer extends Thread {

    private boolean local;
    private String url;
    private String mime;

    public VideoPlayer (boolean l, String u, String m) {
        local = l;
        url = u;
        mime = m;
    }

    public void run () {
        try {
            if (local) {
                InputStream is =
                    getClass().getResourceAsStream (url);
                MediaPlayer.player =
                    Manager.createPlayer(is, mime);
            } else {
```

```
            MediaPlayer.player = Manager.createPlayer(url);
        }

        MediaPlayer.player.realize();
        MediaPlayer.player.prefetch ();

        VideoForm form = new VideoForm ();
        // Or alternatively:
        // VideoForm form = new VideoCanvas ();
        MediaPlayer.display.setCurrent (form);

        form.startPlayer (MediaPlayer.player);
    } catch (Exception e) {
        e.printStackTrace ();
    }
  }
}
```

In the `MediaPlayer` MIDlet, we provide two alternative implementations of the video playback screen: `VideoForm` for the `Form` UI and `VideoCanvas` for the `Canvas` UI. Now, let's check out how the `startPlayer()` method displays the video to the `Form` and `Canvas` screens.

Play Back Video on a Form

The `VideoControl` of a video player can generate an `Item` object, which shows the video window. On creation, the dimensions of the `Item` match the dimensions of the video content.

```
VideoControl video =
  (VideoControl) player.getControl("VideoControl");
Item item = (Item) video.initDisplayMode(
        GUIControl.USE_GUI_PRIMITIVE, null);
```

The `Item` object can be appended to any `Form` as a component widget. For example, we can center the video window on a form using layout attributes or add captions by appending `StringItem` objects before or after the video `Item`. The `VideoForm.startPlayer()` method demonstrates how to set up the player's video control on a `Form` (see Figure 9–6).

```
public class VideoForm extends Form
            implements CommandListener {

  private Player player;
  private Command done;

  public VideoForm () {
```

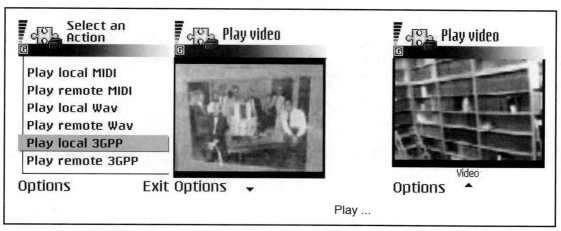

Figure 9–6 Play back video in a Form.

```
      super ("Play video");
      done = new Command("Done", Command.OK, 1);
      addCommand (done);
      setCommandListener (this);
   }

   public void startPlayer (Player p) {
      player = p;
      try {
        // Add the video playback window (item)
        VideoControl video =
          (VideoControl) player.getControl("VideoControl");
        Item item = (Item) video.initDisplayMode(
            GUIControl.USE_GUI_PRIMITIVE, null);
        item.setLayout(Item.LAYOUT_CENTER |
                       Item.LAYOUT_NEWLINE_AFTER);
        append(item);
        // Add a caption
        StringItem s = new StringItem ("", "Video");
        s.setLayout(Item.LAYOUT_CENTER);
        append (s);

        player.start();

      } catch (Exception e) {
        e.printStackTrace();
        append ("An error has occurred");
      }
   }
```

```
public void commandAction(Command c, Displayable s) {
  if (c == done) {
    MediaPlayer.stopPlayer ();
    MediaPlayer.showMenu ();
  }
}
}
```

Play Back Video on a Canvas

The Canvas class gives us direct control over the LCD display and the keypad. It is sometimes desirable to play back video content directly on a Canvas. For example, we could add custom borders to the video window or respond to game key events. The initDisplayMode() method in the VideoControl class initializes the Canvas to display the video. It is called in the Canvas constructor. The video window takes up the entire drawable area of the Canvas. The VideoCanvas class shows how to play back a video file on a Canvas.

```
public class VideoCanvas extends Canvas
                implements PlayerHost, CommandListener {

  private Player player;
  private int width, height;
  private Command done;

  public VideoCanvas () {
    width = getWidth();
    height = getHeight();
    done = new Command("Done", Command.OK, 1);
    addCommand (done);
    setCommandListener (this);
  }

  public void startPlayer (Player p) {
    player = p;

    try {
      VideoControl video =
    (VideoControl) player.getControl("VideoControl");
      video.initDisplayMode(
        VideoControl.USE_DIRECT_VIDEO, this);

      video.setDisplayLocation(2, 2);
      video.setDisplaySize(width - 4, height - 4);
```

```
        player.start ();

    } catch (Exception e) {
      e.printStackTrace();
    }
  }

  public void paint(Graphics g) {

    // Draw a green border around the VideoControl.
    g.setColor(0x00ff00);
    g.drawRect(0, 0, width - 1, height - 1);
    g.drawRect(1, 1, width - 3, height - 3);
  }

  public void commandAction(Command c, Displayable s) {
    if (c == done) {
      MediaPlayer.stopPlayer ();
      MediaPlayer.showMenu ();
    }
  }
}
```

TIP

On the Nokia 6600 and 3650 devices, we recommend that you display VideoControl UI on a Form, since the Form display implementation seems to be more stable and consistent across devices.

Media Capture

For devices equipped with voice recorders or digital cameras, the MMAPI Player class can be used to capture audio clips or snap digital pictures. The media capturing support is currently available only on Series 60 devices and will come soon on future Series 40 devices. In this section, we use a Series 60–based multimedia blog application to demonstrate the media capture mechanisms. The mobile client allows users to take a picture, record a short audio clip, and then send both media files with a text note to a server. The server publishes the entries with timestamps to an HTML Web page in the chronological order. Any user can then view the blog entries from any xHTML-compatible browser on a PC or on a phone. The process is illustrated in Figure 9-7.

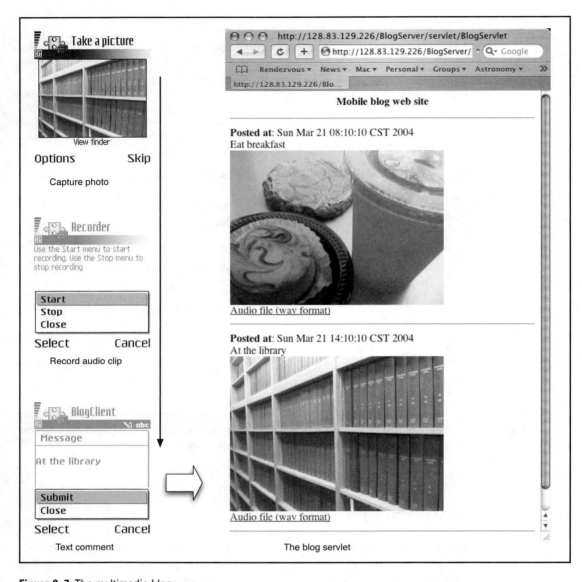

Figure 9–7 The multimedia blog.

NOTE

Blog is the abbreviated term for "Web log." It is a personal Web page that records and publishes a person's daily journal or thoughts.

Capture Image

We can instantiate a video capture Player object by passing the URI locator capture://video to the Manager.createPlayer() factory method. Then, we can get a VideoControl control from the player and display the video UI window to the LCD using the techniques we discussed in the video playback section. Once the player is started, the user sees the live motion video of the camera view in the VideoControl UI. We can then call the VideoControl.getSnapshot() method to take a snapshot and store the photo to a byte array. The argument we pass to the getSnapshot() method determines the type and the dimensions of the resultant image. The following list is specific to Nokia 6600 and 3650 devices.

- The getSnapshot(null) call captures a 160 by 120 PNG image.

- The getSnapshot("encoding=jpeg") call captures a 160 by 120 JPEG image.

- The getSnapshot("width=320&height=240") call captures a 320 by 240 PNG image.

- The getSnapshot("encoding=jpeg&width=320&height=240") call captures a 320 by 240 JPEG image.

Three encoding values, png, jpeg, and bmp, are supported. The gif encoding is recently added to the Nokia 6600 maintenance release. If values are specified for width and height, both must be specified. If the requested dimensions are different from 160 by 120, the image is scaled to the requested width and height. If the aspect ratio requested does not match 4:3 (the default aspect ratio), the resulting image could be distorted. The maximum image size that can be captured depends on the free heap memory available.

NOTE The Series 60 MIDP concept emulator 0.3.1 only supports capturing 160 by 120 PNG images. The emulator uses a stock still image to emulate the camera viewfinder (Figure 9–8).

TIP For security reasons, some of the media capture APIs are restricted. On Nokia 3650, the user has to give explicit permission to the getSnapshot() method call. On Nokia 6600 and other MIDP 2.0 devices, we can sign the MIDlet suite and place it under a trusted domain to suppress security prompts that would otherwise break into the screen.

Figure 9-8 Camera viewfinder on the
Series 60 emulator.

The following code shows how to develop a photo capture screen `CameraView`.
When the user hits the action key or the capture menu, the camera takes a 320
by 240 JPEG snapshot image.

```
public class CameraView extends Form
          implements CommandListener {

  private Command capture;
  private Command skip;

  private Player player = null;
  private VideoControl video = null;

  public CameraView () {
    super ("Take a picture");

    showCamera ();

    capture = new Command ("Capture", Command.OK, 1);
    skip = new Command ("Skip", Command.CANCEL, 1);
    addCommand (capture);
    addCommand (skip);
    setCommandListener (this);
  }

  public void commandAction (Command c, Displayable d) {
    if (c == capture) {
      capture ();
      BlogClient.showPhotoPreview ();
```

```
    } else if (c == skip) {
      player.close ();
      BlogClient.showAudioRecorder ();

    }
  }

  private void showCamera () {
    try {
      player = Manager.createPlayer("capture://video");
      player.realize();

      // Add the video playback window (item)
      video = (VideoControl) player.getControl(
                                   "VideoControl");
      Item item = (Item) video.initDisplayMode(
          GUIControl.USE_GUI_PRIMITIVE, null);
      item.setLayout(Item.LAYOUT_CENTER |
                      Item.LAYOUT_NEWLINE_AFTER);
      append (item);
      // Add a caption
      StringItem s = new StringItem ("", "View finder");
      s.setLayout(Item.LAYOUT_CENTER);
      append (s);

      player.start();

    } catch (Exception e) {
      e.printStackTrace ();
    }
  }

  private void capture () {
    try {
      // PNG, 160x120
      // BlogClient.photoData = video.getSnapshot(null);
      //      OR
      // BlogClient.photoData = video.getSnapshot(
      //      "encoding=png&width=160&height=120");

      // BlogClient.photoPreview = BlogClient.photoData;
      // BlogClient.photoType = "png";

      byte [] tmp = video.getSnapshot(
          "encoding=jpeg&width=320&height=240");
      BlogClient.photoPreview =
```

```
            BlogClient.createPreview(
                Image.createImage(tmp, 0, tmp.length));
        BlogClient.photoData = tmp;
        BlogClient.photoType = "jpg";

        player.stop ();
        player.close ();

      } catch (Exception e) {
        e.printStackTrace ();
        BlogClient.showAlert ("Error", e.getMessage ());
      }
    }
  }
```

The `BlogClient.createPreview()` method resizes the snapshot to a smaller preview image, which fits into the device screen. The method first creates an empty image of the preview size. It then populates the preview image pixel by pixel by sampling the original image. This method creates an approximate thumbnail without parsing the original JPEG image.

```
// Scale down the image by skipping pixels
public static Image createPreview (Image image) {
    int sw = image.getWidth();
    int sh = image.getHeight();

    int pw = 160;
    int ph = pw * sh / sw;

    Image temp = Image.createImage(pw, ph);
    Graphics g = temp.getGraphics();

    for (int y = 0; y < ph; y++) {
      for (int x = 0; x < pw; x++) {
        g.setClip(x, y, 1, 1);
        int dx = x * sw / pw;
        int dy = y * sh / ph;
        g.drawImage(image, x - dx, y - dy,
            Graphics.LEFT | Graphics.TOP);
      }
    }

    Image preview = Image.createImage(temp);
    return preview;
}
```

The `PhotoReview` class shows the review image and asks the user whether to continue.

```
public class PhotoPreview extends Form
                implements CommandListener {

   private Command cancel;
   private Command next;

   public PhotoPreview () {
      super ("Photo Preview");
      cancel = new Command ("Cancel", Command.CANCEL, 1);
      next = new Command ("Next", Command.OK, 1);
      addCommand (cancel);
      addCommand (next);
      setCommandListener (this);

      append (new ImageItem (
          "Image size is " + BlogClient.photoData.length,
          BlogClient.photoPreview,
          ImageItem.LAYOUT_CENTER, "image"));
   }

   public void commandAction (Command c, Displayable d) {
      if (c == cancel) {
         BlogClient.initSession();
         BlogClient.showCamera ();

      } else if (c == next) {
         BlogClient.showAudioRecorder();
      }
   }
}
```

Capture Audio

After the user is satisfied with the photo, she can record an audio message. The audio capture player is instantiated using the `capture://audio` URI locator. Arguments to this string are used to specify audio bitrate and sampling depth. For example, the `capture://audio?rate=8000&bits=16` URI locator string initiates a `Player` object and captures 16-bit sound at 8,000 bits per second. Once we have the `Player` instance, we can get a `RecordControl` control and use its `setRecordStream()` method to assign an `OutputStream` to this control. The default audio output format is the wav format in Nokia 6600 and 3650 devices. The `RecordControl` starts recording once the player enters the started state and stops once the player is stopped.

WARNING Using the `RecordControl` in a video capture player, we can theoretically capture full-motion video clips from the camera. However, currently no video encoding format is supported on any Nokia device.

The source code for the `AudioRecorder` class is listed below. When the user stops the audio capturing player, the program writes out the recorded audio data to a byte array, `audioData`.

```java
public class AudioRecorder extends Form
            implements CommandListener {

  private Command skip;
  private Command start;
  private Command stop;

  private Player player = null;
  private RecordControl recordcontrol = null;
  private ByteArrayOutputStream output = null;


  public AudioRecorder () {
    super ("Audio Recorder");

    skip = new Command ("Skip", Command.CANCEL, 1);
    start = new Command ("Start", Command.OK, 1);
    stop = new Command ("Stop", Command.SCREEN, 1);
    addCommand (skip);
    addCommand (start);
    addCommand (stop);
    setCommandListener (this);

    append ("Use the Start menu to start recording. " +
        "Use the Stop menu to stop recording");
    try {
      player = Manager.createPlayer(
          "capture://audio?rate=8000&bits=16");
      player.realize ();
      recordcontrol =
(RecordControl) player.getControl("RecordControl");
      output = new ByteArrayOutputStream ();
      recordcontrol.setRecordStream(output);

    } catch (Exception e) {
      e.printStackTrace ();
    }
  }
```

```
public void commandAction (Command c, Displayable d) {
  if (c == skip) {
    BlogClient.showMessageForm ();

  } else if (c == start) {
    try {
      recordcontrol.startRecord();
      player.start();
    } catch (Exception e) {
      e.printStackTrace ();
      BlogClient.showAlert ("Error",
          "Cannot start the player. " +
          "Maybe audio recoding is not supported " +
          "on this device. Please skip this step");
    }

  } else if (c == stop) {
    try {
      recordcontrol.commit ();
      player.close();
    } catch (Exception e) {
      e.printStackTrace ();
      BlogClient.showAlert ("Error",
          "Cannot stop the player");
    }
    BlogClient.audioData = output.toByteArray();
    BlogClient.showMessageForm ();
  }
 }
}
```

Submit Blog Entries

After we have gathered the snapshot, audio recording, and short text message data, we can submit it to the server. The code below illustrates how it works. The complete source code with multithread support is available in the BlogClient class.

```
HttpConnection conn = null;
DataInputStream din = null;
DataOutputStream dout = null;

conn = (HttpConnection) Connector.open(url);
conn.setRequestMethod(HttpConnection.POST);

dout = conn.openDataOutputStream ();
```

```
dout.writeInt (PHOTO_AUDIO);
dout.writeUTF (message);
dout.writeUTF (photoType);
dout.writeInt (photoData.length);
dout.write (photoData, 0, photoData.length);
dout.writeInt (audioData.length);
dout.write (audioData, 0, audioData.length);

dout.flush ();
dout.close ();
```

The Blog Servlet

On the server side, the blog servlet intercepts the HTTP POST data in the doPost() method. It stores image and audio data into separate files and appends links to an HTML master file. The doGet() method is invoked when a client accesses the servlet directly from a browser. It assembles and returns an HTML page with up-to-date blog entries. The full source code of the servlet is listed below for your reference.

```
public class BlogServlet extends HttpServlet {
  private static int NO_OBJECT = 0;
  private static int PHOTO_ONLY = 1;
  private static int AUDIO_ONLY = 2;
  private static int PHOTO_AUDIO = 3;

  private static int SUCCESS = 1;
  private static int FAILURE = 2;

  private static String fileroot = null;
  private static String webroot = null;

  public void init() throws ServletException {
    InputStream in =
        getClass().getResourceAsStream("/conf.prop");
    Properties prop = new Properties ();
    try {
      prop.load (in);
      fileroot = prop.getProperty("Fileroot");
      webroot = prop.getProperty("Webroot");
    } catch (Exception e) {
      e.printStackTrace ();
      fileroot = "/root/BlogServer/content/";
      webroot = "/BlogServer/content/";
    }
  }
```

```java
public void doGet(HttpServletRequest request,
                  HttpServletResponse response)
        throws ServletException, IOException {
    response.setContentType("text/html");
    PrintWriter out = response.getWriter();

    out.println(readTextFile("header.html"));
    out.println(readTextFile("entries.html"));
    out.println(readTextFile("footer.html"));

    out.flush ();
    out.close ();
}

public void doPost(HttpServletRequest request,
                   HttpServletResponse response)
        throws ServletException, IOException {

    response.setContentType("application/binary");

    InputStream in = request.getInputStream();
    OutputStream out = response.getOutputStream();
    DataInputStream din = new DataInputStream(in);
    DataOutputStream dout = new DataOutputStream(out);

    String current =
        Long.toString((new Date()).getTime());
    String body = "<b>Posted at</b>: " +
        (new Date()).toString() + "<br/>";
    String filename;

    // Get the opcode
    int opcode = din.readInt();
    // Get the message body
    body += din.readUTF();
    body += "<br/>";

    if (opcode == NO_OBJECT) {
      // Save the message body
      saveMessage (body);
      dout.writeInt(SUCCESS);

    } else if (opcode == PHOTO_ONLY) {
      // Get photo data
      String photoType = din.readUTF ();
      byte [] photoData = receiveObject (din);
```

```
        // Save the photo data
        filename = current + "." + photoType;
        saveObject (photoData, filename);
        body = body + photoHtml(filename);

        // Save the message body
        saveMessage (body);
        dout.writeInt(SUCCESS);

    } else if (opcode == AUDIO_ONLY) {
        // Get the audio data
        byte [] audioData = receiveObject (din);

        // Save the audio data in a file
        filename = current + ".wav";
        saveObject (audioData, filename);
        body = body + audioHtml(filename);

        // Save the message body
        saveMessage (body);
        dout.writeInt(SUCCESS);

    } else if (opcode == PHOTO_AUDIO) {
        // Get the photo data
        String photoType = din.readUTF ();
        byte [] photoData = receiveObject (din);
        // Get the audio data
        byte [] audioData = receiveObject (din);

        // Save the photo data in a file
        filename = current + "." + photoType;
        saveObject (photoData, filename);
        body = body + photoHtml(filename);

        // Save the audio data in a file
        filename = current + ".wav";
        saveObject (audioData, filename);
        body = body + audioHtml(filename);

        // Save the message body
        saveMessage (body);
        dout.writeInt(SUCCESS);

    } else {
        dout.writeInt(FAILURE);
    }
    dout.flush();
```

```java
        dout.close();
        din.close();
        in.close();
        out.close();
    }

    private byte [] receiveObject (DataInputStream din)
                                    throws IOException {
        int length = din.readInt();
        byte [] buf = new byte [length];
        din.readFully (buf);
        return buf;
    }

    private void saveObject (byte [] data, String name)
                                    throws IOException {
        FileOutputStream fout =
            new FileOutputStream(fileroot + name);
        fout.write(data, 0, data.length);
        fout.flush ();
        fout.close ();
    }

    private void saveMessage (String body)
                            throws IOException {
        body = body + "<hr/>";
        FileWriter writer =
            new FileWriter (fileroot + "entries.html", true);
        writer.write(body, 0, body.length());
        writer.flush ();
        writer.close ();
    }

    private String photoHtml (String filename) {
        return "<img src=\"" + webroot + filename +
                "\"/>" + "<br/>";
    }

    private String audioHtml (String filename) {
        return "<a href=\"" + webroot + filename +
            "\">" + "Audio file (wav format)</a>" + "<br/>";
    }

    private String readTextFile (String name)
                            throws IOException {
        StringBuffer result = new StringBuffer ();
        FileReader reader =
```

```
            new FileReader (fileroot + name);

      char [] buf = new char [256];
      int i = 0;
      while ( (i = reader.read(buf)) != -1 ) {
         result.append(buf, 0, i);
      }
      reader.close();
      return result.toString ();
   }
}
```

Summary

In this chapter, we covered the basics of the MMAPI and its implementation on Nokia devices. After studying the two example applications, you should be able to add multimedia playback and audio/video capturing features to your own application.

chapter

10

The Bluetooth API

Understand basic Bluetooth concepts and use Bluetooth API for application communication.

Earlier chapters of this book covered data connectivity and networking in great detail and showed that mobile devices can be members of the worldwide IP space without limitations. It is possible to transmit data between a client handset and a server and between two handsets, and even to have the handset play the role of a server.

The J2ME application developer can choose between HTTP and HTTPS, SMS and MMS, or even sockets, to realize a network-aware client for handsets. With this portfolio of different technologies and transports, it is possible to develop a wide range of applications, from multiuser games and entertainment applications to vertical solutions in the enterprise domain.

The treatment so far has not cared about the physical distance between the endpoints. When connected to the Internet, it often does not matter if the client and server are located in the same room or are spread across the world.

Bluetooth technology delivers a local solution on a more human scale, when an application needs to interact with devices up to about 10 meters apart. It offers lower latency and higher bandwidth than mobile users achieve using their 2.5G or 3G data services, and the user is not billed separately for the data traffic. The following topics are covered in this chapter:

- **Introduction to Bluetooth wireless technology:** explains the fundamental technology and potential of Bluetooth technology in general.

- **Introduction to the Bluetooth API for Java:** explains the Bluetooth API for Java (JABWT, JSR 82) and shows how to use this framework to develop applications.

- **Example Bluetooth application:** our sample Bluetooth application displays the status of the current Bluetooth environment.

- **Nokia development tool support:** discusses Bluetooth emulation support in the Nokia Series 40 Developer Platform 2.0 SDK and issues related to Bluetooth application testing.

After reading this chapter, you will know what Bluetooth is all about and how to include Bluetooth support in your mobile applications.

Introduction to Bluetooth Wireless Technology

Bluetooth defines an open wireless standard for short-range communication among two or more devices. The initial push to define Bluetooth came from the handset and (later) consumer electronics industry, which tried to find better ways to connect devices without the need for more cables and mechanical socket definitions. The founding members of the initial Bluetooth SIG (Special Interest Group) are Ericsson, Intel, IBM, Nokia, and Toshiba. The current membership lists more than 1,000 companies and is still growing.

During the standardization process, it became clear that the technology could be used for more than just cable replacement, and the standard now includes many optional features allowing implementations to differentiate. By combining sets of features in well-defined *profiles*, the standard ensures interoperability between implementations from different vendors.

Depending on the power class, the devices are able to operate in a maximum distance range between 0.10m and 100m, with 10m the most common. Bluetooth offers a maximum data throughput of 1 Mbps using a full duplex transmission with Time-Division Duplex (TDD). Bluetooth uses four physical channels. Two physical channels are used for communicating between devices, a third channel is used for discovering devices, and the fourth one is used for connecting Bluetooth devices.

The signal transmission on each physical radio channel is divided into smaller time units called *slots*. A Bluetooth device transmits its data in packets that are positioned in these slots. The devices that are connected in a Bluetooth network are granted so-called physical links on top of one physical channel. These physical links are the basic transport mechanism that enable higher level logical transport and logical link infrastructure, which is used by the Bluetooth network stack and finally by the application. Each slot can be assigned to a different logical link, or if an application needs more bandwidth, it can be assigned more than one slot in a larger sequence. Each logical link can be used by more than one Bluetooth application when communicating with another device.

The Bluetooth standard supports the transmission of real-time multimedia signals (audio) in parallel to data services. However, this feature is not accessible using JSR-82 (which is the Bluetooth API for Java), and we do not cover it in this chapter.

Bluetooth operates in the unlicensed ISM band at 2.4 GHz (the same band used by WiFi 802.11g), hopping 1,600 times per second among 79 frequencies inside the given band using binary FM modulation. Data integrity is provided through Forward Error Correcting (FEC), Header Error Check (HEC), or Cyclic Error Check (CRC).

Bluetooth devices come in three different power classes (Table 10–1), allowing device designers to balance working range (up to 100m) and power consumption (as little as 1mW). Most devices currently available are Class 2

Table 10–1 Operating Range Varies Depending on the Power Class

Power Class	Transmission Power Rating	Maximum Range
1	100mW (20 dBm)	100m
2	2.5mW (4 dBm)	10m
3	1mW (0 dBm)	0.10m

devices, and since power consumption is of great concern, most mobile devices like handsets are likely to remain so.

With its feature set, Bluetooth sits between IrDA (< 1m, 9600 bps to 16 Mbps) and WiFi (< 100m, 54 Mbps). Since the frequency band of 2.4GHz is globally available, license free, Bluetooth equipment works worldwide. The same band is used for other purposes, including WiFi 802.11b/g, so the Bluetooth standard has been developed with potential interference in mind. A Bluetooth network is still operable even if intermittent interference with other signals occurs.

TIP

A connection using Bluetooth wireless technology is still operable, but transmission speed of all devices involved may degrade dramatically if a WLAN device (IEEE 802.11b, IEEE 802.11g) or a 2.4GHz-based DECT phone is actively operating at the same place and time.

Piconets

Bluetooth arranges single nodes in a dynamic ad hoc network, called a *piconet*, that shares a Bluetooth physical channel. Each node of the piconet carries a unique 48-bit address, very similar to a device-specific MAC address and assigned by the manufacturer from a range controlled by the IEEE Registration Authority. An active member of the piconet gets a temporary 3-bit address (AM_ADDR) that is used in the header of the packet to indicate to which slave the packet is sent. This AM_ADDR should not be confused with the hardcoded 48-bit Bluetooth device address (BD_ADDR).

TIP

To check the Bluetooth device address on a Bluetooth-enabled Nokia handset, type *#2820#.

Each piconet includes one master device, which transmits a piconet-specific clock signal, and up to seven active slave nodes, which synchronize to this signal (see Figure 10–1). The frequency-hopping scheme is determined by the

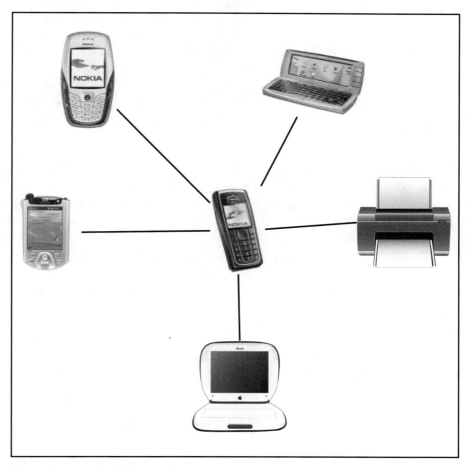

Figure 10–1 A typical piconet with one master in the center and several devices connected as slaves.

Bluetooth device address of the master, and the phase is determined by the Bluetooth clock of the master.

The physical channel in a piconet acts as a transport for one or more logical links. These links could work synchronously, asynchronously, or isochronously between master and one slave (unicast) or between master and all slaves (broadcast). While all slaves are connected with the master using the wireless physical link, it is not possible to connect single slaves directly with each other. Thus, data flows only between the slaves and the master but not directly between slaves. Any device can assume master or slave roles at a certain period of time.

The master can route data between the slaves within a piconet, but the master has to take care of the needed communication and data buffering: routing takes places completely at the application level. This way, any device can route between piconets by connecting to two or more different piconets at once. Such router device is not mandatory to be the master in one of the piconets since a slave can try to connect to specific devices providing at least one specific set of Bluetooth features.

It is possible to run different piconets in the same physical area using a different physical channel and master (clock) to create a *scatternet*. Devices may belong to more than one piconet, but a device can act as a master for only one piconet at a time.

In Figure 10–2, you see different piconets in action. Each Bluetooth device is shown as a node. Node A is the master of one piconet with nodes B, C, D, and E as slaves. Node E is also part of another piconet with node F as the master. Node D, a slave in one piconet, is the master of yet another piconet formed with node J. Node K is currently not connected to any other node, and its device discovery will not find any device, since it is not in the range of the other nodes.

Note that in a piconet, it is necessary for the master device to be within range of all slave devices, but it is not necessary for all slave devices to be within range of each other. For example, in Figure 10–2, nodes B and E could be too far apart to reliably communicate with each other as long as they can each reliably communicate with node A.

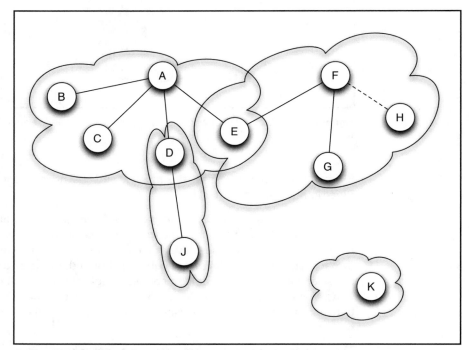

Figure 10–2 It is possible to run various independent piconets in the same area, forming a scatternet.

A connection may be in *normal* mode, *hold* mode, *sniff* mode, or *park* mode. After setup, the connection operates in normal mode and data can be transmitted. In hold mode (currently not supported in Nokia devices), the connection is put on hold for a certain period of time. In sniff mode, data is exchanged only in certain negotiated time intervals to save power consumption. On Nokia devices, sniff mode gets entered if no data is exchanged for 15 consecutive seconds (eventually in the future reduced to 5.2s). Nokia uses a sniff interval of 0.5s. If data transmission is resumed, the device switches back to normal mode instantly. Park mode (currently not supported on Nokia devices) is important if there is a need to communicate with more than seven slave devices. Up to 255 devices could be handled in a piconet, but only seven devices are allowed to be active at any given time. Each active slave device uses a temporary 3-bit AM_ADDR (active member address). The AM_ADDR is only valid as long as the slave is active on the channel. A parked device looses its AM_ADDR, which then could be used to communicate with another device in the piconet. Each device also has a fixed Bluetooth device address (BD_ADDR).

Bluetooth Control Center

The JSR 82 specification defines a Bluetooth Control Center (BCC), which manages the Bluetooth environment for all JSR 82-related clients. The BCC

- Manages security configuration and settings of the device.

- Keeps a list of known or preknown devices and trusted devices.

- May keep additional lists for cached devices, paired devices, and authenticated devices.

The JSR 82 specification defines known or preknown devices as devices with which the local device frequently communicates (DiscoveryAgent.PREKNOWN). Devices that were found via a previous inquiry are cached devices (DiscoveryAgent.CACHED). Paired devices are devices that have exchanged a PIN with the local device and for which link keys are created and stored on the local device. Authenticated devices are devices that have been authenticated.

NOTE The list of paired devices, although available in the native environment, is not accessible from the current implementation of the JSR 82 API on Series 40 devices.

The JSR does not specify an API to access the BCC. On Nokia devices, the BCC is implemented in the device firmware as a black box. There is no API available to access the BCC directly. All interaction between the BCC and the user, such as the process of pairing, is transparent to the Bluetooth application. The application either gets an exception or can proceed.

Security

Bluetooth provides a layered security approach: *pairing* (a part of *authentication*), *authorization*, and *encryption*. The first time two devices attempt to connect to each other, the user of each device gets a message asking if the connection should be allowed. To allow the connection, both devices must use the same PIN code. Based on the PIN, each device generates link keys using cryptographic methods. In the next step, which is transparent to the user, the devices exchange the link keys for authentication as part of a challenge-response protocol. Figure 10–3 shows the pairing process in which the same PIN needs to be used on both devices.

Authentication of Bluetooth devices is based on the initial process of pairing and is only necessary the first time two devices communicate. Both devices may store the result of this process and optionally list the counterpart as a trusted device, since devices can be marked as trusted by the user in the native device user interface. The pairing process is transparent to any Bluetooth application, since it is handled by the BCC itself and is the mandatory first step before any authorization or encryption can take place.

If authentication is needed (the Bluetooth applications or the BCC or a native Bluetooth manager may activate this feature), then both devices exchange data using a challenge-response scheme: Device A sends its challenge to device B. Device B manipulates it using the internal security key (derived during pairing)

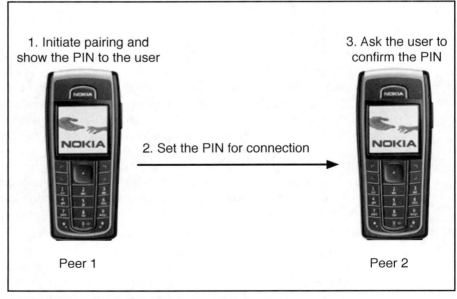

1. Initiate pairing and show the PIN to the user

3. Ask the user to confirm the PIN

2. Set the PIN for connection

Peer 1

Peer 2

Figure 10–3 Pairing uses a secret PIN to allow connection.

and sends back the result. Device A manipulates its own challenge with its internal security key. If both results are the same, device B is authenticated.

Following the successful authentication process, both devices may choose to use encryption. Again, either the BCC or the application client and/or server may activate this option. All data packets are encrypted based on the link keys resulting from a previous pairing/authentication step.

> **NOTE** Bluetooth security applies to the device, not the user of the device. Everyone who has access to the device (legitimate or stolen) has the ability to grant or deny access to it and its services. A Bluetooth connection could also use device authorization on a per-use basis. If needed, the BCC asks the user for permission before the connection request is allowed for the duration of the current session.

In short, security schemes build on each other. If authorization is used, the devices need to already be paired. The BCC makes sure that missing parameters in the actual configuration are filled. That means if a connection needs to be authenticated, but the devices are not paired yet, the BCC leads the users of both devices through the pairing process.

The Bluetooth Protocol Stack

Nokia handsets implement Bluetooth in two major components: the Bluetooth Host and Bluetooth Host Controller. The Bluetooth Host Controller Interface (HCI) sits between these two components. The Bluetooth Controller is the Bluetooth-specific hardware, including the Bluetooth radio; the HCI software connects this hardware to the system environment—it is part of the device firmware. Figure 10–4 shows typical layers in the Bluetooth hardware and firmware.

The interesting parts for application developers are the protocols implemented by the drivers that sit on top of the HCI. The first three protocols in the following list are supported in the JSR-82 implementations provided in Nokia handsets. The last one, although implemented in Nokia Series 40 devices' hardware and native software, is currently not available in the Java runtime.

- **Logical Link Control and Adaptation Protocol (L2CAP):** This is the low-level protocol that is used either directly by applications or by other higher level protocols like SDP. L2CAP is a packet-oriented multiplexing layer. All data-oriented Bluetooth protocols are built on top of L2CAP.

- **Service Discovery Protocol (SDP):** Since a real-life Bluetooth environment consists of a dynamic set of devices and services, it is important to be able to get to know the local Bluetooth environment. The SDP allows the local device to query for the services each remote device provides.

- **RFCOMM:** The RFCOMM protocol provides an emulation of a serial cable and can support multiple concurrent connections to one or more devices.

- **Object Exchange Protocol (OBEX):** This protocol allows packet-oriented data transfers between Bluetooth devices. Nokia devices support OBEX in the native environment. It is currently not available for MIDlets, since the optional API is not implemented in Nokia Devices.

The JSR 82 specification requires support for L2CAP, SDP, and RFCOMM. Java support for OBEX is optional and not currently supported by Nokia. Figure 10–4 shows additional protocols such as the Telephony Control Protocol Specification (TCS binary), which is used in non-GSM Bluetooth devices for voice and data calls. Nokia implements the Headset Profile and Handsfree Profile, which support voice calls. Since OBEX is currently not supported by means of a Java API in Nokia handsets, we do not cover the details in the following sections.

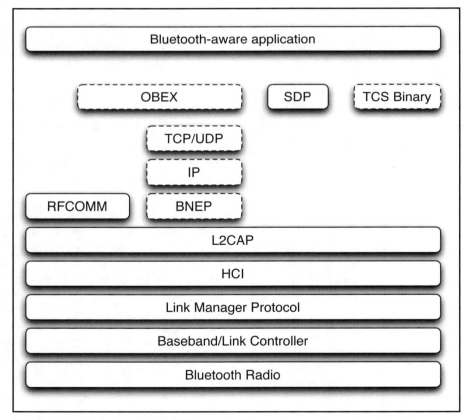

Figure 10–4 Sitting on top of the HCI layer, the Bluetooth protocol stack provides features for Bluetooth applications.

Profiles

The Bluetooth standard uses *profiles* to define vendor-neutral sets of capabilities and features for a wide variety of devices (from simple endpoints like a headphone to a full-blown home entertainment and communication system). All devices supporting a specific profile interact with each other using Bluetooth regardless of vendor. Some profiles are building blocks for other profiles; for example, the Serial Port Profile is based on and expands three different profiles.

The following list shows only some Bluetooth profiles:

- **Generic Access Profile (GAP):** This profile provides the basic features needed for all other profiles. It includes the ability to discover devices and services, establish connections between two or more nodes, and establish security. All Nokia handsets support GAP.

- **Serial Port Profile (SPP):** This profile defines a set of features needed for typical serial communication between two devices in a peer-to-peer setup. It is based on RFCOMM, SDP, and L2CAP and could be used to enable applications to use as emulated serial connection through Bluetooth. All Nokia handsets support SPP.

The following profiles are currently supported by Nokia handsets, but not supported by JSR 82, and are listed only to explain how different profiles are able to build on each other:

- **Generic Object Exchange Profile (GOEP):** This profile is based on SPP and OBEX and is suitable to exchange data objects (files, VCF cards, etc.) between devices. While this profile is supported on the native side, it is not through the JSR 82.

- **Object Push Profile (OPP):** This profile is used to exchange structured objects like address book entries and date book entries. One node acts as an OPP server and the other as an OPP client. The protocol is based on GOEP. While this profile is supported on the native side, it is not through the JSR 82.

- **File Transfer Profile (FTP):** Used to transfer files between devices. One node acts as an FTP server and the other as an FTP client. The protocol is based on GOEP.

As it can be seen, some profiles build on top of lower level profiles. SPP defines a connection between two devices using a serial connection (RFCOMM). Various profiles, such as the Headset, Fax, and LAN profiles, are based on the SPP.

After all this theoretical background, let's now get into the practical handling of Bluetooth networks for Java developers.

The Inquiry Procedure

In the networks for which most of us are accustomed to programming, configuration data (IP address, DHCP server, DNS server, Gateway address, etc.) are sufficient for communication between applications. Since a Bluetooth network follows the rules of dynamic ad hoc networks, there is no way to configure each device with a fixed set of such configuration data up front. Bluetooth devices need to exchange information about each other to set up and operate in a piconet before any data transmission is possible.

The *inquiry* procedure defined in the Bluetooth specification provides the protocol necessary to discover devices within the range of the inquiring device. The information gained through the inquiry process lets systems communicate with each other without prior knowledge about each other. During this process, an application collects the available Bluetooth addresses and the *class of device* (CoD) of potential counterparts. We explain CoD in a bit.

The inquiry process is asymmetrical. After activating the Bluetooth feature, the device is ready to find its counterparts via explicit inquiry requests using a reserved physical Bluetooth channel. Available devices that are configured to be available are discoverable devices.

Since a new device might meet quite a few other Bluetooth devices in the active range, it is possible to run either a global inquiry or a more focused inquiry if the needed service is already very clear. The *General Inquiry Access Code* (GIAC) looks for and makes itself visible to any nearby Bluetooth device. A device in GIAC mode stays in this mode until either the user or the application managing the Bluetooth stack chooses to switch to another mode.

The *Limited Inquiry Access Code* (LIAC) inquiry looks for nearby Bluetooth devices that are in LIAC discoverability mode. LIAC can be enabled only for a limited period of time. This mode could be used, for example, if all players of an interactive game using Bluetooth are starting the game at around the same time. Depending on the implementation, the device either switches back to the prior mode after a limited period of time or stays in LIAC until the modes gets changed again or the MIDlet terminates.

TIP   A device that has enabled LIAC discoverability mode can be discovered by both LIAC and GIAC inquiries.

LIAC inquiry mode is often significantly faster than GIAC inquiry, especially if there are many Bluetooth devices nearby that are in GIAC mode. Because the list of found devices that are in LIAC mode is usually shorter, the following step, service discovery, consumes considerably less time. If the previous mode was NON_DISCOVERABLE, the whole Bluetooth stack is switched off to save energy when LIAC inquiry mode times out. The Bluetooth specification mentions also the *Dedicated Inquiry Access Code* (DIAC), which is used to inquire for certain types of devices—usually from the same manufacturer—to speed up the whole process. DIAC is not implemented in Nokia devices.

Class of Device and Service Discovery

The most important information about a device is defined through the class of device (CoD), which tells everyone around about the types of service that are supported. The CoD defines a major and a minor device class. Following are the major device classes defined by the "Assigned Numbers" section of the Bluetooth specification (*http://www.bluetooth.org*):

- Miscellaneous
- Computer (desktop, PDA, server, etc.)
- Phone (handset, cordless, modem, etc.)
- LAN (networking node)
- Audio/Video (headset, speaker, video display, etc.)
- Peripheral (mouse, keyboard, etc.)
- Imaging (printer, scanner, camera, etc.)
- Uncategorized

For each major device class, there is a set of minor device class attributes that define the given device in greater detail. The following minor class entries are available for the major device class phone:

- Uncategorized
- Cellular
- Cordless
- Smart phone
- Wired modem or voice gateway
- Common ISDN address

TIP

The major device class for Nokia handsets is *phone* and the minor device class for Nokia handsets is *cellular*.

For the major device class LAN, the minor device class entry passes back the actual utilization factor of the device:

- Fully available
- 17% utilized

- 33% utilized

- 50% utilized

- 67% utilized

- 83% utilized

- 99% utilized

- no service available

The minor device class information could be used to select the networking node to connect to according to the actual utilization. If an application running on a Nokia handset needs to stream data to a LAN node, it could poll the minor device number until the utilization drops to a certain level to ensure that the data transmission will be handled without delays to reduce power consumption.

To specify the set of features provided by a Bluetooth device, the standard defines *services*. The services can be used to give an even better picture about the device functionality. The major service classes defined by the Bluetooth specification are as follows:

- Limited Discoverable Mode

- Positioning (GPS, mouse, etc.)

- Networking (LAN, router, etc.)

- Rendering (printer, speaker)

- Capturing (scanner, microphone)

- Object Transfer (structured data source/target)

- Audio (speaker, microphone, headset)

- Telephony (telephone, modem, headset)

- Information (Web server, other servers)

Some service classes could fall into different major classes, so it is important to check for all potential results. A Bluetooth device could use service discovery to query all available devices in the area. Service discovery–related classes are based on the Service Discovery Protocol (SDP).

Java API for Bluetooth

Java programmers can work with Bluetooth devices using JSR 82, an optional API for CLDC-based devices developed under the Java Community Process (JCP). The JSR 82 defines the Java API for Bluetooth—also known as JABWT—

which provides a unified programming environment to access the Bluetooth stack based on Bluetooth specification version 1.1.

Nokia Series 40 Developer Platform 2.0 devices like the Nokia 6230, Nokia Series 60 Developer Platform 2.0 devices, Nokia Series 80 Developer Platform 2.0 devices, and Nokia Series 90 Developer Platform 2.0 devices support JSR 82 (currently without support for OBEX). JABWT adds the classes `javax.bluetooth` and optionally `javax.obex` to the list of available packages.

With JSR 82 in place, it is possible to realize portable MIDlets across a range of devices without the need to reprogram the Bluetooth modules for each device. Besides playing an important role for J2ME (with MIDP and CLDC being a part of this level), JSR-82 has created a lot of interest also in the J2SE camp, and there are ongoing efforts to add JSR 82 support for J2SE (JSR 197). In fact, JSR 82 has been developed to be fundamentally compatible with other Java editions too.

In this section, we will cover the details of the JABWT. We first discuss the Bluetooth initialization process. Then, we cover the Bluetooth connections, device management, and service discovery APIs. A Bluetooth application typically makes use of all those APIs. In the last section "Put Them Together," we use a simple example to show how to pass application data from one Bluetooth device to another. For the impatient readers, you can start from the "Put Them Together" section to see the big picture and then drill down to the APIs.

Bluetooth Initialization

Before any activity can be started using the Bluetooth transport, the underlying stack must be initialized. Depending on the given device, the initialization, or at least part of it, can be defined by using the Bluetooth-specific configuration utility, which is used to enable or disable the Bluetooth stack and to define security options. On the Nokia 6230, for example, choose the Settings menu and then Bluetooth, as in Figure 10–5.

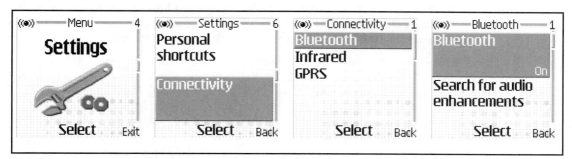

Figure 10–5 Activating the Bluetooth stack on a Series 40 handset.

The Bluetooth submenu allows you to activate the Bluetooth layer, search for audio enhancements (Nokia Bluetooth headset, for example), check for active and paired devices, and define the overall Bluetooth status of the handset (Figure 10–6).

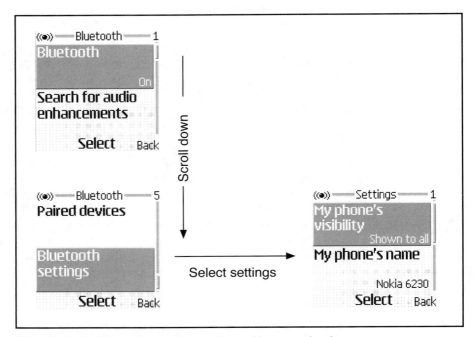

Figure 10–6 The Bluetooth submenu usually provides several options.

If Bluetooth is switched off, the handling from inside the Java application depends on the Platform implementation. In a Series 60 device, a dialog is displayed, asking the user if Bluetooth should be turned on. Series 40 handles this situation differently. If Bluetooth is off, any access to Bluetooth will throw an exception. In this case, the application should inform the user to allow the MIDlet application to turn Bluetooth on in the native UI, as can be seen in the screenshots above, and then to come back to the application.

The Bluetooth configuration menu is also part of the BCC, which is part of the JABWT specification. The BCC makes sure that Bluetooth applications do not interfere with each other. There is no API call available in JABWT to give any application direct access to the BCC. Depending on the implementation, there might be a vendor-specific additional API that provides this feature, but there is no BCC-aware API available on Nokia handsets. The BCC is also responsible for providing access to the read-only device properties. It is possible to read those properties on a Nokia handset, as you will see later on in our Bluetooth demo application.

TIP

Always catch exceptions when using Bluetooth from Java. If the Bluetooth stack is switched off by the user the application may not be able to access the network. Pass on an informative error message to the user.

Bluetooth Connections

With the Bluetooth stack initialized, we can set up connections to and from the devices. Connection is a key concept in JABWT. We can transport both application data and Bluetooth metadata (e.g., device management and discovery information) over these connections.

JABWT leverages the connection interfaces and factory classes in the J2ME Generic Connection Framework (see Chapter 7, "Data Connectivity") for Bluetooth-based data communication. It introduces two new connection types for L2CAP connectivity (`L2CAPConnection` and `L2CAPConnectionNotifier`) but uses an existing connection type for RFCOMM and OBEX (`StreamConnection`). In order to obtain the instances of those `Connection` objects, we need to pass URL connection strings with the `btl2cap://` and `btspp://` schemes, respectively, to the `Connector.open()` factory method. Similar to other data connections in the GCF, the Bluetooth connections can be in the server or client mode depending on the format of the connection URL string.

Note that the server functionality of an application is isolated from the actual working mode the device is running in a piconet: A piconet master could be an application server or the client, and a piconet slave could also fill both roles. It is important to realize that any Bluetooth device that initiates a piconet will be granted permission to be the master. Such a master could still very well play the role of a client in the application level. Each device acts in three different levels: Bluetooth connection level (initiator or acceptor), application level (client or server), and piconet level (master or slave). The initiator of a connection becomes master by default, whereas the acceptor is automatically a slave. If three or more devices are involved, it is reasonable to place the application server on the piconet master. It is possible on certain devices to switch the master and slave roles. To be flexible, an application should also support being a client as well as a server if possible.

Server Connection

To set up a server connection that eventually will be a Bluetooth device service, use the connection URL scheme `btl2cap://` with the target `localhost` to specify the local device and the service string.

```
L2CAPConnectionNotifier server = (L2CAPConnectionNotifier)
  Connector.open ("btl2cap://localhost:0123456789AB")
```

The service string contains both the service UUID (universally unique identifier) and an optional service name—a readable description for the service. The UUID is a 128-bit unsigned integer that uniquely identifies the service provided via this `Connection` in the network. All Bluetooth services have a common base UUID value `0x0000000000001000800000805F9B34FB`. For each service, there is a 16-bit or 32-bit short UUID that can be added to the base value to derive a full length 128-bit UUID for this service. The `UUID` class in the JABWT helps us create long UUIDs from short ones and compare UUIDs. Table 10–2 shows some of the short UUIDs currently in use.

Client Connection

The following code shows how to set up a connection from a client device to a server. Due to the dynamic nature of Bluetooth networks, the server address in the URL string changes with every network, device and service. Fortunately, we rarely need to figure out the server address manually. As we will see later in this chapter, the address is typically automatically obtained in the service discovery process.

```
StreamConnection btcon = (StreamConnection)
   Connector.open ("btspp://0123456789AB:5");

StreamConnection btcon = (StreamConnection)
   Connector.open ("btspp://0123456789AB:5;
      authenticate=true;authorize=false;encrypt=true");

L2CAPConnection btcon = (L2CAPConnection)
   Connector.open ("btl2cap://0123456789AB:1001");
```

Table 10–2 UUIDs in the 16-bit Short Format

Service Name	UUID(16-bit)	Profile
SerialPort	0x1101	Generic Access Profile
LANAccessUsingPPP	0x1102	
DialupNetworking	0x1103	Dial-up Networking Profile
IrMCSync	0x1104	Synchronization Profile
OBEXObjectPush	0x1105	Object Push Profile
OBEXFileTransfer	0x1106	File Transfer Profile
IrMCSyncCommand	0x1107	Synchronization Profile

Table 10–2 UUIDs in the 16-bit Short Format (continued)

Service Name	UUID(16-bit)	Profile
Headset	0x1108	Generic Access Profile
CordlessTelephony	0x1109	Cordless Telephony Profile
AudioSource	0x110A	
AudioSink	0x110B	
A/V_RemoteControlTarget	0x110C	Audio/Video Control Profile
A/V_RemoteControl	0x110E	Audio/Video Control Profile
VideoConferencing	0x110F	Video Conferencing Profile
Intercom	0x1110	Intercom Profile
Fax	0x1111	Fax Profile
HeadsetAudioGateway	0x1112	Generic Access Profile
WAP	0x1113	Interoperability Requirements for Bluetooth as a WAP
Handsfree	0x111E	Handsfree Profile
BasicPrinting	0x1122	Basic Printing Profile
PrintingStatus	0x1123	Basic Printing Profile
HumanInterfaceDeviceService	0x1124	Human Interface Device
Common_ISDN_Access	0x1128	CAPI Message Transport Protocol
VideoConferencingGW	0x1129	Video Conferencing Profile (VCP)
Audio/Video	0x112C	Video Conferencing Profile (VCP)
GenericNetworking	0x1201	
GenericFileTransfer	0x1202	
GenericAudio	0x1203	
GenericTelephony	0x1204	

Connection URL Parameters

According to the GCF specification, the `;name=value` strings appended to the connection URL are the optional parameters for this connection. The connection URL parameters available in JABWT are listed in Table 10-3.

Table 10–3 Bluetooth Connection URL Parameters

Parameter Name	Value	Server or Client	Description
authenticate	true/false	Server and client	Specifies whether the remote device needs to be authenticated via the BCC before the connection can be established.
encrypt	true/false	Server and client	Specifies whether the active link needs to be encrypted.
authorize	true/false	Server only	Specifies whether the connection to the local device needs to be authorized via the BCC before the service could be used.
name	A String value	Server only	Defines the `ServiceName` attribute (see later).
master	true/false	Server and client	Defines if the local device needs to be the connection master. If a device wants to be a master, the URL needs to add the parameter `master=true`. Note that `master=false` does not mean the device wants to be a slave; it means the device does not care about its role.

The BCC always handles the layered security. If a connection specifies encryption and there is no explicit parameter for authentication, authentication gets activated implicitly. A `BluetoothConnectionException` is thrown for invalid parameter combinations and failed security steps.

TIP

If you use L2CAP connections, the Protocol Service Multiplexer (PSM) value needs to be in the range between 0x1001 and 0xFFFF, and it must also be an *odd* value. The PSM is based on ISO 3309 extension mechanism for address fields.

Device Management and Discovery

As we have learned, a key characteristic of Bluetooth network is that its device membership is dynamic. At different times, there are different devices playing different roles in the network. For a Bluetooth application, it is crucial to get information about its neighbor before it can communicate with them over data connections. The JABWT provides an API for device management and discovery.

Get Information about the Local Device

The `LocalDevice` class is used to retrieve and manage the Bluetooth-specific parameters (address and name) and services of the local device. Gaining access to the `LocalDevice` class is often the first step in Bluetooth applications. Since there is only one local device in any Bluetooth application, the `LocalDevice` class follows the singleton pattern. It provides a static factory method `getLocalDevice()` to get access to the `LocalDevice` singleton object.

```
public static LocalDevice getLocalDevice ()
```

The `LocalDevice` class provides public methods to access the device's name, Bluetooth address, and other named Bluetooth properties. As already mentioned, Bluetooth devices use a 6-byte Bluetooth address presented as a 12-character hex string. Table 10-4 lists the named Bluetooth runtime properties that can be queried via the `getProperty()` method. Those properties indicate the capability of the JABWT runtime and hence are important for developing portable applications.

```
String getFriendlyName ()
String getBluetoothAddress ()
String getProperty (String name)
```

An important parameter of the Bluetooth stack is the discovery mode of the device. The `LocalDevice` class allows us to specify whether this device is visible to others and its discovery mode.

```
boolean setDiscoverable (int mode)
int getDiscoverable ()
```

The discovery mode parameter can take one of the following static constant values in the `DiscoveryAgent` class.

- The `NOT_DISCOVERABLE` value indicates that the local device is hidden to all external devices.

- The `GIAC` value sets the device to a permanent (until the next change of discovery status) visible state.

Table 10–4 The JABWT Provides Properties to Access Current Status Values at Runtime

Property Name	Nokia 6230 Value	Description
`bluetooth.api.version`		The version of the JABWT (not the Bluetooth Specification)
`bluetooth.connected.inquiry.scan`	false	Can the device respond to an asynchronous inquiry scan while it has established an active link to another device?
`bluetooth.connected.page.scan`	false	Can the device handle a new connection from another device while it is connected to another device?
`bluetooth.connected.inquiry`	false	Can the local device start an inquiry while it is connected to another device?
`bluetooth.connected.page`	false	Is it possible to connect to another device while there is already an active connection to a remote device?
`bluetooth.master.switch`	true	Is a switch of the master/slave status allowed?
`bluetooth.connected.devices.max`	1	Maximum of connected devices
`bluetooth.sd.attr.retrievable.max`		Maximum of attributes to be retrieved in each `ServiceRecord` (no default)
`bluetooth.l2cap.receiveMTU.max`	672	Maximum MTU size in bytes for L2CAP connections
`bluetooth.sd.trans.max`	1	Maximum of concurrent `ServiceDiscovery` transactions

- The LIAC value allows us to let the device be discoverable either for a specific time window (the specification asks for one minute) and then fall back to the prior state or until the mode is explicitly changed by the application. A device that has enabled LIAC discoverability mode can be discovered by both LIAC and GIAC inquiries. After the MIDlet is terminated, the LIAC mode is automatically removed.

TIP

Series 40 uses `LIAC` mode for support of JSR 82 only. This mode currently does not have any associated time limitation. If the MIDlet switches to `LIAC` mode, it should take care itself to leave the `LIAC` mode after some time.

Finally, the `LocalDevice` class provides access to the `DiscoveryAgent`, which is used to discover other devices and services in the network, and the `ServiceRecord` associated with a server mode `Connection` on the local device. We will cover `DiscoveryAgent` and `ServiceRecord` later in this chapter.

```
DiscoveryAgent getDiscoveryAgent ()
ServiceRecord getRecord (Connection notifier)
void updateRecord (ServiceRecord sr)
```

Discover Devices in the Network

After the status of the local device is known, it is possible to check out the Bluetooth neighborhood for devices. We can use `DiscoveryAgent` and `DiscoveryListener` for this purpose. The nonblocking `startInquiry()` method in the `DiscoveryAgent` class can be used to start looking for devices.

```
// initialize the JABWT stack
lDevice = LocalDevice.getLocalDevice();

// store the reference to the discovery agent (singleton)
lDiscoveryAgent = lDevice.getDiscoveryAgent();

public void startInquiry () {
   // start a Bluetooth inquiry (GIAC mode) by using
   // a DiscoveryListener class to handle the callbacks.
   try {
     lDiscoveryAgent.startInquiry(DiscoveryAgent.GIAC,
                                  new Listener());
   } catch (BluetoothStateException e) {
     // handle exception as appropriate
   }
}
```

For each remote device found in the discovery process, the `DiscoveryAgent` calls the `deviceDiscovered()` method in the `DiscoveryListener` class. A `RemoteDevice` object representing the discovered remote device is passed to the `deviceDiscovered()` method as a call parameter. We must implement our own `DiscoveryListener` to handle the discovered remote devices.

```
public class Listener implements DiscoveryListener {
```

```
// ... ...

   public void deviceDiscovered(RemoteDevice remoteDevice,
                                DeviceClass deviceClass) {
   // process information about the remote device
   }
}
```

The Bluetooth stack has an additional way to handle previously discovered devices. If there had been a connection between devices in the recent past, information about that remote device might be stored in a cache. Devices used on a frequent basis are considered PREKNOWN (currently not implemented in Nokia devices). The list of CACHED devices shows all devices found during the last inquiry and this feature is supported on Series 40 devices.

Depending on the actual implementation, the result of a former startInquiry() method might end up in the cache of the local device. You can use a call to retrieveDevices(int option) with the option CACHED or PREKNOWN to get access to those devices

TIP

The list of CACHED devices shows all found devices from a prior inquiry inside the JSR 82 API. Any devices found through an inquiry process handled outside the JSR 82 API (the native UI, or Series 60 native applications) will not be listed here.

Get Information about Remote Devices

The class RemoteDevice is used to handle information about a remote device. As we have seen, when a remote device is discovered, the DiscoveryAgent instantiates a corresponding RemoteDevice object and passes it to the deviceDiscovered() callback method in DiscoveryListener. We can also instantiate RemoteDevice objects directly from any Bluetooth Connection object. The getRemoteDevice() factory method in the RemoteDevice class simply obtains the object that represents the device on the other end of the Connection.

```
public static RemoteDevice getRemoteDevice (Connection c)
```

TIP

Currently, Series 40 does not support point-to-multipoint connections; therefore, concurrent connections to different devices are not possible. If you need to connect to a device, you must close the former connection first.

After getting the RemoteDevice object, it is possible to retrieve its device name and Bluetooth address.

```
String getFriendlyName ()
String getBluetoothAddress ()
```

We can use the `RemoteDevice` object to set up security permission for the remote device to consume services provided by the local device.

```
// Checks if the remote device is allowed to
// access the local service provided by the connection
boolean authorize (Connection c)

// Checks if the remote device is already authorized
boolean isAuthorized ()

// Authenticates this remote device
boolean Authenticate ()

// Checks of the remote device is already authenticated
boolean isAuthenticated ()

// Turns encryption on or off for the connection
boolean encrypt (Connection c, boolean on)

// Checks if the encryption is turned on
boolean isEncrypted ()

// Checks if this is a trusted device according to the BCC
boolean isTrustedDevice ()
```

NOTE Be aware that any method of the `RemoteDevice` class that throws an `IOException` may also block.

Service Management and Discovery

Each Bluetooth device can serve or consume services provided by other devices. All application data communication happens at the service level. After the details of the local and remote devices are known, the next step is to gain access to the services provided by any of the devices. The service management and discovery API in JABWT works with the GCF to register services when a server connection is opened and to discover client connection URL strings to any service in the local network.

Service Records

The Bluetooth API uses a *Service Discovery Database* (SDDB) to store the available single-device service records, and while it may not be a "real" database (implementation details are not specified in the specification), it just needs to pass back `ServiceRecord` objects to the caller regardless of the internal structure of the stored data. The SDDB consists of `ServiceRecords`, each of which holds one or several `DataElements`. The `DataElements` describe the nature and content of the service record. Each `DataElement` has a corresponding integer attribute ID, which defines the type and semantics of the `DataElement`. The `ServiceRecord` object's `getAttributeValue()` method retrieves the `DataElement` based on the attribute ID. Some attribute IDs are defined in the specification (see Table 10–5). A key method in the `ServiceRecord` class is the `getConnectionURL()` method, which returns the URL connection string for this service. Upon discovering the `ServiceRecord`, the client device can open a Bluetooth connection to the service using that URL string and start to consume the service.

Table 10–5 Reserved Attribute IDs Defining the Type and Semantics of the DataElement

Attribute ID	Attribute Name	Attribute Type
0x0000	ServiceRecordHandle	32-bit unsigned integer
0x0001	ServiceClassIDList	UUID sequence in DataElements
0x0002	ServiceRecordState	32-bit unsigned integer
0x0003	ServiceID	UUID
0x0004	ProtocolDescriptorList	Sequence of UUIDs and parameters in DataElements
0x0005	BrowserGroupList	UUID sequence in DataElements
0x0006	LanguagebaseAttributeIDList	Sequence of DataElements holding language details
0x0007	ServiceInfoTimeToLive	32-bit unsigned integer
0x0008	ServiceAvailability	8-bit unsigned integer
0x0009	BluetoothProfileDescriptorList	UUID sequence in DataElements
0x000a	DocumentationURL	String
0x000b	ClientExecutableURL	String
0x000c	IconURL	String

Each Bluetooth device might support a variety of different services. Information used to advertise a service gets stored in the SDDB. The combination of all services is called a service pattern and is defined by a list of UUIDs for that device.

Register Service for Server Connections

Before a service can be discovered by clients, the server needs to register it locally. Note that any device can be a client or a server or can switch between the role of client and server. Thus, each application needs to register its services internally before they are visible to other peers.

We can use the following steps to register a service locally. A call to `Connector.open()` creates a new `ServiceRecord` and sets initial attributes if a server URL is used. The call returns a `StreamConnectionNotifier` object. We can optionally modify the content of the `ServiceRecord` using the `LocalDevice` object. Then call `acceptAndOpen()` and wait for a external client to discover the service and connect. Finally, we call `notifier.close()` to close the service when we're done.

```
StreamConnectionNotifier notifier;

ServiceRecord servicerecord;
LocalDevice device;

// create a new initial ServiceRecord
notifier = (StreamConnectionNotifier)Connector.open(url);

// get the new ServiceRecord
device = LocalDevice.getLocalDevice();
servicerecord = device.getRecord(notifier);

// now manipulate the record according to your needs

// block for incoming client requests
StreamConnection con = (StreamConnection)
notifier.acceptAndOpen();

// wait ... ...

// finally clean up
notifier.close ();
```

Discover Services

There are at least two ways for a client device to discover services. The first method is to use the `DiscoveryAgent` and `DiscoveryListener` classes to search services asynchronously using a set of UUIDs. This process is very similar to the remote device discovery process we described before. The searchServices() method in the DiscoveryAgent class starts the search.

```
int searchServices (int[] attrSet, UUID[] uuidSet,
                RemoteDevice rd, DiscoveryListener dl)
```

The searchServices() method looks for services on a specific RemoteDevice, which has been discovered earlier. We pass in the list of UUIDs to be searched in the uuidSet array. If the attrSet array is null, the ServiceRecords returned from the search only contain the DataElements with the default attribute IDs, which are attribute IDs from 0x0000 to 0x0004. Otherwise, all DataElements corresponding to the IDs in attrSet will be retrieved in addition to the default ones.

The method searchServices() returns immediately (i.e., nonblocking) with a transaction ID. If you need to stop a running discovery, you can call cancelServiceSearch() and pass in the transaction ID. Once the search is completed, the DiscoveryAgent passes the resultant ServiceRecords to the servicesDiscovered() callback method in the DisocveryListener class. We implement the servicesDiscovered() method to process the discovered services.

```java
public class Listener implements DiscoveryListener {

    // ... ...

    public void servicesDiscovered(int transId,
                                    ServiceRecord[] records) {
        for (int i=0; i < records.length; i++) {
            // Get the connection URL string
            String url = records[i].getConnectionURL ();

            // Open a client connection to the service
            // Connection c = Connector.open (url);
            // ... ...
        }
    }
}
```

The second way to discover service is to look for one and only one specific service according a UUID on all devices in the area using the method selectService() in the DiscoveryAgent class.

```
String selectService (UUID uuid, int security,
                boolean master)
```

If the method finds a match, it returns a connection URL string, which can be used in a subsequent `Connector.open()` call to set up a connection to that service. The security parameter can take static constant values from the `ServiceRecord` class: `NOAUTHENTICATE_NOENCRYPT`, `AUTHENTICATE_NOENCRYPT`, or `AUTHENTICATE_ENCRYPT`. The `master` parameter specifies whether the client must be the master of the connection. This call is blocking and it should be run in its own thread. Depending on the actual implementation (the JSR 82 specification is not clear), the result might vary and take a long time to finalize, so this method should be used carefully.

Put Them Together

Now, we covered the basic concepts and APIs in the JABWT. It is time to put everything together and pass some real data from between Bluetooth devices!

Server

First, we have to set up the server application that accepts and responds to network requests. It primarily involves opening a server connection and then waiting for connections in a loop. Once an incoming connection is received, the server reads the data and processes it. The service record is automatically created when we open the connection. In the following example, we also show how to manipulate the service record inside the application. It is important to run the main server code in its own thread to isolate any networking activities, which could take a while to complete, from the reminder of the application. This way, the application is still responsive to user activities.

```
public class Server {
  boolean done = false;
  LocalDevice device;
  StreamConnectionNotifier server;
  StreamConnection c;
  // ... ...

  public void Server() {
    try {
      // initialize the JABWT stack
      device = LocalDevice.getLocalDevice();
      device.setDiscoverable(DiscoveryAgent.GIAC);

      // start the server code in its own thread
      Thread t = new Thread (this);
      t.start();
    } catch (BluetoothStateException e) {
      e.printStackTrace();
    }
  }
}
```

```
// the server code runs in its own thread
public void run() {
  // human readable name of this service
  String ServiceName = "My BT service";

  // unique UUID for this service.
  UUID uuid = new UUID(0x1202);

  // this is similar to "server socket"
  StreamConnectionNotifier server = null;

  // connection to remote device.
  // similar to "client socket"
  StreamConnection c = null;
  try {
    // Create a server connection object
    // (SPP) in the URL (btspp) and our UUID
    // and friendly service name
    server = (StreamConnectionNotifier)Connector.open(
        "btspp://localhost:" +
        uuid.toString() +
        ";name="+ServiceName);

    // Retrieve the service record which is just
    // created and add one DataElement
    ServiceRecord srec = device.getRecord(server);
    DataElement DE =
        new DataElement(DataElement.DATSEQ);
    // add SerialPort
    DE.addElement(new DataElement(DataElement.UUID,
                            new UUID(0x1101)));
    // add V1
    DE.addElement(new DataElement(DataElement.INT_8,1));
    srec.setAttributeValue(9, DE);
    // update the service record
    device.updateRecord (srec);
  } catch (Exception e) {
    e.printStackTrace();
    return;
  }
  // The server loop
  while(!done) {
    try {
      // start accepting client connection.
      // This method will block until a client connects
      c = server.acceptAndOpen();
```

```
            // retrieve the remote device object
            RemoteDevice rdev =
                RemoteDevice.getRemoteDevice(c);

            // obtain an input stream to the remote service
            DataInputStream in = c.openDataInputStream();

            // read in a string from the string
            String s = in.readUTF();
            log("received data :"+s);

            // work with the data ... ...

            // close current connection, wait for the next one
            c.close();
          } catch (Exception e) {
          e.printStackTrace ();
          return;
        }
      }
    }
  }
}
```

Client

The client just needs to discover the service and then connect to it. The
following example uses the selectService() method to build a connection
URL for the client connection. After the connection is established, we send data
over the server.

```
public class Client {
  public void client() {
    try {
      LocalDevice local = LocalDevice.getLocalDevice();
      DiscoveryAgent agent = local.getDiscoveryAgent();

      // Get the connection URL string
      String url = agent.selectService(
        new UUID("1234", true),
        ServiceRecord.AUTHENTICATE_NOENCRYPT, false);

      if (url != null) {
        try {
          // connect to the server
          StreamConnection scon =
              (StreamConnection) Connector.open(url);
```

```
                    OutputStream out = scon.openOutputStream();
                    out.write("hi, it is me!".getBytes());
                    out.flush();
                    out.close();
                    scon.close();
                } catch (IOException e) {
                    e.printStackTrace ();
                }
            }
        } catch (BluetoothStateException b) {
            // handle exception as appropriate
        }
    }
}
```

TIP

Nokia devices will not send any data to the remote device before its internal buffer is filled or when the `flush()` method is called. The `close()` method will also flush the buffer implicitly.

An Example Bluetooth Application

The code bundle for this book includes the *BTDiscovery* application, which shows how to use device and service discovery to obtain the status of the local device and any remote devices within range. The code is optimized for Series 40 Developer Platform 2.0 devices such as the Nokia 6230 and Series 60 Developer Platform 2.0 devices like the Nokia 6600. The application provides three levels of functionality:

- Display the Bluetooth parameters for the local device

- Discover any remote device and display their parameters

- For any selected remote device, discover and display its Bluetooth services

Let's discuss the three levels in more detail, beginning with the local device. When developing Bluetooth-enabled applications, it makes a lot of sense to check out the Bluetooth parameters of the local device. The Bluetooth API plus the code library used for our BTDiscovery application provide what you need. Start the application, and you will see the greeting form with explanatory text. Select the DeviceInfo option from the Options menu to get the details of the local device (see Figure 10–7). Browse through the list to check out the friendly device name, the current discovery mode, the major and minor device class information, and the Bluetooth property settings.

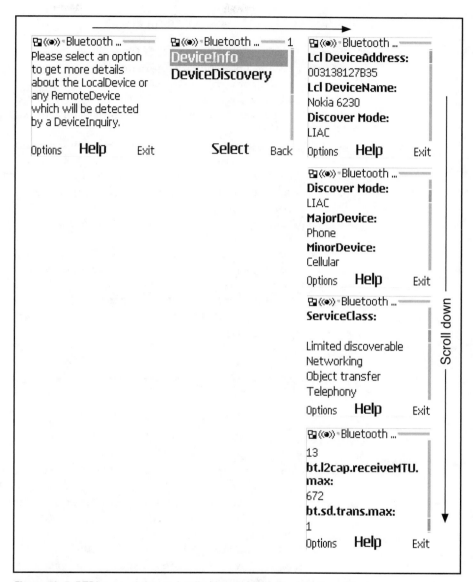

Figure 10–7 BTDiscovery shows detailed information about the LocalDevice.

Here's how the code works. After initializing the Bluetooth stack, it is possible to find out the device's Bluetooth address and friendly name, and to get a reference to `LocalDevice` and the local `DiscoveryAgent`. With `LocalDevice` in place, you can check out the major and minor device number and the service classes available on the local device. The following code fragment gives you the idea. Please refer to the complete example for details:

```java
public void initLocalDevice() {
  try {
    // initialize the JABWT stack
    lDevice = LocalDevice.getLocalDevice();
    // set discovery mode
    if (DiscoveryModeGIAC == true)
      lDevice.setDiscoverable(DiscoveryAgent.GIAC);
    else
      lDevice.setDiscoverable(DiscoveryAgent.LIAC);

    // store the local device address
    lDeviceAdress = lDevice.getBluetoothAddress();
    // store the local device name
    lDeviceName = lDevice.getFriendlyName();

    // store the reference to the discovery agent
    lDiscoveryAgent = lDevice.getDiscoveryAgent();
    BTError = false;
  } catch (BluetoothStateException e) {
    //e.printStackTrace();
    btutil.log(e.toString());
    lDevice = null;
    BTError = true;
    BTErrorMsg = "Bluetooth enabled?";
  }
}

// ... ...

public   void BTDisplayLocalDevice(LocalDevice lDevice) {
  log("Lcl DeviceAddress",lDevice.getBluetoothAddress());
  log("Lcl DeviceName", lDevice.getFriendlyName());
  DeviceClass devClass = lDevice.getDeviceClass();
  if (devClass != null) {
    log("MajorDevice:",
      BTMajorDeviceName(devClass.getMajorDeviceClass()));
    log("MinorDevice:",
      BTMinorDeviceName(devClass.getMajorDeviceClass(),
      devClass.getMinorDeviceClass()));
    log("ServiceClass:","");
    String[] str =
  BTUtil.BTMajorServiceName(devClass.getServiceClasses());
    for (int i = 0; i < str.length; i++) {
      log(str[i]);
    }
  }
}
```

```
// ... ...

public static String BTMajorDeviceName(int device) {
    if ( device == 0x0000 )
        return "Miscellaneous";
    else if ( device == 0x0100)
        return "Computer";
    else if ( device == 0x0200 )
        return "Phone";
    else if ( device == 0x0300 )
        return "LAN";
    // ... ...
}
```

The second major feature of BTDiscovery is the inquiry scan for
RemoteDevices. Choose the DeviceDiscovery option from the menu to start this
procedure. To be able to run the inquiry, the application needs to implement the
methods of the DiscoveryListener class. In our example, we use the main
application class implemented the DiscoveryListener interface.

```
public class BTDiscovery extends MIDlet
        implements CommandListener, DiscoveryListener {
```

We implement the methods deviceDiscovered(), inquiryCompleted(),
servicesDiscovered(), and serviceSearchCompleted() in the
DiscoveryListener interface. During the scan, all found devices are added to
a local list of devices. The local DiscoveryAgent calls deviceDiscovered()
for each found device. It is important to note that the inquiry process could take
a while, and all subsequent steps should be done only after
inquiryCompleted() method is called. Then we can check out the collected
data and prepare for the next steps. In case of an error, it is possible to work
with a partial set of collected data or to get back to square one and try again.

```
void deviceDiscovered(RemoteDevice remoteDevice,
                        DeviceClass deviceClass) {
    // store the device entry as well as the
    // deviceclass entry for further use
    devices.addElement(remoteDevice);
    deviceClasses.addElement(deviceClass);
    btutil.BTDisplayRemoteDevice(remoteDevice,
                                    deviceClass);
}

public void inquiryCompleted(int btInquiryDone) {
    BTInquiry = false; // reset our flag
    switch (btInquiryDone) {
```

```
      case DiscoveryListener.INQUIRY_ERROR:
        btutil.log("Found " + devices.size() +
                     " Elements before error occurred");
        break;
      case DiscoveryListener.INQUIRY_COMPLETED:
        btutil.log("Inquiry done...");
        if (devices.size() > 0) {
          btdevicelist.displaylist();
          display.setCurrent(btdevicelist);
        } else {
          btutil.log ("No Devices found");
        }
        break;
      case DiscoveryListener.INQUIRY_TERMINATED:
        btutil.log("Inquiry terminated");
        break;
      case DiscoveryListener.SERVICE_SEARCH_COMPLETED:
        btutil.log("Service search completed");
        break;
      case
  DiscoveryListener.SERVICE_SEARCH_DEVICE_NOT_REACHABLE:
        btutil.log("Device not reachable");
        break;
      case DiscoveryListener.SERVICE_SEARCH_ERROR:
        btutil.log("Service search error");
        break;
      case DiscoveryListener.SERVICE_SEARCH_NO_RECORDS:
        btutil.log("No devices found");
        break;
    }
  }
}

public void servicesDiscovered(int transId,
             ServiceRecord[] ServiceRecords) {
  for (int i = 0; i < ServiceRecords.length; i++) {
    ServiceRecord record = ServiceRecords[i];
    services.addElement(record);
    btutil.BTDisplayServiceRecord(record);
  }
}

public void serviceSearchCompleted(int transId,
                  int btServiceDiscoveryResult) {
  switch (btServiceDiscoveryResult) {
    case SERVICE_SEARCH_COMPLETED:
      btservicelist.displayservices();
```

```
        display.setCurrent(btservicelist);
        break;
      case SERVICE_SEARCH_ERROR:
        btutil.log("Error searching for services");
        break;
      case SERVICE_SEARCH_NO_RECORDS:
        btutil.log("No service records found");
        break;
      case SERVICE_SEARCH_DEVICE_NOT_REACHABLE:
        btutil.log("Error device not reachable");
        break;
      case SERVICE_SEARCH_TERMINATED:
        btutil.log("Error terminated");
        break;
  }
}
```

Select the DeviceDiscovery option to inquire for the remote devices. After the inquiry process ends, you will see a list of the devices found. If you are using the Series 40 Developer Platform 2.0 SDK, the inquiry will find all running device emulator instances. You can change the friendly name in each emulator window to be able to distinguish the instances. See Figure 10–8.

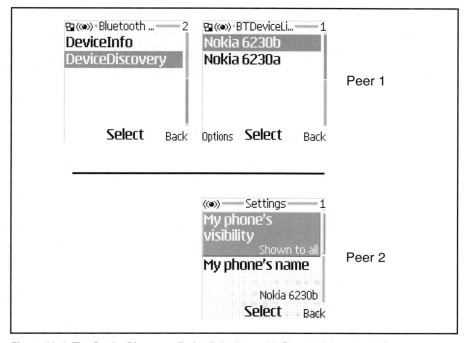

Figure 10–8 The DeviceDiscovery finds all devices with Bluetooth in activated DiscoveryMode. Change the name in the SDK emulator for a more specific name.

The next step is to either find out more details about the services the selected devices provide or get a more detailed look into the Bluetooth parameters. Select Services to find out more about the services. See Figure 10–9 and Figure 10–10.

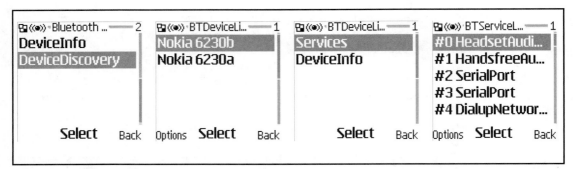

Figure 10–9 For each found device, it is possible to check out the Bluetooth services and Bluetooth-specific details.

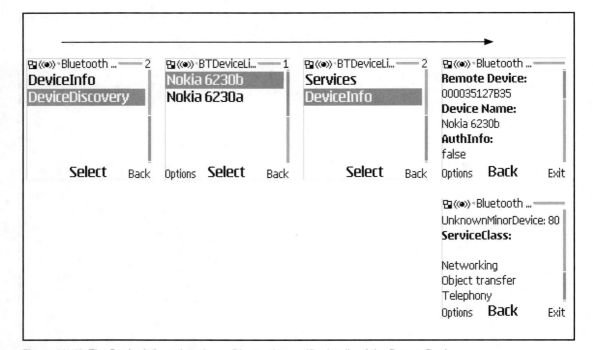

Figure 10–10 The DeviceInfo option shows Bluetooth-specific details of the RemoteDevice.

BTDiscovery uses its own utility class (not part of JSR 82) that provides various methods that pass back readable strings for given major names, minor names, service data structures, and UUIDs for local and remote devices. The utility class makes it easy to check out the Bluetooth neighborhood while developing your own Bluetooth-enabled application.

Nokia Development Tool Support

The Series 40 Developer Platform 2.0 SDK supports full emulation of the Bluetooth network among multiple device emulator instances. It allows us to fully test our Bluetooth applications on the development PC without having to use the real handsets. More information about the Series 40 Developer Platform 2.0 SDK can be found in Chapter 3, "Getting Started."

Figure 10–11 The Series 40 Developer Platform 2.0 SDK emulator uses the Nokia 6230 skin.

To use the Bluetooth-related features on the emulator, you should first make sure to enable the Bluetooth functionality from inside the emulator, as you would do on a real device. We covered this step earlier in the chapter.

To be able to connect from on emulated environment to another emulator, it is important to start the Nokia Connection Framework Lite (NCF), which is part of the Series 40 Developer Platform 2.0 SDK download. Start the NCF by selecting Start| Programs | Nokia Developer Tools| Nokia Connection Framework | Nokia Connectivity Framework Lite. After it is started, the NCF shows an icon in the system tray. After the NCF is completely loaded, start the Series 40 Developer Platform 2.0 SDK emulators either standalone or from the Nokia Developer's Suite for J2ME.

TIP

If you get an error message explaining that the SDK has no MAC address, stop the SDK, stop the NCF, and then restart the NCF. Wait until the NCF has completely started, then start the SDK(s).

If you like to run discovery services from your application to check out other Bluetooth devices, just start one instance of the SDK from the Start | Programs | Nokia Developer Tools | DP 2.0 SDKs | Series 40 | S40 DP 2.0 SDK 1.0. This step starts the SDK emulating the generic device without running a specific application on top. Then start your application. It will discover the emulated device and its services. Of course, you can also start multiple SDK emulators from the Nokia Developer's Suite for J2ME with each emulator instance loaded with a Bluetooth client or server program. If you right-click on the NCF icon in the system tray, you get additional information, including the Bluetooth address for the emulated devices.

After testing your application in the emulated environment, it is very important to thoroughly test the application running on real devices. This is especially true for applications using Bluetooth wireless technology, because there is no typical environment setup for Bluetooth. The time for inquiry and service discovery and also the speed of any single data transfer may depend on a wide variety of external parameters. Examples of such parameters include the number and type of nearby devices that are in range; whether other users or groups are using the same Bluetooth service (in independent sessions of the same application); whether some users are on the edge of device range; whether users move in and out of Bluetooth range; and whether other wireless technologies like WiFi are being used in the same area. To test in this very flexible environment, those parameters should be taken into account using statistical testing methods to gain more knowledge of the application behavior in real-life setups. It should also be clear by now that error handling inside any application is a fundamental prerequisite of a good user experience and application quality.

Summary

Bluetooth is a powerful technology that can be used to connect nearby devices to form ad hoc or even static networks. Bluetooth is very well suited for mobile devices like handsets. Support of JSR 82, the Bluetooth API for Java (JABWT), enables the developer to design portable applications that support Bluetooth over a wide range of J2ME devices. With JSR 82 in place, you can develop peer-to-peer applications like multiuser games or access remote services without the need to connect devices with physical cables. Since it is possible to switch off the Bluetooth stack, power consumption can be optimized.

chapter

11

End-to-End Design Patterns

Learn end-to-end design patterns from a concrete example.

So far in this book, we have covered the basics of smart-client programming using J2ME and MIDP technologies on the Nokia Series 40 Developer Platform. However, knowing a collection of APIs is different from actually using them to write efficient and maintainable mobile applications. It sometimes takes years of experience to figure out what design works best under specific conditions. For beginners, the fastest way to become an expert is to learn from other people's experiences—distilled as design patterns. In this chapter, we use a full end-to-end example application to illustrate important mobile smart-client design patterns. Please note that the design patterns in this chapter focus on media and business applications with turn-based (i.e., screen-based or form-based) workflow. For animation- and timer-based action games and additional design tips, please refer to Chapter 5, "Developing Action Games." In this chapter, we cover the following topics:

- **Introduction to the trivia game example**: shows how the example application works. It gives the background and context of the code examples used in the rest of the chapter.

- **Overall architecture**: discusses the end-to-end architecture of the application. Using code examples, we explain the end-to-end Model-View-Controller design pattern.

- **Object management**: covers object creation and management patterns on the client side. The techniques discussed in this section are widely used to reduce application memory footprint, minimize the garbage collector overhead, and improve code maintainability.

- **Thread management**: introduces an easy-to-use framework for visual worker threads. It drastically improves the user experience when executing lengthy tasks (e.g., network tasks).

- **Remote integration**: discusses how to integrate smart mobile clients with backend services using tightly coupled Remote Procedure Call (RPC) and loosely coupled XML Web Services. The example shows how to delegate part of the application logic to backend servers.

The design patterns and best practices discussed in this chapter help improve the application performance as well as code maintainability. We think those two objectives are both crucial given the hardware constraints of today's devices and the fast evolution of mobile technologies. In the next two chapters, Chapter

12, "Developing Scalable Applications," and Chapter 13, "Debugging and Testing," we discuss how to take advantage of the maintainable architecture of the trivia application to scale it across different devices.

Introduction to the Trivia Game Example

Mobile entertainment applications have long been touted as the killer applications for mobile commerce. Mobile games can be played anytime and anywhere, but typically, a user may have only a couple of minutes of free time to play a game on the go. This usage model means that casual games—that is, games that are low pressure, have short cycles, and can be interrupted at any time—are the most likely to be successful. A particularly interesting example is the trivia game, which asks users questions about celebrities, sports, or other common-interest topics. A user can play one question if she is between meetings or play hundreds if she has an entire afternoon to kill. The game provider can enhance the play experience by building communities and hosting competition among players. In fact, the highly successful U.S. realty TV show, *Who Wants to Be a Millionaire?* is a high-stakes trivia competition. Simple, text-based mobile trivia games have become very successful in Europe and Japan. In this chapter, we expand this concept a little bit and develop a multimedia trivia game on Series 40 devices. It ties together many of the MIDP APIs we have learned so far and introduces several important mobile end-to-end design patterns.

The mobile trivia application is developed using end-to-end Java technologies, including the J2ME/MIDP and J2EE. In Chapter 12, "Developing Scalable Applications," and Chapter 13, "Debugging and Testing," we discuss how to scale the application across different devices and how to manage the development process more efficiently. Figure 11–1 shows a typical multimedia trivia question displayed on the handset.

Feature Overview

Upon starting up, the client displays a navigation menu that mimics the top-level menu on a typical Series 40 device. Each menu option is mapped to a screen, and the user can navigate between the screens using the left and right scroll keys. Figure 11–2 shows these menu options.

If the user selects the New Session menu option, the client connects to a trivia content server and downloads a set of questions. Since the trivia questions are downloaded all at once and cached on the device, the user can play with them offline. Depending on the category and configuration settings under the Preference menu, we can have two types of trivia questions.

- A question can be downloaded with its answer key. After the user selects an answer, the application immediately shows the correct answer. This mode

Figure 11–1 An example trivia question.

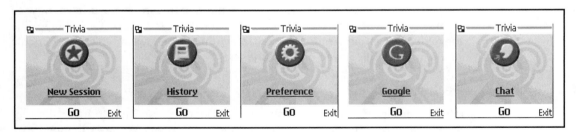

Figure 11–2 Trivia game root menu.

provides instant gratification and helps beginners to learn. If all questions in a session come with answer keys, the session statistics are immediately displayed after the session is finished. Figure 11–3 illustrates how the "instant feedback" question works.

- A question can also be downloaded without the answer key. This mode is suited for trivia competition. After the user answers each question, the user-selected answer is cached to support offline play. Once the session is

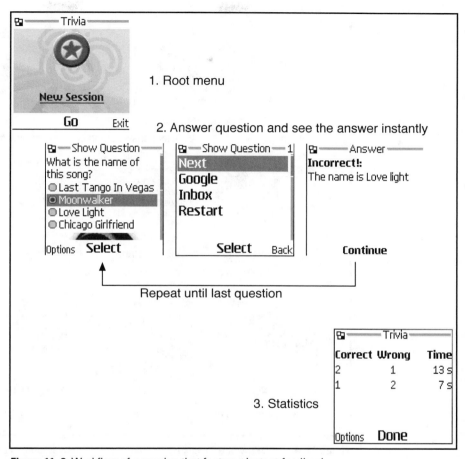

1. Root menu

2. Answer question and see the answer instantly

Repeat until last question

3. Statistics

Figure 11–3 Workflow of a session that features instant feedback.

finished, the client sends all user answers to the trivia server. The server returns the numbers of correct and wrong answers. If the network is not available, the user can postpone the answer check. In this case, a Submit answers menu option would be added to the root menu. Figure 11–4 shows how the workflow of such a trivia session would look.

NOTE

Being able to play the networked multimedia trivia game offline illustrates the benefits of smart clients. Support for the occasionally connected application paradigm is crucial to the application availability in today's wireless networks.

The History menu option shows the statistics of past sessions. It also supports synchronization of the statistics data between the mobile client and the backend server (see Figure 11–5). Since a user may own multiple mobile devices, the

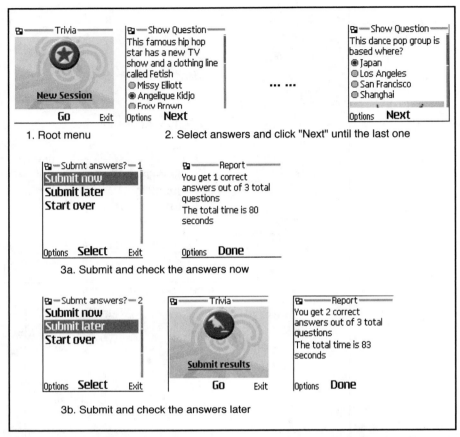

Figure 11–4 Work flow of a trivia session that requires answer check at the backend server.

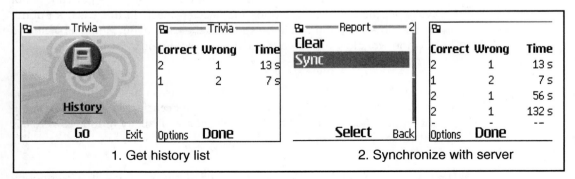

Figure 11–5 Synchronize the score lists.

synchronization feature allows him to have a complete view of the play history from any device he happens to be playing on.

In addition to features directly related to the trivia game, the application also helps the users to research the questions.

- The user can query Internet search engine Google from the Google root menu or at any time within the trivia session via the Google command. Depending on the user's preference setting, the query string is submitted to Google either as a complete phrase or as a collection of separate keywords. The top search results and relevant text snippets are returned and displayed on the device. Figure 11–6 shows a Google search session.

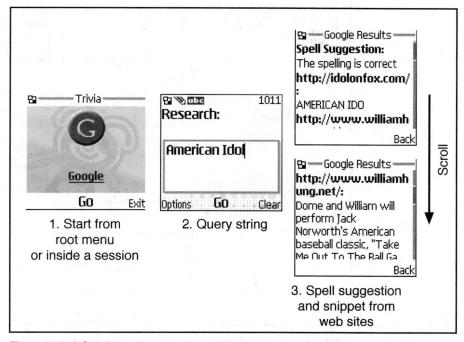

Figure 11–6 A Google session.

- The user can seek help from peers via a built-in messaging client (the Chat root menu or the Inbox command). A player can send text messages to the telephone number associated with any other player. The messaging solution is built on top of the pervasive SMS infrastructure using the WMA (see Chapter 8, "Wireless Messaging"). Figure 11–7 shows how to use the messaging client.

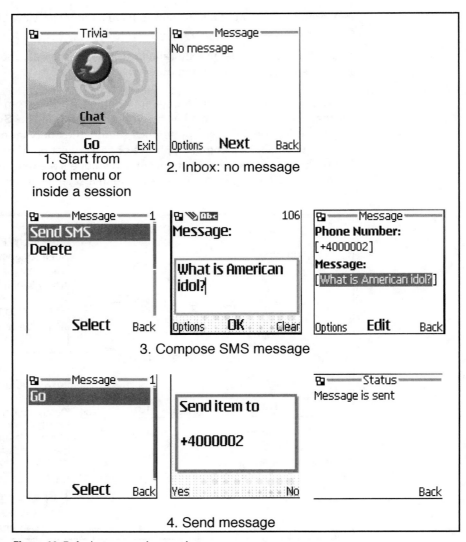

Figure 11–7 A chat messaging session.

Backend Database Setup

The mobile trivia game downloads questions and sends user answers from and to a dedicated server-side application. The server-side application, written in Java servlet, manages and serves the content stored in a database (see Figure 11–8). The database supports efficient data storage and sophisticated queries. It is important to understand the database schema and access mechanism if you wish to deploy the application or understand the query code in the trivia server. Hence, before we move on to discuss the design and implementation of

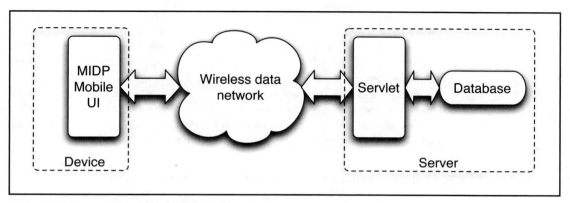

Figure 11–8 The network powered trivia application.

the trivia smart client and companion server, we present a quick overview of the trivia content repository database.

For the sake of simplicity, we chose an open-source Java embedded database engine, HSQLDB, rather than a full-blown commercial database solution as the content repository. In the standalone mode, HSQLDB is just a set of Java libraries that implements the JDBC (Java DataBase Connectivity) API. The server application, programmed as Java servlets, can make JDBC calls to access the in-memory or local file-system data storage managed by HSQLDB. The HSQLDB data store can be directly copied when the application is moved from one machine to another (e.g., when the application is deployed to a production server). There are three tables in the database: the Questions table stores the trivia questions; the Choices table stores all possible choices and associates them with the questions through the matching id field in both tables; the History table stores the statistics data of previous sessions. The database schema is illustrated through the following SQL statements:

```
create table Questions
    (id integer identity, question varchar(4096),
     category varchar(8), answerId integer,
     hasImage integer, hasMusic integer,
     answerHint varchar(4096), sendAnswer integer);

create table Choices
    (id integer identity, questionId integer,
     choiceId integer, choice varchar(4096));

create table History
    (ts bigint, correctNum integer,
     wrongNum integer, time bigint);
```

TIP

The embedded database is perfect for our small example because it is very easy to deploy (just copy the storage file). But embedded databases do not scale well. When there is a lot of content, the embedded database becomes inefficient and hard to manage. In that case, a large client/server-based database management solution, such as Oracle, IBM DB2, and MySQL, is needed. Since we use the standard JDBC and SQL APIs to query the database, our servlet should be independent from the backend database. That is, the servlet code should remain unchanged no matter whether we use an embedded database or a client/server database solution.

The following should be noted about the database structure:

- The `hasImage` and `hasMusic` fields specify the availability of multimedia content associated with this question.

- The `answerHint` field contains a hint to the correct answer. It can be a `null` value.

- The `sendAnswer` field flags whether to give the user any instant feedback after the question is answered. That is related to the two play modes we discussed before.

- The matching values of the `id` field in the `Questions` table and the `questionId` field in the `Choices` table indicate choices following a specific question.

- The `ts` field in the `History` table indicates the start time of the session; the `correctNum` field is the number of correct answers, and the `wrongNum` field is the number of wrong answers; the `time` field is the duration of the session.

- The `ts` field in the first row of the `History` table stores the last synchronization time of the database. It is initialized to value −1.

Multimedia content (such as images and music files) is not stored in the database. We could store arbitrary binary data in a relational database as a BLOB field. But that is unnecessary and degrades the database performance. The hierarchical file system is a better storage for those files. Hence, these media files are stored directly in the file system and named according to the question's ID and named according to the question's ID. For example, the image file for the question with `Questions.id=1` could be named `png/1.png` in the file system.

The HSQLDB software comes with a simple GUI-based management console. Arbitrary SQL statements can be executed through the console. In the downloadable package, the database storage files and multimedia content directories (e.g., the `png/`, `gif/`, and `midi/` directories) are already populated with sample data.

TIP

As a bonus, the HSQLDB also supports Java Stored Procedures. Simple Java function calls can be embedded in SQL statements to manipulate the data in the table or process the results.

Overall Architecture

The most important architectural design pattern used in the trivia example application is the Model-View-Controller (MVC) pattern. In this section, we review this design, discuss its strengths and weaknesses, and analyze how the components work together.

Screen-Switch in Mobile Applications

Most desktop-based applications have a single main window that holds multiple complex UI widgets. The application responds to user actions by updating part of the window display area. However, for mobile applications, this main-window UI paradigm would not work. The mobile device screen is too small for multiple complex widgets. Instead, most mobile applications, especially business forms applications, adopt a screen-switch paradigm: a new screen is generated and displayed in response to each user action. For mobile games, the main game screen is continuously updated during the play session, but the support screens (e.g., menus and preference settings) are still switched back and forth according to the user requests. The `Displayable` class in MIDP is designed to support the screen-switch paradigm. We can have multiple `Displayable` instances in the system and use the `Display.setCurrent()` method to switch between the screens. From the design point of view, there are several approaches to implement the screen-switch navigation model.

- In a simple model, each `Displayable` class has its own UI event listener. Based on the user input, the callback method (e.g., `commandAction()` in `CommandListener` or `keyPressed()` in `Canvas`) instantiates the next `Displayable` screen and hands the control over to the next screen. The problem with this model is that the navigation logic is distributed in multiple classes. The developer has to track multiple points of entry to change the screen and the application state. The application becomes difficult to maintain when there are many screens or complex navigation rules.

- Alternatively, we can have a shared `CommandListener` object for all `Displayable` objects in the system. This way, all the `Command` navigation rules and application state change logic can be centralized. Such shared `CommandListener` class is often the `MIDlet` class itself to reduce the initialization work and provide easy access to the resources data (e.g., JAD attributes). The example application in Chapter 4, "MIDP User Interface," follows this model. The major drawback for this approach is that we cannot easily incorporate the keypad-event-handling callback methods in the

Canvas class (e.g., the keyPressed() method) into the system. In addition, all Displayable screens must use a shared pool of user interaction components (e.g., the Command and ChoiceGroup objects), and that might result in confusing designs in complex systems.

- Or, we can combine the best features of the above two approaches. We can have a separate event listener for each Displayable object. But instead of processing the user request by itself, the event-handling callback method simply delegates to a systemwide controller object that provides centralized support for navigation and state changes. The controller object is typically the MIDlet object itself for the reasons mentioned above. Most of the examples in this book use this approach.

The MVC design pattern is based on the third approach. It aims to simplify the conceptual links between different components in the application. It is a widely used behavior pattern in complex UI applications.

What Is the MVC Pattern?

The MVC pattern divides the application into three layers.

- The model contains the core of the business logic. It maintains the application state and processes all application-specific data to determine state transitions.

- The view presents the model to users. In GUI applications, the view typically consists of a set of display screens. It is the outbound interface of the application.

- The controller links the view to the model. When the user manipulates the view, the controller passes the requests to the model and updates the view after the model responds. It is the inbound interface of the application.

In the multimedia trivia example application, we utilize a single controller for the entire application and a model layer that covers both the mobile client and the server (see Figure 11–9). Key benefits of the MVC pattern are as follows.

- Since the layers are separate from each other, the application is componentized. Each component can be developed and maintained independently by specialists. For example, the view layer can be developed by UI designers, while the model layer can be developed by domain knowledge experts and data modelers. That allows us not only to allocate talent efficiently but also to parallelize the development work and hence shorten the time to market.

- The compartmented layers are easy to test. Automated unit tests can be used extensively in the model layer to ensure functional correctness. User experience tests can be conducted against the view in usability labs before the model is ready (see Chapter 13 for more on the testing topics).

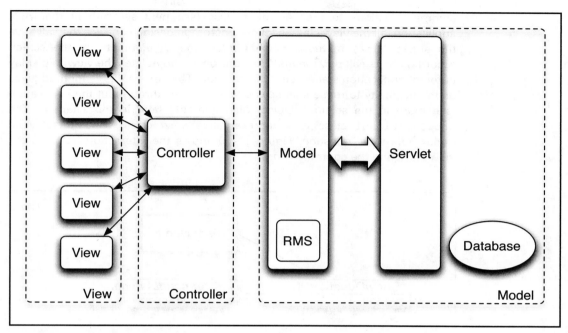

Figure 11–9 The end-to-end MVC pattern.

- The execution flow in an MVC application is well defined. MVC code is easy to understand, since many developers are already familiar with the pattern. That improves the code maintainability and reduces the cost in the long run.

- For applications that require several different user interfaces, we can develop several different views while reusing the same model and controller. As we see in Chapter 12, this simplifies our work to optimize the application for multiple devices within a developer platform series or migrate the application to other developer platform series with different UI requirements.

- As the application gets more complex over time, it may be unavoidable for us to evolve the data model to accommodate the new needs. A separate model layer clearly indicates which classes we need to extend, and the changes are not propagated to other parts of the application. That again promotes code reuse in an object-oriented system.

In order to see how the MVC pattern is implemented in the example application, let's follow the execution logic from view to controller and then to the model.

The View Screens

The view layer consists of MIDP `Displayable` classes under the `com.Series40Book.midp.view` Java package. Each view class has a set of commands and acts as its own command listener, which simply delegates command actions to the controller class (see next section). In the trivia application, all the view classes follow a common design contract: they all have the setStatus() method, which renders the UI elements on the screen according to its call parameters. The controller manipulates the view to display different application states using this method. The setStatus() method gives us the flexibility to reuse instances of view classes throughout the application (see more in the section "Object Management" later in this chapter). The ShowQuestionUI class is a representative view class, which displays a multimedia trivia question. Figure 11–10 shows the interaction between the view class and the controller class.

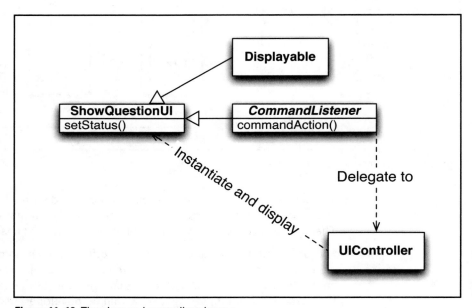

Figure 11–10 The view and controller classes.

Below is the listing of the ShowQuestionUI class in the view layer.

```
public class ShowQuestionUI extends Form
                implements CommandListener {

    private Command restartCommand;
    private Command googleCommand;
    private Command inboxCommand;
    private Command nextCommand;
    private StringItem question;
    private ChoiceGroup choices;
    private ImageItem image;

    public ShowQuestionUI () {
```

```
        super("Show Question");

        restartCommand =
            new Command("Restart", Command.SCREEN, 2);
        googleCommand =
            new Command ("Google", Command.SCREEN, 1);
        inboxCommand =
              new Command("Inbox", Command.SCREEN, 1);
        nextCommand = UIController.nextCommand;
        addCommand(nextCommand);
        addCommand(restartCommand);
        addCommand(googleCommand);
        addCommand(inboxCommand);
        setCommandListener(this);

        question = new StringItem("", "");
        choices = new ChoiceGroup("", Choice.EXCLUSIVE);
        image = new ImageItem("", null,
            ImageItem.LAYOUT_CENTER, "image");

        append (question);
        append (choices);
        append (image);
    }

    // Construct the UI
    public void setStatus (String q, String [] c,
                               byte [] img, byte [] sound) {

        question.setText(q);
        image.setImage(Image.createImage(img, 0, img.length));
        choices =
            new ChoiceGroup("", Choice.EXCLUSIVE, c, null);
        // The second item is the choice group
        set (1, choices);

        SoundPlayer sp = new SoundPlayerImpl ();
        sp.playSound(sound);
    }

    // Delegates to the UIController class
    // Must return immediately
    public void commandAction (Command c, Displayable s) {
      try {
        if (c == restartCommand) {
          UIController.restartQuestion();
        } else if (c == googleCommand) {
```

```
                  UIController.showGoogleQuery(this);
              } else if (c == inboxCommand) {
                  UIController.firstMessage(this);
              } else if (c == nextCommand) {
                  UIController.storeAnswer(
                      choices.getSelectedIndex());
              }
          } catch (Exception e) {
              e.printStackTrace();
              UIController.showAlert("Error",
                                  e.getMessage(), this);
          }
      }
   }
}
```

The Controller

When the user selects a command on the `ShowQuestionUI` screen, its `commandAction()` method delegates the action to a static method in the `UIController` class. The `UIController` class is the controller, and it contains a large number of static methods that handle every possible screen transition. In the `storeAnswer()` method, which handles the Next command in the `ShowQuestionUI` screen, the `UIController` stores the user-selected answer to the question to the data model. Depending on the data model's state after processing the answer, the `storeAnswer()` method constructs the appropriate response screen and displays the screen to the device.

```
public class UIController {

   // Other methods

   public static void storeAnswer (int ans)
                              throws Exception {
      QuestionsNavigator qn =
          QuestionsNavigator.getInstance ();
      int status = qn.storeAnswer(ans + 1);

      if (status == QuestionsNavigator.NA_ANSWER) {
         // No local answer, move on
         nextQuestion ();

      } else {
         // Prepare and show the local answer
         if (answerScreen == null) {
            answerScreen = new ShowAnswerUI ();
         }
```

```
      if (status == QuestionsNavigator.CORRECT_ANSWER) {
        answerScreen.setStatus(true, qn.getAnswerHint());
      } else if (status ==
          QuestionsNavigator.WRONG_ANSWER) {
        answerScreen.setStatus(false, qn.getAnswerHint());
      }

      display.setCurrent(answerScreen);
    }
  }

  // Other methods
}
```

The Model

The `QuestionsNavigator` class referenced in the `UIController`'s `storeAnswer()` method is in the model layer. It models the data structure that represents the questions and answers in the current session. In the `QuestionsNavigator.storeAnswer()` method, the user-selected answer is stored in a hashtable with the question ID. If no answer key is available, the method returns immediately and the `UIController` moves on to the next question in the session. If an answer key is available, the selection is compared with the answer key and the `storeAnswer()` method returns whether the selected answer is correct. Then, the `UIController` displays an instant-feedback screen to the user informing him whether the answer is correct and displays the answer hint, if available. The following listing shows the relevant data fields and methods in the `QuestionsNavigator` class. Other methods in `QuestionsNavigator` are discussed later in this chapter.

```
public abstract class QuestionsNavigator {

  // Memory model of questions and answers in a session
  protected int currentId;
  protected TriviaQuestion currentQuestion;
  protected Hashtable answers;

  protected static String url;
  public long time;

  // Numbers of correct/wrong answers
  public int correctNum;
  public int wrongNum;
  public int totalNum;

  public static int CORRECT_ANSWER = 1;
  public static int WRONG_ANSWER = 2;
```

```
public static int NA_ANSWER = 3;

// Stores the answer for the current question
public int storeAnswer (int ans) {
  answers.put(currentQuestion.questionId,
                new Integer(ans));
  // prepare the return code
  int status = NA_ANSWER;
  if (currentQuestion.sendAnswer) {
    if (currentQuestion.answerId == ans) {
      status = CORRECT_ANSWER;
      correctNum++;
    } else {
      status = WRONG_ANSWER;
      wrongNum++;
    }
  }
  return status;
}

// Other methods
}
```

The TriviaQuestion class represents the memory model of a single question. It not only defines the data fields of the question, but also specifies the mechanism to serialize or deserialize the question to or from a byte array (see Figure 11–11). The byte array can then be stored in an RMS store or transported over the network. Please refer to Chapter 4, "MIDP User Interface," for more information on Java object serialization in MIDP.

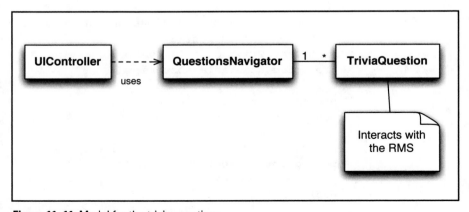

Figure 11–11 Model for the trivia questions.

```java
class TriviaQuestion {

  public String questionId;
  public String question;
  public String [] choices;
  public String answerHint;
  public int answerId;
  public byte [] image;
  public byte [] sound;
  public boolean sendAnswer;

  public TriviaQuestion (String qid, String q,
                         String [] c, String ah, int ai,
                         byte [] i, byte [] s) {
    questionId = qid;
    question = q;
    choices = c;
    answerHint = ah;
    answerId = ai;
    image = i;
    sound =s;
    sendAnswer = false;
  }

  public TriviaQuestion () {

    questionId = null;
    question = "";
    choices = new String [0];
    sendAnswer = false;
    answerHint = "";
    answerId = -1;
    image = null;
    sound =null;

  }

  public byte [] persist () throws Exception {
    byte [] result = new byte [0];

    ByteArrayOutputStream baos = null;
    DataOutputStream dos = null;

    try {
      baos = new ByteArrayOutputStream ();
      dos = new DataOutputStream (baos);
      persist(dos);
```

```
        dos.flush ();
        baos.flush ();
        result = baos.toByteArray();

        dos.close ();
        baos.close ();
    } finally {
      try {
        if (dos != null) dos.close();
        if (baos != null) baos.close ();
      } catch (Exception e) { }
    }
    return result;
}

public void persist (DataOutputStream dos)
                            throws Exception {
    if (questionId != null) {
      // There is nothing to persist
      // if the questionId is missing
      dos.writeUTF(questionId);
      dos.writeUTF(question);
      dos.writeInt(choices.length);
      for (int i = 0; i < choices.length; i++) {
        dos.writeUTF(choices[i]);
      }

      if (image != null) {
        dos.writeBoolean(true);
        dos.writeInt(image.length);
        dos.write(image, 0, image.length);
      } else {
        dos.writeBoolean(false);
      }

      if (sound != null) {
        dos.writeBoolean(true);
        dos.writeInt(sound.length);
        dos.write(sound, 0, sound.length);
      } else {
        dos.writeBoolean(false);
      }

      dos.writeBoolean (sendAnswer);
      if (sendAnswer) {
        dos.writeUTF(answerHint);
        dos.writeInt(answerId);
```

```
      }
    }
  }

  public void load (byte [] entry) throws Exception {
    ByteArrayInputStream bais = null;
    DataInputStream dis = null;

    try {
      bais = new ByteArrayInputStream (entry);
      dis = new DataInputStream (bais);
      load (dis);

      dis.close ();
      bais.close ();
    } finally {
      try {
        if (dis != null) dis.close();
        if (bais != null) bais.close ();
      } catch (Exception e) { }
    }
  }

  public void load (DataInputStream dis)
                            throws Exception {

    questionId = dis.readUTF();
    question = dis.readUTF();
    int numChoices = dis.readInt();
    choices = new String[numChoices];
    for (int i = 0; i < numChoices; i++) {
      choices[i] = dis.readUTF();
    }
    boolean hasImage = dis.readBoolean ();
    if (hasImage) {
      int size = dis.readInt();
      image = new byte [size];
      dis.readFully(image);
    } else {
      image = null;
    }
    boolean hasMusic = dis.readBoolean ();
    if (hasMusic) {
      int size = dis.readInt();
      sound = new byte [size];
      dis.readFully(sound);
    } else {
```

```
            sound = null;
        }
        sendAnswer = dis.readBoolean ();
        if (sendAnswer) {
            answerHint = dis.readUTF();
            answerId = dis.readInt();
        } else {
            answerHint = "";
            answerId = -1;
        }
    }
}
```

In addition to in-memory data model and data serialization management, the model layer of the trivia example application actually extends across the network to the server side. The Java servlet that manages the database and feeds content to the MIDlet is also part of the application business logic and hence belongs to the model layer.

Object Management

One of the key strengths of the Java programming language is that it is fully object oriented. Objects help us conceptualize complex systems and write extensible software components. However, the standard object constructor syntax in Java programming language is often insufficient to precisely describe and constrain the behavior of objects in the system, which results in applications that are either inflexible (too much constraint) or prone to runtime errors (too little constraint). Object creation design patterns help us solve those problems by going around the standard constructor.

In addition, the benefits of an object-oriented system come with potential costs: objects take up the heap memory space; creating and destroying objects require additional CPU cycles. In the Java runtime, the garbage collector monitors each object and automatically frees resources used by discarded objects. The garbage collector is very slow to run. If we create and discard too many objects too frequently, the garbage collector could slow down the application drastically. So, in object-oriented systems, especially on resource constrained devices, it is crucial that we create objects judiciously and manage them efficiently. In this section, we discuss several object-creation and management design patterns that are of particular interest to developers of smart mobile clients.

Static Class

The simplest way to reduce object-related computing overhead is not to create objects at all. As we have seen, the methods in the UIController class are used in every view object. Since there is only one controller in the system, there is no need for multiple UIController instances. In a pure object-oriented design, we could pass a single instance of UIController to every view object. However, that creates a lot of code repetition, which increases the chance of errors and reduces the code readability. So, we choose to make all variables and methods in the UIController class static. This allows us to access UIController methods anywhere in the application and reduces the heap-space usage at the same time. Besides the UIController, this static class pattern is used in several other places in the trivia example application. In this section, we use two static classes in the model layer to illustrate how to use the static class in different scenarios.

NOTE   In most object-oriented systems, static classes are used as a convenient way to provide helper methods, which perform isolated functionalities and normally manage their own states completely within the method.

Stateful Static Class

Although not an object, a static class can maintain state information through static variables. The TheTimer class in the application uses static variables to maintain its state and uses static methods to perform timer functions. Since there is only one application-wide timer, using the static class approach simplifies the code and reduces the runtime overhead.

```
public class TheTimer {

  static private long currentCount;
  static private long startTime;
  static private boolean pauseFlag = false;

  static public void start () {
    startTime = System.currentTimeMillis();
    currentCount = 0;
  }

  static public void pause () {
    if (!pauseFlag) {
      long rightNow = System.currentTimeMillis();
      currentCount += rightNow - startTime;
      startTime = rightNow;
      pauseFlag = true;
    }
  }

  static public void resume () {
```

```
        if (pauseFlag) {
          startTime = System.currentTimeMillis();
          pauseFlag = false;
        }
      }

    static public long report () {
        if (pauseFlag) {
          return currentCount;
        } else {
          long rightNow = System.currentTimeMillis();
          currentCount += rightNow - startTime;
          startTime = rightNow;
          return currentCount;
        }
      }
    }
```

Static Class That Requires Initialization

One problem with the static class is that its state variables cannot be initialized in the constructor, since the constructor is never invoked. One way to get around this is to define a static method that explicitly does the initialization. The application code is required to call that initialization method before it calls any other methods or accesses any data variables in the static class. The init() method in the UIController class initializes display and session variables.

```
public class UIController {

    // Data fields and methods

    private UIController () {
    }

    public static void init (MIDlet m) throws Exception {
        midlet = m;
        isPaused = false;
        needSubmit = false;
        display = Display.getDisplay(midlet);

        QuestionsNavigator.setUrl
    (m.getAppProperty("serverURL"));
        GoogleBrowser.init (m.getAppProperty("serverURL"));
        HistoryManager.init (m.getAppProperty("serverURL"));

        sender = new SenderImpl ();
        inbox = new InboxImpl ();
```

```
    sender.setPort(m.getAppProperty("smsPort"));
    try {
      inbox.setupListener (m.getAppProperty("smsPort"));
    } catch (Exception e) {
      // do nothing
    }

    resume();
  }
  // Other methods
}
```

The HistoryManager class, which manages the score history, also uses the static init() method to initialize. The following listing shows how other static methods in HistoryManager make use of the RMS store initialized in the init() method. A more elegant way to perform state initialization is discussed in the next section.

```
public class HistoryManager {

  private static int [] correctNums = null;
  private static int [] wrongNums = null;
  private static long [] times = null;
  private static long [] timestamps = null;

  private static String storeName = "History";
  // indicates whether the in memory arrays are up to date
  private static boolean isUpToDate = false;
  // the last time this mobile is synced with the backend
  private static long lastSyncTime = -1;

  private static String serverurl;


  private HistoryManager () {
  }

  public static void init (String u) throws Exception {
    serverurl = u;
    RecordStore rs =
        RecordStore.openRecordStore(storeName, true);

    try {
      rs.getRecord(1);

    } catch (Exception e) {
      System.out.println("Starting the history manager");
```

```
        e.printStackTrace ();

        byte [] buf = long2ByteArray(0);
        rs.addRecord(buf, 0, buf.length);
      }

    rs.closeRecordStore ();
  }

  public static void clear () {
    try {
      RecordStore.deleteRecordStore(storeName);
      init (serverurl);
      isUpToDate = false;

    } catch (Exception e) {
      System.out.println("Clear error");
      e.printStackTrace ();
    }
  }

  static public void storeScore(int correctNum,
            int wrongNum, long time) throws Exception {
    // Get the current time stamp
    long timestamp = System.currentTimeMillis();

    RecordStore rs =
        RecordStore.openRecordStore(storeName, true);

    // Add a new score
    ByteArrayOutputStream bos =
        new ByteArrayOutputStream ();
    DataOutputStream dbos = new DataOutputStream (bos);
    dbos.writeInt(correctNum);
    dbos.writeInt(wrongNum);
    dbos.writeLong(time);
    dbos.writeLong(timestamp);
    dbos.flush();
    byte [] buf = bos.toByteArray ();
    dbos.close();
    bos.close();
    rs.addRecord(buf, 0, buf.length);

    rs.closeRecordStore();

    isUpToDate = false;
  }
```

```
  // Other methods
}
```

Factory Methods

The plain old Java object constructor requires us to explicitly specify the class name at compile time. We cannot instantiate objects by just knowing the interfaces in the public API. Once we have the class name, the compiler provides no check on when and where the application code instantiates new instances of that class. The factory methods give us finer control of the object-creation and initialization process. In the example application, we use factory methods to create Singletons or instantiate objects from multiple implementations.

Singleton

The Singleton pattern refers to the design pattern where we only instantiate a class once and reuse the same instance everywhere in the entire application. In our trivia example application, several of the application-state manager classes in the model layer fit this pattern, since the underlying state data is shared across the entire application. Now, you might ask, why don't we just use static classes as discussed above? Compared with static classes, Singletons have the following advantages.

- The static class is difficult to initialize. It is true that we can use the initialization method technique discussed above. However, if the developer forgets to call `init()` before the first use, the compiler will not catch the error. That could result in really hard-to-debug runtime errors.

- Singleton classes can be inherited more easily than the static class. In the subclass, we can relax the Singleton restriction with no side effects. In static classes, however, if an instance of the subclass modifies the static variable, the change propagates across the entire application. Singleton is just more flexible than the static class in an object-oriented system.

- The Singleton pattern can be extended to scenarios where we need two or three instances of a given a class in an application, while the static class cannot.

To enforce the Singleton pattern, we make the constructor private so that no one can instantiate an object without going through the factory method. The `getInstance()` factory method checks whether an instance of this class already exists. If so, it simply returns the existing instance. The `PrefStore` class, which manages the user preference in an RMS store, is listed below.

```
public class PrefStore {
  public String category;
```

```java
public int googleResultsNum;
public int googleTextMargin;
public boolean googleIsPhrase;

private String storeName = "Pref";
private static PrefStore pref = new PrefStore ();

private PrefStore () {
  // If the restore operation fails (e.g., first time
  // start), we resort to default values
  if (!restore ()) {
    setDefaults ();
  }
}

// This is the factory method!
public static PrefStore getInstance () {
  return pref;
}

private void setDefaults () {
  category = "music02";
  googleResultsNum = 5;
  googleTextMargin = 100;
  googleIsPhrase = false;
}

public synchronized void save () throws Exception {
  RecordStore rs =
      RecordStore.openRecordStore(storeName, true);
  ByteArrayOutputStream bos =
      new ByteArrayOutputStream ();
  DataOutputStream dbos = new DataOutputStream (bos);
  dbos.writeUTF(category);
  dbos.writeInt(googleResultsNum);
  dbos.writeInt(googleTextMargin);
  dbos.writeBoolean(googleIsPhrase);

  byte [] buf = bos.toByteArray ();

  // If the record store is new, add a record.
  // If not, reset the first record.
  if (rs.getNumRecords() == 0) {
    rs.addRecord(buf, 0, buf.length);
  } else {
    rs.setRecord(1, buf, 0, buf.length);
  }
```

```
      dbos.close();
      bos.close();
      rs.closeRecordStore();
   }

   // Return false if the operation fails
   public synchronized boolean restore () {
     try {
       RecordStore rs =
           RecordStore.openRecordStore(storeName, true);
       byte [] buf = rs.getRecord(1);
       ByteArrayInputStream bis =
           new ByteArrayInputStream (buf);
       DataInputStream dbis = new DataInputStream (bis);
       category = dbis.readUTF();
       googleResultsNum = dbis.readInt();
       googleTextMargin = dbis.readInt();
       googleIsPhrase = dbis.readBoolean();

       dbis.close();
       bis.close();
       rs.closeRecordStore();
       return true;
     } catch (Exception e) {
       return false;
     }
   }
}
```

Here are some examples of how we use the PrefStore Singleton in the application code.

```
public class UIController {

   // Other methods

   public static void setPref (String category,
             int googleResultsNum, int googleTextMargin,
             boolean googleIsPhrase) {
     PrefStore pref = PrefStore.getInstance ();
     pref.category = category;
     pref.googleResultsNum = googleResultsNum;
     pref.googleTextMargin = googleTextMargin;
     pref.googleIsPhrase = googleIsPhrase;

     try {
```

```
      pref.save ();
    } catch (Exception e) {
      System.out.println("Error saving prefScreen");
      e.printStackTrace();
    }
    resume ();
  }

  public static void showPref() throws Exception {
    if (prefScreen == null) {
      prefScreen = new PrefUI ();
    }
    PrefStore pref = PrefStore.getInstance ();
    prefScreen.setStatus(
        pref.category,
        pref.googleResultsNum,
        pref.googleTextMargin,
        pref.googleIsPhrase);
    display.setCurrent(prefScreen);
  }

  // Other methods
}
```

Select from Multiple Implementations

Recall that the QuestionsNavigator class has several abstract methods. In our example application, we provide two concrete subclasses of the QuestionsNavigator: the QuestionsNavigatorRAM and the Questions NavigatorRMS classes use the heap memory and the RMS to store trivia questions, respectively. The subclasses implement the abstract methods to provide alternative behavior of the QuestionsNavigator object. Now, if we need the in-memory version of the QuestionsNavigator, we can call the QuestionsNavigatorRAM constructor directly in the application code. However, if we need to use the RMS version on some other devices later, we have to go to the application code and change all the explicit references of the QuestionsNavigatorRAM to QuestionsNavigatorRMS. If, in the future, we develop more versions of the QuestionsNavigator implementation, the code base could become hard to maintain. To avoid this problem, we can select the appropriate implementation subclass in QuestionsNavigator's factory method (i.e., the getInstance() method). With this approach, the application does not care about the exact name of the QuestionsNavigator subclass, and there is no need to change the application code when we change the implementation class.

```
public abstract class QuestionsNavigator {

  // ... ...

  private static QuestionsNavigator qn = null;

  public static void setUrl (String u) throws Exception {
    url = u;
  }

  // We could choose different implementation classes
  // in this method
   public static QuestionsNavigator getInstance ()
                            throws Exception
{
    if (url == null || "".equals(url)) {
      throw new Exception ("Please set the URL first");
    }
    if (qn == null) {

      // qn = new QuestionsNavigatorRMS ();
      qn = new QuestionsNavigatorRAM ();
    }
    return qn;
  }

  // ... ...
}
```

Select Implementation at Runtime

Taking the QuestionsNavigator class one step further, we can even select the alternative implementation class at runtime instead of compile time. For instance, in the J2ME Generic Connection Framework (see Chapter 7, "Data Connectivity"), if we want to instantiate a Connection object that knows how to handle HTTP connections, we pass the http:// connection string to the Connector.getConnection() factory method. The factory method selects an underlying implementation class, provided by the device manufacturer, at runtime and returns the resultant objects. That gives us tremendous flexibility in interface designs. The J2ME Mobile Media API (see Chapter 9, "Multimedia") also relied heavily on this design pattern.

Object Pools

To reduce the runtime cost of creating, destroying, and garbage collecting objects repeatedly, we store frequently used objects in the memory all the time. The UIController class maintains a pool of Command objects that all view classes can reuse. For frequently used view screens, the `UIController` also maintains their instances.

```java
public class UIController {

    public static boolean isPaused = false;
    public static boolean needSubmit;
    private static MIDlet midlet;
    public static Display display;

    public static Sender sender;
    private static Inbox inbox;

    // The command pool
    public static Command exitCommand =
        new Command ("Exit", Command.EXIT, 0);
    public static Command backCommand =
        new Command ("Back", Command.BACK, 0);
    public static Command doneCommand =
        new Command ("Done", Command.OK, 0);
    public static Command goCommand =
        new Command ("Go", Command.OK, 0);
    public static Command nextCommand =
        new Command ("Next", Command.OK, 0);

    // The screen pool
    public static ShowQuestionUI questionScreen = null;
    public static ShowAnswerUI answerScreen = null;
    public static SelectActionUI actionScreen =
        new SelectActionUI ();
    public static PrefUI prefScreen = null;
    public static InboxUI inboxScreen = null;

    // Other methods
}
```

We reuse a view object via the `setStatus()` method. The previously discussed `ShowQuestionUI` class is a good example. Here, we show the example of the `InboxUI` class, which displays the inbox screen for the built-in messaging client. Please also notice how it makes use of the pooled `Command` objects.

```java
public class InboxUI extends Form
        implements CommandListener {

    private Command nextCommand;
    private Command deleteCommand;
    private Command backCommand;
```

```java
    private Command sendSMSCommand;

    public InboxUI () {
      super("Message");
      nextCommand = UIController.nextCommand;
      deleteCommand =
          new Command("Delete", Command.SCREEN, 1);
      backCommand = UIController.backCommand;
      sendSMSCommand =
          new Command("Send SMS", Command.SCREEN, 1);

      addCommand(sendSMSCommand);
      addCommand(nextCommand);
      addCommand(deleteCommand);
      addCommand(backCommand);
      setCommandListener(this);
    }

    public void setStatus (String mesg) {
      int n = size ();
      for (int i = 0; i < n; i++) {
        delete (i);
      }
      if (mesg == null || "".equals(mesg)) {
        append("No message");
      } else {
        append(mesg);
      }
    }

    public void commandAction(Command c, Displayable s) {
      try {
        if (c == nextCommand) {
          UIController.nextMessage();
        } else if (c == deleteCommand) {
          UIController.deleteMessage();
        } else if (c == backCommand) {
          UIController.exitMessage();
        } else if (c == sendSMSCommand) {
          UIController.showSMSComposer(this);
        }
      } catch (Exception e) {
        e.printStackTrace();
      }
    }
}
```

The following code shows how the UIController makes use of the cached InboxUI instance variable inboxScreen.

```
public class UIController {

  // Other methods

  public static void firstMessage (Displayable back)
                                           throws Exception {
    backStack.push(back);

    if (inboxScreen == null) {
      inboxScreen = new InboxUI ();
    }
    inboxScreen.setStatus (inbox.firstMessage());
    display.setCurrent(inboxScreen);
  }

  public static void nextMessage () throws Exception {
    if (inboxScreen == null) {
      inboxScreen = new InboxUI ();
    }
    inboxScreen.setStatus (inbox.nextMessage());
    display.setCurrent(inboxScreen);
  }

  public static void deleteMessage () throws Exception {
    if (inboxScreen == null) {
      inboxScreen = new InboxUI ();
    }
    inbox.deleteMessage ();

    inboxScreen.setStatus (inbox.nextMessage());
    display.setCurrent(inboxScreen);
  }

  public static void exitMessage () throws Exception {
    inbox.cleanUp();
    showBack();
  }

  // Other methods
}
```

Implement a Back Screen Stack

One of the most popular features in screen-based applications is the back key that allows the user to navigate backwards to previous screens. In the trivia application, we do not have a universal back key. However, we do have back keys on screens in the Chat and Google modules. When the user opens the chat inbox or starts a Google research query in the middle of a question session, he expects to return to the question at which he left off. The back screens are stored in a three-object stack in the UIController class. The stack has only three objects for easy management—in our application, we only need to go back a maximum of three steps. The Stack class has two methods: the push() method pushes a new back screen into the stack. If the stack is full, the oldest screen is discarded. The pop() method retrieves the last back screen from the stack. A very simplistic implementation of the Stack is listed as follows.

```
public class Stack {

  private Displayable [] screens;

  public Stack () {
    screens = new Displayable [3];
  }

  // Push a new back screen into the stack
  public void push (Displayable d) {
    screens[2] = screens[1];
    screens[1] = screens[0];
    screens[0] = d;
  }

  // Retrieve the last "back" screen
  public Displayable pop () {
    Displayable result = screens[0];
    screens[0] = screens[1];
    screens[1] = screens[2];
    screens[2] = null;
    return result;
  }
}
```

WARNING

Since the back screen stack lives in the static controller, it has a very long lifetime. That means screen instances in the stack are not garbage collected. We should design our stack carefully with a limited depth to avoid memory leak situations.

When the `ShowQuestionUI` screen's Google command key is pressed, the command handler passes the `ShowQuestionUI` screen itself to the controller method, which pushes the screen into the back stack and switches the view to the `GoogleQueryUI` screen. The same thing happens when the system switches from the `GoogleQueryUI` screen to the `GoogleResultUI` screen. When the Back command on the `GoogleQueryUI` or `GoogleResultUI` screen is pressed, the controller pops out the last screen in the `backStack` and displays it. Listed below are the relevant code segments in the view classes.

```java
public class ShowQuestionUI extends Form
            implements CommandListener {

  // ... ...
  public void commandAction (Command c, Displayable s) {
      // ... ...
      } else if (c == googleCommand) {
        UIController.showGoogleQuery(this);
      // ... ...
  }
  // ... ...
}

public class GoogleQueryUI extends TextBox
                implements CommandListener {

  // ... ...
  public void commandAction(Command c, Displayable s) {
    try {
      if (c == goCommand) {
        UIController.getGoogleResults(getString(), this);
      } else if (c == backCommand) {
        UIController.showBack();
      }
    } catch (Exception e) {
      e.printStackTrace();
    }
  }
}

public class GoogleResultUI extends Form
                implements CommandListener {
  // ... ...
  public void commandAction (Command c, Displayable s) {
    try {
      if (c == backCommand) {
        UIController.showBack();
      }
```

```
    } catch (Exception e) {
      e.printStackTrace();
    }
  }
}
```

Here are the relevant code segments in the controller to manipulate the back screen stack.

```
public class UIController {

  // ... ...

  public static Stack backStack = new Stack ();

  public static void showGoogleQuery (Displayable back)
                                              throws Exception {
    backStack.push(back);

    GoogleQueryUI show = new GoogleQueryUI ();
    QuestionsNavigator qn =
        QuestionsNavigator.getInstance ();
    show.setStatus(qn.getQuestion());
    display.setCurrent(show);
  }

  public static void getGoogleResults (String keywords,
                                        Displayable back) {
    backStack.push(back);

    WorkerRunnable worker =
        new GoogleSearchWorker (keywords);
    WaitScreen wait = new WaitScreen (worker);

    display.setCurrent(wait);
  }

  public static void showBack () throws Exception {
    display.setCurrent(backStack.pop());
  }
  // ... ...
}
```

Thread Management

Methods in the `UIController` class are responsible for screen switches. For simple tasks, the process is normally to take information from the previous screen, process it in the model layer, and then display the next screen. For tasks that take a long time (e.g., network operations), we have to use separate worker threads to avoid blocking of the main UI thread. In Chapters 7, 8, and 9, we show several simple examples of visual threads. In this section, we discuss the visual thread solutions from the design pattern point of view. We introduce a generic visual thread framework that supports both progress bar and text message feedbacks. The key design element in the framework is the interface between the thread and the wait screen. Figure 11–12 shows the components in the framework.

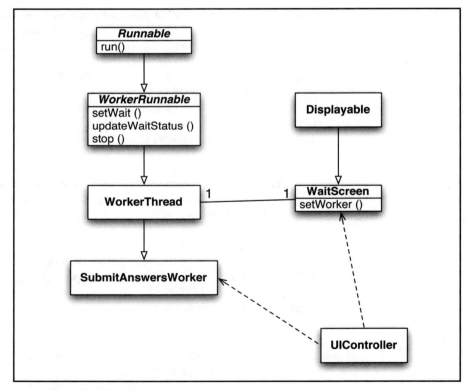

Figure 11–12 The visual thread framework.

The following code shows how to use the framework. You just need to instantiate a worker thread object, associate it with the `WaitScreen` object, and switch the view to display the `WaitScreen`. Figure 11–13 shows the visual thread's `WaitScreen` in action.

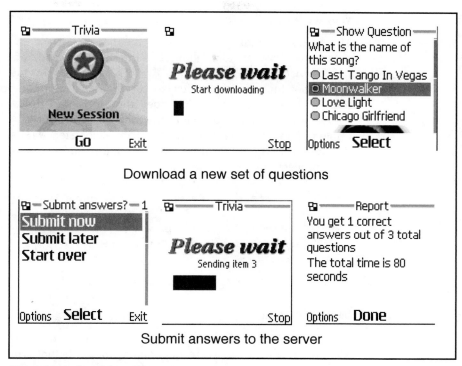

Figure 11–13 Examples of visual threads.

```
public class UIController {

  // Other methods

  public static void submit () {
     // Setup and start the thread
     WorkerRunnable worker = new SubmitAnswersWorker ();
     WaitScreen wait = new WaitScreen ();
     wait.setWorker (worker);

     // Display the wait screen
     display.setCurrent(wait);

     // Make changes to other related UI items
     actionScreen.setStatus(false, needSubmit);
  }

  // Other methods
}
```

WorkerRunnable

The `WorkerRunnable` interface is the base interface in the framework. It extends the Java standard `Runnable` interface with additional methods specific to the visual worker thread. All worker threads in the framework must implement those methods. It also serves as an interface between the actual thread implementation, which does the work, and the `WaitScreen`, which supports user interaction while the work is in progress. A `WorkerRunnable` implementation holds a reference to its associated `WaitScreen` so that the thread can update the display via the `updateWaitStatus()` method as the work processes.

```
public interface WorkerRunnable extends Runnable {

  void setWait (WaitScreen w);
  void updateWaitStatus (String mesg);
  void stop ();
}
```

WorkerThread

For the methods declared in the `WorkerRunnable`, only `run()` (inherited from `Runnable`) and `stop()` are dependent on the actual worker task. All other methods support interactions with visual components (i.e., the `WaitScreen` class) and hence are common to all worker threads. The `WorkerThread` abstract class implements the shared methods to reduce code duplication. All concrete worker thread classes in this framework extend the `WorkerThread` class.

```
public abstract class WorkerThread
          implements WorkerRunnable {

  public WaitScreen wait;
  protected int count = 0;
  protected boolean stopped = false;

  public WorkerThread () {
  }

  public void setWait (WaitScreen w) {
    wait = w;
  }

  public void updateWaitStatus (String mesg) {
    count++;
    wait.message = mesg;
    wait.setCount(count);
```

```
    }
}
```

WaitScreen

The WaitScreen class represents the screen that notifies the user about the progress of the worker thread. The WaitScreen.setWorker() method associates the WaitScreen object with the WorkerThread and starts the thread. The WaitScreen provides a Stop command for the user to stop the worker thread if possible. The worker thread calls the WaitScreen.setCount() method to update the numerical value of the progress bar on the WaitScreen. The setCount() method also forces the screen to redraw itself.

```java
public class WaitScreen extends Canvas
                implements CommandListener {

  private int maxCount = 10;
  private int count = 0;
  public String message = "";

  private Command stop;
  private Image img;
  private WorkerRunnable worker;

  int width = getWidth ();
  int height = getHeight ();

  public WaitScreen () {
    try {
      img = Image.createImage("/" + "wait.png");
    } catch (Exception e) {
      e.printStackTrace ();
      img = null;
    }
    stop = new Command ("Stop", Command.EXIT, 1);
    addCommand (stop);
    setCommandListener (this);
  }

  public void setWorker (WorkerRunnable w) {
    worker = w;

    // The worker updates the current screen
    worker.setWait(this);
    Thread t = new Thread(worker);
    t.start ();
  }
```

```
public void setCount (int value) {
  count = value % maxCount;
  repaint ();
  serviceRepaints ();
}

public void commandAction (Command c, Displayable d) {
  if (c == stop) {
    worker.stop ();
  }
}

public void paint (Graphics g) {
  g.setColor(0xffffff);
  g.fillRect(0,   0, width, height);
  g.setColor(0x000000);

  g.drawImage (img, width / 2, height / 3,
          Graphics.HCENTER | Graphics.VCENTER);

  int buffer = 10; // Pixels at both ends of the bar

  int endX = buffer +
        ((width - (2 * buffer)) * count / maxCount);
  g.setColor(0, 0, 255);
  int startY = height * 2 / 3;
  g.fillRect(buffer, startY,
              endX-buffer, 15);

  g.setFont(Font.getFont(Font.FACE_PROPORTIONAL,
      Font.STYLE_PLAIN, Font.SIZE_SMALL));
  g.drawString (message, width/2, height*2/3 - 10,
          Graphics.BASELINE | Graphics.HCENTER);
  return;
  }
}
```

A Concrete Worker Thread Implementation

A concrete worker thread extends the WorkerThread abstract class and provides implementations for the run() and stop() methods. The thread does all its work in the run() method and updates the WaitScreen by calling updateWaitStatus() periodically. After the work is done, the WaitScreen view is switched to the next screen before the run() method returns. The stop() method is invoked when the user clicks on the Stop command soft key on the WaitScreen. It flags the run() method to stop at the next check point and switches the screen to the main menu instead of the result screen.

The following listing shows the implementation of the SubmitAnswersWorker class. We need to update the WaitScreen status from within the QuestionsNavigator.submit() method, as it handles the time-consuming network operation. Hence, we pass the worker object to the submit() method.

```java
class SubmitAnswersWorker extends WorkerThread {

    public void run () {
        UIController.needSubmit = false;
        try {
            // run the network handler
            QuestionsNavigator qn =
                QuestionsNavigator.getInstance ();

            updateWaitStatus("Starting submitting");
            qn.submit(this);

            updateWaitStatus ("Generate the report screen");
            ResultUI result = new ResultUI ();
            result.setStatus(
                qn.correctNum,
                qn.wrongNum,
                qn.time);

            updateWaitStatus ("Update the history");
            HistoryManager.storeScore(
                qn.correctNum,
                qn.wrongNum,
                qn.time);

            if (!stopped) {
                UIController.display.setCurrent(result);
            }
        } catch (Exception e) {
            e.printStackTrace ();
            if (!stopped) {
                UIController.actionScreen.setStatus(false, true);
                UIController.showAlert("Failed",
                    e.getMessage(), UIController.actionScreen);
            }
        }
    }

    public void stop () {
```

```
        stopped = true;
        UIController.display.setCurrent (
                UIController.actionScreen);
    }
}
```

Network Integration

Like most other mobile enterprise and entertainment applications, the trivia game is driven by backend servers. The server has access to large content databases and other computational resources that are unable to fit into small devices. In Chapters 6 and 7, we introduced techniques to serialize Java value objects and pass them across the network to or from servers. However, for complex applications, we need a more organized approach to make the communication code robust and maintainable. In this section, we discuss some important integration design choices we made in the trivia application.

RPC Protocol

In complex applications, there are multiple integration points between the MIDlet on the device and servlet on the backend server. For example, in the trivia application, the MIDlet downloads questions, submits answers, synchronizes scores, and queries Google services. A uniform RPC protocol helps us to clearly document those interactions, which provides a better design view and avoids confusion during the implementation process. Under this design, each MIDlet request is a stream of bytes starting with a two-byte operation code. The request is passed through an HTTP connection. Each operation code corresponds to a remote method on the server side. There is only one servlet in the system to process all user requests. Upon receiving the request, the servlet first parses out the operation code and then dispatches to the appropriate method. The call parameters of the remote method are serialized Java values in the rest of the request stream. Please refer to Chapter 6 to learn about how to serialize Java values to byte streams using the `DataOuputStream` class. The return values are again serialized and returned to the MIDlet in the HTTP response.

TIP

The RPC servlet is a facade that captures all requests and dispatches them to different subsystems for processing. That hides the complexity inside the remote system and exposes a clean interface to the client.

On the Mobile Client Side

The `OpCodes` class in the MIDlet defines the operation codes. The RPC-processing servlet also has a copy of those operation codes.

```
public class OpCodes {
  public static int DOWNLOAD = 1;
  public static int SUBMIT = 2;
  public static int GOOGLE = 3;
  public static int SYNC01 = 4;
  public static int SYNC02 = 5;
}
```

The `QuestionsNavigator.submit()` method illustrates an RPC transaction from the client side. It first passes the operation code to indicate the RPC method it wants to invoke. The call parameters that follow are the number of questions, the question IDs, and the user-selected answers for each question. The servlet returns the number of correct and wrong answers.

```
public abstract class QuestionsNavigator {

  // ... ...
  public void submit (WorkerRunnable worker)
                                 throws Exception {

    HttpConnection conn = null;
    DataInputStream hdin = null;
    DataOutputStream hdout = null;

    try {
      conn = (HttpConnection) Connector.open( url );
      conn.setRequestMethod(HttpConnection.POST);
      hdout = conn.openDataOutputStream();
      hdout.writeInt(OpCodes.SUBMIT); // Submit opcode

      int numAnswers = answers.size ();
      hdout.writeInt(numAnswers);

      Enumeration enu = answers.keys ();
      int i = 0;
      while (enu.hasMoreElements()) {
        i++;
        worker.updateWaitStatus ("Sending item " + i);
        String questionId = (String) enu.nextElement();
        hdout.writeUTF(questionId);
        hdout.writeInt(((Integer)
             answers.get(questionId)).intValue());
      }
      hdout.flush();

      hdin = conn.openDataInputStream();
      correctNum = hdin.readInt();
```

```
      wrongNum = hdin.readInt();

    } catch (Exception e) {
      e.printStackTrace();
      throw new Exception ("Submit failed");
    } finally {
      try {
        if (conn != null) conn.close();
        if (hdout != null) hdout.close();
        if (hdin != null) hdin.close();
      } catch (Exception e) {}
    }
  }
  // ... ...
}
```

On the Server Side

On the server side, the `MIDPTrivia` servlet dispatches the RPC to appropriate methods based on the operation code.

```
public class MIDPTrivia extends HttpServlet {

  private static int DOWNLOAD = 1;
  private static int SUBMIT = 2;
  private static int GOOGLE = 3;
  private static int SYNC01 = 4;
  private static int SYNC02 = 5;
  private static String googleKey;
  private static String fileroot;

  // ... ...

public void doPost(HttpServletRequest request,
                   HttpServletResponse response)
           throws ServletException, IOException {

    response.setContentType("application/binary");
    try {
      InputStream in = request.getInputStream();
      OutputStream out = response.getOutputStream();
      DataInputStream din = new DataInputStream(in);
      DataOutputStream dout = new DataOutputStream(out);

      int opcode = din.readInt ();
      if ( opcode == DOWNLOAD) {
        processDownload (din, dout);
```

```
        } else if ( opcode == SUBMIT) {
          processSubmit (din, dout);
        } else if ( opcode == GOOGLE) {
          processGoogle (din, dout);
        } else if ( opcode == SYNC01) {
          processSync01 (din, dout);
        } else if ( opcode == SYNC02) {
          processSync02 (din, dout);
        } else {
          throw new Exception("wrong op code");
        }
        din.close();
        dout.close();
        in.close();
        out.close();

      } catch (Exception e) {
        e.printStackTrace();
      }
    }

    // ... ...
}
```

The target RPC method `processSubmit()` parses the call parameters and does the requested work.

```
public class MIDPTrivia extends HttpServlet {

    // ... ...

    private void processSubmit (DataInputStream din,
                DataOutputStream dout) throws Exception {
      Connection c =
        DriverManager.getConnection ("jdbc:hsqldb:" +
                        fileroot + "TriviaDB", "sa", "");
      int correctNum = 0, totalNum = 0, answer = 0;
      String questionId = null;
      PreparedStatement pstmt =
          c.prepareStatement("select id from " +
              "Questions where id=? and answerId=?",
              ResultSet.TYPE_SCROLL_INSENSITIVE,
              ResultSet.CONCUR_READ_ONLY);
      int size = din.readInt();
      for (int i = 0; i < size; i++) {
        questionId = din.readUTF();
        answer = din.readInt();
```

```
      pstmt.setString(1, questionId);
      pstmt.setString(2, Integer.toString(answer));
      ResultSet rs = pstmt.executeQuery();
      if (rs.next()) correctNum++;
      totalNum++;
    }
    dout.writeInt(correctNum);
    dout.writeInt(totalNum - correctNum);
    dout.flush();
    pstmt.close();
    c.close();
  }
}
```

NOTE

The RPC is synchronous in nature. The mobile application must have active network connections for the RPC to succeed. For occasionally connected smart clients, we can design mechanisms to schedule RPCs flexibly. Figure 11–4 shows how the trivia MIDlet allows the user to postpone submitting answers to the server if the network is temporarily unavailable.

Synchronization

A key architectural design pattern of mobile applications is data synchronization. Mobile clients can synchronize with backend servers or with each other. Synchronization is different from synchronous RPC in the sense that it does not require always-on network connections. The smart client can operate on its own data for extended periods and only synchronize when the network is available.

WARNING

Of course, the synchronization pattern does not apply to real-time application data. However, the vast majority of mobile applications do not require real-time data access. For example, the hugely popular personal information management and email applications on PDA devices are all based on synchronization with PCs.

In addition, the synchronization paradigm makes it easy to support multiple devices in the same application. In the case of our trivia application, the user might play the game from different devices. It would be nice if we could access the game scores from any device. We do this by synchronizing each device's score list with the server (see Figure 11–14). The synchronization process works as follows.

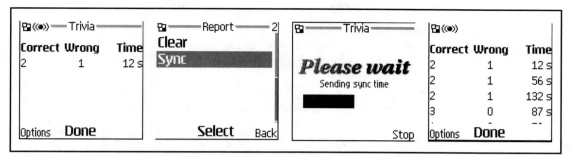

Figure 11–14 The two-step synchronization process.

- The client sends the timestamp of the last synchronization event on this device to the server.
- The server returns all records that are more recent than the client's last synchronization time. It also returns the server's last synchronization timestamp.
- The client inserts the new server records into its database and returns all its local records that are later than the server's last synchronization time.
- The server inserts the new records to its database.

On the Client Side

In the MIDlet, the `synchronize()` method in the `HistoryManager` class handles the synchronization process. It initializes two HTTP transactions to send and receive the most recent synchronization timestamps as well as updated score records.

```
public class HistoryManager {

    // ... ...

    static public void synchronize (WorkerRunnable worker)
                                             throws Exception {

        RecordStore rs =
            RecordStore.openRecordStore(storeName, true);

        worker.updateWaitStatus ("Getting last sync time");
        // get the last sync time stamp
        lastSyncTime = byteArray2Long(rs.getRecord(1));
        worker.updateWaitStatus("Client last sync: " +
                                    lastSyncTime);
        readFromRMS ();
```

```
HttpConnection conn = null;
DataInputStream hdin = null;
DataOutputStream hdout = null;

try {
  worker.updateWaitStatus ("Opening connection");
  conn = (HttpConnection) Connector.open(serverurl);
  conn.setRequestMethod(HttpConnection.POST);
  hdout = conn.openDataOutputStream();
  worker.updateWaitStatus ("Sending sync time");
  hdout.writeInt(OpCodes.SYNC01); // Submit opcode
  // POST the time stamp to the HTTP sync site
  hdout.writeLong(lastSyncTime);
  hdout.flush();

  worker.updateWaitStatus ("Getting server set");
  hdin = conn.openDataInputStream();
  // GET the server sync time stamp
  long serverSyncTime = hdin.readLong();
  worker.updateWaitStatus("Server last sync: " +
                          serverSyncTime);
  // GET the server update list
  int size = hdin.readInt();
  worker.updateWaitStatus("Size from server: "+size);

  for (int i = 0; i < size; i++) {
    worker.updateWaitStatus ("Getting item " + i);
    int correctNum = hdin.readInt();
    int wrongNum = hdin.readInt();
    long time = hdin.readLong();
    long ts = hdin.readLong();
    // Insert the server update list into the RMS
    ByteArrayOutputStream bos =
        new ByteArrayOutputStream ();
    DataOutputStream dbos =
        new DataOutputStream (bos);
    dbos.writeInt(correctNum);
    dbos.writeInt(wrongNum);
    dbos.writeLong(time);
    dbos.writeLong(ts);
    dbos.flush();
    byte [] buf = bos.toByteArray ();
    dbos.close();
    bos.close();
    rs.addRecord(buf, 0, buf.length);
  }
```

```
// Close everything
hdin.close();
hdout.close();
conn.close();

// Determine the client update list size
worker.updateWaitStatus ("Determine client set");
size = 0;
for (int i = 0; i < timestamps.length; i++) {
  if (timestamps[i] > serverSyncTime) {
    size++;
  }
}

// POST the client update list
worker.updateWaitStatus ("Writing to the server");
conn = (HttpConnection) Connector.open(serverurl);
conn.setRequestMethod(HttpConnection.POST);
hdout = conn.openDataOutputStream();
hdout.writeInt(OpCodes.SYNC02); // Submit opcode
hdout.writeInt(size);

for (int i = 0; i < timestamps.length; i++) {
  if (timestamps[i] > serverSyncTime) {
    worker.updateWaitStatus ("Sending item " + i);
    hdout.writeInt(correctNums[i]);
    hdout.writeInt(wrongNums[i]);
    hdout.writeLong(times[i]);
    hdout.writeLong(timestamps[i]);
  }
}
hdout.flush();
// Close everything
hdout.close();
conn.close();

// Update the "last sync time" timestamp,
// which is the first record in the store
long timestamp = System.currentTimeMillis();
byte [] buf = long2ByteArray(timestamp);
rs.setRecord(1, buf, 0, buf.length);
worker.updateWaitStatus("Update sync: " +
                        timestamp);

// Close the record store
rs.closeRecordStore();
```

```
      isUpToDate = false;

   } catch (Exception e) {
     e.printStackTrace();
     throw new Exception ("Connection error");
   } finally {
     try {
       if (conn != null) conn.close();
       if (hdout != null) hdout.close();
       if (hdin != null) hdin.close();
     } catch (Exception e) {}
   }
 }

 // ... ...
}
```

On the Server Side

Inside the MIDPTrivia servlet, the processSync01() and processSync02()
methods process the two-step synchronization requests.

```
public class MIDPTrivia extends HttpServlet {

 // ... ...

 private void processSync01 (DataInputStream din,
            DataOutputStream dout) throws Exception {

   long clientSyncTime = din.readLong();

   Connection c =
     DriverManager.getConnection ("jdbc:hsqldb:" +
                  fileroot + "TriviaDB", "sa", "");
   Statement stmt = c.createStatement(
       ResultSet.TYPE_SCROLL_INSENSITIVE,
       ResultSet.CONCUR_READ_ONLY);

   // Get the server sync time stamp
   ResultSet rs = stmt.executeQuery("select ts from " +
                    "History where time < 0");
   rs.next();
   long serverSyncTime = rs.getLong(1);
   rs.close();

   // Get the size of the update list
   ResultSet rs1 =
```

```
                    stmt.executeQuery("select ts, correctNum, " +
                    "wrongNum, time " + " from History " +
                    "where ts > " + clientSyncTime +
                    " and time > 0");
        int size = 0;
        while (rs1.next()) size++;
        rs1.beforeFirst();

        // Return the time stamp,
        // update list size and the list itself
        dout.writeLong(serverSyncTime);
        dout.writeInt(size);
        while (rs1.next()) {
          dout.writeInt (rs1.getInt(2));
          dout.writeInt (rs1.getInt(3));
          dout.writeLong (rs1.getLong(4));
          dout.writeLong (rs1.getLong(1));
        }
        dout.flush();
        rs1.close();
        stmt.close();
        c.close();
    }

    private void processSync02 (DataInputStream din,
                DataOutputStream dout) throws Exception {

      Connection c =
        DriverManager.getConnection ("jdbc:hsqldb:" +
          fileroot + "TriviaDB", "sa", "");
      PreparedStatement pstmt =
          c.prepareStatement("insert into History " +
              "(ts, correctNum, wrongNum, time) " +
              "values (?, ?, ?, ?)",
              ResultSet.TYPE_SCROLL_INSENSITIVE,
              ResultSet.CONCUR_READ_ONLY);
      int size = din.readInt();
      for (int i = 0; i < size; i++) {
        pstmt.setInt (2, din.readInt());
        pstmt.setInt (3, din.readInt());
        pstmt.setLong (4, din.readLong());
        pstmt.setLong (1, din.readLong());
        pstmt.executeUpdate();
      }
      pstmt.close();

      Statement stmt = c.createStatement(
```

```
                    ResultSet.TYPE_SCROLL_INSENSITIVE,
                    ResultSet.CONCUR_READ_ONLY);
        stmt.executeUpdate("update History set ts=" +
                            System.currentTimeMillis() +
                            " where time < 0");
        stmt.close();
        c.close();
    }

    // ... ...
}
```

Web Service Gateway

So far, we discussed how to connect MIDlets to specialized backend servlets. This is a powerful paradigm. However, most existing enterprise systems are not specially designed for mobile clients. A growing trend in the industry is expose services through XML-based Web Service interfaces. For example, Google offers its search service as a Web Service over the Internet. The key benefit of Web Services is its standards-based open interface. The SOAP protocol, which is widely used in Web Service systems to exchange objects between endpoints, is an XML-based open protocol standardized by the W3C. A published SOAP interface allows third-party clients to interface with the Web Service with minimal amount of integration-specific code. This reduces system complexity and speeds up the development process. In this book, we do not cover the details of Web Services, but you may refer to Eric Newcomer's book *Understanding Web Services: XML, WSDL, SOAP, and UDDI* (Addison-Wesley, 2002).

However, it has been difficult to consume Web Services on a mobile device, since XML processing is a computationally intensive task. Popular open source XML libraries for J2ME (e.g., kXML, kSOAP, and minXML) increase the JAR size by 10kb to 50kb and significantly increase the response time on slow CPUs. In addition, the XML data format uses plain text to describe data structures, which is not optimized for bandwidth efficiency. One way to solve these problems is to build a special gateway servlet for Web Services (see Figure 11–15). The servlet knows how to talk with the target Web Service using XML/SOAP. It translates the XML-based requests and responses to binary streams that can be easily digested by the J2ME client. In the trivia application, we demonstrate how to build such a Web Services gateway servlet for the Google Web Service.

NOTE   The J2ME Web Services API (JSR 172) is a specification for XML parsers and SOAP Web Services clients on mobile devices. It has just become a formal Java specification in 2004. Currently, no Nokia device supports the JSR 172 API in firmware. Nokia is still evaluating whether and when to support this API on future Series 40 devices.

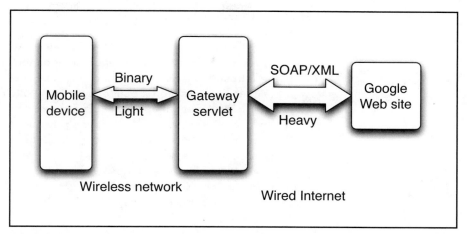

Figure 11–15 Web Services gateway.

On the Client Side

The GoogleBrowser class in the MIDlet shows how to use the gateway servlet from the client side. It is just like any other RPC client. It sends in the query string and search options, and receives the spell suggestions and search results.

```
public class GoogleBrowser {

  public static String spellSugg;
  public static String [] urls;
  public static String [] snippets;
  private static String serverurl;

  private GoogleBrowser () {
  }

  public static void init (String u) {
    serverurl = u;
    spellSugg = "No Suggestion";
    urls = new String [0];
    snippets = new String [0];
  }

  public static void search (String keywords,
        boolean isPhrase, int maxBuffer, int maxResults,
              WorkerRunnable worker) throws Exception {
    HttpConnection conn = null;
    DataInputStream hdin = null;
```

```
      DataOutputStream hdout = null;

      try {
        worker.updateWaitStatus ("Opening connection");
        conn = (HttpConnection) Connector.open(serverurl);
        conn.setRequestMethod(HttpConnection.POST);
        hdout = conn.openDataOutputStream();
        worker.updateWaitStatus ("Sending request");
        hdout.writeInt(OpCodes.GOOGLE); // Submit opcode
        hdout.writeUTF(keywords);
        hdout.writeBoolean(isPhrase);
        hdout.writeInt(maxBuffer);
        hdout.writeInt(maxResults);
        hdout.flush();

        worker.updateWaitStatus ("Spell checking");
        hdin = conn.openDataInputStream();
        spellSugg = hdin.readUTF();
        int size = hdin.readInt();
        snippets = new String [size];
        urls = new String [size];

        for (int i = 0; i < size; i++) {
          worker.updateWaitStatus ("Downloading item "+i);
          urls[i] = hdin.readUTF();
          snippets[i] = hdin.readUTF();
        }
      } catch (Exception e) {
        e.printStackTrace();
        throw new Exception ("Connection error");
      } finally {
        try {
          if (conn != null) conn.close();
          if (hdout != null) hdout.close();
          if (hdin != null) hdin.close();
        } catch (Exception e) {}
      }
    }
  }
```

On the Server Side

The processGoogle() method in the MIDPTrivia servlet delegates the Google query to a Facade class that consolidates all Google-related functions.

```
public class MIDPTrivia extends HttpServlet {
```

```
// ... ...

private void processGoogle (DataInputStream din,
            DataOutputStream dout) throws Exception {
   String keywords = din.readUTF();
   boolean isPhrase = din.readBoolean();
   int maxBuffer = din.readInt();
   int maxResults = din.readInt();

   Facade f = new Facade (googleKey);
   f.getResults(keywords, isPhrase,
                maxBuffer, maxResults);

   dout.writeUTF(f.spellSugg);
   dout.writeInt(f.urls.length);
   for (int i = 0; i < f.urls.length; i++) {
      dout.writeUTF(f.urls[i]);
      dout.writeUTF(f.snippets[i]);
   }
   dout.flush();
}

// ... ...
}
```

The `Facade.getResults()` method calls the `GoogleUtil` class's `search()`, `getSpellSugg()`, and `getCache()` methods to query Google. The other methods in the `Facade` class process the Google results and optimize them for mobile network and display. Much of the work in the `Facade` class is CPU- and network-intensive. It is a conscious design choice to put them on the server side rather than on the mobile client.

```
public class Facade {

   public String spellSugg;
   public String [] snippets;
   public String [] urls;

   private String key;

   public Facade (String k) {
      key = k;
   }

   public void getResults (String keywords,
      boolean isPhrase, int maxBuffer, int maxResults) {
      try {
```

```java
    String query = keywords;
    if (isPhrase) {
      query = reformatPhraseQuery(keywords);
    }

    spellSugg = GoogleUtil.getSpellSugg(key, query);
    if (spellSugg == null || "".equals(spellSugg)
                          || "null".equals(spellSugg)) {
      spellSugg = "The spelling is correct";
    }
    urls = GoogleUtil.search(key, query, maxResults);
    snippets = new String [urls.length];

    for (int i = 0; i < urls.length; i++) {
      String cache = GoogleUtil.getCache(key, urls[i]);
      cache = stripTags(cache);
      String snippet = cutSnippet (cache, maxBuffer,
                                   keywords, isPhrase);
      if (snippet == null || "".equals(snippet)) {
        snippets[i] = "No snippet";
      } else {
        snippets[i] = snippet;
      }
    }
  } catch (Exception e) {
    e.printStackTrace();
    System.out.println("Error in getResults");
    spellSugg = "error";
    snippets = null;
  }
}

private String reformatPhraseQuery (String keywords) {
  StringTokenizer st = new StringTokenizer(keywords);
  StringBuffer sb = new StringBuffer ();
  sb.append("\"");
  while (st.hasMoreTokens()) {
    sb.append("+").append(st.nextToken()).append(" ");
  }
  String result = sb.toString().trim();
  result = result + "\"";
  return result;
}

private String stripTags (String cache) {
  StringBuffer cacheBuffer = new StringBuffer(cache);
  int start, end;
```

```java
      while ((start = cacheBuffer.indexOf("<")) != -1) {
        end = cacheBuffer.indexOf(">", start);
        if (end == -1) {
          break;
        } else {
          cacheBuffer.replace(start, end + 1, " ");
        }
      }
      if ((end = cacheBuffer.indexOf(
                    "responsible for its content.")) != -1){
        end = end + 29;
        cacheBuffer.replace(0, end, "");
      }
      while ((start = cacheBuffer.indexOf("\n")) != -1 ||
             (start = cacheBuffer.indexOf("\r")) != -1 ||
             (start = cacheBuffer.indexOf("\t")) != -1) {
        end = start + 1;
        cacheBuffer.replace(start, end, " ");
      }
      while ((start = cacheBuffer.indexOf(" ")) !=-1){
        end = start + 6;
        cacheBuffer.replace(start, end, " ");
      }
      while ((start = cacheBuffer.indexOf("  ")) != -1) {
        end = start + 2;
        cacheBuffer.replace(start, end, " ");
      }
      return cacheBuffer.toString().trim();
    }

    private String cutSnippet (String cache, int maxBuffer,
                    String keywords, boolean isPhrase) {
      int start = 0;
      int end = 0;
      int index = -1;
      if (isPhrase) {
        index = cache.toUpperCase().indexOf(
                        keywords.toUpperCase());
        if ( index != -1) {
          index += keywords.length() / 2;
        }
      } else {
        StringTokenizer st = new StringTokenizer(keywords);
        while (st.hasMoreTokens()) {
          String word = st.nextToken ();
          index = cache.toUpperCase().indexOf(
                        word.toUpperCase());
```

```
        if (index != -1) {
          index = index + word.length() / 2;
          break;
        }
      }
    }

    if (index == -1) {
      return null;
    }

    start = index - maxBuffer / 2;
    end = index + maxBuffer / 2;
    if (start < 0) start = 0;
    if (end > cache.length() - 1)
        end = cache.length() - 1;

    return cache.substring(start, end);
  }
}
```

Static methods in the `GoogleUtil` class query Google Web Services. The `GoogleSearch` class parses the SOAP messages used to access Google functionalities, and `GoogleSearchResult` class represents a search result. The Google access classes, under the `com.google.soap.search` Java package, are provided by Google's developer toolkit, which is available for free download from Google's Web site. You can also find more documentation on how to use the Google API for more complex tasks in the toolkit.

```
public class GoogleUtil {

  private static String encoding = "UTF-8";

  // Returns a list of URLs
  public static String [] search (String key,
      String keywords, int maxResults) throws Exception {
    GoogleSearch search = new GoogleSearch();
    search.setKey(key);
    search.setMaxResults(maxResults);
    search.setQueryString(keywords);
    GoogleSearchResult result = search.doSearch();
    GoogleSearchResultElement [] elements =
        result.getResultElements();
    String [] ret = new String [elements.length];
    for (int i = 0; i < elements.length; i++) {
      ret[i] = elements[i].getURL();
    }
```

```
      return ret;
   }

   // Get the base64 decoded google cache
   public static String getCache (String key,
                           String url) throws Exception {
      GoogleSearch search = new GoogleSearch();
      search.setKey(key);
      search.setOutputEncoding (encoding);
      return new String (search.doGetCachedPage(url),
                           encoding);
   }

   public static String getSpellSugg (String key,
                           String word) throws Exception {
      GoogleSearch search = new GoogleSearch();
      search.setKey(key);
      return search.doSpellingSuggestion(word);
   }
}
```

Summary

In this chapter, we used the multimedia trivia game as an example to demonstrate common design patterns and implementation techniques in complex networked mobile applications. We covered the end-to-end MVC pattern, object management, visual worker threads, and the efficient use of network servers.

chapter

12

Developing Scalable Applications

Design techniques and tools to make your application run on any Java devices.

Although all Nokia Developer Platforms support Java technology, a single MIDlet will not necessarily run on all Nokia devices without modification. Even where it would be possible to build such a MIDlet, using a one-size-fits-all approach is likely to produce a MIDlet that runs marginally well on all devices and may not successfully compete against better-optimized applications. On one hand, some of today's mobile devices have limited capabilities that require aggressive optimization from application developers (e.g., to reduce the JAR file size to fit into the 64KB limit of earlier Series 40 devices). On the other hand, the newest devices offer richer API sets and larger address spaces, and a user who pays a premium price for a high-end phone is unlikely to be satisfied with an application that does not exploit the device's capabilities.

The variation in devices requires us to individually optimize for each device we target, but that does not mean we need to develop an application over and over. As a general rule, about 80 percent of a typical development effort is devoted to generating core code that works across the entire population of target devices; the other 20 percent is spent migrating features between platform families and optimizing the code for specific devices. If we approach the optimization process strategically, the increased workload will be more than compensated by an increased market potential.

As a result of the develop/optimize process, for a MIDlet project, we could generate multiple versions of the JAD and JAR file pair, each optimized for a specific handset or a specific group of handsets. For very simple applications, we might be able to build each JAD and JAR file pair from scratch or by branching from a common source. However, for complex applications, manually keeping track of multiple source code repositories with lots of duplicated code manually is impractical and error prone. We need a solution to scale a single maintainable code base to match multiple target device optimization requirements. In this chapter, we introduce important strategies, designs, and tools to develop and manage scalable mobile applications. Key topics covered in this chapter include the following:

- **Develop and optimize:** covers the recommended application development process from Forum Nokia. We discuss the required optimization for Series 40 and Series 60 devices. We will also introduce coding best practices in the develop phase to minimize future code changes in the optimize phase.

- **Replaceable modules:** discusses how to use replaceable modules to customize both the UI presentation and logical behavior of an application for different devices.

- **Preprocessor and postprocessor:** uses the open source J2ME build tool, Antenna, to illustrate how to generate different versions of the source code from the same code base and then optimize the results automatically. Antenna is an open source extension to the Apache Ant project.

The most important tool we use in this chapter is Apache Ant and its Antenna extension. If you are not familiar with Ant, please refer to Chapter 3, "Getting Started," for an introduction. Most examples in this chapter are based on the trivia game sample code discussed in Chapter 11, "End-to-End Design Patterns."

Develop and Optimize

The Nokia Developer Platforms promote the develop-and-optimize process for application development. The application development process starts from marketing research and requirement analysis. Based on the requirements and available developer skills, we can select an enabler technology upon which we can develop the application. For Nokia devices, the enabler technology must be supported by the Nokia Developer Platforms. For example, if our application requires rich user interfaces and offline capabilities, and has to run on a large number of devices, the Java MIDP platform is the most sensible choice. For more information about how to choose the right technology for your application, please refer to Chapter 2, "Introducing Nokia Developer Platforms." In this chapter, we focus on applications based on the Java MIDP technology.

After choosing the enabler technology, we can build a generic version of the target application, which has all the core features and only requires the technology enablers contained in one of the developer platform major releases. We can begin to test this generic application by selecting a target device that includes only the base platform software. For example, we could begin developing for Series 40 Developer Platform 1.0 and work with the Nokia 7210, or we could start with Series 40 Developer Platform 2.0 and work with the Nokia 6230.

For beginning developers, we suggest starting from the Nokia Series 60 devices since they have less resource constraints and generally support more Java APIs. As your development skill matures (e.g., after studying this book), you can port and optimize your applications to the more restrictive Series 40 devices. For experienced developers, you can start from Series 40 devices and define the "must-have" features on those devices. That helps to ensure that your application runs well on the largest number of phones. Then, you can scale it up to Series 60 devices by adding more features and relaxing resource consumption requirements.

TIP

Porting applications to Series 40 devices is a major challenge facing mobile application developers. On one hand, the Nokia Series 40 devices have by far the largest market share compared with other Java-based mobile phones. For any application that targets the mass market, Series 40 support is crucial for reaching the critical mass. On the other hand, Series 40 software often needs to be heavily optimized in order to run efficiently on the limited hardware.

With the generic version of the application ready, we should now compile a list of all devices that we want to target. Then, based on each device's unique characteristics, we optimize the application for the best compromise of features and user experience. The key challenges are to have a consistent optimization strategy and leverage tools to automate the process. In this section, we discuss typical device-to-device variations that might need optimization. We also cover key techniques that we can use in the generic application to reduce the required optimization work down the road.

Screen Characteristics

The display screen is a major differentiating factor for devices. A compelling mobile application must display well on all target devices. This is one of the most important optimization tasks. The good news is that the MIDP API has several built-in methods to help us write screen-agnostic applications early on in the develop phase.

As we discussed in Chapter 2, Nokia devices have a variety of screen sizes. For example, a typical Series 40 device has a 128 by 128 screen, while a typical Series 60 device has a 176 by 208 screen. In MIDP's `Displayable` abstract class, the `getHeight()` and `getWidth()` methods return the values of the usable screen size. To minimize manual device-to-device optimization work in the future, we should use those methods wisely. On a low-level `Canvas`, we should position images, text strings, and other components proportionally to the screen size. For example, we can place an image at coordinate `[getWidth()/2, getHeight()/2]` rather than at `[64, 64]` to ensure that it is at center screen for all target devices. On a high-level `Form` in an MIDP 2.0 application, we can use the `Item.LAYOUT_CENTER` layout attribute to place an item at the center of the row. For more information about the layout management in MIDP 2.0, please refer to Chapter 4, "MIDP User Interface."

Choosing the right icon images is also important for a professional-looking display screen. Since images in the MIDP are bitmap based, they do not scale well. It is important that we use the right image sizes for screen size. An icon designed for a Series 60 screen would look too big on a Series 40 device. In the `Display` class, we can query the optimal sizes of the icon images using the getBestImageWidth() and getBestImageHeight() methods (MIDP 2.0 only). These methods take in the type for the desired icon image as arguments. In the MIDP 2.0, available icon types are LIST_ELEMENT, CHOICE_GROUP_ELEMENT, and ALERT. These recommended image dimensions can be used outside of the high-level user interface as well. For example, when we need to assemble a Canvas in a game, the LIST_ELEMENT size is a good sprite image size for a foreground character, and the ALERT size is probably suitable for a landscape object in the background. In a business or media application, we often display images from the server on a form. We can pass the return values of those methods to the server and ask the server to provide the correct display images.

Besides different screen sizes, different device displays also support different color depths and transparency levels. The numColors() and numAlphaLevels() methods in the Display class return the number of colors and alpha levels supported on this device.

TIP

We do not have to specify the exact font size for text strings on a Canvas or in a StringItem. The font attributes defined in the MIDP API are automatically adjusted to the correct absolute font size for the underlying device. For example, the Font.SIZE_SMALL attribute typically corresponds to the 9-pt size on a Series 40 device and the 12-pt size on a Series 60 device. For more information about fonts in Series 40 devices, please refer to Chapter 4.

Memory Constraints

A mobile device is typically memory constrained. The memory limits include the maximum JAR file size, the available heap memory, and the available RMS store space.

JAR Size Limit

Most Series 40 Developer Platform 1.0 devices can only install MIDlet JAR files smaller than 64KB. The current Series 40 Developer Platform 2.0 devices (e.g., Nokia 6230 and Nokia 5140) support 128KB JAR files. Most Series 60, 80, and 90 devices do not impose an upper limit for the JAR file as long as the device has sufficient memory to store them. If the generic version of our application exceeds the target device's JAR file size limit, we can do the following:

- **Optimize the internal structure to reduce the footprint**. This is often done at the cost of performance. For example, we can download images from the Web at runtime rather than bundle them in the JAR file.

- **Take out nonessential features.** For example, in the trivia application in Chapter 11, "End-to-End Design Patterns," we can take out the Chat and Google features without hurting the application's core value.

- **Reduce the use of high-resolution images and large multimedia files.** On Nokia devices, we could consider using JPEG images, which offer better compression for photos, instead of png images in some cases. We could also consider using MIDI files for music instead of wav files.

Heap Memory

Each device has a different amount of heap memory available for Java applications. Early Series 40 Developer Platform 1.0 devices have about 200KB of heap space, while newer devices can have several megabytes. If the memory is used up and the garbage collector cannot free sufficient memory space in time, the application crashes with an `OutOfMemoryError`. To limit heap-memory usage, we could reduce the number of large images or players for large media files. We could also reduce the size of static object pools, such as the back screen stack described in Chapter 11. Sometimes, the heap-memory shortage is caused by the application simply being too busy to run the garbage collector. In order to keep the garbage collector up to date, we can call the `System.gc()` method explicitly after large objects go out of scope. Please note that we trade performance for memory usage by calling `System.gc()` explicitly, since the method runs slowly and does not return until it finishes the garbage collecting work.

RMS Space

Series 40 devices typically can accommodate only small RMS stores (20KB or more) for local persistent storage. Series 60 and above devices can have RMS stores as big as their physical memory, which is several megabytes. So, if we have an image manipulation application on Series 60 devices, we could store the manipulated image data in the RMS store. But if we scale it to Series 40 devices, we have to add a network component to persist large amounts of data to the network server.

API Availability

The J2ME platform is quickly evolving. New API specifications and new devices implementing those APIs come out every couple of months. If we develop the generic version of the application based on the MIDP 2.0 API, which is available on Series 40 Developer Platform 2.0, we will encounter some unsupported APIs when trying to run it on Developer Platform 1.0 devices, which are based on MIDP 1.0. API differences between MIDP 2.0 and 1.0 are covered in previous chapters of this book. The key point is that we are likely to encounter API-level code changes when optimizing the application for different devices.

Even within the same Developer Platform, different devices have different MIDP extension APIs. Here are some example devices in the Series 40 Developer Platform 1.0.

- Nokia 7210 only supports MIDP 1.0 plus the Nokia UI API extension package.

- Nokia 6800 supports MIDP 1.0, Nokia UI API, and the Wireless Messaging API (WMA).

- Nokia 3410 supports MIDP 1.0, Nokia UI API, and a Nokia-specific SMS package (Nokia SMS API) that predates the WMA.

- Nokia 3300 supports MIDP 1.0, Nokia UI API, WMA, and the Mobile Media API (MMAPI).

Although all Series 40 Developer Platform 2.0 devices support MIDP 2.0, WMA, MMAPI, and the Bluetooth API, they could support different versions of the add-on API packages. For example, the WMA 2.0 would add features for accessing MMS (Multimedia Messaging Services) messages from the Java runtime. Future devices could further support other J2ME APIs that just come out of the JSR process. Examples of those upcoming APIs include the Location API, FileConnection and PIM APIs, and Mobile 3D Graphics API. For more information on Nokia Java roadmaps, please refer to Chapter 2.

NOTE Even if two devices implement the same set of APIs, there may be subtle variations in behavior. For example, a known issue on the behavior of one device may be corrected in the firmware release used in a later device. Many of these known issues are documented on the Forum Nokia Web site.

Protocol Availability

The factory class design pattern (see Chapter 11) is frequently used in J2ME to increase the flexibility of the API. The idea is to use URI locator strings instead of formal class names to select and instantiate classes. The benefit is that the different devices can choose to support different URL protocols (i.e., schemes) while staying within the same API framework. The caveat is that we have to consider such device-to-device variations during the optimization process. The MMAPI and GCF are the two most important factory-class-based APIs on Nokia devices.

The MMAPI

As we saw in Chapter 9, "Multimedia," the MMAPI gives its implementing devices a lot of freedom to support various content protocols and types. For example, the Nokia 6600 device supports video playback and camera access from the MMAPI, while the Nokia 6230 allows neither. On the other hand, the Nokia 6600 supports fewer audio playback controls compared with the Nokia 6230. We can find out the exact media protocols and content types supported on a particular device at runtime via the `getSupportedContentTypes()` and `getSupportedProtocols()` methods in the `Manager` class. We can pass the supported content types discovered at runtime to the networked server to download the correct content for the current device. This way, we do not have to modify the hardcoded content types for each device in the optimization process.

For maximum portability, we recommend that you put all method calls to the MMAPI in one thread.

The GCF

Series 40 Developer Platform 1.0 and 2.0 devices both support the GCF. However, the supported connection protocols vary between devices. If the generic version of the application utilizes the HTTPS protocol for secure communication, we should change to custom crypto libraries (e.g., the Phaos SSL library for J2ME http://www.phaos.com/) when porting to Series 40 Developer Platform 1.0 devices.

Behavior of UI Components

To scale an application from Series 40 to Series 60 or from MIDP 1.0 to MIDP 2.0, we often need to adjust the behavior of certain UI components to make it run smoothly. For example, the Series 60 MIDP implementation appends a Close command to the Options menu. If the user selects that command, the application quits unconditionally. If our application already implements a Close command, it will run fine on Series 40 devices but show duplicated commands on Series 60 devices. Another example is the display of long text in List and ChoiceGroup items. On MIDP 1.0 devices, the long text is automatically wrapped; on MIDP 2.0 devices, the Choice.setFitPolicy() method is used to control the wrapping behavior. The MIDP 2.0 devices also allow us to use popup menus to substitute for radio button selection lists to save screen real estate.

Thread Behavior

The MIDP execution environment is inherently multithreaded. Differences in thread implementations can cause very visible differences in application behavior. For example, on some devices, the Display.setCurrent() method changes the display to the next screen immediately, while others are not updated until the system is idle. Both behaviors are permitted by the MIDP specification. That could cause problems when we need to switch multiple screens over a short period. Please refer to the visual worker thread implementation in Chapter 7, "Data Connectivity," for a concrete example of this problem and a possible solution. Similarly, when we update an Item on a Form, some implementations reflect the changes on the screen immediately, while others do not. In addition, it is a known issue that some Series 60 devices do not properly abort all user-initiated threads when the application is terminated. For applications optimized for those devices, we have to manually notify all user-initiated running threads to exit.

Languages and Cultures

Devices released in different markets support different languages and data display conventions (e.g., the time and date format). The multimedia content can also be optimized for audiences with different cultural backgrounds. For example, when a Chinese user plays a game, she would probably prefer Chinese pop music to American hip-hop in the background. On Nokia devices, the user can choose the default language and culture mode by selecting from the system menu. The MIDlet can call the `System.getProperty("microedition.locale")` method to find out which language/culture setting the user has selected and then customize the display or multimedia content. For example, the return value en-US indicates American English; es-US indicates American Spanish; zh-CN indicates simplified Chinese; and fi-FI indicates Finnish.

Bundling multiple versions of the content for different languages and cultures inflates the size of the deployment JAR file. A better solution is to make different versions of the JAR file and make them available to users in different markets. Alternatively, if the MIDlet primarily downloads content from a server, we can use a single generic JAR file and configure the server to provide the appropriate content based on the `Content-Language` header of the HTTP request from the client, which is set to be the value of the `microedition.locale` system property using the following snippet.

```
HttpConnection c = (HttpConnection) Connector.open(url);
c.setRequestProperty("User-Agent", "My agent");
c.setRequestProperty("Content-Language",
        System.getProperty("microedition.locale"));
// Use c to access the server at url
```

Replaceable Modules

From the above analysis, we can see that much of the optimization work involves choosing the right media files, selecting the right feature sets, and/or re-implementing the same application behaviors with alternative APIs or programming techniques. However, it is tedious and error prone to manually keep track of the custom modifications for each target in the development and deployment process. In this section, we introduce a systematic approach to organize the device-specific optimization in replaceable resource and code modules, and then automate the building process. The automated process allows us to adopt agile development methodologies and produces robust code. The approach discussed in this section is based on the Apache Ant build system, which we have used throughout this book. If you need to refresh your memory on Ant, please refer to Chapter 3. We will enhance the Ant build script for the multimedia trivia application (Chapter 11) to illustrate how to optimize the trivia application for multiple devices. The new build script, which we discuss in this section, is the file `build2.xml` in the downloadable source code bundle of the trivia application.

Customized JAD Files

The JAD file can provide vital information about the MIDlet to the device AMS during the installation process. However, the value of the JAD file is not limited to the MIDlet installation. As we described in Chapter 3, the MIDlet can call the `MIDlet.getAppProperty()` method to retrieve the value of any named attribute (i.e., key) in the JAD file at runtime. As a result, we can use the JAD file to customize the behavior of the application for a specific group of users or devices without changing the JAR file. For example, the trivia MIDlet utilizes content servers for trivia questions. For users in different countries, we may want to use localized databases for culture-specific questions and use local servers to reduce the latency. The following example JAD file passes a trivia server URL in the United Kingdom to the MIDlet, and it can be made available to UK customers. There is no need to modify the build script for the JAR file to use custom JAD files.

```
Manifest-Version: 1.0
MIDlet-1: Trivia, ,com.Series40Book.midp.TriviaMidlet
MIDlet-Name: Trivia Game
MIDlet-Version: 1.0.10
MIDlet-Jar-Size: 57923
MIDlet-Jar-URL: Trivia.jar
MIDlet-Vendor: Nokia
MicroEdition-Configuration: CLDC-1.0
MicroEdition-Profile: MIDP-2.0
serverURL: http://host.in.UK/Trivia/servlet/MIDPTrivia
smsPort: 8765
```

WARNING   We can deploy MIDlet JAR files to the devices using Symbian OS (not for Series 40 devices) via infrared, Bluetooth, or MMS without the accompanying JAD file. In this case, custom attributes in the JAD file are lost. A workaround is to define the attributes in the manifest file and swap the custom manifest file for each build target.

Resource File Modules

As we discussed, each device-optimized JAR file needs to be bundled with an optimized set of images, media files, and localized text files. In the Ant build script we used so far in the book, we have always placed such resource files in a separate `res/` directory. For multiple device targets, we can simply make a subdirectory under `res/` for each device. For example, we might place larger background images under the `res/6600` directory to suit the larger screens on

Nokia 6600 devices. Before building the JAR file, we can copy the appropriate set of resource files to the stage directory. The snippet below shows the relevant parts of the build2.xml file for the trivia MIDP client to build a target for the Nokia 6600 device. The pre6600 task copies the Nokia 6600 specific resource files from the res/6600 directory to the directory containing pre-verified class files. It is invoked from the build6600 task, which actually builds the Nokia 6600 deployment JAR.

```
<target name="pre6600" depends="prepare">
    ... ...
  <copy todir="${pvclasses}">
    <fileset dir="res/6600" />
  </copy>
</target>


    ... ...

<target name="build6600" depends="init">
  <antcall target="pre6600" />
  <antcall target="compile" />
  <antcall target="preverify" />
  <antcall target="package" />
</target>
```

By combining the custom JAD files with the alternative resource files, we can use device-specific resource files that have filenames different from those in the generic version. For example, the generic version might have a wav audio file music.wav, but the target device only supports MIDI playback and hence has to use the music.mid file. We can insert an AudioFileSuffix attribute in the JAD file. It takes value .wav for devices that support wav playback and value .mid for devices that only support MIDI. The MIDlet uses this attribute to assemble the media filename at runtime. This way, we can avoid hardcoding device-specific filenames into the source code.

```
InputStream is = this.getClass().getResourceAsStream (
                "music" + getAppProperty("AudioFileSuffix"));
Player player = Manager.createPlayer(is, null);
```

Source Code Modules

Alternative resource files can satisfy only part of our optimization needs, as they do not alter the behavior of the application. For example, if the generic application is written against the MIDP 1.0 API and we want to take advantage of a new MIDP 2.0 API on a target device, we need to rewrite part of the code. We also need to rewrite the UI code to optimize Canvas-based applications for devices with very different screen sizes. Positioning components using proportional values of the screen width and height does not always work perfectly, especially if the target screen is significantly larger or smaller than the generic screen tested.

The simplest way to optimize the source code for each target device is just to replace the relevant generic source files with device-specific ones before we compile. We can do it in the stage area just as we did for the alternative resource files. However, the caveat of this approach is that the replaceable classes in the application should not intertwine with other classes. In Java, we must have one source code file per class, and hence the replacement source file must implement all the functionalities of the generic class it replaces. The clear separation of classes reduces code duplication, which is the main source of errors, inconsistencies, and hard-to-maintain repositories.

A good way to modularize classes is via the use of the Model-View-Controller (MVC) design pattern as illustrated in the trivia example. Under the MVC architecture, each view class represents one screen. All business logic is routed through the controller to the model layer. We can easily replace any view class and change the view without impacting other parts of the application. For example, we can replace the ShowQuestionUI.java to use a popup menu for choices instead of radio buttons. The Nokia 6600 version of the ShowQuestionUI.java file is placed in the src/6600 directory and copied over to the stage area (the ${tmp}/src directory) by the pre6600 task in the build2.xml Ant script. It overwrites the generic version of the same file in the stage area, which is copied earlier by the prepare task. We could also replace the SelectActionUI.java file to use simple List menus rather than Series 40–style screen-based menu items. For devices that need drastic UI changes from the generic device, we can even replace the entire view layer to develop a completely new look and feel of the application while reusing all the business logic code.

Another example of the replaceable source code module is the alternative version of the WaitScreen.java class in the src/SafeWait directory. The generic version of the WaitScreen class starts the worker thread in its setWorker() method (see Chapter 11). But as we discussed in Chapter 7, it is sometimes safer to start the thread in the paint() method to make sure that the wait screen is displayed while the thread is running. The new WaitScreen class starts its worker from the paint() method, and the pre6600 task uses it to overwrite the generic version.

```
<target name="prepare" depends="clean">
    ... ...
  <copy todir="${tmp}/src">
    <fileset dir="src/generic" />
  </copy>
</target>


<!--
    copy over device specific source files to
```

```
     overwrite the generic ones
-->
<target name="pre6600" depends="prepare">
   ... ...
  <copy todir="${tmp}/src" overwrite="true">
    <fileset dir="src/6600" />
    <fileset dir="src/SafeWait" />
  </copy>
</target>
```

```
   ... ...
```

Figure 12–1 shows the build workflow with custom JAD files, replaceable resource files, and replaceable source code.

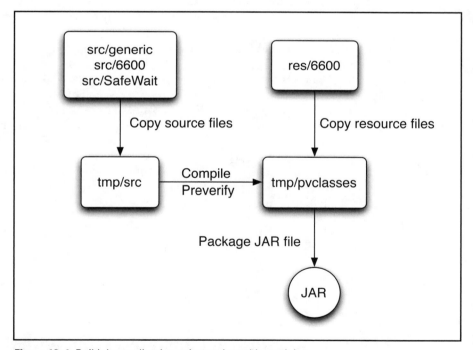

Figure 12–1 Build the application using replaceable modules.

Replacing Part of a Class

Through careful design, we can use the replaceable source code module approach to provide alternative implementations of specified methods in a class instead of replacing the class completely. An example is the QuestionsNavigator class in the trivia example application. On devices with large RMS storage space, we would like to store all downloaded questions with multimedia files in an RMS store, but for devices with limited RMS space, we would store the questions in the heap memory. Depending on the deployment device, we need to implement several methods in the QuestionsNavigator class differently. What we could do is declare those methods as abstract and provide alternative implementations in two concrete subclasses. In Chapter 11, we used different class names for the subclasses (QuestionsNavigatorRMS and QuestionsNavigatorRAM) to avoid name conflict in the same package. Using the replaceable source code module approach, we can use the same class name QuestionsNavigatorImpl for both subclasses and store different versions of the QuestionsNavigatorImpl.java file in device-specific source directories. Similar to what we did with the replaceable view classes, we would simply copy the device-specific version of the QuestionsNavigatorImpl.java file to the stage directory (e.g., the ${tmp}/src directory) before compiling. The application calls the QuestionsNavigator.getInstance() factory method to obtain an instance of the QuestionsNavigator class. In a general scenario, we can invoke the subclass's constructor directly to instantiate instances.

```
public abstract class QuestionsNavigator {

  public static QuestionsNavigator getInstance ()
                                       throws Exception {
    if (url == null || "".equals(url)) {
      throw new Exception ("Please set the URL first");
    }
    if (qn == null) {
      qn = new QuestionsNavigatorImpl ();
    }
    return qn;
  }

  // ... ...

}
```

Preprocessing and Postprocessing with Antenna

The techniques discussed in the previous section allow developers to optimize the application for specific target devices by utilizing customized versions of JAD files, media files, source code modules, or even methods in a class. Since all the optimization was done by replacing existing files in the generic version of the application, we do not need to compromise on the application footprint as a result. However, if we need to make finely grained modifications to the source code, the above techniques become increasingly hard to use and could lead to inefficient applications. For example, if we have many method-level optimizations, we would require many abstract classes. That leads to at least three problems:

- Since the Java programming language only supports single inheritance, it limits our ability to reuse those implementation classes in the future. It breaks the natural inheritance structure.

- Since the class inheritance structure is no longer designed around the application logic but dictated by the optimization needs, the application source code becomes hard to understand and maintain.

- The extra abstract classes and implementation classes use more symbols and ultimately increase the JAR file size.

In addition, none of the techniques discussed in the previous section allows us to optimize within a method. To make finely grained changes inside the source code, we might have to resort to the tried-and-true method from the pre-Java software development world: code preprocessing and postprocessing. The preprocessor goes through the source code files before compiling and determines which code segment to exclude from compiling based on some external conditions. The postprocessor goes through the compiled executable file (i.e., the JAR file in the Java world) and removes any unused classes, including those in the bundled API libraries, to reduce the application's footprint. The preprocessing and postprocessing steps complement each other: in order to support preprocessing, the code repository must support all possible scenarios (i.e., all target devices) and hence include all the classes we might need. But for a specific target device, the preprocessed source code would probably not utilize all classes in the classpath and hence require the postprocessing step to purge the unused classes. In this section, we introduce a popular open source J2ME tool for code preprocessing and postprocessing: Antenna. The best part is that Antenna is based on Ant and hence can be fully integrated into our existing build process. In this section, we further enhance the build script for the trivia application using Antenna. The new script file is `build3.xml` in the trivia application (see Chapter 11) code bundle.

Introducing Antenna

One of the key strengths of the Ant build system is its extensibility. The standard Ant package supports common build tasks such as file copying, compiling, and JAR packaging. Through an open API, developers can define and implement custom Ant tasks using the Java programming language. Each Ant custom task implementation consists of an XML element definition and an associated Java class. In the `build.xml` file, we can use the custom XML element to specify custom tasks in the workflow. When the Ant execution engine encounters the custom XML element, it locates and executes the associated Java class. Ant allows any Java developer to extend and customize the build system to do anything that can be implemented in Java. For more information about Ant's extension API, please refer to the Ant documentation.

The Antenna project develops a collection of custom Ant tasks that help us build J2ME applications smoothly. Antenna is open source software developed by Jörg Pleumann. It is freely available for download and redistribution from its Web site at `http://antenna.sourceforge.net/`. In this book, we cover Antenna version 0.9.12 released in April 2004. In order to run Antenna, we have to install the following third-party software:

- **Ant version 1.5.0 or above:** You can download Ant software free of charge from its Web site at `http://ant.apache.org/`. For more information about how to install and use Ant, please refer to Chapter 3.

- **Sun J2ME Wireless Toolkit (WTK):** Antenna uses tools in the Sun WTK to compile, preverify, and package J2ME applications. We need WTK 1.x for MIDP 1.0 development and WTK 2.x for MIDP 2.x development. You can download WTK free of charge from its Web site at `http://java.sun.com/ products/j2mewtoolkit/` and then run the installer. In the future, Antenna will be able to work with Nokia device SDKs as well.

- **ProGuard or RetroGuard obfuscator:** Antenna allows us to obfuscate the compiled Java bytecode during the build process. But Antenna does not provide an obfuscator itself. It has to rely on third-party obfuscators. Antenna works with RetroGuard (`http://www.retrologic.com/`) and ProGuard (`http://proguard.sourceforge.net/`). Both are open source software freely available from their Web sites. You have to place the downloaded JAR file in Ant's `lib` directory or under the current classpath.

NOTE
As an open source project released under the Lesser GNU Public License (LGPL), Antenna relies on its user community to fix bugs and add new features. If you make improvements to Antenna during your work, you are strongly encouraged to make the source code patch available to the community. Contact information about patch submission is available from Antenna's Web site.

Installing Antenna

Once the Antenna JAR file is downloaded, simply place it either in the current Java classpath or in the Ant's `lib/` directory on your computer (e.g., `C:\Java\Ant\lib\`). Then, in the `build3.xml` file, we can add the following lines of code to make Antenna tasks and the Sun J2ME WTK available to the Ant runtime. The optional properties specify the runtime versions and whether MIDP extension APIs are enabled. Those properties should be self-explanatory.

```
<!-- Required lines -->

<taskdef resource="antenna.properties"/>
<property name="wtk.home" value="C:\Java\WTK21\"/>
```

```
<!-- The following are optional attributes -->

<!-- Default value is "1.0", available in WTK 2.1+ -->
<property name="wtk.cldc.version" value="1.1"/>

<!-- Default value is "2.0" for WTK 2.x -->
<property name="wtk.midp.version" value="2.0"/>

<!-- Default value is "false", available in WTK 2.x -->
<property name="wtk.mmapi.enabled" value="true"/>

<!-- Default value is "false", available in WTK 2.x -->
<property name="wtk.wma.enabled" value="true"/>

<!-- Support for J2ME Web Service API -->
<!-- Default value is "false", available in WTK 2.1+ -->
<property name="wtk.j2mews.enabled" value="false"/>
```

Antenna Tasks

Antenna defines 10 J2ME specific Ant tasks, listed in Table 12–1.

Table 12–1 Ant tasks Supported by the Antenna Package

Task	Description
wtkjad	Creates a new JAD based on the task attribute values or updates an existing one. In particular, it updates the values for the MIDlet-Jar-Url and MIDlet-Jar-Size keys automatically. This task can also increase the value of the MIDlet-Version key automatically.
wtkbuild	Extends the Ant's standard javac task to support MIDP-specific bootclasspath and bytecode preverification.
wtkpackage	Extends the Ant's standard jar task to package the JAR file with compiled bytecode and library classes. It can optionally update the JAD file as the WtkJad task does. It also allows preverification and obfuscation of the classes in the JAR file.
wtkmakeprc	Generates Palm OS installation packages for a MIDlet suite.
wtkrun	Runs a MIDlet suite in the WTK's generic device emulator.
wtkpreverify	Preverifies the compiled bytecode for device deployment.

Table 12–1 Ant tasks Supported by the Antenna Package (continued)

Task	Description
`wtkobfuscate`	Obfuscates a JAR file. It is discussed in detail later in this chapter.
`wtksmartlink`	Postprocesses a JAR file to remove unused classes. It is discussed in detail later in this chapter.
`wtkpreprocess`	Preprocesses the source code for conditional compilation. It is discussed in detail later in this chapter.
`wtkdeploy`	Uploads the MIDlet suite to a remote OTA server for later download.

Preprocessing

The `wtkpreprocess` task in Antenna is used for source code preprocessing.

Preprocessor Directives

The Java language itself does not support preprocessing directives. Instead of defining a new syntax for additional language keywords, we embed Antenna-defined directives in the source code as comments. This way, we can still compile the source code without preprocessing and edit the code in Java-aware editors or IDE tools. All Antenna directives must be placed in line-style comments. The directive must immediately follow the `//` characters, and there should be no Java code to the left of the `//` in the same line.

Since our primary goal in J2ME application preprocessing is to achieve conditional compilation for different target devices, the Antenna directives support if-then blocks for code inclusion based on the values of boolean identifiers or complex identifier expressions. In addition, the `#include` directive can be used to include the content of an external source file. That makes it easier for us to optimize individual methods for different devices using the replaceable module approach discussed earlier in this chapter, because we can now have a partial class implementation in a separate source code file. The available directives are listed in Table 12–2. In practice, we can have a special source code file that sets the values for all identifiers used in the application. Each target device's source code directory contains a different version of the identifier definition file that reflects the preprocessing needed for this device. Then, we can replace the generic version of the identifier definition file with the device-specific one at build time using the techniques described earlier in this chapter.

Table 12–2 Antenna Preprocessing Directives

Directive	Description
`#define <identifier>`	Defines an identifier. This directive makes the identifier have a `true` value in subsequent evaluation directives.
`#undefine <identifier>`	Undefines an identifier. This directive makes the identifier have a `false` value in subsequent evaluation directives.
`#ifdef <identifier>`	Evaluates whether the identifier is `true` (i.e., defined). If so, the following code segment until the `#endif` or `#else` directive is included in compilation.
`#ifndef <identifier>`	Evaluates whether the identifier is `false` (i.e., never defined or undefined). If so, the following code segment until the `#endif` or `#else` directive is included in compilation.
`#else`	Constructs the if-else blocks.
`#elifdef <identifier>`	Evaluates whether an identifier is `true` for further logic branches in an `else` directive.
`#elifndef <identifier>`	Evaluates whether an identifier is `false` for further logic branches in an else directive.
`#endif`	Indicates the end of an if-then block.
`#if <expression>`	Evaluates an expression for an if-then block. The expression can consist of multiple identifiers, parentheses, and popular logical operators such as `&&`, `||`, `^`, and `!`.
`#elif <expression>`	Evaluates an expression for further logic branches in an `else` directive.
`#include <filename>`	Includes the contents of an external source code file.
`#endinclude`	Matches the `#include` directive for technical reasons.

Examples of Directive Usage

In this section, we show the usage of three example directives we defined for the trivia application. We use the S60 directive to indicate whether the target build is for Series 60 devices; the WMA directive to indicate whether the target should include the chat messaging module; and the LargeRMS directive to indicate whether the device supports large RMS storage and hence can use RMS to store trivia questions.

The following code snippet shows that we add an Exit command to the screen if the device is Series 40. If the device is Series 60, the AMS implementation automatically adds a Close command to exit the application.

```
//#ifndef S60
{
  exitCommand = UIController.exitCommand;
  addCommand (exitCommand);
}
//#endif
```

TIP

Notice that we used { and } brackets to include code that can be conditionally included for compilation. This helps us to keep the indentation clear and the code more readable in a modern code editor. In addition, it is a best practice to place the code for the most common scenario in the last block. This way, if we do not preprocess the code and compile directly, the last block overrides all the previous ones.

The WMA directive is used in UIController, SelectActionUI, and ShowQuestionUI classes in the enhanced trivia application example (see Chapter 11). If the chat module is not supported, we will not start the SMS server and not display the Chat option in the menus. Here, we do not actually remove the chat module's implementation classes themselves. We just eliminate the interface access points. Late in this chapter, we discuss how postprocessing can help us further reduce the application footprint.

```
public class UIController {

  ... ...

  public static void init (MIDlet m) throws Exception {

    ... ...

    //#if WMA
    {
      sender = new SenderImpl ();
```

```
        inbox = new InboxImpl ();
        sender.setPort(m.getAppProperty("smsPort"));
        try {
          inbox.setupListener (m.getAppProperty("smsPort"));
        } catch (Exception e) {
          // do nothing
        }
      }
      //#endif


      ... ...
    }

public class SelectActionUI extends Canvas
                    implements CommandListener {

  ... ...

  private void takeAction () {
    try {
      if (state == resumeSessState) {
        ... ...
      } else if (state == chatState) {
        //#if WMA
        {
          UIController.firstMessage(this);
        }
        //#endif
      }
    } catch (Exception e) {
      ... ...
    }
  }

  private boolean isValidState (int state) {

    ... ...

    //#if !WMA
    {
      if ((state == chatState)) {
        result = false;
      }
    }
    //#else
    {
      if ((state == chatState)) {
```

```
                result = true;
            }
        }
        //#endif

        return result;
    }
}

public class ShowQuestionUI extends Form
                implements CommandListener {

    public ShowQuestionUI () {

        ... ...

        //#if WMA
        {
            inboxCommand =
                new Command("Inbox", Command.SCREEN, 1);
            addCommand(inboxCommand);
        }
        //#endif

        ... ...
    }

    public void commandAction (Command c, Displayable s) {
        try {
            if (c == restartCommand) {
                ... ...
            } else if (c == inboxCommand) {
                //#if WMA
                {
                    UIController.firstMessage(this);
                }
                //#endif
            } else if (c == nextCommand) {
                ... ...
            }
        } catch (Exception e) {
            ... ...
        }
    }
}
```

In the `QuestionsNavigator` class discussed in Chapter 11, we used a factory method to select from different implementations. Now, we can do it more smartly using the `LargeRMS` directive.

```
public abstract class QuestionsNavigator {

  // ... ...

  // We could choose different implementation classes
  // in this method
  public static QuestionsNavigator getInstance ()
                                        throws Exception {
    if (url == null || "".equals(url)) {
      throw new Exception ("Please set the URL first");
    }

    if (qn == null) {
      //#if LargeRMS
      {
        qn = new QuestionsNavigatorRMS ();
      }
      //#else
      {
        qn = new QuestionsNavigatorRAM ();
      }
      //#endif
    }
    return qn;
  }

  // ... ...
}
```

The wtkpreprocess Task

Antenna's `wtkpreprocess` task preprocesses the source code. Using its symbol's attribute, we can pass in a list of initially defined directives for each file. The directives are separated by commas. This is often a cleaner solution than using dedicated and replaceable source files to hold the directive definitions.

The following `build3.xml` snippet shows how to assemble the source code files in the `${tmp}/org` directory, preprocess the files and output to the `${tmp}/src` directory, and then move on with compilation, packaging, and postprocessing from the `${tmp}/src` directory. For the generic build target (the `buildGeneric` task), only the `WMA` directive is defined. For the Nokia 6600

build target (the `build6600` task), the `WMA`, `S60` and `LargeRMS` directives are all
defined.

```xml
<target name="prepare" depends="clean">

    ... ...

  <copy todir="${tmp}/org">
    <fileset dir="src/generic" />
  </copy>
</target>

<target name="preGeneric" depends="prepare">
  <!-- Resource module -->
  <copy todir="${tmpclasses}">
    <fileset dir="res/generic" />
  </copy>
</target>

<target name="buildGeneric" depends="init">
  <antcall target="preGeneric" />
  <wtkpreprocess srcdir="${tmp}/org"
                 destdir="${tmp}/src"
                 symbols="WMA" />
  <antcall target="compile" />
  <antcall target="package" />
  <antcall target="postprocess" />
  <antcall target="preverify" />
</target>

<target name="pre6600" depends="prepare">
  <!-- Source code module -->
  <copy todir="${tmp}/org" overwrite="true">
    <fileset dir="src/6600" />
    <fileset dir="src/SafeWait" />
  </copy>
  <!-- Resource module -->
  <copy todir="${tmpclasses}">
    <fileset dir="res/6600" />
  </copy>
</target>

<target name="build6600" depends="init">
  <antcall target="pre6600" />
  <wtkpreprocess srcdir="${tmp}/org"
                 destdir="${tmp}/src"
                 symbols="WMA,S60,LargeRMS" />
```

```
    <antcall target="compile" />
    <antcall target="package" />
    <antcall target="postprocess" />
    <antcall target="preverify" />
</target>
```

Postprocessing

The postprocessing gets rid of unused classes in the JAR file to reduce the application footprint. Unused classes might get into the JAR file via two ways:

- Our application might use a third-party library. We typically include the entire library in the MIDlet suite JAR file in the build process. However, in reality, we often use only some of classes in the library.

- When a preprocessor is used, some of the application code might be excluded from the compilation, and some of the classes in the source code might never get used. For example, in the QuestionsNavigator class discussed in the previous section, either the QuestionsNavigatorRMS or the QuestionsNavigatorRAM class is never used depending on the device target settings.

Since most postprocessors work only with standard Java bytecode, not the J2ME preverified bytecode, we need to first package the JAR file, postprocess it, and then preverify it. The wtkpreverify task in Antenna supports preverification directly from the JAR file. The wtkpreverify task could also update the MIDlet-Jar-Size attribute in the JAD file automatically to reflect the preverified JAR file size.

```
<!-- Preverify from the post-processed JARs -->
<target name="preverify" depends="init">
  <wtkpreverify jarfile="bin/${projname}.jar"
                jadfile="bin/${projname}.jad" />
</target>
```

The postprocess task invokes two Antenna tasks: the wtksmartlink for smart linking and wtkobfuscate for bytecode obfuscation.

Smart Linking

The wtksmartlink task in Antenna starts from the public MIDlet classes specified in the JAD file. It builds a tree of class dependencies of all classes used the MIDlet classes. Then, it compares the tree with all classes scanned from the JAR file and deletes the unused ones from the JAR file. Since the wtksmartlink task changes the JAR file size, it updates the JAD file's MIDlet-Jar-Size attribute value automatically.

```
<wtksmartlink jarfile="bin/${projname}.jar"
              jadfile="bin/${projname}.jad" />
```

Since the `wtksmartlink` task analyzes the bytecode to derive the class dependency diagram, it may mistakenly delete classes that are instantiated by the class loader via their full names. In this case, we can nest the `<preserve class="class name"/>` elements inside the `wtksmartlink` task to explicitly prevent certain classes from being deleted.

One limitation of the `wtksmartlink` task is that it only analyzes the static dependence of classes. It does not delete unused methods and statements inside a class. Hence, it could fail to delete classes that are never reached in the execution flow but are still referenced by the unused statements. For example, when we do not define the `WMA` preprocessing directive, none of the SMS messaging–related classes are accessible from the MIDlet, but the `wtksmartlink` task would not delete those classes, since they are still referenced from the unused methods in the `UIController` class. The ProGuard obfuscator discussed in the next section provides a better solution.

Bytecode Obfuscation

Bytecode obfuscation is an important technique to protect intellectual properties and reduce the application footprint. The concept behind bytecode obfuscation is simple: the obfuscator goes through the bytecode in a JAR file and replaces all the class names, method names, and variable names with short, illogical symbols. For example, the class name `QuestionsNavigatorRMS` might be obfuscated to `Q2`. For the execution engine, the obfuscated program is identical to the original one, since the relationships among the symbols stay the same. Bytecode obfuscation has the following benefits:

- It is very difficult for a hacker to take an obfuscated JAR file, decompile it, and figure out how the program works. The reason is that obfuscated symbols give little clue to the intended use of classes, methods, and variables in the application.

- By replacing long symbols with short ones, obfuscation reduces the size of the JAR file.

Antenna's `wtkobfuscate` task utilizes the ProGuard or RetroGuard obfuscator to obfuscate a JAR file. An added bonus for ProGuard is that it actually analyzes the execution flow to figure out the unused classes, methods, and statements. For example, if we do not pass the `WMA` directive to the preprocessor, ProGuard deletes all the SMS messaging–related implementation classes from the JAR file after obfuscation. ProGuard does everything the Antenna smart linker does. So, with the ProGuard obfuscator, we do not need to invoke the `wtksmartlink` task.

Of course, in a MIDlet suite JAR, we cannot obfuscate all class names. The public MIDlet class names specified in the JAD file cannot be obfuscated.

Otherwise, the device AMS would not be able load the correct MIDlet class at startup. The wtkobfuscate task uses a JAD file to figure out MIDlet class names to preserve during the process. It also updates the MIDlet-Jar-Size attribute in a specified JAD file afterwards.

```
<wtkobfuscate jarfile="bin/${projname}.jar"
              jadfile="bin/${projname}.jad"
              obfuscator="proguard" />
```

As in the wtksmartlink task, the wtkobfuscate task can also take nested <preserve> elements to preserve the original names of specified classes. Figure 12–2 shows the workflow of an Antenna build script with both replaceable modules and code preprocessors and postprocessors.

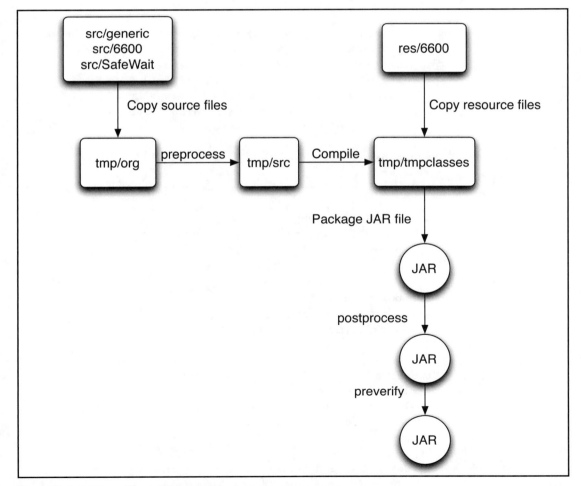

Figure 12–2 Build workflow with preprocessors and postprocessors.

WARNING

Obfuscators do not always work correctly. It is known that some obfuscators could produce bytecode that crashes the MIDlet on the device. When this happens, we should always first verify the correctness of the source code using the unobfuscated JAR file. Then, based on the error message, we could design workarounds. For example, the `getWidth()` and `getHeight()` method calls in the `Displayable` class often do not work correctly after obfuscation. We could hardcode the screen size of the specific deployment device into the source code as a workaround.

The build3.xml File

In this section, we give a full listing of the `build3.xml` file for your reference.

```
<project name="Trivia" default="all">

  <taskdef resource="antenna.properties"/>
  <property name="wtk.home" value="C:\Java\WTK21\"/>
  <property name="wtk.cldc.version" value="1.1"/>
  <property name="wtk.midp.version" value="2.0"/>
  <property name="wtk.mmapi.enabled" value="true"/>
  <property name="wtk.wma.enabled" value="true"/>
  <property name="wtk.j2mews.enabled" value="false"/>

  <target name="init">
    <tstamp/>
    <property name="projname" value="Trivia" />

    <property name="SDK"
      value="C:/Nokia/Devices/Nokia_S40_DP20_SDK_1_0" />
    <property name="midpclasses"
      value="${SDK}/lib/classes.zip" />

    <property name="tmp" value="temp" />
    <property name="tmpclasses"
      value="${tmp}/tmpclasses" />
  </target>

  <target name="clean" depends="init">
    <delete dir="${tmp}" />
    <delete file="bin/${projname}.jar" />
    <delete file="bin/*.sh" />
  </target>

  <!-- Setup build directory structure and copy over
       the generic source files -->
  <target name="prepare" depends="clean">
```

```
      <mkdir dir="${tmp}" />
      <mkdir dir="${tmpclasses}" />
      <mkdir dir="${tmp}/org" />
      <mkdir dir="${tmp}/src" />

      <copy todir="${tmp}/org">
        <fileset dir="src/generic" />
      </copy>
    </target>

    <!-- Example of preparing for a specific target -->
    <target name="preTarget" depends="prepare">

      <!-- Optional: Copy over the library classes -->
      <unzip dest="${tmpclasses}">
        <fileset dir="lib/targetname">
          <include name="**/*.zip"/>
          <include name="**/*.jar"/>
        </fileset>
      </unzip>
      <delete dir="${tmpclasses}/META-INF" />

      <!-- Optional: Copy over the replaceable
           source modules -->
      <copy todir="${tmp}/org" overwrite="true">
        <fileset dir="src/targetname" />
      </copy>

      <!-- Optional: Copy over the replaceable
           resource files -->
      <copy todir="${tmpclasses}">
        <fileset dir="res/targetname" />
      </copy>
    </target>

    <!-- Compile from the source file -->
    <target name="compile" depends="init">
      <javac srcdir="${tmp}/src" destdir="${tmpclasses}"
             bootclasspath="${midpclasses}"
      >
        <classpath>
          <pathelement path="${tmpclasses}"/>
          <pathelement path="${midpclasses}"/>
        </classpath>
      </javac>
    </target>
```

```
<!-- Package the preverified class
     and resource files -->
<target name="package" depends="init">
  <wtkpackage jarfile="bin/${projname}.jar"
              jadfile="bin/${projname}.jad"
              basedir="${tmpclasses}"
              manifest="bin/${projname}.MF"
  />
</target>

<!-- Smart link and obfuscate the JAR file -->
<target name="postprocess" depends="init">
  <wtksmartlink jarfile="bin/${projname}.jar"
                jadfile="bin/${projname}.jad" />

  <wtkobfuscate jarfile="bin/${projname}.jar"
                jadfile="bin/${projname}.jad"
                obfuscator="proguard" />
</target>

<!-- Preverify from the post-processed JARs -->
<target name="preverify" depends="init">
  <wtkpreverify jarfile="bin/${projname}.jar"
                jadfile="bin/${projname}.jad" />
</target>

<!-- Example of built for a specific target -->
<target name="buildTarget" depends="init">
  <antcall target="preTarget" />
  <!-- pre-process -->
  <wtkpreprocess srcdir="${tmp}/org"
                 destdir="${tmp}/src"
                 symbols="S60,DP20" />

  <antcall target="compile" />
  <antcall target="package" />
  <antcall target="postprocess" />
  <antcall target="preverify" />
</target>

<!-- Now the real build targets -->

<!-- The generic build task -->
<target name="preGeneric" depends="prepare">
  <copy todir="${tmpclasses}">
    <fileset dir="res/generic" />
  </copy>
```

```xml
  </target>
  <target name="buildGeneric" depends="init">
    <antcall target="preGeneric" />
    <wtkpreprocess srcdir="${tmp}/org"
                   destdir="${tmp}/src"
                   symbols="WMA" />
    <antcall target="compile" />
    <antcall target="package" />
    <antcall target="postprocess" />
    <antcall target="preverify" />
  </target>

  <!-- The build task for unit tests -->
  <target name="preUnitTests" depends="prepare">
    <delete dir="${tmpclasses}" />
    <mkdir dir="${tmpclasses}" />
    <unzip dest="${tmpclasses}">
      <fileset dir="lib/UnitTests">
        <include name="**/*.zip"/>
        <include name="**/*.jar"/>
      </fileset>
    </unzip>
    <delete dir="${tmpclasses}/META-INF" />

    <copy todir="${tmp}/org" overwrite="true">
      <fileset dir="src/UnitTests" />
    </copy>

    <copy todir="${tmpclasses}">
      <fileset dir="res/generic" />
    </copy>
  </target>
  <target name="buildUnitTests" depends="init">
    <antcall target="preUnitTests" />
    <wtkpreprocess srcdir="${tmp}/org"
                   destdir="${tmp}/src"
                   symbols="WMA" />
    <antcall target="compile" />
    <antcall target="package" />
    <antcall target="postprocess" />
    <antcall target="preverify" />
  </target>

  <target name="pre6600" depends="prepare">
    <copy todir="${tmp}/org" overwrite="true">
      <fileset dir="src/6600" />
      <fileset dir="src/SafeWait" />
```

```
      </copy>
      <copy todir="${tmpclasses}">
        <fileset dir="res/6600" />
      </copy>
    </target>
    <target name="build6600" depends="init">
      <antcall target="pre6600" />
      <wtkpreprocess srcdir="${tmp}/org"
                     destdir="${tmp}/src"
                     symbols="WMA,S60,LargeRMS" />
      <antcall target="compile" />
      <antcall target="package" />
      <antcall target="postprocess" />
      <antcall target="preverify" />
    </target>


    <target name="all" depends="buildGeneric"/>

</project>
```

Summary

In this chapter, we covered topics on how to scale an MIDP application to suit multiple target devices. We discussed key areas that require device-specific optimization and how to write the generic version of the application to minimize the need for future optimization. Using the replaceable media file and source code modules, we can complete most of the necessary optimization tasks. For the finely grained modifications to the source code, we can utilize Antenna's source code preprocessor. We also covered Antenna's bytecode postprocessor and obfuscator that complement the preprocessor.

chapter

13

Debugging
and Testing

Develop commercial quality mobile applications.

A key component in Forum Nokia's develop-and-optimize approach is the iterative debugging and testing process. Compared with desktop application users, mobile users are less tolerant of application errors and poor UI designs. If the mobile application crashes, runs too slowly, or is not intuitive to use, the user simply moves on and does not use it anymore. On the other hand, debugging and testing for multiple target devices is a very tedious task. In this chapter, we cover some tools and approaches that make the debugging and testing process as smooth as possible. The topics include the following:

- **Debugging**: covers the basics of MIDlet debugging. We introduce tools and methods to debug MIDlets on both emulators and devices.

- **Unit testing**: introduces how unit tests and agile development methods can help us reduce the debugging work and improve the application design. We cover a J2ME-based unit testing framework.

- **Usability testing guidelines**: discusses principles and best practices for MIDlet usability testing with end users.

The techniques discussed in this chapter can be applied to applications of all sizes. We use the `PrefStore` class in the trivia application as an example to show how to debug and test an individual Java class. The `PrefStore` class saves and restores preference information to and from the RMS record store. It is relatively independent from the rest of the trivia example application. Hence, for busy readers, Chapter 11, "End-to-End Design Patterns," and Chapter 12, "Developing Scalable Applications," are not prerequisites for this chapter. You only need to go over the relevant code sections of `PrefStore` in Chapter 11 before starting this chapter.

Debugging

The debugging process is to find errors in the code. There are three types of common errors:

- Compiler errors are typically language syntax errors or errors caused by missing libraries. They are relatively easy to fix, since the compiler gives precise information about the nature of the error and its location in the code.

- Runtime errors cause the program to fail or terminate prematurely. Runtime errors result from problems that do not occur until the code is being executed. For example, trying to open a file that does not exist, attempting to divide by zero, or trying to use null objects are errors that cannot be caught at compile time. In Java, the runtime errors typically cause the JVM to throw uncaught Java `Exception` or `Error` objects containing the error message and then quit. Runtime errors can be difficult to find because they may occur in rarely used execution paths. Exhaustive testing is often required to detect those errors. They can also be difficult to fix, since we need to peek into the live program and know the precise state of the objects when the error occurs.

- Logic errors are nonfatal problems with the design or implementation of your application. Although the program statements may not throw exceptions, they do not produce the results you intended. For example, logic errors can occur when variables contain incorrect values or when the algorithm misbehaves under boundary conditions. Logic errors can be hard to detect, since there are no obvious signs. The application runs as if everything is fine, and we have to check the input and output values to find out about the error. Debugging logic errors requires us to re-create the execution scenario and peek into the application state.

In this section, we focus on the basic debugging techniques for runtime and logic errors.

Basic Techniques

Developers can use specialized debuggers in their development environment to debug programs. The debugger can be integrated in IDE tools or available as a standalone utility. The debugger can set breakpoints in the execution flow and inspect current values of local and global variables. There are two ways for the debugger program to communicate with the debuggee program.

- The debugger can directly communicate with the JVM that runs the target application via a native interface called the Java Virtual Machine Debugger Interface (JVMDI). In this scenario, the debugger and debuggee programs must reside on the same machine.

- The debugger and debuggee can communicate via a data protocol called Java Debug Wire Protocol (JDWP). The JDWP data can be passed over network connections.

Both the JVMDI and JDWP are optional features for the JVM. Not all JVMs can interoperate with debuggers. Currently, most MIDP VMs in Nokia devices do not support the JVMDI or JDWP interfaces due to the requirement of small footprints. Hence, we cannot debug Nokia MIDlets directly from physical devices yet. Some Nokia device emulators, most noticeably the Series 40 Developer Platform 2.0 SDK emulator, do support Java debuggers. The Nokia Developer's Suite (NDS, see Chapter 3) for J2ME's Eclipse IDE plugin allows us to debug MIDlets running in those emulators from within the Eclipse IDE.

WARNING

The Java debugger support in NDS for J2ME v2.2 has several known issues. For example, you can only set break points at the method level and cannot step into methods. Please refer to the NDS documentation that comes with the installation package.

Compared with dedicated Java debuggers, a more generic and portable debugging technique is to use the tried-and-true print-statements. We can strategically place the print statements in the code to print out the current state

Figure 13–1 Standard output in the lower right panel of the Nokia Developer Suite for J2ME.

of the application. For example, the statement can simply indicate that a certain execution stage has been reached (e.g., "Record store opened") or it can print out the values of relevant variables (e.g. "Category is music02"). For more sophisticated use, we can print out the return values of the Runtime .freeMemory() and System.currentTimeMillis() method calls to profile and optimize the performance of the application. When running on the emulator, we can use the System.out.println() method to print to the standard output.

- If the emulator is started from the Nokia Developer's Suite for J2ME, the print statements output to the log panel at the lower right of the NDS main window (see Figure 13–1).

- If the emulator is the Nokia Series 40 Developer Platform 2.0 SDK emulator, the print statements also output to the log panel in the System Diagnostics window (see Figure 13–2).

- If the emulator is started from a terminal (or shell) window via command line, the print statements output to the terminal. (Note: this is not the case for the Series 40 Developer Platform 2.0 SDK emulator.)

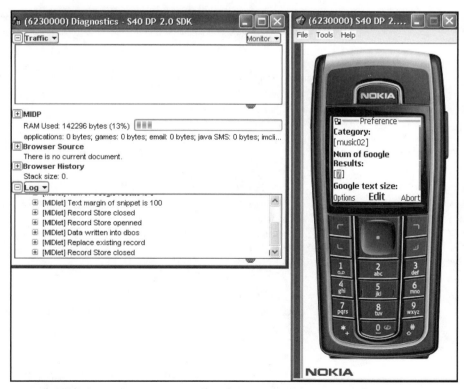

Figure 13–2 Standard output in diagnostic window of the Nokia Series 40 Developer Platform 2.0 SDK emulator.

NOTE   The Nokia Series 40 Developer Platform 2.0 SDK device emulator has a very useful profiler that shows the memory use and network traffic of the current MIDlet in real time.

In addition to the basic `System.out.println()` statement, we can also use the `Exception.printStackTrace()` method to print the error messages in exceptions caught in the execution process. Like the `println()` method, the `printStackTrace()` method also prints to the standard output. The following listing shows the `PrefStore.restore()` method (discussed in Chapter 11, "End-to-End Design Patterns") with debugging print statements. Since the print statements increase the size of the bytecode, we should eliminate them before releasing the MIDlet JAR file. Hence, we enclose them in the `DEBUG` preprocessor tag. The Ant script to build the debug and release versions of the sample trivia application is the `build4.xml` file (tasks `buildDebug` and `buildRelease`, respectively). Please see Chapter 12 for more information about the preprocessor and the construction of the Ant tasks.

```
public class PrefStore {

    public String category;
    public int googleResultsNum;
    public int googleTextMargin;
    public boolean googleIsPhrase;

    private String storeName = "Pref";

    // ... ...

    // Return false if the operation fails
    public synchronized boolean restore () {
      try {
        RecordStore rs =
            RecordStore.openRecordStore(storeName, true);
        //#if DEBUG
        System.out.println("Record Store opened");
        //#endif

        byte [] buf = rs.getRecord(1);
        //#if DEBUG
        System.out.println("Record Store retrieved");
        //#endif

        ByteArrayInputStream bis =
            new ByteArrayInputStream (buf);
        DataInputStream dbis = new DataInputStream (bis);
        category = dbis.readUTF();
```

```
//#if DEBUG
System.out.println("Category is " + category);
//#endif
googleResultsNum = dbis.readInt();
//#if DEBUG
System.out.println("Num of Google results is " +
    googleResultsNum);
//#endif
googleTextMargin = dbis.readInt();
//#if DEBUG
System.out.println("Text margin of snippet is " +
    googleTextMargin);
//#endif
googleIsPhrase = dbis.readBoolean();

dbis.close();
bis.close();
rs.closeRecordStore();
//#if DEBUG
System.out.println("Record Store closed");
//#endif
return true;

} catch (Exception e) {
    //#if DEBUG
    e.printStackTrace ();
    //#endif
    return false;
}
}
}
```

NOTE

If the MIDlet crashes with a runtime error, the error message in the uncaught exception or error is displayed to the standard output as well as on the device user interface.

On-Device Logging with MIDPLogger

The print statements work well on PC device emulators. However, emulator results are not always accurate. Many Nokia devices do not have their own emulators, and we have to debug with a similar device's emulator or even a *concept emulator* that is based on the MIDP reference implementation. For devices that do have emulator support, the emulator only accurately emulates one of the many software revisions the device has in its life cycle. Even if the emulator correctly emulates both the device hardware and software, it is still nearly impossible to emulate the wireless network environment (e.g., the slow and unreliable connections), the slow mobile processors, and the in-hand UI experience. Given the above the reasons, it is important that we debug our MIDlets on target devices before releasing them.

On real devices, there is no "standard output," and the print statements do not have any effect. We need an alternative way to log the debugging messages. The open source `MIDPLogger` utility is a logging framework that allows us to redirect the debugging output to the device's RMS stores. The `MIDPLogger` does more than replace the `println()` and `printStackTrace()` methods. It allows us to specify the relative importance of the logged information using logging levels. Using a special viewer MIDlet bundled within the same MIDlet suite as the target MIDlet, we can view the debugging information after we run the target MIDlet. The viewer MIDlet also supports management of the log storage space (e.g., to delete log entries).

To use the `MIDPLogger` utility in your programs, you first need to include the two source code files `MIDPLogger.java` and `MIDPLogViewer.java` in your source code path. The first class is the log library, and the second is the viewer MIDlet. We can instantiate a `MIDPLogger` object via the following constructor method.

```
public MIDPLogger (int logLevel, boolean toConsole,
                                  boolean incLogName)
```

The `logLevel` argument controls the level of information written to the log storage. Its value can be any of `MIDPLogger.DEBUG`, `MIDPLogger.INFO`, `MIDPLogger.WARNING`, `MIDPLogger.ERROR`, `MIDPLogger.EXPRESS`, and `MIDPLogger.NONE`. If the `toConsole` argument is `true`, the log information is printed to the standard output as well. The `incLogName` argument controls whether the output contains the log-level name. Still using the code example shown in Chapter 11, "End-to-End Design Patterns," the following snippet shows that we modified the `TriviaMidlet`'s `startApp()` and `destroyApp()` methods to instantiate and close a `MIDPLogger` object. The `MIDPLogger` object is a public static object that is available anywhere in the MIDlet code throughout the MIDlet life cycle.

```
public class TriviaMidlet extends MIDlet {

  public static MIDPLogger logger;

  protected void startApp() {
    try {
      // ... ...

      logger =
        new MIDPLogger (MIDPLogger.DEBUG, false, true);
```

```
      } catch (Exception e) {
        e.printStackTrace();
      }
    }

    protected void destroyApp(boolean unconditional) {
      logger.close ();
    }

    // ... ...
  }
```

WARNING

The MIDPLogger log levels are defined as protected static final variables in the 1.0.5 version of the software. We have to change them to public in order to access them from our MIDlets.

We can now call the MIDPLogger.write() method to write out debugging information. The following snippet of the modified PrefStore.restore() method shows how the write() method can replace the println() and printStackTrace() methods. We used different debug levels to differentiate messages of different levels of importance.

```
public class PrefStore {

  public String category;
  public int googleResultsNum;
  public int googleTextMargin;
  public boolean googleIsPhrase;

  private String storeName = "Pref";

  // ... ...

  // Return false if the operation fails
  public synchronized boolean restore () {
    try {
      RecordStore rs =
          RecordStore.openRecordStore(storeName, true);
      TriviaMidlet.logger.write(
        "Record store opened", MIDPLogger.INFO);

      byte [] buf = rs.getRecord(1);
      TriviaMidlet.logger.write(
        "Record retrieved", MIDPLogger.DEBUG);
```

```
        ByteArrayInputStream bis =
            new ByteArrayInputStream (buf);
        DataInputStream dbis = new DataInputStream (bis);
        category = dbis.readUTF();
        TriviaMidlet.logger.write(
          "Category is "+category, MIDPLogger.DEBUG);
        googleResultsNum = dbis.readInt();
        TriviaMidlet.logger.write(
          "Num of Google results is " + googleResultsNum,
          MIDPLogger.DEBUG);
        googleTextMargin = dbis.readInt();
        TriviaMidlet.logger.write(
          "Snippet text margin is " + googleTextMargin,
          MIDPLogger.DEBUG);
        googleIsPhrase = dbis.readBoolean();

        dbis.close();
        bis.close();
        rs.closeRecordStore();
        TriviaMidlet.logger.write(
          "Record store closed", MIDPLogger.DEBUG);
        return true;

    } catch (Exception e) {
      TriviaMidlet.logger.write(
        e.getMessage(), MIDPLogger.ERROR);
      return false;
    }
  }
}
```

In order to view the logged information in the RMS store, we need to use the MIDPLogViewer MIDlet. The default security policy of MIDP states that only MIDlets in the same MIDlet suite can share RMS stores. So, we have to bundle the MIDPLogViewer in the same JAR file as the TriviaMidlet and provide a MIDlet attribute entry for MIDPLogViewer in the JAD and manifest files. The MIDPLogger compatible versions of TriviaMidlet and PrefStore classes as well as the MIDPLogger and MIDPLogViewer classes are available in the src/MIDPLogger directory of the trivia example application. The TriviaMIDPLogger.jar target is built by the buildMIDPLogger task in build4.xml script (see Chapter 12 for how to construct the custom Ant build file). The Ant task uses the bin/TriviaMIDPLogger.MF file as the manifest file for the additional MIDPLogViewer MIDlet attribute. Figure 13–3 shows the MIDPLogViewer in action.

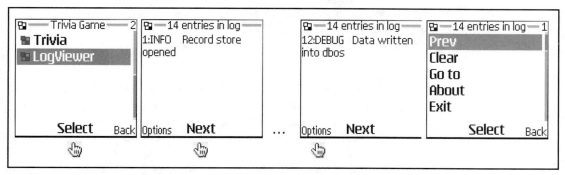

Figure 13-3 Run the MIDPLogViewer MIDlet after the trivia MIDlet to view the log entries.

TIP The `MIDPLogger` utility adds about 4KB to the final JAR file. This might prove too big for projects with JAR files already very close to the limit imposed by the device. If the device is MIDP 2.0 based, we can customize the `MIDPLogger` classes to share the log storage across different MIDlet suites. This way, we can place the `MIDPLogViewer` class in another JAR file.

WARNING The `MIDPLogger` utility is licensed under the GNU General Public License (GPL), which requires that all derivative work be made open source under GPL as well. It is not clear whether a MIDlet that bundles and uses `MIDPLogger` constitutes derivative work. So, use it at your own risk. However, the point of this section is to illustrate the approach `MIDPLogger` uses to solve the on-device debugging problem. It is easy to write your own on-device logging framework from scratch if the `MIDPLogger` licensing is an issue.

Unit Testing

The print and log statements help us in debugging MIDlets. Unit testing is designed to prevent errors from happening in the first place and drastically cut down the need for debugging. A unit test method feeds arguments into an application method and compares the actual output with the expected output. A successful unit test result indicates that a method in the target application is behaving as expected. In MIDlet applications, unit tests can be applied to test objects and methods in the business logic or data management layers. As we demonstrated in the trivia example application, the MVC design allows us to cleanly separate the business layer from the UI layer. In this section, we cover how to use the J2MEUnit framework to run unit tests against the business layer objects. The J2MEUnit framework is based on the widely popular JUnit unit testing framework available in J2SE.

NOTE   We cannot run JUnit directly on mobile devices, since the Java reflection API is not supported in CLDC/MIDP.

TIP   Agile development methodologies call for a test-first development approach. This approach is to first write all the unit tests from the specification to define the expected behavior of the application and boundary conditions. Then, developers start to design and develop the application, and get it to pass the unit tests one by one. After the application passes all unit tests, the development work is done and there is little need for debugging. Since the frequently run unit tests always ensure the correctness of the application's external behavior, this process allows us to make small incremental changes to the internal design with confidence. The test-first approach allows us to defer design decisions until late in the development process and reduces the cost associated with over- or under-designs.

Assert

The basic process of running a unit test is to invoke the public method being tested with predetermined arguments and compare the outcome with the expected values. The `assert` methods in the J2MEUnit framework provide the basic functionalities to compare the values.

```
// Asserts that the two values are the same.
assertEquals (String mesg, long expected, long actual)
assertEquals (String mesg, Object expected, Object actual)

// Asserts that the object is null.
assertNull (String mesg, Object object)

// Asserts that expected and actual refer to the same
// object.
assertSame (String mesg, Object expected, Object actual)

// Asserts the given boolean expression is true.
assertTrue (String mesg, boolean condition)

// Fails this test immediately
fail (String mesg)
```

In a test method, we can have any number of `assert` statements. If any of the `assert` statements fails (or the `fail()` statement is reached), the framework logs a failure for this test method and moves on to the next test method.

TestCase

In a typical J2MEUnit project, every class that needs to be tested has an associated test class. The test class extends the `TestCase` class in the framework. For example, the test class `PrefStoreTest` is designed to test the `PrefStore` class in the trivia example application. The basic functional unit in a test class is the test method, which typically tests a single public method in the target class. The test method invokes the public method with a set of typical or boundary input parameter values. Then it compares the output with the expected output using the `assert` statement discussed above. Ideally, the test class should have at least one test method for each public method in the target class. The naming convention of the test method is `testXXX()`, where XXX is the name of public method it tests.

The unit test methods are independent from each other. We must be able to run any combination of test methods in any order in our test project. That requires us to restore the test environment between tests. For example, we might need to instantiate a fresh instance of the target class or restore the shared object to its initial state. In the J2MEUnit framework, we can simply provide implementations to the `setUp()` and `tearDown()` methods in the `TestCase` class to initialize and finalize the test environment between tests. When the framework runs the tests, the test method calls are sandwiched between the `setUp()` and `tearDown()` calls.

```
setUp ();
   testMethod1 ();
tearDown ();

setUp ();
   testMethod2 ();
tearDown ();

... ...
```

The following listing shows how to implement the test methods for the `PrefStore` class. We not only test the `save()` and `restore()` methods separately to see if they break when the preference record is saved or restored multiple times, we also test the two methods together to see if the `restore()` method can recover the data just saved.

```
public class PrefStoreTest extends TestCase {

  protected PrefStore pref;

  public PrefStoreTest () {
  }
```

```java
        public PrefStoreTest (String sTestName,
                              TestMethod rTestMethod) {
          super(sTestName, rTestMethod);
        }

        // ... ...

        public void testSave() {
          try {
            // Save once
            pref.save ();
            // Save twice
            pref.save ();
          } catch (Exception e) {
            fail ("Cannot save" + e.getMessage());
            e.printStackTrace ();
          }
        }

        public void testRestore () {
          // Restore once
          assertTrue(pref.restore ());
          // Restore twice
          assertTrue(pref.restore ());
        }

        public void testSaveRestore () {
          try {
            pref.save ();
          } catch (Exception e) {
            fail ("Cannot save" + e.getMessage());
          }
          // Assign random values
          pref.category = "random";
          pref.googleIsPhrase = false;
          pref.googleResultsNum = -1;
          pref.googleTextMargin = 20;

          assertTrue(pref.restore ());
          // Verify the setUp values are restored
          assertEquals(pref.category, "music02");
          assertTrue(pref.googleIsPhrase);
          assertEquals(pref.googleResultsNum, 10);
          assertEquals(pref.googleTextMargin, 100);
        }

        public void setUp () {
```

```
    pref = PrefStore.getInstance ();
    pref.category = "music02";
    pref.googleIsPhrase = true;
    pref.googleResultsNum = 10;
    pref.googleTextMargin = 100;
  }

  public void tearDown () {
    pref = null;
  }
}
```

TestSuite

In a `TestCase` class, we can have test methods and other support methods. In the J2SE version of JUnit, the testing framework automatically figures out which methods are the test methods via Java reflection using the `testXXX()` naming convention. In J2MEUnit, there is no reflection support, so we have to manually specify which methods in a `TestCase` class are test methods via the `TestCase.suite()` method, which returns a `TestSuite` object containing all the tests. We can add each test method into the `TestSuite` via an anonymous class. The following listing shows how we construct a `TestSuite` for the `PrefStoreTest` class.

```
public class PrefStoreTest extends TestCase {

  // ... ...

  public Test suite() {
    TestSuite aSuite = new TestSuite();

    aSuite.addTest(
      new PrefStoreTest("testSave",
        new TestMethod() {
          public void run(TestCase tc) {
            ((PrefStoreTest) tc).testSave();
          }
        }
    ));

    aSuite.addTest(
      new PrefStoreTest("testRestore",
        new TestMethod() {
          public void run(TestCase tc) {
            ((PrefStoreTest) tc).testRestore();
          }
        }
```

```
        ));

    aSuite.addTest(
      new PrefStoreTest("testSaveRestore",
        new TestMethod() {
          public void run(TestCase tc) {
            ((PrefStoreTest) tc).testSaveRestore();
          }
        }
    ));

    return aSuite;
  }

  // ... ...
}
```

The `TestAll.suite()` method assembles all test suites into a master suite
that can be invoked from the test runner MIDlet (see next section). In an
application, we can have multiple master suites, each with a selected subset of
the test cases to suit different scenarios. For example, when the network is not
available, we'd probably skip the network-related tests.

```
public class TestAll extends TestCase {

    public TestAll() {
        super("null");
    }

    public TestAll(String name)    {
        super(name);
    }

    public Test suite()     {
        TestSuite suite = new TestSuite();

        suite.addTest(new PrefStoreTest().suite());

        // Add more test cases ...

        return suite;
    }
}
```

TestRunner

The `TestRunner` class in J2MEUnit runs the `TestSuite`. It invokes the test methods in the suite one by one with the correct `setUp()` and `tearDown()` calls between them. If a test method fails an assertion, the `TestRunner` records the failure and its message. After all the test methods are completed, the `TestRunner` visually presents the results to the developer on the device's screen. The `TestRunner` class itself is a MIDlet. We can simply extend it and override the `startApp()` method to start the test using the full Java class name of the `TestCase` class that assembles the needed `TestSuite`. Figure 13–4 shows the screen output after we run the `TestAll` test suite.

```
public class TestMidlet extends TestRunner {

    public TestMidlet()    {
    }

    protected void startApp()    {
        start(new String[]
           {"com.Series40Book.midp.tests.TestAll"});
    }
}
```

The source code for `PrefStoreTest`, `TestAll`, and `TestMidlet` classes is available in the `src/UnitTests` directory of the trivia example application. The `buildUnitTests` task in the `build4.xml` script builds the unit testing target in the `TriviaTests.jar` file using the necessary source code and manifest files (see Chapter 12 for suggestions on how to construct the custom Ant build file).

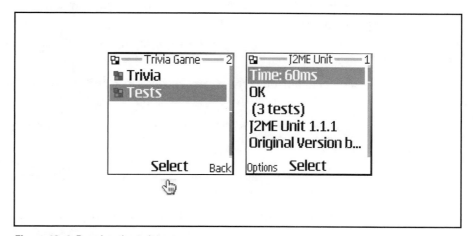

Figure 13–4 Running the unit tests.

UI Testing Guidelines

Unit testing has its limits. For most mobile smart clients, a large portion of the application code is UI-related. But it is difficult to unit test user interfaces. A UI testing framework requires a runner program that automatically executes user actions specified in a script file, programmatically generates the UI events, and then feeds the events to the main thread of the application to be tested. On MIDP devices, we also need to worry about the MIDlet life cycle. Even if such a framework is technically possible, it is probably too big to be useful on any Series 40 devices that limit the JAR file size to 64KB or 128KB. So, our method to test an MIDP user interface still involves having a human tester manually go through the execution branches using a story script.

On the other hand, UI testing is much more than just ensuring functional correctness. It is equally important to test human experiences with the user interface, such as the placement of UI components, text labels, response time, and alert messages. Feedbacks on user experiences can only be generated from human testing. In this section, we list some of the important things to consider when testing your MIDlets.

- The MIDlet should work correctly even though the environment changes (e.g., the network connection drops). Errors should be handled gracefully or presented to users in easy-to-understand messages.

- The network connections are closed when they are no longer in use.

- The Bluetooth device and service discoveries are efficient. Use Limited Inquiry Access Code (LIAC) to speed up the discovery procedure if feasible. The Bluetooth connection should be turned off if it is not needed for a long time.

- In RMS operations, the user is informed if important data is about to be overwritten.

- All main functions of the application can easily be accessed through the main menu.

- Each functionality works as described in the documentation and in the application's Instructions section.

- Each screen appears for the length of time that is necessary to read its information.

- The consistency of the following features is maintained throughout the application: terms, layout, colors (or reverted colors), soft key labels, vibration, and sounds.

- Menus are grouped logically, and menu structures are not too deep.

- It is possible to exit the application from the main menu.

- Soft key labels reflect the style of the user interface of the particular Developer Platform.

- The label related to the right soft key refers to Back, Quit, Exit, Cancel, Clear, or other "negative/backward" functions.

- The middle soft key can have only positive functioning commands.

- The most probable action (highest priority for the Command) that the user may take next should be mapped to middle soft key.

- Each sound has a distinctive meaning.

- Sound settings do not affect the usability of the application.

For more information on application testing guidelines, please refer to the "Developer Platforms Guidelines for Testing J2ME Applications" document on Forum Nokia. In addition, Forum Nokia document "Series 40 Developer Platform 2.0: Usability Guidelines for J2ME Games" deals specially with testing issues for J2ME games.

Summary

In this chapter, we discussed the key strategies and tools for debugging and testing J2ME/MIDP applications on Nokia devices. Those techniques are key to increased software productivity and quality assurance for commercially successful applications.

chapter

14

Multimedia Messaging Service

Use Multimedia Messaging Services (MMS) to deliver content-rich applications.

MMS technology is a key component of the Nokia Series 40 Developer Platform. All Series 40 Developer Platform devices are capable of receiving and sending MMS messages. The device-native MMS client integrates with other native applications, such as the address book and camera controls, to provide a smooth multimedia experience for users. With the majority of wireless operators already offering MMS data services, MMS is quickly gaining popularity, and it offers a major revenue opportunity for developers and content providers. In this chapter, we discuss how to develop MMS applications. The topics include the following:

- **Messaging services:** covers the basics of MMS, its network infrastructure, and business opportunities. We discuss the modes of MMS applications. Since most MMS applications reside on a PC (or on a server), not on a handset, we discuss how to send and receive MMS messages from the PC side.

- **Authoring MMS messages:** covers how to create MMS messages on a PC. We discuss the MMS client characteristics for Nokia devices, the basics of SMIL, and how to use Nokia's MMS content authoring tools.

- **The Nokia Mobile Server Services API Library:** introduces the Java APIs for Nokia MMSC servers. We can use those APIs to develop external MMSC applications for any External Application InterFace (EAIF) or MM7 standard compatible MMSCs.

After studying this chapter, you will be able to grasp the key concepts of MMS and how to get started with Nokia tools and devices.

Messaging Services

MMS extends the text-based Short Message Service (SMS) to multimedia content. While SMS is limited to text and to basic graphic content with Smart Messaging, MMS is able to encapsulate virtually any media file, including text, photographs, video, screen savers, ring tones, audio files, and animations. However, it should be noted that suitable content is constrained by the media-handling capabilities of individual devices (see the next section for Nokia device characteristics). MMS is often described as the next-generation messaging service. MMS can be used by consumers to message friends, family, and business colleagues—essentially providing peer-to-peer messaging. MMS can also be used by content providers to deliver content or application functionality through an operator's Multimedia Messaging Service Center (MMSC).

Many mobile devices on the market, including all Nokia Series 40 and Series 60 mobile phones, already support MMS. Most operators deliver phones preconfigured for their MMS service. Users with MMS-capable phones purchased before their operator offered MMS service can configure their phones, either using over-the-air (OTA) configuration, usually initiated from a Web support site, or manually. For example, the Web site `https://secure.mouse2mobile.com/clients/nokia/americas/mms/` can send the MMS configuration directly to any MMS subscriber phone in North America via WAP Push. The user just needs to accept and save the message for the settings to take effect. The Nokia Web site provides links to MMS configurator services in other parts of the world as well. To access those services, point your browser to `http://www.nokia.com/` and select the menu's Support | Phone Support | Settings.

MMS Benefits and Opportunities

Consumers benefit from MMS technology by having the opportunity to experience richer entertainment and information content. For instance, applications are available that allow consumers to send their friends animated greeting cards instead of simple text messages.

For developers, the possibilities for creating exciting new entertainment applications using MMS are virtually limitless. MMS provides services for everything from downloading and playing music, storing pictures and creating online photo albums, to composing and editing animations and greeting cards to send to friends.

Network operators also benefit from MMS because they charge consumers directly for the MMS services, indirectly for the bandwidth used to deliver the services, or recoup their investment by decreasing subscriber turnover rate. Operators actively seek value-added MMS services that can justify premium pricing. There are ample opportunities for developers to structure revenue share deals with operators based on applications that generate MMS usage and demand for data bandwidth.

The MMS Infrastructure

A key component of the MMS infrastructure is the MMSC server. Nokia is a major manufacturer of MMSCs. From the developer's and user's perspectives, the MMSC is very much like an email server in the Internet infrastructure. The sender sends her message to the MMSC operated by her mobile network operator. Depending on the receipt phone number in the message header, the MMSC routes the message to the target MMSC operated by the recipient's network operator. The communication between the MMSCs is typically through the wired Internet using the standard HTTP and email protocols. The recipient

MMSC first sends a WAP Push message to the recipient device notifying it of the incoming MMS message. The message provides a location to download the media content. The MMS-enabled device is automatically triggered to download the media content via WAP in the background. Once the message is completely downloaded and assembled, the device alerts the user and launches the MMS viewer application. Delivery of MMS messages is designed to be immediate but can be delayed by heavy loads on servers or by network congestion. On the current GPRS networks, it is not uncommon for an MMS message to take more than 15 minutes to be delivered to its recipient. The above process is illustrated in Figure 14–1.

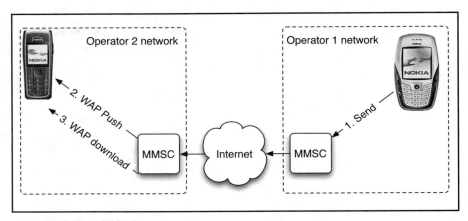

Figure 14–1 The MMS infrastructure.

NOTE   An MMS recipient address could also be an email address. In this case, the originating MMSC delivers the message directly to the recipient's email server using the SMTP protocol. The MMS message appears to be an email message with media file attachments in the recipient's email reader application.

Since the MMS relies on a packet data network to receive WAP Push and automatically download the media content, it requires at least a 2.5G wireless data network (i.e., either a GSM GPRS or a CDMA 1x network). The network operators and device manufacturers can both impose a limit on the maximum MMS message size. Large messages are slow to download. They could overrun the device's limited memory and offer no obvious user-experience improvements over smaller messages on the phone's limited display and audio hardware. In addition, since wireless data services are typically charged according to the bandwidth usage, unsolicited large messages are actually a security threat to users. Most wireless operators limit MMS message sizes from

30KB to 180KB. The Nokia devices have MMS size limits from 45KB to 100KB. Later in this chapter, we discuss the MMS characteristics of Nokia devices, including information about the maximum MMS size on different devices.

MMSC Access

To deliver MMS messages from our applications to the end users, it is crucial for us to gain access to the network operator's MMSC servers. However, operators, especially in the United States, often maintain tight control over their MMSCs. Only authorized parties are allowed to connect to the MMSC. Although making MMSCs talk with each other is technically simple, interoperability is a difficult business issue even between big operators themselves. As a result, it is not always possible to send MMS messages across different networks. For developers, the issue is more complicated, since we have to make a business deal for MMSC access with each major operator in order to reach a broad range of end users. We expect network operators to gradually open their MMSCs to third-party developers in the future as the MMS technology and business model mature. Forum Nokia helps developers to gain access to live MMSCs in Europe, Asia, and North America via the Nokia Developer Hub program. The MMSC typically exposes its service to external applications via an HTTP-based interface. Two data protocols are supported by Nokia MMSC servers.

- The External Application InterFace (EAIF) is a binary data protocol over HTTP. It is a nonstandard protocol supported by all Nokia MMSC servers.

- The MM7 protocol is an XML Web Services standard used to access MMSCs and defined by the 3GPP. The MM7 protocol should be supported by most new MMSC servers in the future.

The detailed specifications of EAIF and MM7 are not important to MMS application developers, since the Nokia Mobile Server Services Library provides an easy-to-use Java API to wrap around those protocols. We introduce the Java API in a later section in this chapter.

An alternative way to access MMSCs is through commercial MMS gateway services, such as the `http://www.csoft.co.uk/` Web Service. The gateway service provider has negotiated contracts with multiple operators. It exposes a simple HTTP-based interface to developers. For a small subscription fee, we can send MMS messages directly from our backend applications. The MMS message is enclosed in a .mms file. We can just upload it via HTTP POST to the gateway server and the gateway sends it to the target phone number. Later in this chapter, we cover how to generate .mms files from Nokia content authoring tools.

MMS Application Modes

MMS applications can interact with users in several different ways. For MMS developers, it is important to understand the application modes and choose the best message delivery mechanisms.

Peer-to-Peer Messaging Mode

MMS enables mobile users to send multimedia messages to each other. For example, a user with a camera phone can send photos to peers via MMS. In this mode, the users typically use the MMS client software that is factory-installed on the handset. With the current generation Series 40 devices, the native MMS client software is not programmatically accessible and hence there is little opportunity for developers. However, two new developments in the near future might change the landscape for this type of applications drastically.

- The J2ME File I/O API (JSR 75) will provide access to the native file system on the device. That would allow a J2ME application to exchange media files with the native MMS client. For example, we can retrieve media files from MMS messages and use them in J2ME applications.

- The J2ME Wireless Messaging API 2.0 (JSR 205) will enable J2ME applications to send MMS messages directly to each other. Together with MMAPI, it could open exciting new opportunities for peer-to-peer smart-client applications. For more information on the WMA 2.0, please refer to Chapter 8, "Wireless Messaging."

The Terminating Mode

An MMS terminating application receives messages. A good example is the mobile photo blog application. The camera phone takes a picture, composes the MMS message, and sends it to the server. The server extracts the photo from the message, processes it, and makes it available from the blog Web site. The terminating application can receive the MMS message either by integrating with the MMSC or through a standard email account.

When integrated with an MMSC, the terminating application is associated with a special phone number easily accessible to users. In this case, the terminating application is typically an HTTP server that listens for incoming connections. The phone number, server address, and port number are registered in the operator's MMSC route table. When the user sends an MMS message to the registered number, the MMSC connects to the terminating application's server and posts the message content over HTTP using Nokia's EAIF protocol or the standard MM7 protocol. Direct integration with the MMSC allows us to take full advantage of the MMSC features (e.g., to use easy-to-remember special phone numbers). But, as we have discussed, it is also difficult and potentially costly to sign business arrangements with the operators to gain the MMSC access.

An easier and cheaper approach is to receive MMS messages via your own email servers. The MMS client on Nokia devices can send messages to email addresses. We can write an application that polls the email server periodically to retrieve the messages. The JavaMail API provides a standard and easy-to-use API to retrieve messages via any email protocol and parse the multimedia parts of the message.

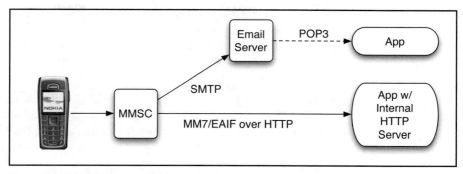

Figure 14–2 The terminating MMS applications.

The terminating application mode is illustrated in Figure 14–2.

The Originating Mode

An originating application sends MMS messages to mobile devices. An example for such an application is a mobile content provisioning service. The user could call in or use her mobile Web browser to order a picture or a ringtone. The originating MMS application would send the media file to the phone once the payment is received. As we have discussed, the MMS application could send MMS messages to handsets via direct integration with the MMSC (EAIF or MM7 over HTTP, or the Nokia Mobile Server Services Library) or via MMS gateways (HTTP upload of .mms files). The originating application mode is illustrated in Figure 14–3.

The Originating-Terminating Mode

An originating-terminating application can both send out MMS messages and receive MMS messages. An example is an MMS-based mobile trivia

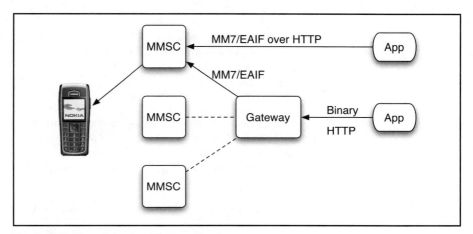

Figure 14–3 The originating MMS applications.

application. The backend application sends questions to the handset, and the user responds by replying with the choice number in the message body. However, we have to note that the current MMS infrastructure does not provide sufficient support for highly interactive applications, since it could take a long time for the message to deliver.

The easiest way to develop originating-terminating applications is to integrate with MMSCs. However, it is also possible to use mixed originating and terminating solutions. For example, we can send out MMS messages via mobile MMS gateways and receive replies via a special email address.

Authoring MMS Messages

MMS messages are the core of any MMS application. The MMS messages carry the rich media content. They are delivered to the user's handset and played back by the MMS viewer application on the device. We start our discussion by introducing the MMS characteristics of Nokia devices.

Nokia Device Characteristics for MMS

An MMS message consists of several text or multimedia components. There are many kinds of media content, and not all MMS-compatible devices support all media types. Table 14–1 lists the MIME types and media filename suffixes supported on Nokia Series 40 and Series 60 Developer Platform devices. The symbols are as follows.

- N/A indicates that this media type is not supported on this class of device.

- S/R indicates that both sending and receiving are supported. The user can view the media file in the on-device MMS viewer application.

- R indicates that receiving is supported and the user can view the media files in the MMS viewer.

- R1 indicates that this media type file can be received in an MMS message but has to be saved to the device memory and opened by another application.

 NOTE   For Series 60 devices, we can pass Java applications (JAR and JAD files) and WML content in MMS messages. This content can be saved to the device memory and then opened by the Java Application Management Software and the WML/xHTML browser application.

For older specialized Series 40 devices, there are several notable exceptions to Table14–1. In particular,

Table 14–1 Supported MIME Types on Nokia MMS Handsets

MIME Type or File Name Suffix	Series 40 DP 1.0	Series 40 DP 2.0	Series 60 DP 1.0	Series 60 DP 2.0
image/jpeg, baseline (*.jpeg, *.jpg)	S/R	S/R	S/R	S/R
image/jpeg, progressive	N/A	N/A	S/R	S/R
image/gif, static (*.gif)	S/R	S/R	S/R	S/R
image/gif, animated (*.gif)	S/R	S/R	S/R	S/R
image/png (*.png)	S/R	S/R	S/R	S/R
image/bmp (*.bmp)	S/R	S/R	R1	R1
image/vnd.wap.wbmp (*.wbmp)	S/R	S/R	S/R	S/R
image/vnd.nok-wallpaper (*.jpg, *.gif)	R	R	R	R
application/vnd.Nokia.ringing-tone	R	R	R1	R1
audio/amr (*.amr)	N/A	S/R	S/R	S/R
audio/x-amr (*.amr)	N/A	N/A	S/R	S/R
audio/amr-wb (*.awb)	N/A	N/A	N/A	R
audio/x-wav	N/A	N/A	S/R	S/R
audio/midi (*.mid)	R	R	R	R
audio/sp-midi (*.mid)	R	R	R	R
text/plain	S/R	S/R	S/R	S/R
text/x-vCard	N/A	N/A	R1	R1
text/x-vCalendar	N/A	N/A	R1	R1
application/java-archive (*.jar)	N/A	N/A	R1	R1
application/x-java-archive (*.jar)	N/A	N/A	R1	R1
application/vnd.wap.wmlc	N/A	N/A	R1	R1
application/vnd.wap.wmlscriptc	N/A	N/A	R1	R1
application/vnd.wap.wbxml	N/A	N/A	R1	R1
text/vnd.sun.j2me.app-descriptor (*.jad)	N/A	N/A	R1	R1
video/3gpp (*.3gp)	N/A	S/R	S/R	S/R
Max message size	45KB	100KB	100KB	100KB

- The Nokia 6650 and 3105 devices support progressive jpeg images.

- The Nokia 6220, 6650, 6820, and 7200 devices support 3gpp video files.

- The Nokia 3200, 6220, 6650, 6810, 6820, and 7200 devices support amr audio files, and they support MMS message sizes up to 100KB.

For the exact and most up-to-date MMS specifications for Nokia devices, please refer to the "Messaging Characteristics in Nokia Phones" document published on Forum Nokia. In addition to supporting the individual media types, some Nokia devices support an MMS presentation component that ties together the media file attachments in the MMS message. We discuss MMS presentation in the next section.

A Quick Introduction to SMIL

The MMS presentation component is written in an XML-based markup language called Synchronized Multimedia Integration Language (SMIL). SMIL is supported on Series 40 Developer Platform 2.0 devices as well as all Series 60 Developer Platform devices. In a nutshell, the SMIL part in an MMS message provides instructions to the MMS client on how to present the other multimedia parts in the same message. It works similarly to the way HTML Web pages provide rendering instructions to Web browsers. For example, it can specify how images or video clips can be laid out on the screen. More interestingly, the SMIL can specify timing information of the presentation. For example, the SMIL presentation can play back an audio file for a specified period of time while an image is displayed. We can also use SMIL to program a timed slide show through the images attached in the MMS message. Without the SMIL component, the MMS message will be displayed as a series of discrete media objects in the viewer, which the user can step through using the device's scroll key. Figure 14–4 shows an MMS message with image and audio components but no SMIL presentation. Figure 14–5 shows how the SMIL presentation ties the two media parts together by playing back the audio while displaying the image. Hence, SMIL allows us to compose sophisticated MMS messages that produce an excellent user experience.

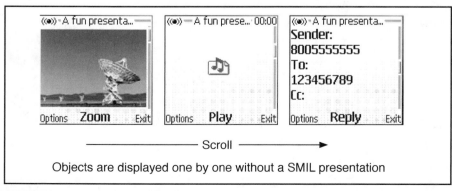

Figure 14–4 Objects in an MMS message without the SMIL presentation.

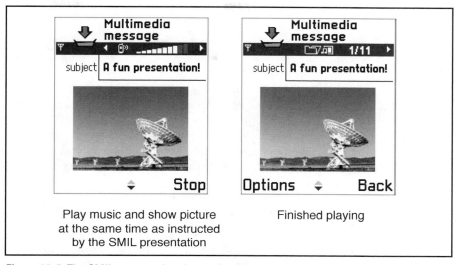

Figure 14–5 The SMIL presentation ties media objects in a message together.

The SMIL Document Structure

A SMIL document is a properly formatted XML document. The entire document must be enclosed inside a pair of `<smil></smil>` tags. The root `<smil>` element has the following two children elements.

- The `<head>` element defines shared information across the document, such as the screen layout and available transition effects. For simple MMS messages, we can ignore the `<head>` element altogether. The use of the `<head>` element is discussed later in this section.

- The `<body>` element contains the instructions on how the media files should be played back. It is required in all SMIL documents.

Two types of playback elements can be used inside the `<body>` element: the parallel and sequential playback elements.

The Playback Control Elements

The `<par>` element in a SMIL document encloses media elements that are played parallel to each other. For example, we can play a music clip while at the same time displaying a picture on the screen (see the following listing).

```
<smil>
  <body>
    <par>
      <img src="photo01.png" dur="5s" />
      <audio src="music.mid" />
```

```
      </par>
    </body>
  </smil>
```

The playback length of the `<par>` element is by default the longest media child element. We can alter this behavior by changing the value of the `endsync` attribute. For example, `endsync="first"` would cause the `<par>` element to stop when the first media element is stopped. We could also specify an arbitrary playback length for the `<par>` element using the `dur` attribute. For example, the attribute value `dur="5s"` would cause the playback to stop after 5 seconds. The `begin` attribute can be used to specify the initial delay before the playback is started. The `repeatCount` attribute specifies how many times this element should be repeated, with the value `indefinite` indicating an indefinite playback loop until the user interrupts it.

We can also play back media elements in sequence using the `<seq>` element in SMIL. That is analogous to a slide show (see the listing below).

```
<smil>
  <body>
    <seq>
      <text src="welcome.txt" dur="3s" />
      <img src="photo01.png" dur="5s" />
      <img src="photo02.png" dur="5s" />
    </seq>
  </body>
</smil>
```

The `begin`, `dur`, and `repeatCount` attributes can also be used together with the `<seq>` element. The `<par>` and `<seq>` elements can be nested in a SMIL document. For example, we can have a picture slide show with a single music track or a slide show with a different music clip for each picture. See the sample code at the end of this section for an example of nested `<par>` and `<seq>` elements.

The Media Elements

The media elements inside the `<par>` or `<seq>` elements indicate what media files to play and how to play them. We saw the image and audio media elements in the above examples. Table 14–2 lists the media elements defined in SMIL. The `src` attribute specifies the referenced media filename, and the `dur` attribute specifies the duration of the playback. The media object type must be one of those supported by the device's MMS viewer.

Layout Management

As we mentioned, the `<head>` element in a SMIL document can be used to hold definitions of shared attributes. For example, we can specify how the screen should be divided into display areas using the `<layout>` element. Each display

Table 14–2 Media Elements in SMIL

Element	Description
`<animation>`	Defines a reference to an animation object stored as vector graphics or in another animated format.
`<audio>`	Defines a reference to an audio object stored as recorded audio.
`<brush>`	Defines a fill color or a fill pattern in the specified screen area.
`<img>`	Defines a reference to an image object.
`<text>`	Defines a reference to a text object stored as a text file.
`<textstream>`	Defines a reference to a text object stored as a text stream.
`<video>`	Defines a reference to a video object stored as a recorded video clip.

area is specified by a `<region>` element inside `<layout>`. The `top`, `left`, `bottom`, and `right` attributes of the `<region>` element specify the position of the display area; the `width` and `height` attributes specify the size of the display area. The `<root-layout>` element is a sibling of `<region>` elements, and it specifies the overall screen size. Using the `<par>` element, we can display multiple media objects at the same time on the screen. The following example shows a photo with a line of text caption below it.

```
<smil>
  <head>
    <layout>
      <root-layout width="128" height="128" />
      <region id="main" width="128" height="110"
                        z-index="0"/>
      <region id="text" top="111" width="128"
                height="18" z-index="1"/>
    </layout>
  </head>

  <body>
    <par>
      <img src="photo01.png" region="main" />
      <text src="photo01.txt" region="text" />
    </par>
  </body>
</smil>
```

In addition to layouts, we can also define transition effects between <seq> children elements in the <head> element. SMIL has a number of predefined transition effects to use when we change from slide to slide. For more information, please refer to the SMIL specification available from http://www.w3.org/AudioVideo/.

A Music Slide Show Example

Combining all we learned above, the following listing shows a SMIL presentation that runs a picture slide show with background music. Each of the pictures stays on the screen for a different length of time.

```
<smil>
  <head>
    <layout>
      <root-layout width="128" height="128" />
      <region id="main" width="128" height="110"
                                      z-index="0"/>
      <region id="text" top="111" width="128"
                        height="18" z-index="1"/>
    </layout>
  </head>

  <body>
    <par>
      <audio src="music.mid" />
      <seq>
        <par dur="5s">
          <img src="photo01.png" region="main" />
          <text src="photo01.txt" region="text" />
        </par>
        <par dur="7s">
          <img src="photo02.png" region="main" />
          <text src="photo02.txt" region="text" />
        </par>
      </seq>
    </par>
  </body>
</smil>
```

Nokia Developer's Suite for MMS

The Nokia Developer's Suite (NDS) for MMS is a content authoring tool that allows us to test SMIL-based MMS messages to device emulators. The user interface of the software is very simple. Upon starting up, the program locates all the suitable device SDKs installed on the current computer and lists them in the lower right panel. We can click on the Start New button to create new SDK emulator instances (see Figure 14–6).

NOTE We have to start the Nokia Connectivity Framework in order to send messages from the NDS for MMS to the Series 40 Developer Platform 2.0 SDK emulator.

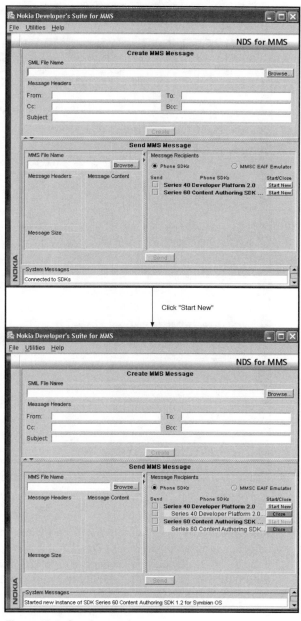

Figure 14–6 Starting emulators.

Then, we can select a SMIL file in the top panel and fill in the route and message header information. We click on the Create button to create a new .mms file that has all the media elements embedded. The .mms file is saved in the same directory as the .smil file, and it can be sent as a standalone message to commercial MMSC gateway services. We can see the content of the generated .mms file in the lower left panel (see Figure 14–7).

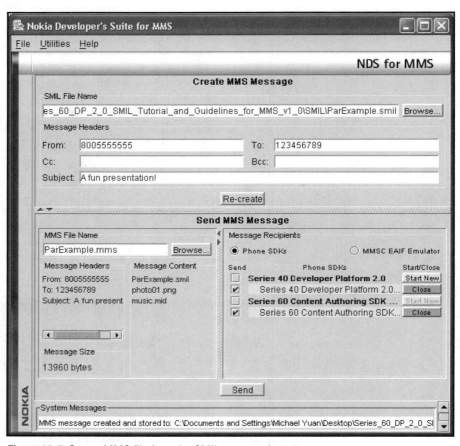

Figure 14–7 Create MMS file from the SMIL presentation.

After the .mms file is created, we can click on the Send button to send it to selected emulator instances. The emulator displays a new message alert (see Figure 14–8). Once we accept the alert, the MMS viewer application is automatically launched to display the message.

Figure 14–8 New messaging alerts.

Unfortunately, the version 1.0 of the Series 40 Developer Platform 2.0 SDK does not yet support SMIL presentation properly. Until this known issue is resolved, to test your SMIL presentations properly on the PC, we recommend installing the free RealOne media player and opening the SMIL file from there.

Nokia Mobile Server Services Library

Now we have composed the MMS messages. It is time to deliver them to the phones via the MMSC servers. Although we could use gateway services or email servers to send and receive MMS messages without direct interaction with the MMSC, direct MMSC access is always preferred whenever possible because MMSC provides more reliable services and richer features.

As we have discussed, MMSC servers expose their programmatic access interfaces to Internet applications via protocols such as EAIF and MM7, both of which are built on top of the ubiquitous HTTP. Programming to interact with the MMSC HTTP interfaces requires the manual manipulation of many headers and serialized content. It is a tedious task, and the protocols are complex and convoluted. To make life easier for backend developers, Nokia has released a Java library called Nokia Mobile Server Services API and Library that encapsulates most MMSC functions as Java API calls. (The library is available as a free download from the Forum Nokia Web site at `http://www.forum.nokia.com/nokia_mobile_server/`). Since the MM7 protocol is a 3GPP standard adopted by most major MMSC vendors, this Java API library works with many MMSC products, including those from Nokia, Openwave, Ericsson, and more. The Nokia Mobile Server Services Library actually contains two sets of Java APIs for the MMSC.

• The Nokia API is a proprietary API developed and used by Nokia over the years. It is being phased out but still supported because there are older MMS applications written with this API.

• The Server API for Mobile Services (SAMS) API is a new Java API standardized by the Java Community Process (JSR 212). It is supported by multiple vendors.

Both APIs support both the EAIF and MM7 protocols. In fact, the two Java APIs provide almost identical functional support for MMSC servers. In this section, we show the basic use of both APIs. Together with Nokia Mobile Server Services Library, we can also download Nokia's MMSC emulator. The emulator runs on its embedded JBoss open source Java application server and has an Eclipse framework-based administrative client. The MMSC emulator can route messages between external applications and Series 40 Developer Platform 2.0 SDK device emulators. The detailed usage and administration of the MMSC server emulator is beyond the scope of this book. Interested readers can refer to its user and administrator guide.

Instantiating the Driver

Using the abstract factory pattern, the library provides support for both EAIF and MM7 protocols. The difference between the Nokia API and the SAMS API is primarily in the syntax used to call the factory methods and the configuration files passed.

Using the Nokia API

The `MMSDriverFactory` class in the library creates connection objects to the MMSC server, as shown below.

```
// create a driver engine instance using parameters
// from a local configuration file "Driver.prop".
factory = MMSDriverFactory.getInstance(
                "file:///Nokia/Driver.prop");
engine  = factory.createEngine();
// enable the engine so it can send/receive messages
engine.connect();

// do the work ... ...

engine.disconnect();
```

Using the SAMS API

In the SAMS API, the factory class is `ServiceFactory`. We have to pass the generic SAMS configuration file and the implementation-specific driver configuration file to the service object.

```
// The basic SAMS system properties
System.setProperty("javax.sams.config.file",
                    "file:///Nokia/SAMS.prop");

// Get service and open session
ServiceFactory sf = new ServiceFactory();
service = sf.getService(MessagingSession.class, "MMS");

Properties props = new Properties();
props.load(
   new FileInputStream("file:///Nokia/Driver.prop"));

messagingSession =
   (MessagingSession)service.openSession(props);

// do the work ... ...

service.closeSession(messagingSession);
```

Connection Configuration

The factory methods are passed configuration files containing the names of the API implementation classes and connection information about the remote MMSC.

Using the Nokia API

The `Driver.prop` file specifies the driver properties. The property file for an EAIF driver might be similar to that shown below.

```
# The implementation class name for driver factory
mmsc.Factory.Implementation =
com.nokia.mobile.services.driver.mms.eaif.MMSDriverFactoryImpl
# Specifies the port number of the MMSC
mmsc.Engine.MMSCURL = http://mmschost:41020
# Specifies the port to listen on
mmsc.Engine.server.port = 61020
# Determines what mode an engine is to work in.
mmsc.Engine.mode = originating
# ... Other configuration options ...
```

The property file for a MM7 driver might be similar to that shown below.

```
# The implementation class name for driver factory
mmsc.Factory.Implementation =
com.nokia.mobile.services.driver.mms.mm7.MM7DriverFactory
# The URL for the MMSC's MM7 Web Service
mmsc.Engine.MMSCURL =
http://user:pass@host:8180/axis/services/MMSService
# Specifies port to listen to for terminating mode
mmsc.Engine.axis.server.port = 8000
# Determines what mode the engine Will be working in.
mmsc.Engine.mode=originating
# Value added service provider (VASP) ID
mmsc.Engine.MM7.VASPID = com.provider
# Value added service (VAS) ID
mmsc.Engine.MM7.VASID = pictureService
# ... Other configuration options ...
```

Using the SAMS API

The SAMS configuration file SAMS.prop contains system properties indicating the names of the API implementation classes. The following listing should be one line in the SAMS.prop file.

```
javax.sams.messaging.MessagingSession=
MMS:com.nokia.mobile.services.sams.messaging.
mms.MmsMessagingServiceImpl;
SMS:com.nokia.mobile.services.sams.messaging.
sms.SmsMessagingServiceImpl
```

Then, we can use the same EAIF and MM7 Driver.prop configuration files as those used in the Nokia API example.

Sending Messages

In this section, we discuss how to send MMS messages with or without the SMIL presentation part, using the library. We also cover the API to send SMS messages.

Simple Messaging with Nokia API

Simple messages contain several multimedia parts, each independent from each other, and no SMIL presentation file. We can construct the message from a list of files in the local file system using the `MMSDriverFactory` factory class, set the recipient address, and then simply call the `MMSEngine.send()` method to send it. The library guesses the appropriate MIME types for the files. We can also construct message parts using the `ContentPart` class and manually add them to the `MMSMessage` object. The `ContentPart.setContent()` method takes two arguments. The first one is the string content for a text part or the path to a multimedia file. The second argument is the MIME type of the part.

```
//Table of URLs of files to be attached to MMS.
// Full file path URLs for each file is used.
String contentPath = "file:///myContent/";
String attachments[] = {
  contentPath + "yellow.jpg",
  contentPath + "house.jpg",
  contentPath + "bridge.jpg"
};

MMSDriverFactory factory;
MMSEngine engine;
// Create the engine and start it ... ...

MMSMessage toSend = factory.createMMSMessage(attachments);
// this is to be a message with unrelated parts
toSend.setContentType(MimePart.CT_MULTIPART_MIXED);

// Optional: we can add some content parts "by hand"
// Add a text part
ContentPart cp = new ContentPart();
cp.setCharEncoding("UTF-8");
cp.setContent("Hi! Have fun!", "text/plain");
toSend.getMultipart().addPart(cp);
// Add another image file
cp.setContent(contentPath + "mesg.png", "image/png");
toSend.getMultipart().addPart(cp);

// Set message parameters
// Can also take CC and BCC address lists
```

```
toSend.setTO(new MMSAddress("18005555555/TYPE=PLMN"));
toSend.setFROM(new MMSAddress("18005555554/TYPE=PLMN"));
toSend.setSubject("This is the subject line");

// Send the message
engine.send(toSend);
```

SMIL Message with Nokia API

Sending MMS messages with a SMIL presentation part is more complex than sending simple MMS messages. On the file system, we can easily distinguish the SMIL file based on its filename suffix and locate all the media files referenced in the SMIL file based on the URLs and filenames. However, once those files are read out and assembled into an MMS message, they become `ContentPart` objects, and their filename information is lost. We have to programmatically specify which part of the message is used for the SMIL presentation and how the media filenames referenced in the SMIL document correspond to the content parts in message. To do that, we use metadata (or attributes) for `ContentPart` and `MMSMessage` objects.

We first need to set the content type attribute of the `MMSMessage` as `MimePart.CT_MULTIPART_RELATED`, which indicates that some of the parts are referred to by other parts (e.g., the SMIL part). Then, we assign a `content ID` attribute for each part in the message. The SMIL part's ID is then set to be the `presentation ID` attribute of the `MMSMessage`. Each message part also has a content location attribute that indicates the name of the file referred to in the SMIL presentation part. The following code first builds an `MMSMessage` from a list of media files and then modifies the attributes for each part programmatically via the `MMSMessage` interface.

```
//Table of URLs of files to be attached to MMS.
// Full file path URLs for each file is used.
String contentPath = "file:///myContent/";
String attachments[] = {
  contentPath + "frog.txt",
  contentPath + "frog.smil",
  contentPath + "frog.gif"
};

MMSDriverFactory factory;
MMSEngine engine;
// Create the engine and start it ... ...

MMSMessage toSend = factory.createMMSMessage(attachments);
// this is to be a message with related parts (SMIL)
toSend.setContentType(MimePart.CT_MULTIPART_RELATED);
```

```
// Get all content parts and set/modify
// some parameters for each of them;
MultipartMimeContent contentParts = toSend.getMultipart();

// Get the first content part
ContentPart cp = (ContentPart)contentParts.getBodyPart(0);
cp.setContentID( "<CID00>" );
cp.setContentLocation( "frog.txt" );
cp.setContentType( "text/plain" );

// This part is to be the presentation part (SMIL)
cp = (ContentPart)contentParts.getBodyPart(1);
cp.setContentID( "<CID01>" );
cp.setContentLocation( "frog.smil" );
cp.setContentType( "application/smil" );

// Get the last part
cp = (ContentPart)contentParts.getBodyPart(2);
cp.setContentID( "<CID02>" );
cp.setContentLocation( "frog.gif" );
cp.setContentType( "image/gif" );

// Set the 'id' of the SMIL presentation part
toSend.setPresentationId( "<CID01>" );


// Set message parameters
toSend.setTO(new MMSAddress("18005555555/TYPE=PLMN"));
toSend.setFROM(new MMSAddress("18005555554/TYPE=PLMN"));
toSend.setSubject("This is the subject line");

// send message to MMSC
engine.send(toBeSentMsg);
```

SMIL Message with SAMS API

Overall, the SAMS API is very similar to the Nokia MMS API. A noticeable difference is that the SAMS API does not provide convenience methods to convert file paths directly to messages or message parts. You have to explicitly read the media file or convert the text string into byte arrays before you can assemble the message. The following method is a simple example of how to read in a file.

```
public byte[] getFileAsBytes(String filename)
                                throws Exception {
  FileInputStream fis = new FileInputStream(filename);
  byte[] result = new byte[fis.available()];
```

```
    fis.read(result);
    return result;
}
```

In the SAMS API, an empty MMS message is instantiated by passing its implementation class to the `MessagingSession.getMessage()` factory method. We can assign recipient addresses to the to, cc and bcc lists. Each of those lists is an array of `MmsAddress` objects, even if there is only one recipient address. Each content part is manually added to the `MmsMessage` object as a `ContentPart` object. The `ContentPart` constructor takes five arguments:

1. The first argument is a byte array holding the content of the part.

2. The second argument is the MIME type of the content.

3. The third argument is the part ID for internal reference. For example, we can specify which `ContentPart` is the SMIL presentation of this message by passing its ID to the `MmsMessage.setPresentationId()` method. The ID for each part must be unique within the message.

4. The fourth argument is the URL location of the part as referred to from the SMIL document. It can be `null` if there is no SMIL presentation in the message.

5. The fifth argument is the character encoding of the content. It can be `null` for nontext content.

```
String contentPath = "file:///myContent/";

MessagingSession session;
// Initialize the MessagingSession ... ...

// Create the message
MmsMessage toSend =
    (MmsMessage)session.getMessage(MmsMessage.class);

// Create the sender address
Address sender = new Address(Address.ADDRESS_TYPE_MSISDN,
                             "18005555554");
toSend.setSender(sender);

// Create the To address list
// We can also use CC_ADDRESS and BCC_ADDRESS lists
MmsAddress[] receiversTo = new MmsAddress[1];
receiversTo[0] =
    new MmsAddress(Address.ADDRESS_TYPE_MSISDN,
                   "18005555555");
toSend.setReceivers(MmsMessage.TO_ADDRESS, receiversTo);
```

```
// Create the subject line
toSend.setSubject("This is the subject!");

// Set content
javax.sams.messaging.mms.ContentPart[] cp =
  new javax.sams.messaging.mms.ContentPart[3];

cp[0] = new ContentPart("Hello SMIL".getBytes(),
                        "text/plain", "id0",
                        "frog.txt", // referenced in SMIL
                        "ASCII");

byte[] smil = getFileAsBytes(contentPath + "frog.smil");
cp[1] = new ContentPart(smil, "application/smil", "id1",
                        "frog.smil", null);

byte[] picture = getFileAsBytes(contentPath + "frog.gif");
cp[2] = new ContentPart(picture, "image/gif", "id2",
                        "frog.gif", // referenced in SMIL
                        null);

m.setContents(cp);

// Point to the id of the presentation part
m.setPresentationId("id1");

session.send(toSend);
```

SMS Message with SAMS API

The Nokia Server Services SDK Java library supports access to not only the MMSC but also the SMSC for server-side SMS messaging. In this section, we cover the syntax for the SAMS API. To send a simple text SMS message is straightforward.

```
MessagingSession session;
// Initialize the MessagingSession ... ...

// Create the message
TextMessage toSend =
  (TextMessage)session.getMessage(TextMessage.class);

// Create the sender address
Address sender = new Address (
    Address.ADDRESS_TYPE_MSISDN, "18005555554");
toSend.setSender(sender);
```

```
// Create the receiver address
Address receiver = new Address(
    Address.ADDRESS_TYPE_MSISDN, "18005555555");
toSend.setReceiver(receiver);

// Create the message
m.setText("Hello SAMS. Current date is: " +
        (new Date()));

// Send it!
session.send(m);
```

In addition to text-based SMS messages, we can send binary SMS messages using the SAMS API. Binary SMS messages can carry basic images such as the operator's logo.

```
MessagingSession session;
// Initialize the MessagingSession ... ...

// Create the message
BinaryMessage toSend =
    (BinaryMessage)session.getMessage(BinaryMessage.class);

// Create the sender address
Address sender = new Address (
    Address.ADDRESS_TYPE_MSISDN, "18005555554");
toSend.setSender(sender);

// Create the receiver address
Address receiver = new Address(
    Address.ADDRESS_TYPE_MSISDN, "18005555555");
toSend.setReceiver(receiver);

// Create the message
toSend.setContent(
    getFileAsBytes("file:///mylogo.otb"));

// Send message to the port for operator logo
m.setDestinationPort(0x158A);

// Send it!
session.send(m);
```

Receiving Messages

In this section, we cover how to receive MMS messages directly from the MMSC server.

Using the Nokia API

In the following listing, we illustrate how to receive an MMS message and parse its content for application use. The `engine.receive()` method call opens a server socket at the port number specified by the configuration file and waits for the MMSC to connect when a new MMS message is received. The method does not return until it receives a message. So, in the external application, we should run it in a background thread. The Nokia API also provides an asynchronous API for receiving messages.

```
MMSDriverFactory factory;
MMSEngine engine;
// Create the engine and start it ... ...

// This method will block until it receives a message
MMSMessage receivedMsg = engine.receive();

// Decode the reply message
// The from address
String from = receivedMsg.getFROM().toString();
// The subject line
String subject = receivedMsg.getSubject();

// process from, subject and any other message attributes
// ... ...

// Get the content parts
MultipartMimeContent contentParts =
              receivedMsg.getMultipart();
// Iterate through the content parts
for (int i = 0; i < contentParts.size(); i++) {
  ContentPart cp =
    (ContentPart) contentParts.getBodyPart(i);
  if (cp.getContentType().equals("application/text") {
    String content = cp.getContent ();
    // process text content ... ...
  } else {
    byte [] content = cp.getContent ();
    // process binary content based on the ID, location
    // and MIME type ... ...
  }
}
```

Using the SAMS API

In the SAMS API, receiving messages is primarily done asynchronously through a `MessageListener` callback interface. The following code shows how to add a `MessageListener` to the `MessageSession`.

```
MessagingSession session;
// Initialize the MessagingSession ... ...

// Set messaging listener to receive MMS messages
MessageListenerHandler mlh =
    session.getMessageListenerHandler();
MessageListener ml1 = new MyMessageListener();
mlh.addMessageListener(ml1, new DefaultMmsFilter());

// Before we close session, all incoming messages
// will be processed by ml1.onMessage()
```

The `onMessage()` method in the `MessageListener` implementation class is invoked for each incoming MMS message. We need to provide the `onMessage()` implementation for our application needs.

```
public class ExampleMessageListener
        implements MessageListener {

  // Invoked when a new message arrives
  public void onMessage(Message message)
    throws InvalidArgumentException, ServiceException {

    if ( message instanceof MmsMessage ) {
      MmsMessage receivedMsg = (MmsMessage) message;

      ContentPart[] contentParts =
          receivedMsg.getContents();
      for (int i=0; i<contentParts.length; i++) {
        try {
          ContentPart cp = contentParts[i];
          if (cp.getCharEncoding() != null) {
            // This part is text
            String content = new String(cp.getContent(),
                              cp.getCharEncoding());
            // process the content string ... ...
          } else {
            // This part is binary
            byte [] content = cp.getContent ();
            // process the binary content based on the
            // MIME type in cp.getType ()
```

```
            // ... ...
        }
    } catch (Exception e) {
        // Handle error ... ...
    }
}
} else {
    // This is not an MmsMessage
    // Throw an error ... ...
}
}
}
```

Summary

In this chapter, we introduced the basic concepts of MMS and discussed how to develop compelling MMS content using SMIL. Ideally, our MMS application should integrate directly with the wireless operator's MMSC server using Java APIs provided by the Nokia Mobile Server Services Library. However, since the MMS service is still very young, direct MMSC access for individual developers might prove difficult at this time. In this case, we should leverage the MMS gateway services and standard Internet email servers to send and receive MMS messages in our applications.

chapter

15

Browser Applications

Use pervasive browser-based technologies to reach the maximum number of users.

WAP and mobile browsers are among the first killer applications for the mobile Internet. After years of adoption, most mobile phones today have factory-installed WAP browsers, and WAP data service is readily available from almost all mobile network operators. The pervasiveness of WAP makes it a great channel to deliver content to a large number of users. WAP is also used as a mechanism to provision Java applications, MMS content, and push messages. Topics covered in this chapter include the following:

- **Browser applications:** discusses the benefits and limitations of browser-based applications. We introduce the WAP technology stack.

- **Authoring mobile browser content:** covers the browser characteristics of Nokia devices, markup languages for WAP content, and Nokia development tools.

- **Advanced WAP features:** covers mobile-specific, value-added services provided by the WAP gateway and mobile browsers.

Of course, the full description of WAP is beyond the scope of this book. In this chapter, we introduce the basics of WAP infrastructure and applications with special focus on Nokia Series 40 devices.

Browser Applications

Since the late 1990s, browser-based Web applications have become increasingly popular as a form to deliver software services to end users. At the same time, the mobile Internet is also emerging as a powerful network platform. Web browsers on mobile phones enable Web site developers to make their applications available to mobile users as well. Mobile browser-based applications have played essential roles in the early period of mobile commerce.

The Thin-Client paradigm

As we discussed in Chapter 2, "Introducing Nokia Developer Platforms," browser-based applications are thin-client applications. The pros and cons of the thin-client applications compared with the Java-based smart-client applications are described in Chapter 2 as well. To summarize, the greatest advantage of browser-based applications is that they are pervasively available. All Nokia developer platforms include WAP browsers, as do the vast majority of phones from other manufacturers; most network operators provide WAP data services at a low cost; almost all Web-content authoring tools now support mobile browser content; many popular dynamic Web site development frameworks support mobile browsers. In addition, browser-based applications are very easy to deploy. We simply need to update the Web site, and there is no need to install new client software on the user side. That guarantees all users are in sync with the latest version of the software at all times.

However, the greatest limitation of browser-based applications is their over-reliance on the network. Compared to the wired Internet, mobile networks are slow and unreliable with high latency and expensive bandwidth. Browser-based applications require uninterrupted connection and frequent network round trips, which can result in a poor user experience. Furthermore, the lightweight mobile browsers only render simple content markup languages, which currently cannot support complex UI elements. For example, it would be impossible to build a good action game with the browser alone.

The WAP Infrastructure

Mobile handsets connect to the wired Internet via a WAP gateway. The gateway acts as a proxy for network traffic between the mobile client and the general Internet (e.g., the HTTP or TCP/IP traffic to access Internet servers; see Figure 15–1). For instance, if your mobile phone downloads a Web page from an Internet Web server, the server's access log shows a visit from your WAP gateway's IP address rather than from your mobile phone's direct IP address. All the IP network connections made from a J2ME client are also routed through the WAP gateway. Nokia's devices support two different wireless protocol stacks.

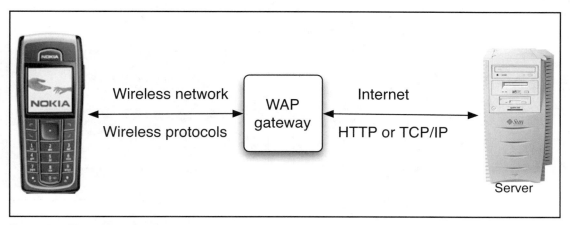

Figure 15–1 The WAP architecture.

The WAP and HTTP Stack

The WAP specification defines a complete stack of protocols layered upon each other to transport application data in the wireless network environment. Figure 15–2 shows the layers of WAP protocols and their relationship with the data protocols in the wired Internet. On top of all data communication protocols, the Wireless Application Environment (WAE) defines the valid application data that can be correctly rendered on the device browsers. The WAE is the WAP layer with which most content developers need to be familiar. The Wireless Markup Language (WML) and WMLScripts are both defined in the WAE. The data protocols beneath the WAE handle the actual connections and data flows that carry the WAE contents. We do not discuss the details of the data protocols except for two important points that are relevant to application developers.

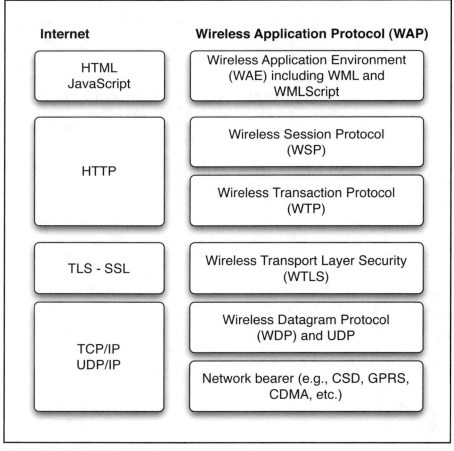

Figure 15–2 The WAP protocol stack.

- The Wireless Session Protocol (WSP) handles session-oriented and stateful connections. The WAP gateway translates the WSP traffic to HTTP to interface with the Internet servers, and vice versa. The WSP is specially optimized for the slow and long latency wireless networks. Common HTTP headers, such as Cookies and Authenticate, are passed transparently between HTTP and WSP.

- The optional Wireless Transport Layer Security (WTLS) protocol underneath the WSP layer allows devices to encrypt their data traffic for secure communication. The WAP gateway can translate the encrypted data to HTTPS, and vice versa.

Since the WSP is specifically modeled after the HTTP protocol, the WSP-based WAP gateway only supports HTTP-based content from the mobile browser. A key drawback of the WSP is that it only allows small data files (less than 30KB). For large messages, the underlying WTP could split the messages into a number of smaller datagrams and selectively retransmit failed datagrams. This functionality is called Segmentation and Reassembly (SAR), and it is defined as an optional feature by the WAP Forum. To use SAR, both the device and the WAP gateway must support this feature. The use of SAR improves over-the-air efficiency for downloading large messages to the phone and makes content downloading and MMS transfer faster and more reliable.

Most Series 40 Developer Platform 1.0 devices utilize the WAP 1.2.1 protocol stack (HTTP and WSP) for data network access. Those devices typically support SAR for large file transfer.

The Wireless Profiled TCP/IP Stack

A second wireless protocol stack, which is defined in the WAP 2.0 specification and is widely used in more recent devices, uses the WAP gateway as a proxy for TCP/IP traffic instead of HTTP traffic, from the Internet to the wireless network. On the wireless network side, the data protocol is called the wireless profiled TCP/IP, which is optimized for wireless environments and can operate with standard TCP/IP implementations on the Internet. Wireless profiled TCP/IP is more reliable, with improved error-handling capabilities when compared to normal TCP/IP, and has lower connection setup times. Wireless profiled TCP/IP enables connections with larger data file sizes than WSP. Since the HTTP is built on top of TCP/IP, we can easily implement HTTP applications using the wireless profiled TCP/IP. In this case, the WAP gateway is completely transparent to HTTP traffic. But more importantly, the wireless profiled TCP/IP enables us to reach beyond HTTP into network application areas that require the power and flexibility of TCP/IP. Examples of those areas include MIDP 2.0 networking, media streaming, instant messaging, and presence.

Another key benefit of the wireless profiled TCP/IP over WSP is improved security via end-to-end HTTPS. As we discussed, in the WSP stack, the device could use the underlying WTLS to communicate encrypted data to the WAP gateway. The gateway then needs to decrypt the data and re-encrypt it with HTTPS before sending it off to the Internet. Under this setup, the data is temporarily available as plain text on the gateway during the translation, and that poses a security risk. TCP/IP enables the usage of Transport Layer Security (TLS) all the way from the terminal to the origin server. Based on the Internet security protocol (SSL), TLS is a standard for enabling secure Internet connections, and it is the basis for HTTPS.

Some newer Series 40 Developer Platform 1.0 devices, such as Nokia 6220, 6650, 6810, 7200, and 7600, as well as all Series 40 Developer Platform 2.0 devices, use the wireless profiled TCP/IP protocol.

TIP

Since the WAP gateway acts as a proxy for all the HTTP connections between the WAP device and the Internet content server, the content server sees all the HTTP requests originating from the same IP address (i.e., the gateway's IP address). Nokia's WAP gateway could reveal the WAP client's mobile phone by adding an X-Nokia-MSISDN header to all HTTP requests originated from a mobile device. This header helps the server application to keep track of users, maintain block lists, and generate useful log files. Different WAP gateway products might have different names for the "phone number" header. Mobile operators could also disable this feature in their networks. So, check your WAP gateway's and the mobile operator's developer manuals to find out more before you develop applications that rely on this feature.

Authoring Mobile Browser Content

Authoring content for browser-based mobile applications requires understanding of the device browsers and the standards-based markup languages. In this section, we discuss the features and capabilities of the browser software on Nokia devices.

Nokia Device Browsers

For Nokia devices that support the WAP 1.2.1 protocol stack (WSP and HTTP), including most Series 40 Developer Platform 1.0 devices, their built-in browsers support content authored in the WML version 1.3. For Nokia devices that support the wireless profiled TCP/IP protocol stack, including newer Series 40 Developer Platform 1.0 devices and Series 40 Developer Platform 2.0 devices, their built-in browsers support both WML 1.3 and XHTML Mobile Profile (MP) 1.0 as content markup languages.

All Nokia browsers support HTTP Cookies and Authentication headers. HTTPS is supported either through the WTLS layer for WSP stack devices or directly through the TCP/IP protocol for TCP/IP devices. HTTP POST for uploading forms or other content is also supported.

The browser utilizes the device memory space to cache Web pages and store bookmarks. Caching makes previously visited pages quick to access, as there is no need to reload them. The user can empty the cache by selecting Clear Cache in the Options list in the browser. The cache stored in the client can be controlled by HTTP headers. The "no-cache" HTTP header directive can be set by the HTTP server to indicate that the pages are not to be cached. On the Series 40 Developer Platform 2.0 browsers, the cache and storage size are limited only by the free memory space of the device. On Series 40 Developer Platform 1.0 browsers, the cache size ranges from 10KB to 200KB. Earlier devices also impose maximum sizes for WML decks and XHTML MP pages they can display. For more detailed information on the browser characteristics for each device, please refer to the "Browser Characteristics in Nokia GSM Devices" document on Forum Nokia.

TIP

Nokia device browsers can add User Agent Profile headers to their HTTP requests to identify the client device to the server. That allows the server to customize the content presentation for the specific client. For example, the Nokia 6230 device's user agent header is `Nokia6230/1.0 (xx.yy)`, where the `xx.yy` indicates the software version number of this device. When the server receives such a header, it knows that the client browser is capable of displaying XHTML MP.

WML Versus XHTML MP

Nokia browsers support WML or XHTML MP content. WML has a syntax structure similar to the widely used HTML for Internet Web pages. It has several tags that are specially designed to format content for small screens. For example, the `<card>` tag is used to divide content into multiple screens, and the `<do>` tag is used to map soft key actions. WML is supported on all Nokia Developer Platform devices, including the early Series 40 Developer Platform 1.0 devices. However, in 2002, the Internet standard body W3C decided to consolidate numerous browser markup languages and use XHTML MP, which is a subset of XHTML, to replace WML. Although XHTML MP is also often referred to as WML 2.0, it is not compatible with older versions of WML. We discuss the technical differences between XHTML MP and WML later in this section. The XHTML MP has the following advantages over WML.

- It has more text formatting tags to take advantage of the rich display capabilities of modern mobile browsers.

- It provides a presentation and navigation model consistent with PC-based browser applications. That gives the users a similar experience across devices.

- It allows XHTML-compatible PC-based browsers to display mobile content directly and hence promotes interoperability and code reuse.

- It makes life easier for toolkit developers and Web site authors, since there are fewer confusing standards to support.

Most Nokia Developer Platform devices support both WML and XHTML MP. We should use XHTML MP instead of WML whenever possible. Detailed documentation of WML and XHTML MP tags and syntax are beyond the scope of this book. Interested readers can refer to the "WAP Service Developer's Guide for Nokia Series 40 Phones with WML Browser" and "Series 40 Developer Platform: Designing XHTML Mobile Profile Content" documents on Forum Nokia. In this section, we highlight some key differences between WML and XHTML MP.

- The root element of a WML document is the `<wml>` element. The `<wml>` root can contain several `<card>` elements to hold the display content. Each `<card>` element represents a page of content and has a unique ID. We can navigate between `<card>` pages by linking to the target page's ID. The "deck of cards" structure allows the device to download several pages of content at once and then display them offline. An XHTML MP document has only one `<body>` element under the `<html>` root to hold the content.

- The biggest advantage of XHTML MP over WML is its support for WAP CSS. Using CSS and the style attributes supported in most XHTML MP tags, we can customize how the content elements are rendered. For example, a `<p style="color:red">` element would render the enclosed text paragraph in red color. We can customize the color, borders, margin, alignment, and many other attributes of the rendered content via styles. The separation between the presentation style and content is key to the design of modern Web pages. Interested readers can find out more information about how to use CSS together with XHTML from the "Series 40 Developer Platform: Designing XHTML Mobile Profile Content" document on Forum Nokia.

- Earlier Series 40 Developer Platform 1.0 devices (e.g., Nokia 7210) only support simple text formatting tags in WML, such as `<p>`, `<br>`, and `<pre>`. Later Series 40 Developer Platform 1.0 and 2.0 devices added emphasis support for different font sizes (e.g., `<big>` and `<small>`) and font faces (e.g., `<i>`, `<b>`, and `<u>`) in WML. XHTML MP further added support for content dividers (e.g., `<div>`), indentation (e.g., `<blockquote>`), and logical presentation tags. For example, in XHTML MP, we can use `<h1>` to `<h6>` tags to specify different levels of headlines. The exact presentation style of those headlines can be defined in custom style sheets.

- In WML, we can customize the soft key menus using the `<do>` element. This option is not available in XHTML MP. We can, however, map `<a>` links to any key on the key pad in both languages.

- Both WML and XHTML MP support tables. In WML, the cell sizes are automatically determined according to their content. The browser provides the necessary scroll control if the table is longer or wider than the screen itself. In XHTML MP, we have the option to manually specify the column width in pixels or as a percentage of the screen width.

- Earlier versions of WML in Series 40 Developer Platform 1.0 do not support the width, height, and alignment attributes in the <img> tag. The Developer Platform 2.0 version of WML and XHTML MP both support those attributes.

- XHTML MP supports list elements (e.g., <ol>, <ul>, <li>, etc.), which are absent in WML.

How About WMLScript?

WMLScript is a client-side scripting language similar to JavaScript. It extends the WML and allows the user to perform simple information processing inside the browser without round trips to the server. Most Nokia devices support WMLScript 1.2. WMLScript can be called from anywhere within WML code. WMLScript communicates with WML markup context via variables. In XHTML applications, it is recommended that we implement all user interactions, such as input validation, on the server side, although it would incur more network round trips. Server-based solutions are more interoperable across browsers on different devices.

WMLScript is compiled by the gateway when the HTTP data is being translated into WSP data. Such a compilation step does not take place in WAP gateways that translate TCP/IP to wireless profiled TCP/IP. Since the TCP/IP-based Series 40 Developer Platform 2.0 browser does not support uncompiled WMLScript content, the WMLScript must be stored in compiled form (wmlsc) on the origin server for those client devices. Furthermore, the origin server must be configured to recognize a new file extension and associate it with the MIME type application/vnd.wap.wmlsc.

Content Download and Upload

The browsers allow users to download objects on the Web page (e.g., photos) and save them into the on-device storage (e.g., the gallery) for future use. Figure 15–3 shows that after setting the focus of the browser to a media object (using the navigation keys), we can use the Options menu to open the object with a native application or simply save it to the gallery. In fact, downloading via WAP is the most important mechanism to provision content, such as ringtones, wallpapers, and Java applications, over-the-air (OTA).

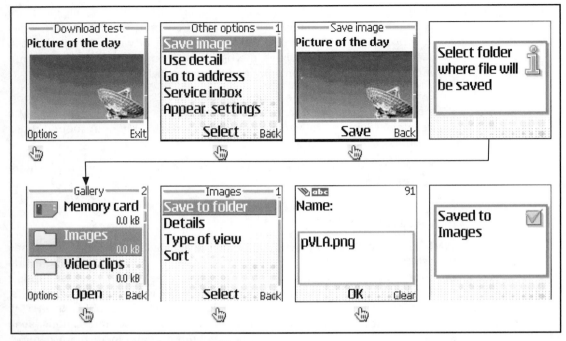

Figure 15–3 Download media files from a Web page.

<table>
<tr><td>NOTE</td><td>The OTA installation of Java MIDlets (see Chapter 3) requires the device browser to download the JAD file and then invoke the Java Application Management Software (AMS) to process it.</td></tr>
</table>

We can also upload media files from the local storage to a remote server using WML or XHTML MP forms. The file type `<input>` element in a `<form>` element is displayed like a textbox in the browser. When the user selects to edit it, she is prompted to choose a file from the gallery. The name of the selected file is filled into the field. When the user clicks on the Submit button, it is posted to the remote HTTP site. Various server-side toolkits can be used to retrieve the submitted file from the HTTP request. The following code shows the relevant code in the page, and Figure 15–4 shows what happens on the device. The `processor.php` in the form's `action` attribute is the relative URL from this page to the server-side PHP script that receives and processes the uploaded file.

```
<html>
  <head>
    <title>Upload test</title>
  </head>
  <body>
    <h3>Please upload</h3>
    <form action="processor.php" method="post">
```

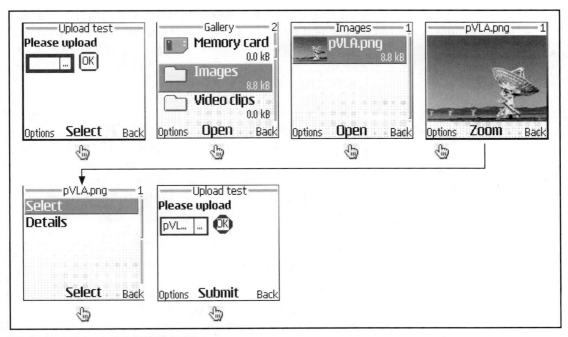

Figure 15–4 Upload media file via the browser.

```
        <input type="file"/>
        <input type="submit" name="submit" value="OK"/>
      </form>
    </body>
</html>
```

Not all downloaded content can be uploaded to third-party servers (or sent out as MMS messages) due to copyright protection issues. Nokia devices limit the user's ability to resend the downloaded content according to MIME types. Typically, the device does not permit forwarding the downloaded Java applications, wallpapers, ringtones, or operator logos. The permission policy varies from device to device. Interested readers should refer to the "Browser Characteristics in Nokia GSM Devices" document on Forum Nokia for the detailed information on each device. For newer Series 40 devices that implement the OMA DRM specifications, the content provider can have finely grained control over the forwarding policies beyond the simple MIME types.

Nokia Browser Developer Tools

Forum Nokia provides several tools for developing and testing browser-based applications. All of these tools are freely available for download from the Forum Nokia Web site's tools section. The device emulator in the Series 40 Developer Platform 2.0 SDK emulates the browser application on the PC. You can just start the device emulator from the SDK menu, navigate the browser application using the scroll keys, and enter the Internet address of your Web page (see Figure 15–5). The SDK emulator is sufficient for most developers to test their Web sites without a real device with live data connections.

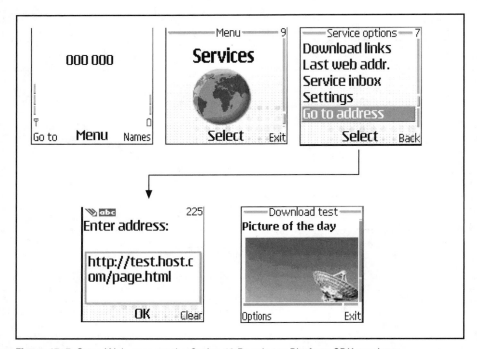

Figure 15–5 Get a Web page on the Series 40 Developer Platform SDK emulator.

The Nokia Mobile Internet Toolkit (NMIT) provides an editor for WML and XHTML MP pages. You can use it to validate the tag syntax and then launch a browser emulator to test the page. Figure 15–6 shows the "new file" dialog box NMIT and part of the WML page editor.

The Nokia WAP Gateway Simulator and Nokia WML Browser Emulator are two products that work together to emulate the entire end-to-end WAP infrastructure on the development PC. They are useful to developers who wish to interact with the WAP gateway. Through the traffic monitor, you can see exactly how HTTP traffic is translated into WSP, and vice versa.

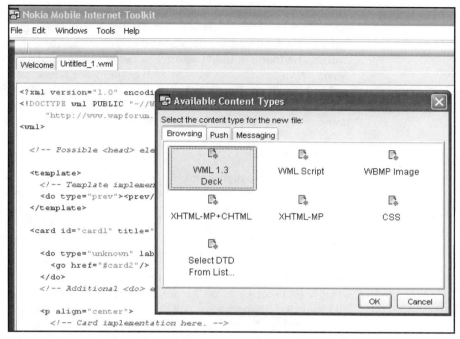

Figure 15–6 The Nokia Mobile Internet Toolkit supported file formats and editor.

Advanced WAP Features

The WAP gateway is more than just a transparent proxy between the Internet and mobile browsers. It can provide services that are specific to the wireless environment. Similarly, the mobile browser can provide value-added services to users to take advantage of the entire integrated device. In this section, we discuss advanced WAP gateway and Nokia browser features and how to leverage them in our applications.

Push

The Push Proxy Gateway (PPG) component in the WAP gateway server allows Internet applications to push messages to the handsets. Examples of such messages include new emails, changes in stock prices, flight schedule changes, and news headlines. Unlike SMS, where the message text is the content, the text in a WAP Push message is typically a URL indicating further downloadable content. The user can view indicated content by using the Service Inbox and the browser. In fact, as we discussed in Chapter 14, "Multimedia Messaging Service," the MMS content is provisioned using the WAP Push mechanism.

The Internet application submits the push content to the gateway via the Push Access Protocol (PAP) over HTTP. The PAP is an XML-like standard protocol defined by WAP Forum. Details of the PAP are beyond the scope of this book and can be found in the "Getting Started With WAP Push" document on Forum Nokia. Java libraries to handle PAP content are freely available from several vendors, such as Openwave. The Forum Nokia Developer Hub provides free access to WAP gateways around the world. Now, let's check out the two most common types of WAP Push messages.

Service Indication

The Service Indication content type enables an alert message to be sent to users. A Service Indication must contain at least the text to be displayed to the user and a URL address of content that may be dynamically generated for each push message in the application server. In addition to text and a URL address, the service indication can optionally contain the following information: creation date and time, expiration date and time, ID, and priority.

Each Service Indication has a Service Indication ID, which is used to uniquely identify different kinds of Service Indications. Service providers set the Service Indication IDs for messages. The ID allows reception of multiple Service Indications with the same URL address and priority level. If the received Service Indication has the same ID as the one stored in memory, the received Service Indication replaces the stored one only if it is newer. Priority levels define how the received messages are ordered in the Service Inbox and also whether the user is notified about the received Service Indication. Nokia devices support the following priority levels and their corresponding actions.

- **signal-high:** A notification is displayed, and an SMS alert tone is sounded.
- **signal-medium:** A notification is displayed, and an SMS alert tone is sounded.
- **signal-low:** No notification is displayed. The message is silently stored in the Service Inbox.
- **signal-none:** The Service Indication is discarded, and the user is not notified.
- **delete:** The Service Indication of the same ID in the Service Inbox, if any, is replaced by the new message. If there is no message of the same ID in the Service Inbox, the received message is discarded without user notification.

Service Loading

The Service Loading content type enables a URL address to be sent to a device, which then "pulls" the content at that URL from the origin server without the user specifically requesting it. As the user may be busy doing other things when service-loading content is received, the intrusiveness level can be set. Service Loading is not supported on all terminals, especially older Series 40 Developer Platform 1.0 devices. A Service Loading content type has one mandatory `href` attribute and one optional `action` attribute. The `href` attribute is the URL of the service application to be loaded, and the `action` attribute specifies the action that should be taken after pulling the service application. There are three possible values for the `action` attribute:

- **execute-low**: The application is executed in a nonintrusive manner.

- **execute-high**: The application is executed and may result in user-intrusive behavior.

- **cache**: The application is not executed. It is placed in cache if cache exists.

Wireless Telephony Applications Interface (WTAI)

The dual-mode browser incorporated in Series 40 Developer Platform 2.0 supports three Wireless Telephony Applications Interface (WTAI) public library functions: making a call while browsing, sending DTMF tones, and saving numbers and names to the phone book.

Making a Phone Call

The `WTAPublic.MakeCall(number)` function can be invoked from within a WMLScript to make a voice phone call. In a WML or XHTML page, we use a specially formatted URL link to trigger the `MakeCall` function. If the user clicks on the following link, the phone calls number 123456789.

```
<a href="wtai://wp/mc;+123456789">Call 123 456789</a>
```

When a `MakeCall` function is executed, the user is asked to confirm that the dial-up is to be made. If the phone number about to be called does not exist in the phone book, a confirmation query with the phone number is displayed. If the number exists in the phone book, a confirmation query is displayed with the name fetched from the phone book. If the user accepts making the phone call, another confirmation query is displayed with the text "Quit browsing?" (Exact text depends on the local language.) If the user accepts both queries, the browser session is terminated and the browser application closes down. The call is then initiated. When the call is terminated, the phone is in idle state. If the user rejects the latter confirmation query, the call is initiated from within the browser display, and the user can browse cached content during the call. If the user is browsing over a GPRS connection, the connection is suspended while the phone call is active.

Sending a DTMF Tone

The device can send a sequence of touch tones by executing a WTAI function called `WTAPublic.SendDTMF(sequence)` in the WMLScript. The user must have an active voice call in session when the `SendDTMF` method is invoked. Just like the `MakeCall` function, we can assign the `SendDTMF` function to a link. When the user clicks on the following link, the phone sends the touch tones of the key sequence 123*456# over the currently active voice call.

```
<a href="wtai://wp/sd;123*456#">Touch tone 123*456#</a>
```

After the touch tone sequence has been sent, the user returns to the active page where she initiated the sending. The voice call remains active.

Adding a Phone Book Entry

The WTAPublic.AddPBEntry(number, name) function offers an easy way to store a phone number and corresponding name onto the phone book application from a WMLScript. The AddPBEntry function can also be invoked via the following URL link.

```
<a href="wtai://wp/ap;+123456789;Home">Home</a>
```

When the user activates an AddPBEntry function and the content author has declared a name and a number, the phone displays a confirmation query with the text "Save name?" When the user accepts the confirmation query, another confirmation query with the text "With number +123456789" is displayed, and the number is stored in the phone book application. When saving is complete, the currently active page is displayed again. The user does not have to be online or have any voice calls active in order to use the AddPBEntry function.

Wallet

The wallet application is a secure space in the terminal where consumers can store personal information and easily retrieve that information while browsing, enhancing the user friendliness of a range of mobile services. The wallet supports the Electronic Commerce Modeling Language (ECML) specification, which is an open Internet standard (IETF RFC 2706) for digital wallets and online merchants that facilitates automatic exchange of transaction information. In addition to transferring credit card information, ECML can be used whenever applications need a common method for transferring information such as an address.

Consumers can store a wide range of personal information into the wallet, including, for instance, payment card details for making convenient mobile payments as well as billing and shipping addresses. Data in the wallet is encrypted and accessible only with a wallet PIN code.

Among the Series 40 phones that have an XHTML browser, the Nokia 6220 phone is the first to include a new, advanced version of the wallet application. Not only has the user interface been improved, but wallet 2.0 also has additional features, such as access cards and support for OTA card downloading.

The new wallet enables users to create access cards, including the user name and password to a mobile service, and then easily use wallet data when this information is requested in an XHTML page, eliminating the need to memorize user names and passwords to different services and to enter them manually each time he or she logs in to the service. Another major new feature is the ability to download payment, loyalty, address, and access card information OTA to the wallet. OTA card downloading greatly enhances the use and usability of the wallet because it allows service providers to send card information to the user, and there is no need to type it in manually.

Summary

In this chapter, we discussed the key concepts behind browser-based mobile applications and its key enabling technology: WAP. WAP devices that support TCP/IP and XHTML MP can deliver rich content and applications to mobile users. We also covered some of the advanced topics in WAP and browser-based applications.

Index

B

S

X

Z

Register
Your Book

at www.awprofessional.com/register

You may be eligible to receive:

- Advance notice of forthcoming editions of the book
- Related book recommendations
- Chapter excerpts and supplements of forthcoming titles
- Information about special contests and promotions throughout the year
- Notices and reminders about author appearances, tradeshows, and online chats with special guests

Contact us

If you are interested in writing a book or reviewing manuscripts prior to publication, please write to us at:

Editorial Department
Addison-Wesley Professional
75 Arlington Street, Suite 300
Boston, MA 02116 USA
Email: AWPro@aw.com

Visit us on the Web: http://www.awprofessional.com